0/00

 St. Louis Community College

Forest Park
Florissant Valley
Meramec

Instructional Resources
St. Louis, Missouri

THE
UTE INDIANS
of UTAH, COLORADO, and NEW MEXICO

THE

UTE INDIANS

OF UTAH, COLORADO, AND NEW MEXICO

VIRGINIA MCCONNELL SIMMONS

UNIVERSITY PRESS OF COLORADO

Copyright © 2000 by the University Press of Colorado

International Standard Book Number 0-87081-571-7

Published by the University Press of Colorado
5589 Arapahoe Avenue, Suite 206C
Boulder, Colorado 80303

The University Press of Colorado is a cooperative publishing enterprise supported, in part, by Adams State College, Colorado State University, Fort Lewis College, Mesa State College, Metropolitan State College of Denver, University of Colorado, University of Northern Colorado, University of Southern Colorado, and Western State College of Colorado.

The paper used in this publication meets the minimum requirements of the American National Standard for Information Sciences—Permanence of Paper for Printed Library Materials. ANSI Z39.48-1984

Library of Congress Cataloging-in-Publication Data

Simmons, Virginia McConnell, 1928–
    The Ute Indians of Utah, Colorado, and New Mexico / Virginia McConnell Simmons.
      p. cm.
    Includes bibliographical references and index.
    ISBN 0-87081-571-7 (alk. paper)
    1. Ute Indians—History. 2. Ute Indians—Government relations. 3. Ute Indians—Social life and customs. I. Title

    E99.U8 S55 2000
    979'.0049745—dc21   99-088408

09 08 07 06 05 04 03 02 01 00   10 9 8 7 6 5 4 3 2 1

For the Núu-ci

Contents

▼ ▼ ▼

Illustrations

▼ ▼ ▼

Maps

▼   ▼   ▼

Maps drafted by Yvonne Halburian

Preface

▾ ▾ ▾

Although numerous archaeological and ethnological papers, historical articles, books, folktales, and fictional accounts about Ute Indians exist, this tribe is less well known than many other North American Indian tribes. Lack of familiarity appears to have been caused, at least in part, by the absence of readily available scholarly studies, as well as by neglect of the Utes in regional histories. What is generally known and retold to the point of redundancy can be found in articles and books—especially in accounts of dramatic episodes, such as the Meeker Massacre and the Posey War, or about renowned individuals such as Chief Ouray and Chipeta or Walkara.

This history has been undertaken in an attempt to provide an overview of the Ute Indians beyond the often repeated and, unfortunately, often incorrect hearsay. I found myself delving into the excellent scholarly literature that does abound, despite its unfamiliarity to general readers, and reading countless imaginative accounts that have contributed to misinformation about Ute Indians. Everything had to be evaluated in terms of its potential contribution to an accurate, balanced history of the Ute people. Perhaps I did not succeed in winnowing out all of the misinformation, and I may well have contributed some of my own, for which I apologize.

This study makes apparent the fact that Ute Indians have been longtime, widespread occupants of Utah, Colorado, and northern New Mexico. They warrant recognition as successful adapters to diverse and sometimes harsh environments—not only the Rocky Mountains and other choice habitats such as the Utah Valley and Colorado's intermontane parks and valleys but also arid and semiarid portions of the Great

Basin and the Colorado Plateau. They even made sorties into the central and southern short-grass prairies.

Several excellent studies have concentrated on specific aspects of Ute material culture. For readers wishing to learn more about archaeology and ethnology than this single volume offers, I recommend especially the bibliographical entries by Sally Crum, Joel C. Janetski, Joseph G. Jorgensen, Marvin K. Opler, Anne M. Smith, and Omer C. Stewart, as well as the material in Volume 11 of the Smithsonian Institution's *Handbook of North American Indians*. Ute tales have been collected and published by the Southern Ute and the Uintah-Ouray Ute tribes and by Smith. Wick R. Miller is the accepted authority on Native American linguistics. Existing literature on several neighboring and related tribes gave me information and insights and is recommended to others who wish to understand Ute history.

A difficulty students of Ute Indians encounter is the incomplete and often contradictory nature of information about bands or groups and their distribution. Such problems can be attributed to the fact that Ute groups did not remain permanently within fixed boundaries or even territorial circuits, which appear to have been overly emphasized by some scholars. In addition, after Ute Indians acquired horses, became increasingly mobile, or were assigned to reservations, they became increasingly fluid, shifting their group affiliations or entering into temporary associations. My conclusions about the groups, their names, and their territories are as accurate as seems possible at this late date when much information has been lost. I hope this history has avoided as many such pitfalls as possible rather than having added to them.

Another source of confusion results from the fact that Ute Indians often had more than one name and that spellings vary, not only in the proper names of bands or groups but also in the names of individuals and places. Much variation arose when early white recorders attempted to put into English orthography the phonetically unfamiliar sounds of the unwritten Ute language. As a result, it is fairly common to find a variety of spellings in different publications, within one article, or even on a single page in a work. I have tried to use the most commonly accepted spellings of proper nouns, with alternates indicated when necessary and with translations as well. Readers with a special interest in language are referred to the publications of the Southern Ute Tribe's Ute Language Program, which offers a grammar, a dictionary, and a collection of narratives in the native language.

Because an overview such as mine would lack context without the geographical setting of events, this account begins with a description of the varied lands of the Utes. I then summarize information about the misty origins of this people, a subject that unfortunately offers more questions than absolute answers but that still allows us to reach a few relatively safe conclusions. Most of the history is given chronologically, from Spanish contact to the early twentieth century through the Reorganization Act of 1934 and the work of the Indian Claims Commission. The volume concludes with changing conditions in the twentieth century.

Acknowledgments

▼ ▼ ▼

In compiling this history, I owe a great debt to countless institutions, archives, and individuals. No work of this type would be possible without them.

Invaluable resources have been located at university and college libraries and in public archives. These include the New Mexico State Records Center and Archives, the Museum of New Mexico Division of Anthropology, Archives of the Archdiocese of Santa Fe, the Colorado Historical Society's Stephen H. Hart Library, the Denver Public Library's Western History Department, National Archives of the Rocky Mountain Region, Fort Lewis College's Center of Southwest Studies, Archives of the University of Colorado at Boulder Libraries, the Utah State Historical Society Library, the University of Utah's Marriott Library, Southern Utah University's Reid Library, the University of New Mexico's Zimmerman Library, the American Heritage Center at the University of Wyoming, and The Colorado College's Tutt Library.

Numerous less-well-known museums and public libraries, scattered throughout the study area, also provided useful information. These include Colorado's State Ute Museum at Montrose, the Southern Ute Museum at Ignacio, Denver Museum of Natural History Library, the Denver Museum of Art Library, Colorado Springs Pioneers Museum, Durango Public Library, Buddy Werner Library at Steamboat Springs, Grand County Museum at Hot Sulphur Springs, the Museum of Northwest Colorado at Craig, the Museum of Western Colorado at Grand Junction, Rangely Museum, Jackson County Public Library at Walden, Vernal's Western Heritage Museum and Uintah County Library, Manti's Family History Center, Kit Carson House in Taos, Fort Union National Monument archives, and Fort Garland State Museum.

Correspondence with the late Myra Ellen Jenkins of Santa Fe and the late George P. Hammond of Berkeley, California, was not only useful but also inspiring. The sharing of information by such respected people was one of the joys of my research, and the contributions made to Western American history by these people and others during their lifetimes is immeasurable. I became aware of how much new work like mine owes to many who are gone.

Among the many helpful individuals with whom I worked on this project, special thanks are extended to Robert G. Lewis, Esq., who generously contributed not only his knowledge about vintage photographs and photographers but also access to images in his private collection. Archaeologists Steven G. Baker of Centuries Research in Montrose, Jack Pfertsh of Mancos, Ken Frye of Del Norte, Vince Spero of Rio Grande National Forest, David Breternitz of Dove Creek, and Dennis Stanford of the Smithsonian Institution shared information freely. Throughout my numerous journeys to conduct research, I was aided by individuals like Levitt Christensen of Kanosh, Stan Bronson of Blanding, William L. Chenoweth of Grand Junction, Allen Kane of the U.S. Forest Service, Celinda Kaelin of Florissant, Bob Wiseman and Richard Duran of Las Vegas, Nevada, D. L. Birchfield of Oklahoma City, Robert S. McPherson of Eastern Utah State College, Paul Reddin at Mesa State College, and Duane Smith at Fort Lewis College. Serendipitous encounters included a conversation with a gracious Paiute Indian, Blanche, near Parowan and correspondence from Barbara Ekker at Hanksville.

Without the capable help of many archivists and librarians, research for this volume would have been impossible. I am indebted to them for their professional help. Among these individuals were Robert Kelly of the Interlibrary Loan Department at Adams State College; librarians and archivists Ginny Kiefer, Mary Davis, Sharon Euler, and Kelly Murphy in Colorado Springs; Todd Ellison and Catherine Conrad at the Center of Southwest Studies; Judy Prosser-Armstrong and a score of other regional museum archivists, all of whom were competent and helpful; David Hays, Cassandra M. Volpe, and Sylvia Bugbee at the University of Colorado in Boulder; Eric Bittner and Eileen Bolger at the National Archives and Records Center, Rocky Mountain Region; Laura Holt at the Museum of New Mexico's Laboratory of Anthropology; Rebecca Linz, Barbara Dey, and especially Debra Neiswonger at the Colorado Historical Society; Eleanor Gehres and her proficient staff at the Denver Public Library; Joseph Sánchez at the Spanish Colonial Research Center in Albuquerque; and Robert Torrez, New Mexico's state historian in Santa Fe.

I also wish to acknowledge assistance from my family members, Thomas and Catherine McConnell, who read the manuscript and provided valuable critical comments to improve its clarity. Susan and Gvidas Sakys provided hospitality, without which extended research in the Denver and Boulder area would have been difficult.

Most especially, I acknowledge the gracious assistance of Ute Indians who conversed with me, among them Alden Naranjo of the Southern Ute Tribe, Norman Lopez of the Ute Mountain Ute Tribe, and Larry Cesspooch and Clifford Duncan of the Ute Indian Tribe of the Uintah and Ouray Reservation. Without their insights and patience, my understanding of many subjects would have gone astray. Any lingering errors are the author's.

Last but far from least, my appreciation is extended to Luther Wilson, director of the University Press of Colorado, and to Laura Furney, the press's editorial and production manager, for their expertise and interest in this publication.

THE
UTE INDIANS
OF UTAH, COLORADO, AND NEW MEXICO

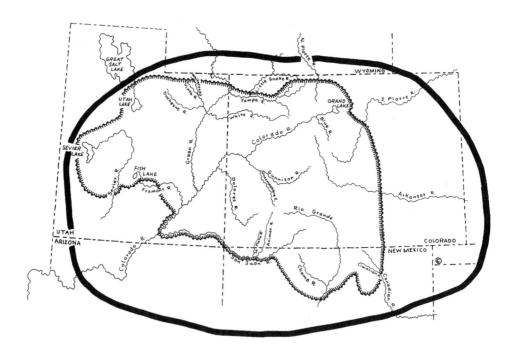

Ute Indian territory, with surrounding area used in hunting, trading, and warfare.

1

▾ ▾ ▾

Mother Earth, Father Sky

In the Ute Indians' traditional view of the natural world, Father Sky created the sun, moon, stars, and Earth. Mother Earth provides what is needed by those who show reverence and respect. For Utes, there was a vast and varied land—sometimes gentle and sometimes severe—where they survived by living respectfully in harmony with their environment, whatever it might be.

Before there were people, Senawahv, the Creator, made buffalo and deer, berries and piñon nut trees, and everything the people would need to live. Then he cut up sticks and put them in a bag. He meant for the sticks to be different peoples to whom he would give equal portions of the land and its good things, but Coyote, the curious trickster, opened the bag to see what was inside, and people scrambled forth in disorder, speaking many tongues. Senawahv looked inside and saw the remaining people, the Utes, and he declared that they would be so brave and strong that they would be able to defeat all others.[1]

The land Senawahv gave to the Utes encompassed part of the eastern Great Basin in Utah; a large portion of the Colorado Plateau in Utah as well as all of it in Colorado; all of the Rocky Mountains within Colorado, north to the Yampa River, and within northernmost New Mexico; and the eastern edge of the mountains where the High Plains abruptly meet them, from Colorado's South Platte River south to New Mexico's Mora River. The topography of the mighty sweep of land looked much as it had when humans first occupied it about 10,000 or 12,000 years ago.

Legends notwithstanding, geologists tell us that the land as we know it was billions of years in the making. The Ancestral Rockies go back hundreds of millions of years. Later, a great inland sea, dinosaurs, and forests of giant ferns came and went, followed eventually by the building of today's Rocky Mountains, the "shining mountains," about sixty million years ago. Next came enormous volcanic activity, further changing the face of the land and leaving basalt and lava flows in the Great Basin, northern New Mexico, and south-central Colorado.

Later, the Great Ice Age descended on the Northern Hemisphere. Although the ice cap did not extend as far south as Utah and Colorado, glaciers covered the mountains. During this time, evaporation lowered sea levels. In the far North, a previously drowned land bridge permitted the migration of Paleo-Indians, who entered the North American continent and hunted megafauna with atlatls and spears.

As the climate warmed again, the land bridges closed. Glaciers retreated, carving and polishing the mountains and depositing moraines of boulder and gravel. Melting water filled lakes, the largest of which was Utah's Lake Bonneville—about 150 miles wide and 350 miles long and covering all of western Utah. When its natural dam in Idaho gave way, Lake Bonneville drained and left broad, dry terraces and remnant bodies of water such as briny Great Salt Lake, which dwarfs all other remnants, and Sevier Lake. Where sufficient fresh water from the mountains on the east reached a lake, it was fresh, as is the case with Utah Lake, which, in turn, empties into Great Salt Lake through the Jordan River.

The Great Basin, where Lake Bonneville was located, is part of an immense alkaline desert, reaching from Utah's Wasatch Range on the east to the Sierra Nevada on the west. The basin occupies most of the western half of Utah, nearly all of Nevada, and portions of eastern California, Oregon, and Idaho. The only river outlet is Nevada's Humboldt. The province has low annual precipitation—five inches or less—with constant dusty winds, searing summers, and bitter winters. This inhospitable demeanor is relieved by north-south–trending ranges of hills and mountains that sustain animal life and vegetation, although in Utah most of these hills and mountains in the basin are too short and low to provide for many people.

Nevertheless, the hunter-gatherers of this province—members of what is called the Desert Culture—survived even in recent history by carefully observing the seasons, weather, and available resources of the Great Basin. They moved about in small, territorial groups, and they traveled light, in constant search of food—lizards, grasshoppers, crickets, ants, larvae, rats, mice, snakes, prairie dogs, jackrabbits, and cottontails to supplement grass seeds and roots. In historic times, the occupants were Western Shoshones and Gosiutes (Goshutes), or "Digger

Indians" as some have called them. Despite the poverty of their natural resources, through remarkable ability these hunter-gatherers survived in a hostile environment.

Ancestors of today's Utes probably lived at one time in the basin's deserts and later traveled there from time to time. In the historic period their western boundary ran southwest from the Jordan River around Utah Lake and west of Sevier Lake before angling southeast. Although indefinite, the southern boundary in Utah is thought to have been near Beaver or a little farther north at what is called the "Rim" between Kanosh and Cove Fort.[2]

Utah's Utes enjoyed the largesse of the wetlands around lakes and the streams feeding into them, especially the rich environs of Utah Lake, where Provo now stands. Here were reeds and rushes, cattails, willows, grasses and sedges, numerous forbs and roots, fish in great abundance, geese, ducks, birds' eggs, beaver, muskrats, badgers, skunks, deer, and rabbits—a cornucopia.

The Utes also favored the fringe of the Wasatch Front—at elevations of 4,000 to 5,000 feet—where streams exited. Here were grasses, sagebrush, willows, alder, cottonwoods, chokecherries, serviceberries, some bison, pronghorn antelope, mule deer, beaver, sage hens, and coyotes, among many other flora and fauna. Up the slopes, moving through life zones from the Upper Sonoran to Alpine, the mountains offered the Utes a vertical buffet, limited only by the seasons. There were deer, elk, mountain lions, black bears, mountain sheep, fox, martens, squirrels, and other small species. On the mountain slopes piñon pines (called *cedars* in Utah), junipers, shrubby maple, ponderosas, bristle cones, aspens, fir, and spruce provided firewood, lodgepoles, and pine nuts. Everything one could want for food, shelter, clothing, medicines, and tools was at hand near the banks of Provo Canyon, the Spanish Fork, the Sevier River, Corn Creek, and the slopes of the Wasatch. The name of this range means "mountain pass," and routes offered by passes and river canyons were another of the area's advantages.

The north-south–trending Wasatch Range, whose highest peaks are 12,000 feet above sea level, forms a barrier when storms blow eastward across the Great Basin. Heavy precipitation falls on the mountains, up to two hundred inches of snow in winter, for example, causing a rain shadow to the east. In the vast uplift of the Colorado Plateau Province, east of the Wasatch, are component plateaus of various heights, some of which rise high enough to capture rain and snow and are crowned with forests and lakes, game, and abundant vegetation. Fish Lake is the largest of the bountiful plateau lakes that attracted the Indians.

Beyond the Wasatch a few mountains are found. To the north, the Uinta Range (near the pine canyons), reaching 13,000 feet—even higher than the Wasatch—offers good resources, but dry conditions at low elevations reduced the desirability of the canyons and foothills for prolonged occupation by Indians. In southeast Utah are found the isolated dome ranges of the La Sals (called the Elk Mountains by some early people), the Blue Mountains (also known as the Abajos, meaning "low"), and the Henry Mountains, providing welcome oases in the country lying east toward the Colorado border. The La Sals are the second-highest peaks in Utah. Bison occurred in the valleys as well as in the Uinta Basin, but not in large numbers.

On the whole, this was a hazardous region for foot travelers, who found little water, vegetation, and other resources. The Uinta Basin has a few rivers, the most important being the Strawberry, Uinta, Whiterocks, and Duchesne, the last-named emptying the water of them all into the Green River (once called the Seedskeedee-Agee after the prairie chickens of the area). South of the Uinta Basin lies the Tavaputs Plateau, meaning "the land of the sun." This plateau is a badlands of barren, eroded cliffs, carrying some bunchgrass but little else. South of it is the sweeping, nearly waterless Castle Valley of Emery County, a land of dazzling escarpments best enjoyed from the security of an air-conditioned automobile and a modern highway. Summer temperatures of 110 degrees are not uncommon in this region. Coming off the San Rafael Swell, which rises here, is a muddy river, the San Rafael, that empties into the Green. Clearer and more reliable is the Fremont River, but between the two lie miles of sand and barren, deeply eroded cliffs resembling multihued layer cakes with few streams or springs. Around Capitol Reef, the rocks in Waterpocket Fold provided natural pockets of rainwater, or "tanks," for those few nomads who penetrated this rugged area.[3]

Nearly waterless but awesome, the "standing up country" of Canyonlands lies between the plateau's deserts and the southeastern corner of Utah. Getting from one side to the other through the tangle of eroded needles, domes, crevices, arches, and impassable chasms once presented a seemingly impossible challenge, but some tough people were able to do so. Utes, Southern Paiutes, and Navajos were able to reach and traverse the Colorado River, sometimes using crude rafts. The Spanish Domínguez-Escalante expedition was directed by Indians to the Ute Ford, later called the Crossing of the Fathers, now under Lake Powell. Upriver, just north of Moab, was a commonly used ford, and north of Canyonlands the Green could be crossed about three miles above the town of Green

River, Utah, at a point called Ute Crossing. The river could also be forded about two miles below the mouth of the Duchesne River, as well as six miles above Jensen, near Dinosaur National Monument—where Domínguez and Escalante forded with the guidance of a Ute—as well as at a point south of Flaming Gorge.[4]

There are no indications that Utes or other aboriginal peoples had an inkling about the Mesozoic giants sleeping in the earth near the Green River at Dinosaur Monument or in other locations like the red rocks near present-day Morrison, Colorado, although the Utes often camped there and enjoyed soothing baths in the mud springs. Further, no evidence shows that the fossil fuels of northeast Utah and northwest, southwest, west-central, and central Colorado were used, with the exception of an oil seep near Cañon City, Colorado, where the black ooze relieved injuries, aches, and pains of Utes camping in a nearby cave. The Utes were unaware of the wealth of coal in Carbon County, Utah, and in Colorado's Moffat, Routt, Gunnison, Fremont, and Las Animas Counties. Undiscovered were the oil and gas of Utah's Uintah and San Juan Counties, Colorado's La Plata and Montezuma Counties, and New Mexico's San Juan County.

The crest of the Uintas, west of Dinosaur National Monument, was a flexible northern boundary of Ute country, and the beautiful Yampa River, which joins the Green in the canyons of the monument, provided a similar border farther east. Sometimes called the Bear River in early days, the Yampa River's name refers to a plant of the area, whose roots were a favorite food of Utes and Comanches, the latter coming to the area from the north in pre-horse times. Both tribes had groups called Yamparikas, "yampa eaters." North of the Yampa is Brown's Park or Hole, part of Colorado's Washakie Basin, where the Utes' enemies from the north made even Senawahv's favorites cautious and scarce. The Little Snake River east of Brown's Park offered a wide valley where Utes and hostile neighboring tribes from Wyoming often fought during hunting excursions.

Most of northwest Colorado consists of semiarid steppe, broken up by the Roan Plateau, which includes the stark Book Cliffs, and the Axial and Piceance Basins. Higher elevations are capped with forests like those on the White River Plateau, better known as the Flattops. From the Flattops down to the Green River flows the White River, or Smoking River as the Utes called it. It was an important pathway. The White River's confluence with the Green is at the ford just south of the mouth of the Duchesne in the Wonsits Valley (meaning "antelope"), so the neighborhood was a crossroad of trails traveled by early Indians and subsequently by trappers, traders, and explorers. In west-central Colorado the Colorado River was an obstacle to those who needed to cross it, but a few fords, known to Indians, could be found above Westwater Canyon, at Grand Junction, and near DeBeque.

Dinosaur beds along the Colorado River contain many fossils, whereas the colorful sandstone cliffs and canyons of Colorado National Monument, prominent west of Grand Junction, contain petrified wood—a potential subject for Indian legends. The mighty forces of the Gunnison and Colorado Rivers join at Grand Junction. Between the two rivers looms the great hulk of Grand Mesa with its thick forests, lakes, and game of many kinds—a favorite haunt of aboriginal peoples and modern hunters alike. To the south is the long uplift of the Uncompahgre Plateau (meaning "red water source" or "lake"). North of the plateau lies Unaweap Valley ("red canyon"), and southwest is the Paradox Basin of uranium mining fame, with the Dolores River flowing through it. The terrain from this basin rises through slick rock and piñon-juniper country to meet the La Sals, Canyonlands, and the sage plains around the Abajos in Utah.

The far southwest corner of Colorado is dominated by dry washes, Sleeping Ute Mountain, countless ancient stone structures, and Mesa Verde, where Anasazis (Ancestral Puebloans) dwelled before Ute people occupied the area. The small amount of flowing water in the Four Corners area flows down the sandy beds, primarily in the Mancos River, McElmo Creek, and Montezuma Creek—all seeking the San Juan River in northwest New Mexico. The San Juan River was an indefinite southern boundary of the early Utes. To the east along the state line is the San Juan Basin, where oil and gas are now extracted, as they are also in the Four Corners area. Through the San Juan Basin flow the San Juan River's tributaries—the Piedra, Navajo, Los Piños, Florida, Animas, and La Plata—all of which begin in Colorado's snowy mountains.

Skirting the Navajos' Gobernador region, Ute territory continued to the southeast—down the Chama River and sandy hills, pastel cliffs, and forested, yellow-soiled Tierra Amarilla country to the Rio Grande and the heart of the northern Pueblo Indian region in New Mexico. Northward on both sides of the Rio Grande, piñon-juniper woodland ascends the Taos Plateau to Colorado's San Luis Valley and New Mexico's Taos Valley and Red River area. In this area the Rio Grande cuts a deep gorge, an obstacle to east-west travel, although Indians were able to create footpaths down the steep embankments to cross the river. To the east is the Sangre de Cristo Range, containing New Mexico's highest peaks and some of Colorado's 14,000 footers.

North and northeast of the San Juan Basin, relatively low hogbacks and hills of sandstone and shale tilt toward the heady heights of the mineral-rich La Plata and San Juan Mountains. In these 13,000- and 14,000-foot volcanic peaks lay treasures of gold and silver that would lure hordes of white newcomers to usurp the Indians' land. The silvery San Juans, as they are sometimes called, are so rugged and beautiful that it is impossible to suppose the Utes ignored aesthetics as they went about their rounds of hunting and gathering. Surely they loved these mountains passionately in autumn, in "Indian summer," when golden aspen leaves framed jagged summits, gleaming with their early snow, and the sun, shining out of a cerulean heaven, still breathed warm on Ute shoulders. When it was time to descend, it was not far to the Uncompahgre Valley to the north or the Animas to the south, both favorite winter campgrounds.

To the north of the San Juans are the West Elk and the Elk Mountains—which should not be confused with Utah's pseudonymous La Sals—offering outstanding hunting and, unfortunately for the Utes, more seductive minerals that would bring whites. Knee-deep wildflowers bloom in profusion, turning valleys and woodlands into magnificent gardens in summer while scrub oak and aspens weave Persian carpets in fall. The breathtaking Elk Mountains, volcanic like the San Juans, lie between the Gunnison Valley on the south and the famous Maroon Bells on the north. Colorado's Rockies were rich in plant and animal resources similar to those in Utah's high elevations.

To the east in the mineral belt are the soaring Sawatch Range and the Mosquito Range. Several of Colorado's summits over 14,000 feet lie in these two groups, including Mount Elbert, the highest. Altitude would prove no deterrent to gold and silver miners, though. Between the Sawatch and the Mosquitoes are the headwaters of the Arkansas River, flowing south for several miles in a valley formed by a deep fault before it turns east toward the Royal Gorge and the Great Plains.

This fault, called the Rio Grande Rift, continues south from the Upper Arkansas River through the San Luis Valley and New Mexico, funneling the waters of the Rio Grande for much of this distance. The semiarid climate and cold winters of the San Luis Valley belie its value as good hunting land for bison, deer, and pronghorn antelope in former times, and wetlands in its basin attracted great numbers of waterfowl. Not only Utes but also Pueblo peoples visited this area and held it sacred. Tewa people believed one of the lakes was their place of origin, and Navajos made pilgrimages to Blanca Peak, rising to over 14,000 feet elevation in the Sangre de Cristos, as it was their sacred mountain of the east. The San Juan Mountains lie on the west side of the San Luis Valley, and the high, ragged Sangre de Cristo Range extends down the east side and into New Mexico as far as Santa Fe.

Three other large mountain parks, like bowls in a sea of mountains, are found in Colorado. Better watered but smaller than the San Luis Valley are South Park (or Bayou Salado), Middle Park, and North Park, all prized as hunting grounds by the Utes. From North Park, the North Platte flows toward Wyoming, creating a thoroughfare for Utes and enemy Plains tribes. In addition to many bison, deer, elk, and pronghorns in these parks, beaver awaited trappers. The streams also contained flakes of gold, promising veins and lodes to prospectors who one day would swarm into the parks and their surrounding peaks. To the west of South Park is the Mosquito Range. The Gore and Park Ranges bound the west sides of Middle Park and North Park.

To the east of the Sangre de Cristos in Colorado are the Wet Mountains, which drop off to grassy foothills and the Great Plains. In similar fashion the Front Range separates the northern two-thirds of Colorado's mountains from the plains, which begin at elevations of about 4,000 to 6,000 feet about sea level—approximately the same as the base of the Wasatch Front, with similar natural resources, far to the west. Hogbacks of sandstone, like those at Red Rocks near Denver, were tilted to the west as the Rockies rose. With the exception of these hogbacks, the eastern foothills in early times were well supplied with grasses, yucca, cacti, oak thickets, wild turkeys, game, rattlesnakes, the ubiquitous all-purpose rabbit, and other small mammals. Huge herds of bison, perhaps as many as sixty million, roamed the plains. The base of the Rockies was the eastern edge of Ute country, and this margin was often the meeting place of mountain Utes heading east to hunt bison on the plains and Plains Indians heading west to fight Utes for control of territory. When bison were vanishing from the western edge of the plains and from Utah by the 1840s, these animals still could be found in the mountain parks, which then became more hotly contested as hunting grounds.

Along the Front Range, numerous rivers cut routes of travel for the mountain Utes and their Plains enemies. Among these routes, in New Mexico the Cimarron and Canadian Rivers were important. In southern Colorado there were the Apishipa, Purgatoire, Huerfano, and Arkansas. Farther north were Fountain Creek, Plum Creek, the South Platte, Clear Creek, Boulder Creek, the St. Vrain, Big Thompson, and Cache la Poudre.

In addition to the four major parks, other mountain valleys attracted Utes and their enemies. There were the Wet Mountain Valley between the Sangre de Cristos and the Wet Mountains, the Upper Arkansas,

Taylor Park, the Gunnison and Yampa Valleys, among countless others. Utah's Wasatch Range also has many inviting valleys such as those around the Sevier and San Pete Rivers, Heber City, and particularly the Strawberry Valley at the west end of the Uinta Basin.

Expeditions to these locations were seasonal activities of hunter-gatherers, who traveled within circuits as animals migrated or emerged from their wintering grounds and as various plant foods matured. The Utes described the different elevations as Lower Earth, Middle Earth, and Upper Earth.[5] Lower Earth consisted of low valleys and places such as the bottom of the Royal Gorge or Canyonlands. Middle Earth, also known as the Blue Earth, whose Ute name, Saguguachipa, has evolved to Saguache and Sawatch, took in mountain valleys and parks and their foothills. These do, indeed, appear blue at times from a distance. Upper Earth included high, rocky ridges and peaks.[6] A few lofty trails and game drives have been located by archaeologists, but it is impossible to determine positively which of these were used by Utes and which by earlier hunters. Seeds, berries, roots, and nuts had to be harvested from early summer into autumn by women and girls in Middle Earth.

The geography of these circuits was based on knowledge handed down from generation to generation by family members who could remember and predict where and when harvesting and hunting would be good and how to travel from one site to another. Depending as they did on natural resources for survival, Utes did not wantonly change or destroy those resources but instead respected them. This is the underlying philosophy when Native Americans today warn that everyone must respect Mother Earth if we are to survive. Everything is interrelated, and everything—even inanimate rock—has its place. It is all part of the Circle of Life. As former Southern Ute Tribal Chairman Clement Frost has said, "The land does not belong to us. We belong to the land. We utilized the land for our survival."[7]

The piñon-juniper zone offers an especially rich diversity of plants and animals. At an elevation of 5,000 to 7,000 feet or slightly higher, its climate tends to be a little warmer than the surrounding valley floors, where cold air settles. Winter camps were often located in this zone, where animals seeking shelter from snowbound elevations above and exposed valleys below also winter.

After their supply of food had been secured, the Utes retired to campgrounds where many small family groups could come together and enjoy some hard-won comforts and social intercourse. Such locations in post-horse times required sufficient food and water for ponies, so river bottoms with cottonwoods were often popular sites.

Hot springs also attracted winter camps with opportunities for soothing, healing baths. The Rockies have many geothermal and mineral springs. For example, in central Colorado the Roaring Fork Valley alone has about a hundred, and near the mouth of this river is renowned Glenwood Springs. Other well-known hot springs in Colorado are those at Ouray and Pagosa Springs, Mount Princeton, Poncha Springs, Hot Sulphur Springs, Steamboat Springs, Juniper Warm Spring, and Manitou Springs. Countless smaller springs are found throughout the former Ute territory in Colorado, New Mexico, and Utah. Large or small, wherever such springs are found it can be assumed that they were enjoyed by the Utes. Many springs also had religious significance.

Well-worn trails converged on these locations, as they did also at river crossings, such places requiring alertness to ascertain who else might be in the area. These were locations where unplanned, undesirable encounters might occur. Away from such sites, pre-horse family groups could travel their traditional annual circuits with fair assurance of security, for the hunting territories of each group were usually respected except in times of scarcity of resources.[8] After Indians had obtained horses, competition became much more common and intense, however.

Ute territory contained a vast, still identifiable network of paths, some following game trails in their origins and some becoming the routes of driveways for livestock or, more recently, of modern highways. Nearly every mountain pass, high or low, had a trail. Maps today are liberally sprinkled with numerous Ute Passes and Ute Creeks or the names of head men and bands. Mountains and plateaus also carry such names. A designation like the Dog Trail near Trail Ridge Road in Rocky Mountain National Park reveals how some early Utes moved about, with dogs dragging small travois or carrying light loads. Other names, like Cochetopa Pass, come from Indian words. Bison once migrated across this pass between the San Luis and Gunnison Valleys. *Kúcu* is the Ute word for bison, and with assorted phonetic variations the pass has become Cochetopa. At one time it also was Anglicized as the "Buffalo Pass" or "Buffalo Crossing."

Thousands of panels of petroglyphs and pictographs are like road signs, advertising trails and campsites and suggesting events that occurred along the way. Famed Newspaper Rock between Moab and Monticello, Utah, for example, testifies to the adventures of both prehistoric peoples and horse-mounted Utes near a reliable spring of water.

In late winter or early spring, Utes came over the trails from winter camps for their biggest gathering. It was the season when the most powerful and fearsome animal the Utes knew, the bear, was awakening from hibernation. It was the season when the first hint of green touched the plants. It was the season of the Bear Dance.

Long, long ago, before anyone can remember, a hunter encountered a bear leaving its winter den. The bear told the young man that Ute hunters would be successful and their women would be fertile, assuring the strength of their tribe, if his people would dance the Bear Dance. Ever after, they greeted the new cycle of life with this dance. They still do.

The Circle of Life continues.

2

▼ ▼ ▼

The Núu-ci

"We were always here," say the Utes, reluctant to discuss their history, even their myths. Equally obscure is the archaeological story that might reveal when and how this tribe came to occupy its present territory.

About eight millennia before Ute Indians appeared in North America, hunters and gatherers of the Archaic Stage, which lasted until about A.D. 500, appeared in North America. Ute people, who also were hunters and gatherers with a similar lifestyle, are believed to have come from Mexico into what is now the southwestern part of the United States in about A.D. 1000. Whether Ute sites are in the Great Basin, the Colorado Plateau, or the Central and Southern Rockies, archaeologists have had difficulty distinguishing between Late Archaic and Early Ute occupation. Even on Colorado's Uncompahgre Plateau, where it was once thought a continuum between the two cultures might be proved, archaeologists have been unable to provide convincing material evidence of such a link.[1]

Additional confusion arises in connection with Ancestral Puebloans, or Anasazi, and Fremont People, who were called Mo-cutz (Moquis), meaning "the dead ones," by the Utes. Belonging to the Formative Stage, these two cultures existed in the Great Basin and on the Colorado Plateau prior to the arrival of the Utes. The agricultural way of life of the Anasazi, who occupied the Four Corners region, differed markedly from that of the Utes.

On the other hand, the Fremont People, occupying eastern and northeastern Utah and northwestern Colorado with several geographic variants, combined hunting and gathering with sedentary and agricultural activities. It has been speculated but not proven that late Fremonts possibly reverted to the Desert Culture, indistinguishable from the Ute way of life, but archaeological investigations have been unable to link the Fremonts and the Utes, although they overlapped geographically in some areas.[2] Firm chronology has been the stumbling block.

Utes deny any knowledge of the Anasazis' departure from the Four Corners region, which took place about A.D. 1300–1350. Although early in the twentieth century Jesse Fewkes reported that Utes told of their killing many ancient people in McElmo Canyon around Battle Rock, archaeologists have found no evidence of such conflicts there or elsewhere in former Anasazi country.[3] The arrival of Utes, Navajos, and Apaches at about this time often has been suggested as a reason the Anasazis vacated the region, but climatic changes and depletion of natural resources are more widely accepted causes, and the same explanations, not warfare, might also account for the disappearance of the Fremonts.

It is generally agreed that the Utes as a recognizable people began to appear about A.D. 1000–1200 in the southern part of the Great Basin, roughly where eastern California and southern Nevada meet. The Southern Paiute Tribe, closely related to the Utes, has an origin myth placing its beginnings east of Death Valley and north of Las Vegas in Nevada. According to this myth, Coyote brought a sack of sticks from the south to Pahranagat, where the Paiutes, Utes, Shoshones, and Mookweetch (Hopi or Anasazi) escaped from the sack.[4]

Today, most authorities agree that Uto-Aztecan people moved north from Mexico, this migration beginning perhaps as long ago as 2000 B.C.[5] Some continued to raise corn, beans, and squash as their people had done previously, but everyone depended on hunting and gathering, surviving with the techniques of the Desert Culture in a harsh environment.[6] Although a few scholars believe the next wave of dispersal began in the central Great Basin, the most commonly accepted theory is that it began in the Death Valley area: Shoshones went north, Utes went northeast, and Southern Paiutes "stayed in this country," as that tribe says. In an effort to trace the spread, prehistoric twined and coiled basketry from the Great Basin has been submitted as physical evidence.[7]

Today's distribution of related tribes fans out through the Great Basin to Idaho and southeast Oregon, to southern Wyoming, and to Colorado's mountains and adjacent New Mexico. Utes were present in the Four Corners region by A.D. 1300 and rapidly completed their spread across Colorado's Rocky Mountains within a century or two.

The most reliable link among these people is the Uto-Aztecan linguistic family, shared by Utes and others who are traced to the Great Basin. Three main linguistic branches of this family are Nahuatlan, used by Aztecs, Toltecs, and other early people; Sonoran, of northern Mexico; and Shoshonean, the branch brought into the Great Basin. Distant linguistic relatives of Utes include Mexico's Tarahumaras and Arizona's Hopis. The Shoshonean branch began to spread out from the area of Death Valley about A.D. 1000, with diversity increasing as the distance between groups of people grew. Eventually, three linguistic divisions of the Shoshonean emerged west of the Rockies, these being the Mono-Bannock division, which includes Monos, Northern Paiutes, Snakes, and Bannocks; the Shoshone-Comanche-Koso (Panamint) division, which includes Comanches, Gosiutes, Shoshones, and a small number of California's Indians; and the Ute-Chemehuevi division, which includes the Southern Paiutes, Kawaiisus, Chemehuevis, and Utes.[8] Another way to classify the Shoshonean linguistic branch has been Western, Eastern, Central, and Southern Numic—the last being used by Southern Paiutes, Chemehuevis, and Utes.[9] Currently, the most common classification is simply Western, Central, and Southern Numic.[10]

Despite dialectic differences among various groups, the relatedness of language from division to division is apparent. It is because of these similarities that the spread of peoples into and beyond the Great Basin is believed to be relatively recent.

Regardless of linguistic divisions, the language is called Numic, and its speakers are called the Numic people. This name is based on the similarity of words used for *people*. With some variations among Utes, the word for people is *Núu-ci*, which can mean any humans or Indians according to the strict definition of the word but which usually refers specifically to the Ute people.[11]

Utes often call themselves "Nuche" and other variants, such as "Nooche," as well as the more common word *Ute*. This word appears to be a Spanish corruption of the name *Guaguatu* or *Guaputa*, used by Jemez Indians when they told Spaniards about some Indians who talked like Mexican Indians and who came to the Interior Province with the conquistadors. Spaniards then spoke of Utes and all other people who spoke Shoshonean dialects as Yutas.[12] Several variant spellings have appeared. Hopis speak of Ute Indians as Utaws or Yotas, and Shoshones have called them Yoo'tawtch.

After the Utes had acquired horses and thus had more contact with different American Indian tribes, they also used sign language, or gesture speech, to communicate. In the northern and eastern parts of their territory, where more frequent encounters with Plains Indians took place, sign language was better known than in remote locations such as the Four Corners, however.[13]

While they were limited to foot travel for centuries, the Utes' out-ward spread was gradual. Nevertheless, seeking uncontested territory and optimum natural resources, Utes had become the principal occupi-ers of their huge domain by 1598 when Spaniards first colonized New Spain's northern province. Adaptations to the starkly contrasting envi-ronments within Ute country directly influenced differences among Ute groups of the Great Basin, the Colorado Plateau, and the Central and Southern Rockies. Adaptation to a particular environment could also result in similarities among unrelated groups, though. Consequently, it is sometimes difficult to distinguish who occupied a site—whether Na-vajos or Utes in the San Juan Basin, along the Chama River, or on the Uncompahgre Plateau, for instance—or to attempt to draw clear bound-aries between such groups.[14] Even more difficult is the attempt to place boundaries between the Utes and Southern Paiutes of southern and southeastern Utah. In contrast, territorial boundaries to the north, east, and southeast were better known but still were blurred, especially after Utes and neighboring tribes became mounted. The physical appearance of Utes, who are typically dark-skinned, stocky, and less than five feet nine inches tall, appears to have been affected by intermixture with other peoples, as some Utes are six feet or more in height.

Estimates of maximum Ute population range from 5,000 to 10,000 at the time of first white contact. Utes traveled in many small groups of extended family members. These clans were identified by the name of a current headman, a preferred geographic area, a favorite food source, or some special trait. Examples of such names linger in English as the Elk Mountain Utes, the Rabbit Eaters, the Fish Utes, or the Capotes ("blan-ket wearers"). Occasionally, names given by outsiders were derogatory, as when one group was called the "humping Utes" because of their sexual activity or "lizards" because of their hot, dry homeland and food source. Although in early times a single chief might lead a family clan, he did not head a large band, much less an entire tribe. A special leader was designated for a specific undertaking such as fishing, warfare, hunting, or deciding when to move camp.

Except at places where very large harvests of fish, game, or nuts were available, large numbers of people did not come together in summer and fall. After the harvest in winter, several hundred people might come together. This was the time for visiting and for the telling of the old legends. Most popular sites for winter encampments were near rivers and creeks. In New Mexico they were found at Abiquiú, Taos, and Cimarrón. In Colorado they were at today's Pueblo, Colorado Springs, Denver, and Fort Collins along the Front Range and at Yampa, Meeker,

Grand Junction, Montrose, and Delta deeper in the mountains.[15] Among known locations elsewhere were today's Fort Duchesne and Provo in Utah.

In addition to seasonal migration, individuals occasionally moved from one group to another and even from one tribe to another as a result of intermarriage, captivity, quarrels, and, later, displacement by white settlement and removal to reservations. The perception that a band always had the same name, location, and constituency has led to many misconceptions that overlook this fluidity, which became pronounced after Utes acquired horses.

Some, though not all, names of bands known today resulted from the need of the United States bureaucracy to departmentalize, compartmentalize, and label its wards after agencies and reservations were created. For more than a century now, Ute tribes have been called Northern and Southern, with the Ute Indian Tribe of the Uintah and Ouray Reservation, Utah, comprising the former and the Southern Ute Tribe and the Ute Mountain Ute Tribe comprising the latter, but these terms are inadequate in describing prereservation Utes. To take into account differences in cultural characteristics, anthropologists now tend to speak of Western (west of the Green River) and Eastern Utes (east of the Green River), but even this terminology does not fit all Utes.

Despite these many hurdles, it is necessary and possible to provide some names of the people who occupied various geographical territories. The following brief summaries will give some understanding of the groups encountered after white contact, at which time the term *band* became commonly used.

In southwestern Utah, not far from where it is assumed Utes first emerged as a people, were found Pahvants, called Barbones or bearded "Yutas" when the Domínguez-Escalante expedition encountered them in 1776. The expedition's journal speculated that these people might have been descendants of Spaniards, who had beards. Barbones were also distinguished by polished bones worn in their noses—a practice shared by their bearded neighbors, the Timpanogots, to the north around Utah Lake. These two groups spoke the same dialect, the explorers noted. Barbones ranged from the Sevier River south to today's Beaver, Utah. South of them were Southern Paiutes, called Yutas Cobardes, the "timid Utes," by the Spaniards.[16]

Pahvant Utes (Pavant, Parant, Pahva-ntits, and other spellings) historically occupied the area around Sevier Lake and Clear Lake, as well as lush meadows at the foot of the mountains. *Pah* means "much water," and these water people enjoyed fish and waterfowl along with the

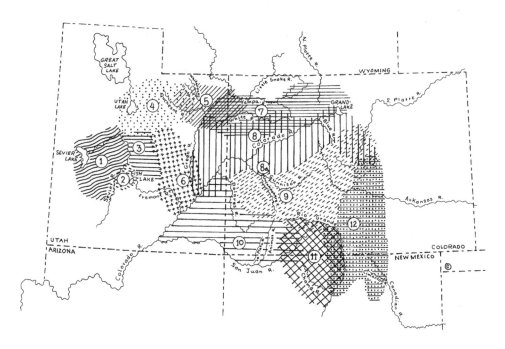

Distribution of Ute Indian bands: 1. Pahvant, 2. Moanunt, 3. Sanpits, 4. Timpanogots, 5. Uintah, 6. Seuvarits, 7. Yampa, 8. Parianuche, 8a. Sabuagana, 9. Tabeguache, 10. Weenuche, 11. Capote, 12. Muache.

wild plants and game of the watershed. After some intermixture with Paiutes from the south, Pahvants farmed along Corn Creek both before and after contact with white people. Following the removal of Pahvants to the Uintah Valley Reservation in the Uinta Basin, some of this group returned to southern Utah near Kanosh where they had earlier lived and shared their home with off-reservation Southern Paiutes. Residents of the area have mistakenly called all of these people Paiutes.[17]

To the southeast of the Pahvants were Moanunts (Moavinunts) who lived near Bicknell, Marysvale, Red Lake, and elsewhere south of Salina. A group of Moanunts summered at Fish Lake, trapping and netting fish and hunting, and were called Fish Utes. As they intermixed with Paiutes, some were called "half-Ute" and "half-Paiute." They spent their winters at Koosharem. Some Fish Utes, who went south to raid Paiutes for captives in prereservation times, were regarded by the latter as a superior people who were rich and who knew special dances and crafts.[18] A few of these people went to the Uintah Valley Reservation, but others who did not eventually located around Koosharem, Richfield, and Kanosh. Even in the twentieth century they still returned seasonally to their cherished Fish Lake.

An unnamed group from around Parowan and Panguitch hunted at times as far east as the Waterpocket Fold in the Capitol Reef area. They also were called variously Paiutes or "half-Utes."[19]

To the west of the Pahvants were Southern Paiute Piedes and Shoshonean Gosiutes, or Goshutes. Although some intermixture did occur, "Diggers" were looked down on by their Ute neighbors, who preyed on the Piedes and Gosiutes for captives.[20]

East of the Pahvants were the "tule people," the Sanpits (Sahpeech, Sawmpeet, San Pitch, San Pete) who occupied the upper valley of the Sevier River where Manti and Mount Pleasant are situated. Early white observers considered this group to be comparatively poor and sometimes called them "Diggers," but the Sanpits enjoyed good hunting territory and were far from destitute. They sometimes roamed far afield to the southeast. Sanpits were eventually relocated to the Uintah Reservation.

The largest group of Utah's Utes were those at Utah Lake, or Lake Timpanogots, where they harvested large quantities of fish and shared social activities. Possibly an amalgamation of some members of neighboring peoples, these Utes have usually been called the Timpanogots (Toompahnahwach), although the Domínguez-Escalante party called them Lagunas, "lake people," and Come Pecado, "fish eaters."[21] Timpanogots means "rocky," a word once applied to the Provo River as well as to a nearby peak in the Wasatch Range.

When the Spaniards arrived at Utah Lake in September 1776, they found villages of Timpanogots all along the shores. Some of these people dispersed to hunt and fish in the Uinta Basin and elsewhere, but they, like other Western Utes, remained less mobile than Eastern Utes until the 1800s when horses were acquired in Utah. The villagers at the lake were peaceful people when the Domínguez-Escalante expedition visited them in 1776. After settlement by Euro-Americans, the Timpanogots were scattered among other Ute groups who were removed to the Uintah Valley Reservation.[22] In the 1930s Kurump Longhair told an interviewer that in early years her Duncan family had traveled north as far as Fort Bridger, Wyoming, south into Utah's Thistle Valley, and sometimes into the Utah Valley, but they wintered in the Uinta Basin from Vernal to Strawberry Reservoir. She called her people the "timpana-nuuci."[23]

No single band or tribe of Native Americans claimed the land east of Great Salt Lake, where many groups traded. North about thirty-five miles in the Ogden-Logan area was the territory of the Cumumbas, or

Weber Utes, who were a mixture of Ute and Shoshone. Their speech was also a mixture of the two, and their name means "talks different."[24] Still, Fred Conetah's excellent history of the Northern Utes includes Cumumbas among the major Ute groups, perhaps because some were sent to the Uintah Valley Reservation with other Utah Indians. Other Cumumbas went to a Shoshone reservation, though.

The crest of the east-west trend of the Uinta Mountains was traditionally accepted as the northern boundary of the Utes, with Wyoming's Shoshones occupying land beyond the range. The Uintah Utes (Uinta-atsm, Uintanuntsm, Yoowetuh) occupied the Uinta Basin, the region around the Green River, and the Tavaputs Plateau. Originally, Uintahs were less numerous than some other Ute groups, but after the creation of the Uintah Valley Reservation for Utah's Utes in the 1860s, bands who moved there increased the total population, all then being called collectively the Uintah Band. It included Pahvants, Sanpits, Timpanogots, Shoshonean Cumumbas, and a small fragment of the Seuvarits.

Seuvarits (Sheberitch, Sahyehpeech) had focused their activities chiefly in the area between Castle Valley on the west and the Monticello-Moab area on the east. Because of this presence around the La Sal Mountains, once called the Elk Mountains, these people were called the Elk Mountain Utes by their agents, one of whom reported that besides the Utah contingent his Elk Mountain Band included some others from Colorado and Arizona.[25] Probably those from Colorado were Weenuches and those from Arizona Southern Paiutes. The Southern Paiute name for the Elk Mountain people is Suhuh'vawduhuts, Anglicized to Sheberitch, meaning "squawbush water people."[26] When some Seuvarits went to the Uintah Valley Reservation, others went to Arizona. In 1930 Daisy Ais, an elderly woman who said her father was a Seuvarits, reported that most of the band had died in an epidemic in the early 1870s.[27]

In Colorado's northwest sector, a large number of Yampa Utes (Yamparikas, Yampaticas, Yahpudttka), the "root eaters," lived primarily south of the Yampa (Bear) River and north of the White River. Independent by nature, the Yampas traveled far and wide, hunting on the Little Snake River in southern Wyoming, on Colorado's Flattops, and in both Middle Park and North Park. Some visited the Uinta Basin, too. On the north, horse-mounted Comanches and eventually Arapahos would deter the Yampas' wanderings and territorial claims.

In 1776 Sabuagana Utes were found at Grand Mesa and northward into the Douglas Creek area by Domínguez and Escalante. Their cartographer, Don Bernardo Miera y Pacheco, placed "Zaguegunas" north and northeast of the La Sal Mountains. Most likely, this was the group later known as the Parianuches (Parianuc, Pahdteeahnooch, Parasanuch), the "elk people," later called the Grand River Utes.[28] Their territory extended into eastern Utah and up the Colorado River (formerly called the Grand River) to their winter resort at Glenwood Springs, onto Grand Mesa and the Flattops, up the Roaring Fork (the Bunkara), and into the mountains to the headwaters.

After the establishment of an agency on the White River near Meeker in the 1860s, both Yampas and Parianuches, or Grand River Utes, were assigned to it. Together, these bands were subsequently called the White River Band. Until then, there were no Utes with this name. White River Utes were removed to the Uintah Reservation in 1881 in the aftermath of the Meeker Massacre. The Uncompahgre Utes also were sent to Utah, where additional reservation land was provided for them on the Ouray Reservation. The Uintah and Ouray Reservations soon were consolidated.

Originally, the Uncompahgres were called the Tabeguaches (Taveewach, Taviwach), their territory being south of the Parianuches. The Domínguez-Escalante expedition learned that "Tabehuachis" lived near the Dolores River and Disappointment Creek and mentioned that the Sierra de los Tabehuachis, known today as the Uncompahgre Plateau, was their particular territory.[29] Popular wintering grounds of this band were in the Uncompahgre Valley and between Montrose and Grand Junction along the Gunnison River, called the Tomichi by Utes. This group ranged far afield, as far away as North Park even, but more often they traveled to South Park, the Upper Arkansas Valley, the San Luis Valley, and Colorado's Elk Mountains. Following the creation of agencies and of ever shrinking reservations in southwestern Colorado, the Tabeguaches became known as the Uncompahgre Utes after their last agency in Colorado was established in the Uncompahgre Valley in the 1870s. Along with the White River Utes, the Uncompahgres were removed to Utah following the Meeker Massacre.

The group occupying southwestern Colorado and, to some extent, southeastern Utah was the Weenuches (Weeminuche, Weminuche, Wiminuche). The present spelling, used now by the Weenuches themselves, avoids a derisive implication and has been adopted in this text. The name *Weenuche* means "long time ago people."[30] The group occupied mountains, mesas, and valleys west of the San Juan Mountains and north of the San Juan River in southwest Colorado and southeast Utah, as far north as the Blue Mountains.[31] To the north in Colorado the Weenuches overlapped with the Tabeguaches, and in the southwest they overlapped with Southern Paiutes as well as Navajos. Navajos south of the San Juan River and their Ute neighbors usually were not on friendly terms, and mutual trespass into one another's territory resulted in raids and battles throughout the Four Corners region. Occasionally, Weenuches planted small crops of corn, as did their neighbors to the south.

East of the Continental Divide in southern Colorado and northern New Mexico were two Ute groups—the Capotes and the Muaches, who now comprise the Southern Ute Tribe. The name of the Capotes (Capota, Kapota, Kaputa), meaning "blanket" or "cloak" in Spanish, might have been derived from the Jemez word *Guaputa*. These Utes lived along New Mexico's Chama River, on the eastern slopes of the southern San Juan Mountains, and in the southwestern portion of the San Luis Valley.

Typically, the territory of the Muaches (Mouache, Moache, Mowatsi, Muhuachi), meaning "cedar bark people" in Ute, is described as being located east of the Sangre de Cristos in New Mexico, along the Front Range in Colorado, in the Wet Mountain Valley, in the southeastern part of the San Luis Valley, and around Taos.[32] In 1765 the Rivera expedition reportedly came upon some "Mauchi Utes" in the Dolores River area of southwestern Colorado.[33] Moreover, the Miera map made only a few years later shows "Muchaches Yutas" on the nearby Mancos River, and Escalante's journal mentioned "Muchaches" country south of Disappointment Creek, while north of it were the "Tabehuachi." Possibly, these Muaches were simply travelers, but reports of their presence in southwestern Colorado raise an unresolved question about early distribution.

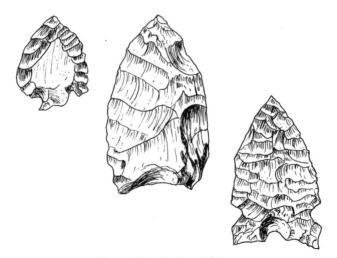

Typical Ute Indian lithics.

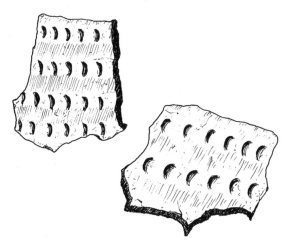

Shards of Ute Indian brownware pottery.

When a Southern Ute agency and reservation were established in the 1870s, Weenuches, Muaches, and Capotes were assigned there. Later the Weenuches were given the western portion of the reservation, and eventually they became the Ute Mountain Ute Tribe, separate from the Southern Ute Tribe composed of Muaches and Capotes. Now enrolled with the Weenuches are Utes mixed with some Southern Paiutes of the San Juan Band and some Navajos. Occupying the area around White Mesa and Allen Canyon near Blanding, Utah, they are designated as White Mesa Utes.

Generally, one might assume that early Utes who traveled on foot made few changes in affiliation from one group to another. Depending on the natural resources to be found during their seasonal circuits, Utes sought familiar habitats offering water, shelter, game, and wild plants. As they moved about they came to well-known rock shelters, caves, or places where they could erect brush shelters and tepees on sunny benches and hills, a short distance from, rather than directly adjacent to, water. Hunting camps might be located in wooded areas, but villages were most often in open areas, with shelters usually facing south or east.

Ute sites may contain wickiup poles leaning against a tree; scaffolds for hunting, burial platforms, or vision quests; eagle traps; grooves worn in rocks where tools were sharpened or tepee poles were smoothed; small, notched projectile points, other lithic tools, and countless flakes; manos and metates used for grinding; small amounts of ceramic brownware; and rock art. Many sites have multiple components, evidence that for thousands of years people of different cultures were attracted to certain localities with suitable natural resources and that in historical times people of different tribes lived in "Ute country."

Making use of natural resources, Utes provided necessities—shelter, tools, food, medicine, and clothing. Although some dry caves and over-hangs offered protection, brush shelters, wickiups, and tepees were more common. Utes around the Great Basin's lakes and marshes used grasses, willows, and rushes to thatch round-topped huts with a framework of strong twigs or stems, bent concentrically and tied in place with plant fibers. With no nearby supplies of wood, these Utes burned bulrushes as fuel, too. A windscreen of brush might surround a group of shelters as protection from cold or dusty winds. Other Utes besides the Great Basin people also made brush shelters, even after tepees and cabins became common. Smaller versions were built for sweat baths and for menstrual huts where women were required to remain during their menstrual cycles. Open-sided brush shelters were used for summer sunshades or cooking and are still frequently found in the yards of modern Ute homes.

There were many alternatives for the conical, skin-covered tepees that are a stereotype for Native American shelters. In the foothills and on mesas, Ute wickiups sometimes consisted of several poles leaning against a tree trunk or strong branch, although others were freestanding. In piñon-juniper country the poles might be rather crooked, whereas aspens, cottonwoods, and lodgepole pines provided straight building material. Often, the poles were heavily covered with boughs, but sometimes the poles were stacked so closely that little additional packing was needed.

When tepees were used, the skin covers sometimes consisted of up to ten elk hides, sewn together and placed over a conical framework of poles. With a diameter of fifteen or seventeen feet, these tepees could house half a dozen or more individuals. There is no reliable evidence that pre-horse Utes possessed these large elk-skin tepees or those made with bison hides, although humans and dogs might have transported small shelters.[34] At a later time, when Utes did have large tepees, they were carried on packhorses, with poles lashed to the animals' sides. Plains-type travois came into use later.

Tepees offered some conveniences. For instance, an adjustable flap could be moved with a pole to allow smoke from the central hearth to be ventilated out the top. Dew claws attached to the entrance flap served as a door knocker. A small tripod outside the entrance held valued possessions, such as a saddle or a shield made of bison hide, to identify the owner. Another tripod might support a mat of tules or willow twigs serving as his backrest. Inside the shelter, mattresses of juniper bark, evergreen boughs, or willow or tule mats were covered with rabbit-skin blankets or bison robes for beds. By the late 1800s a few Utes were living in cabins built of logs or adobe bricks, and by the 1900s most Utes who still had tepees were using canvas covers. Some also had canvas tents.

Utes also relied solely on natural resources for food, and they exploited whatever animal and plant foods were available. Around Utah Lake, Fish Lake, and other bodies of water in Utah, Utes used rafts made of bulrushes to fish, catch waterfowl, and collect eggs. The Indians also fished with hooks, sometimes fashioned from tiny ribs of mice, but fish were more commonly harvested in weirs, traps, and nets or even by hand when fish were abundant.

Utes did not hunt bison in large numbers until after horses were acquired. There were small numbers of bison in Western Ute territory, especially in the Uinta Basin, but many more roamed to the north in southern Wyoming, on Colorado's plateaus and mountain valleys, and primarily, of course, on the Plains. Bison could be killed by stampeding them or spearing them in bogs or brush corrals. Game animals most commonly sought by Utes were deer, bighorn sheep, elk, and pronghorn antelope. Black bears were feared, but there was no taboo preventing the killing or eating of bears, and the prowess of anyone who killed a grizzly bear was held in high esteem. Small animals including beaver, gophers, lizards, and insects were eaten, but rabbits—caught with nets and snares made of plant fibers, traps woven of willow, nooses, and clubs—were most abundant.[35] Large birds such as ducks, geese, cranes, sage hens, grouse, and wild turkeys were taken for food, feathers, and bones. When communal hunts took place, a hunt chief was designated as leader of the activity. Customs carrying religious connotations accompanied the killing of animals, and an adolescent boy's first big hunt was a rite of passage, with the species he killed becoming a symbol of his character.[36]

Bows and arrows had been used in North America for several hundred years prior to the presence of Ute Indians, and these weapons provided the principal way Utes killed animals, although some spears were also used for hunting and fishing. The earliest Ute bows were made from the horns of mountain sheep. Single- and double-curved wooden bows followed.[37] These bows were made chiefly from chokecherry, serviceberry, mountain mahogany, or juniper and were wrapped with sinew. Twisted sinew provided bow strings. Arrows made of chokecherry, serviceberry, currant, juniper, and other woods were scraped, heated, and straightened between rocks before being trimmed with bird feathers and attached with sinew and glue produced from animal hide or horn. Fletches and painted designs identified the owner of an arrow and, thus, a successful hunter or warrior. Ute arrowheads were small and usually side notched. They were made of many materials—such as chert, jasper, obsidian, basalt, even feldspar, and by the 1800s iron and glass. Good material for knapping arrowheads came from well-known quarries within Ute country and was carried with the Indians in small chunks, called preforms, for manufacturing points.

After a hunt, women did most butchering. They also did the cooking by roasting or by simmering food in waterproofed baskets into which heated stones were dropped. Women preserved meat and fish by drying or smoking them. Salt was also a preservative that could be collected at places such as flats around Utah's saline lakes, Brine Creek, the La Sal (meaning "salt") Mountains, Paradox Valley, and South Park's Salt Creek.

Although some early Utes may have traded occasionally with Puebloan people for corn, beans, and squash, as did later Utes, they depended chiefly on gathering wild plant foods for survival, so much so that it might be better to call these Indians gatherer-hunters rather than hunter-gatherers. Women collected harvests in baskets made from squawbush, willow, and red osier dogwood. Ute women crafted excellent coiled baskets and twined baskets of various shapes and sizes to fit their needs. There were burden baskets and berry baskets, as well as baskets for cooking, water jugs, winnowing trays, seed beaters, bowls, dippers, and even shades for cradleboards to protect babies while their mothers worked. The most characteristic basket was the *kanosh*, a round-bottomed, narrow-necked water jug coated with pitch to make it watertight.[38] Wooden ladles and bowls were created from horns or from knots of trees. Only rarely did Ute women make ceramic pots, using a paddle-and-anvil technique when they did.[39] To meet their needs throughout the long year, women made rawhide bags, or parfleches, in which to store and transport their food.

A lexicon of plant names would be necessary to cite all of the berries, roots, shoots, pollens, flowers, leaves, and nuts that nourished the Utes. Among the staples were Indian ricegrass and sunflower seeds; sego and mariposa lily bulbs and wild onions; all the tender parts of bulrushes and cattails; roots of wild potatoes and yampa; cactus and yucca fruits; chokecherries, serviceberries, buffaloberries, squawberries, and currants; acorns and piñon nuts; the inner bark of ponderosa pines, cottonwoods, and aspens; and in spring the sweet sap tapped from aspens.

The largest part of women's time was occupied with harvesting and preparing food. Some of these foods were eaten raw, but others were cooked in soups, made into infusions, roasted, or dried for later consumption. Seeds and other dry products were ground on stone metates with manos to make gruels and flatbreads or cakes.

Besides providing nourishment, native plants also represented a pharmacy of remedies for wounds and illnesses. Leaving scars that can still be seen on old ponderosa pines, Utes peeled the outer bark of trees to obtain the inner bark for making poultices for cuts or for teas that, it was hoped, would cure anything from stomach and heart troubles to venereal diseases and smallpox.[40] Bark, roots, and galls of oak, aspen bark, ephedra, horsetail, sagebrush, mountain mahogany, osha root, and hundreds of herbs became medicines that might prevent or cure diseases, wounds, or poisonings. Not only plants but also animal materials—such as ground-up ants—and minerals, oil seeps, and mud provided internal or externals aids.

Clothing, another necessity, also came from the land's natural resources. In central Utah in September, Escalante observed Ute men wearing buckskin jackets and leggings, whereas women wore only aprons made of twined sagebrush bark, tules, or deerskin. In cold weather, however, Utes—adults and children—wrapped themselves in blankets woven of rabbit or other soft fur by twisting long strips of skin and intertwining them on a foundation of fiber. As late as the nineteenth century, in winter some Utes still wore wraps of bearskin or smaller, pieced skins of animals such as wolf, mountain lion, wolverine, bobcat, beaver, otter, rabbit, and deer.[41] Overshoes with the animals' hair left to the inside provided some warmth and could also be stuffed with sagebrush or other material for extra insulation. Small snowshoes helped Indians move over the snow.

In most seasons men wore fringed buckskin shirts, breech clouts, and long leggings tied to a belt. Women wore fringed doeskin dresses. The men's shirts consisted of two skins if sleeveless plus another skin if sleeves were provided, sewn with sinew. A typical dress consisted of two skins sewn together at the shoulders and sides, with a belt from which hung bags containing personal possessions. Desert Utes wore sandals made of yucca or sagebrush fibers or went barefoot, whereas in early times other men wore soft-soled moccasins. Later, they had hard-soled moccasins made from buffalo or elk skins.[42] Women's moccasins and knee-length leggings were made as one piece, pulled on like stockings. Children wore a belt around their garments, and sometimes a strap was attached to the belt so a mother could snatch a child quickly when danger appeared.

Paint on faces, clothing, and bags was the most common form of ornamentation among early Utes. Men wore their hair in two braids, which lay in front of their shoulders, and the braids might be intertwined with strips of fur, such as otter. Headdresses made of feathers, bird skins, or fur were worn at dances and ceremonies. Without ornaments, women's hair was parted in the middle and hung loose, although some women wore small basket hats, occasionally with feather decoration, for dances. Shampoo was created by rubbing pieces of yucca root in water. Men might decorate their shirts with long strands of hair, and women might embellish their dresses with elk teeth, but otherwise clothing had little adornment until the reservation era, when beadwork became popular. A little quillwork came into use, and jingles, cut from the tin lids of baking powder cans, were attached to dance garments. Contrary to what is shown in many portraits, ceremonial clothing was stored away and brought out only for special occasions to avoid the dirt, smoke, and grease that soiled everyday apparel.

Although men made excellent ropes from sinew and strips of rawhide, quivers for arrows, scabbards for knives, and other accessories, preparing skins was women's work, from scraping them clean of flesh and hair to tanning them with animal brains, staking them on the ground to stretch and dry, smoking them if a yellow hue was desired, and making many finished products. Women made garments and moccasins, rawhide parfleches for food storage, and small tanned leather bags for possessions such as awls, medicinal herbs, mirrors, flints, tobacco, and, later, ration tickets. Some Mexican-style, high-canteled saddles, consisting of a wooden frame covered with elk skin, were used by women. Ute women were famous for tanning skins, and their beautiful velvety products were important in trade with other Indian tribes and with white people.

As white traders came to the land, many tools the Indians had fashioned from stone, wood, and bone were replaced with metal trade goods such as knives, needles, fish hooks, axes, kettles, and projectile points. Devastating to Ute survival, though, was the arrival of settlers on land that had provided water, shelter, food, medicine, and clothing. The native people had adapted to a wide variety of ecosystems, from deserts and lakes to the plateaus and mountains of Utah, Colorado, and New Mexico. Even their myths and the animistic view of the world of which the Núu-ci were part were tied to the land. When Spaniards arrived in northern New Mexico in 1598, Utes could not imagine the changes that would soon transform their way of life.

3

▼ ▼ ▼

The Coming of the White Man
(1598–1821)

Led by Governor and Captain General Juan de Oñate, in 1598 the Spanish invaders were an astonishing spectacle with their horses, riders in metal and leather armor, firearms and long swords, friars in long robes, and Mexican Indian servants herding thousands of head of sheep, goats, and cattle. These first European colonists arrived at the southern edge of Ute territory and advanced as far north as San Juan Pueblo, near the confluence of New Mexico's Chama River with the Rio Grande. Utes soon learned about the unusual newcomers from the Pueblo people, who traded with Utes at San Juan, Taos, and Picuris[1] and learned that the Spaniards were requisitioning food and blankets from Pueblos, forcing them into slave labor, baptizing them into a new religion, and taking many to Mexico as slaves.

Before long, foreigners rode north into La Tierra de los Yutas, too, to hunt bison in the San Luis Valley and to seek silver and gold. In 1637 the first recorded battle took place there between Utes and Spaniards, and eighty Ute prisoners were taken south to Santa Fe where they, along with Jicarilla Apache captives, were forced into labor in Governor Luis de Rosas's textile workshop.[2] In 1640 some Utes escaped from Santa Fe and took their first horses, the beginning of a new era for the nomads.

As more horses were captured in following decades, the way of life of the Eastern Utes changed dramatically. The small, fast ponies thrived on native grasses in mountain valleys and on the plains and multiplied quickly without attempts at selective breeding. Mounted Utes reveled in their new ability to move greater distances than had previously been possible for their subsistence. They even traveled as far east as the panhandles of Texas and Oklahoma, and seasonal circuits within their

traditional territory widened. When wintering, larger groups could sustain themselves with supplies packed on their beasts of burden.

Gatherings of many tepees called for more structured leadership,
although both groups and leadership remained fluid, suiting the impera-
tives and impulses of family clans. Social life in winter encampments
offered a chance to tell the tribe's legends, to dance, gamble, race on foot
or on horseback, and gossip while the prized ponies grazed nearby or
browsed on piles of cottonwood branches gathered by the women.

The Utes' material culture changed, too. In addition to being able
to move heavy hide tepees from place to place, Utes added horse trappings to their most highly valued possessions—acquired as trade items,
as loot from raids, or as the handiwork of Ute men. Often they rode
bareback, or leather pads sufficed for saddles with short stirrups, allowing riders to guide their horses with their knees and leaving hands free
for shooting arrows rapidly. Quickly the proud, vigorous Utes became
renowned for their skill as horsemen, as well as for their large herds.
Ownership of ponies became the Ute Indians' principal symbol of wealth
and source of pride.

Cultural exchange increased between tribes, who met for trading
and socializing.[3] Horses enabled more frequent excursions to the pueblos for trading, and Pueblo Indians—who also were acquiring horses—
came to the Utes more often. Trading increased at Spanish settlements.
At the same time, more raids took place against Jicarilla Apaches, who
occupied the plains to the east, and against Navajos, who occupied lands
to the southwest. These foes also acquired horses and became raiders.

In 1670 Spaniards arranged a peace accord with Utes to stop raids,
but this treaty did not deter Utes from siding with the Pueblo Indians in
the 1680 revolt, when the Spaniards were driven out of New Mexico.
During the Spaniards' ensuing twelve-year absence, Utes took advantage of opportunities to acquire more horses and to raid pueblos, some of
whose people fled as far east as Kansas and as far west as the Hopi mesas,
where the uninvited Puebloans were allowed to remain after they helped
to fight off Ute aggressors who were attacking the Hopis.[4]

When Spaniards, led by Don Diego de Vargas, returned to Nuevo
Mexico in 1692, expeditions were undertaken to reestablish control
among the pueblos, where the people were fearful not only of the Spanish but also of the Utes. Even at the Hopi villages, Vargas saw mounted
Utes.[5] On one excursion in 1694, Vargas traveled north into the San
Luis Valley, and, surprisingly, the three hundred Utes he met there were
on foot, not on horses. These Utes signaled to each other news about
the army's presence with smoke signals and then attacked. After eight

Utes were killed and six soldiers were wounded, Vargas was able to hold a council with the Indians and to pacify them by smoking and distributing a few gifts. The Utes apologized, saying that the troops had been mistaken for Pueblo Indians who had been coming north to hunt, disguised in Spanish garments. Vargas invited the Utes to come to Santa Fe to trade, as they had done before the Pueblo Revolt.[6] His efforts were, at best, partly successful in controlling for a time the volatile mix of native people on Spain's northern frontier.

By 1700 many horses had been traded or had drifted north through Eastern Ute country into Comanche hands. These horsemen began moving east across southern Wyoming and south through the plains of eastern Colorado and finally New Mexico, where they arrived by 1705.[7] Here they enjoyed access to horses without Ute middlemen. The Comanches, who rapidly became a fearsome tribe, pressed against Jicarilla Apaches in southeastern Colorado and northeastern New Mexico. As a result, the mix of Utes, Apaches, Navajos, Pueblos, and Spaniards became unpredictable. Usually, Utes teamed up with Comanches to trade and raid. At Taos in 1706, Juan de Ulibari learned that Utes and Comanches were planning an attack, which, although it did not take place, alerted the government to the existence of an alarming new alliance of these two groups.[8] These foes plagued new Spanish-Mexican outposts, where land grants were being made in hopes of attracting settlers. Trade in slaves also accelerated because official policy approved ransoming of captives to prevent their being maimed or murdered by their captors—a successful kind of blackmail used by the captors.

As a defense against Utes, Comanches, and Jicarilla Apaches, pueblos such as Picuris and San Juan allied themselves with their former enemies, the Spanish, and became auxiliaries when punitive expeditions were sent out. Consequently, Utes and Comanches sought a peace accord with the Spaniards.[9] Nevertheless, depredations continued, with Jicarillas becoming a new target, until 1716. Following an attack on Taos Pueblo, Spanish forces went after the aggressors, killed 150 Ute men, and sold 350 Ute women into slavery in Mexico.[10]

But raids continued, most actions being by small groups of Muaches. A mestizo at Arroyo Hondo was wounded with arrows. A slave boy and the livestock he was tending at Embudo were run off the land. A Pueblo Indian was killed by a party of about forty Utes. Apaches protested an attack by Utes and Comanches, who killed many men and took the women and children captive. Governor Antonio Valverde y Cosio, eventually mounting a campaign against both Utes and Comanches, pursued the troublemakers onto the plains as far as the Arkansas River but captured none of the elusive "barbarous Indian gentiles."[11] Next, the Utes turned their energy against Navajos in New Mexico's Gobernador district, east of Farmington, while Comanches were wresting control of the High Plains from the Jicarilla Apaches. Apaches already had acquired firearms from Frenchmen on the eastern plains, and during warfare with Apaches in the 1720s Comanches also obtained some.

This constant turmoil among the tribes in New Mexico, combined with the threat of French intrusions from the east, led the provincial government at Santa Fe to invite Utes, Comanches, and also Jicarilla Apaches to come to Taos for friendly trade. Any hopes for peace and tranquillity were short-lived, however, as the balance of power on the plains was again upset. The new players were Kiowa Apaches, who were gradually moving south from the Black Hills area with a great supply of horses and equally great skill as horsemen. As Comanches and Kiowas became allies, Utes and Jicarilla Apaches joined forces in both offense and defense.

To protect settlements at the edges of population centers, in the mid-1730s the government at Santa Fe resorted to establishing *genízaros* at outlying locations, such as Abiquiú and Ojo Caliente. *Genízaros* were former captives from various tribes who had been baptized and had developed a measure of acculturation, along with Spanish names, and were allowed to live as free persons, engaging in subsistence farming in and around the outposts. They provided a front line of contact with Utes and other nomadic tribes. Some *genízaros*, who spoke both Spanish and Indian tongues, were engaged as interpreters, guides, and traders. Although the government attempted to enforce regulations prohibiting freelance operations, illicit trading opportunities attracted Indians to the outlying settlements. For instance, in 1735 restless Utes were camping near Ojo Caliente while Comanches were swapping buffalo robes for much-desired knives, called *belduques*, with an unlicensed Hispanic trader. The following year Utes raided an area near Abiquiú and successfully eluded a militia of settlers and Indians mustered at Santa Cruz.[12]

Abiquiú was located on the Chama River, the principal Indian trail to and from the northwest. As an active trading site, the village hosted an annual fair to which Utes came. Despite this arrangement, raiding for livestock, crops, and captives continued around both Abiquiú and Ojo Caliente. Independent parties of Capotes, Sabuaganas, Muaches, and Comanches took part in these attacks during the 1730s and 1740s. After a raid in 1747 in which an old woman was killed and many women and children were taken captive, surviving settlers abandoned both villages. An army of five hundred troops, sent out in pursuit of suspected

Capote and Comanche raiders, recovered a thousand head of livestock, including horses, and took 206 prisoners, but nervous settlers convinced the government that they should be allowed to leave their homes for a safer location.[13] These settlements were not reestablished until 1754.

By the late 1740s the Ute-Comanche alliance was breaking down, while Utes and Jicarilla Apaches collaborated increasingly in hit-and-run raids. They centered their activities in the Taos area and among the valleys and foothills of the Sangre de Cristo Mountains down to the margin of the plains. The allies also engaged Navajos around the San Juan River and pushed them west, away from Capote territory and into northeast Arizona. In an effort to ensure the friendship of Utes and other tribes, Spanish officials gave presents, a practice Indians came to expect from future governments as well.

Spaniards were not the only foreigners of concern to the Utes. The French were upsetting intertribal relations. In 1744 thirty-three Frenchmen had ventured into the headwaters of the Canadian River and traded guns to Comanches.[14] These Indians, who had become "lords of the plains" in less than half a century, blocked Utes and Jicarillas from enjoying similar trade associations with the French. Furthermore, Spanish bans against trading firearms meant Native Americans in the mountains had small quantities of those weapons. A few were obtained in raids, but they were of little use without ammunition.

During this period, with Utes continuing to steal large numbers of livestock in the Rio Grande Valley, New Mexico's governor met with Ute leaders and tried to reach an agreement whereby the Utes would discipline their renegade raiders. When this plan failed, militias of soldiers and settlers went after the offenders, many of whom were captured or killed. As a result, hostilities with Hispaños increased. At the same time, Utes were also fighting Comanches.

Exhausted, some Utes went to Taos in 1750 and asked for peace.[15] Two years later the governor met with Chiquito, Don Tomás, and Barrigon, representatives of the Muaches, Capotes, and Sabuaganas, respectively, to establish a trade agreement. This resolution of the trouble on the northern frontier allowed settlers to return in 1754.

The northern communities again drew nomadic Indians' commerce, but Taos was now the hub of their trade. In addition to enjoying a peaceful interlude, the colonists gained a reliable source of trade goods, which were essential because the settlers depended on hides, deer and bison meat, and slaves supplied by the Utes. The Utes, in turn, wanted horses above all else, in addition to corn, flour, tobacco, blankets, horse trappings, metal utensils, and tools—especially knives. The Utes had learned to fashion projectile points from metal, so this material was of benefit beyond its normal uses.

Generally, the rate of exchange was understood without haggling. A buckskin shirt brought a bushel of corn. A female captive, about twelve to twenty years old, was worth two horses plus odds and ends such as tobacco and trinkets. Young men of similar ages could be had for only one horse. This disparity indicated the greater usefulness of girls, who would be assigned endless household tasks such as grinding corn, cooking, cleaning, washing, weaving, and making soap. Boys' jobs consisted chiefly of herding and doing field work. Once taken into a household, the captives were baptized, but they were still usually treated as persons of lower caste.[16]

Between 1700 and 1760 the majority of captives were Apaches, with fewer numbers of Navajos and Hopis. In 1760 at Taos, Muaches captured about three hundred Comanche women, who we might assume were traded into bondage. In comparison, not many Utes were captured, and, consequently, few Utes were baptized during this period. Utes had become so intimidating that in 1761, Comanches seeking peace at Santa Fe requested an escort for their return to Taos.[17] Later the same year, when Comanches attacked Taos and local people killed four hundred of them, opportunistic Utes made off with a thousand horses from the Comanches and settlers.

Through such episodes, Utes helped to keep Comanches in check. More often friendly than unfriendly toward the Spanish now, Utes continued to be allowed to trade at settlements—especially Taos, Abiquiú, and Santa Cruz. This relatively peaceful state made land grants on the frontier seem desirable to colonists, who sometimes traveled up the Chama River and occasionally into west-central Colorado to meet Indians for trading. Also, in 1762 the relinquishment of France's claims in Louisiana to Spain had relaxed worries about French intrusions into New Mexico from the east.

With this comparative calm, authorized exploration into the northwestern portion of the Spanish province began in 1765, when the governor gave Juan María Antonio Rivera permission to go to Ute territory in search of silver. The immediate cause of this belated undertaking, more than a century and a half after Oñate's arrival in New Mexico, resulted from the appearance of a Ute, Cuero de Lobo, who had ridden into Abiquiú with a chunk of silver to trade. As Rivera journeyed into *tierra incognito*, he kept a journal, shedding light for posterity on the whereabouts and activities of Utes. Rivera's route followed the well-traveled Ute path up the Chama River to the San Juan, Animas, and

Dolores Rivers—a route that would be called the Spanish Trail several decades later. His expedition investigated the La Plata Mountains and saw many "Yuta" villages with occupants who were experienced in dealing with Spaniards. Some of these Utes had traded in Spanish settlements, and a chief called Largo wanted a horse in exchange for accompanying the expedition. He was denied the opportunity.

During a second expedition conducted by Rivera, while traveling northwest from Abiquiú, the group met Muache Utes with Cabézon, their leader. The expedition gave the Utes gifts as a token of friendship. Later, at a Muache village near the Dolores River, "Payuchis" (probably Weenuches rather than Southern Paiutes, as is sometimes thought) entered the camp and fought unsuccessfully for the privilege of guiding Rivera. Farther to the north, before crossing the Uncompahgre Plateau, Rivera found three more Muache villages.

These references to Muaches, at a considerable distance from what is usually described as their normal territory, cannot be explained with existing information about the early distribution of Ute groups. Basing its knowledge on Rivera's reports, in 1776 the Domínguez-Escalante expedition also placed Muaches in southwestern Colorado. Neither Rivera nor the Domínguez-Escalante journal mentioned Capotes or Weenuches, across whose territories the expeditions should have crossed if the usual theories about distribution are correct.

North of the Uncompahgre Plateau, Rivera came to a friendly Tabeguache village called Passochi, where he smoked and exchanged gifts with the leader, Tonampechi. The visit by the Spaniards interrupted plans for ceremonies intended to celebrate a recent victory over Comanches. Tonampechi warned of unfriendly Comanches to the north but eventually agreed to lead Rivera if he would wait until the victory celebration and feasting were completed.

With the Tabeguache guiding them, the party moved on from water hole to water hole until they reached the Gunnison River. During this journey Rivera was told about other people who lived near a big lake, ate their children, had beards, and wore buckskin clothing. Although we have no evidence that they ate their children, these people were presumably Timpanogots Utes.

Next, Rivera met Sabuaganas Utes, whom he called Saguagans. Their chief was Cuchara. They said they had been in a battle with Spaniards, all of whom had been killed. Despite the Sabuaganas' fears that Rivera might want to avenge those deaths, the Utes and Spaniards camped together and traded before Rivera's party set out for the Colorado River. A day or two out, he came to another village of Sabuaganas, who said they had recently fought Comanches.[18] The accounts in Rivera's journal reveal that Utes in west-central Colorado were not as isolated in the 1760s as one might suppose and that they were experienced in fighting Comanches.

Comanches, meanwhile, were continuing their depredations around Spanish settlements as well, despite the combined efforts of Utes, Jicarillas, Pueblos, and Hispaños to fend them off and to recover stolen property. In 1773 a militia pursued them into the San Luis Valley and brought back two hundred horses, but the next year the Comanches retaliated by striking the settlements repeatedly with increased fury.

On another front, Utes and Navajos were fighting again in the early 1770s, but as this conflict simmered down both tribes combined to fight the Hopis. In 1776 Utes were openly at war with the Hopis.[19] Because Hopis were Christianized and therefore were the king's subjects, this warfare was an active concern of the Spaniards but posed no obstacle to an ambitious expedition undertaken that year by Fray Francisco Atanasio Domínguez and Fray Silvestre Vélez de Escalante.

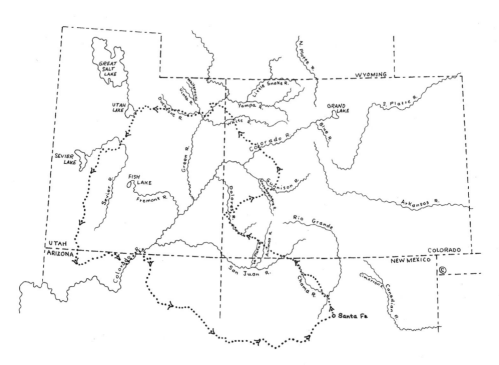

Route of the 1776 Domínguez-Escalante expedition.

The two were seeking a connecting route between the Franciscan missions in New Mexico and those in Alta California, as well as opportunities for future missions along the way. Clearly, the padres were not interested in trading with Indians, as they forbade their companions to bring trade goods with them. They were also uninterested in finding precious metals, as they refused to detour from their path to inspect silver ore, which one of their men—formerly a companion of Rivera— knew was located in the La Platas. Their curiosity was aroused, however, by Rivera's mention of the people he had met and by legends about Teguayo in the Great Basin with pueblos like apartment houses and the great Lake Copala, where some native people said they had originated.[20] These mysteries drew the priests onto a northerly route.

With Domínguez as leader, the duty of maintaining a journal during the trip fell to Escalante. His account provides firsthand observations of Utes whom the expedition encountered in western Colorado, northeastern Utah, and the eastern Great Basin. The journal contains the first accurate and detailed descriptions of the land they traversed and of its Ute occupants.[21]

In addition to Domínguez and Escalante, the party consisted of eight men including Spanish soldiers and their Indian servants, guides, and, notably, Don Bernardo Miera y Pacheco, a retired soldier and astronomer who would create the first map of the interior territory, including locations of "Yuta" bands the group met or of whom they heard. Engaged as guide and interpreter was Andrés Muñiz, who knew the Ute language and some of the land because he had accompanied Rivera in 1765 and had traded with Utes as far north as the Gunnison and Colorado Rivers. Another member of the party was Lucrecio Muñiz, brother of Andrés, who spoke Ute and might have been in Ute country previously as a trader. Two *genízaro* adventurers from Abiquiú soon fell in with the party, and Ute guides were added along the way.

The expedition set out on August 1, 1776, on the well-known trail up the Chama River. Entering Ute country beyond the Navajo River, they crossed what would become the Southern Ute Reservation a century later. Escalante described it as "good land for farming with the aid of irrigation." Having forded the Animas River near Durango, the group proceeded on a clear trail to the Dolores River near the town of Dolores, then northwest over sagebrush-covered plains, where they were puzzled by an impoundment of water that had been covered over with wood and rocks. They concluded that "some misfortune" had befallen Utes at this spot.

After again descending to the river below Slick Rock, the expedition followed recent Indian tracks, believed to be those of Tabeguaches.

While searching for a way out of the Dolores's sandstone canyon, the group came to Disappointment Creek, then called Rio de las Paralíticas, or the River of the Paralytics, which the guide noted was the dividing point between "Tabehuichi" and "Muhuachi" Utes. This tributary had been named by previous travelers who had found three Ute women with a kind of paralysis camping there. An explanation for their ailment and the encampment might be that the women suffered from arthritis and were soaking their joints in a bath made with streamside Cow Parsnip, a common folk treatment for arthritis as well as for some forms of paralysis.

Once out of the Dolores's confines, the expedition traveled east-northeast to La Sierra de los Tabehuaches, the Uncompahgre Plateau. Ascending it, they discovered a stone rampart, made by a "Tabehuachi Yuta," it was assumed, of rocks taken from a nearby ancient ruin. Later the same day the Spaniards' party was overtaken by a Ute who was traveling from Abiquiú. Everyone stopped to eat and to smoke tobacco with this Tabeguache wayfarer. Through their interpreter they asked where the "Tabehuachis," "Muhuachis," and Sabuaganas were located and learned that the Sabuaganas were "in their own country," where, indeed, they were soon met by the Spaniards. As for the "Tabehuachis," they were said to be located in scattered groups throughout the area. Apparently, nothing was learned about the "Muhuachis."

The Ute guest agreed to guide the party the next afternoon to a Sabuagana headman who Andrés knew liked Spaniards. This Ute's services would have to wait, though, until the following afternoon. When the Ute, now named Atanacio after Domínguez, returned the next day, he brought his wife and two other women—probably his wives—with two infants and three older children. The friendly women gave the explorers jerked meat and dried manzanita berries and in turn received flour from the expedition's larder. Atanacio then received two *belduques* and sixteen strings of beads that he requested for his work, and the women and children left.

The men descended the Uncompahgre Plateau into the Uncompahgre Valley. Utes called the river the Ancapagari because of the red water in its upper reaches. The party camped next to a marsh where, a century later, Ute Chief Ouray's home would stand south of Montrose.

Taking a well-worn trail down the valley to the Gunnison River just east of Delta, the men camped near a Sabuagana village, where Andrés and Atanasio asked for guides from among the occupants. The village was being visited by "Lagunas," also called "Timpanogotzis," who happened to be visiting. The presence of Timpanogots so far from home in a Sabuagana camp suggests not only that the former were already involved in trading in 1776 but also that the latter may have acted as middlemen when they did business at New Mexican settlements. Five Sabuaganas came to the expedition's camp, where they ate, smoked, and described recent conflicts with Yamparika Comanches. The Utes warned the Spaniards that they too would have trouble if they continued northward. The following day another meeting took place, this one attended by five Sabuaganas and one Timpanogots who was persuaded to become a guide when he was offered a blanket, a *belduque,* and some white glass beads. He was called Silvestre, Escalante's name.

The party set out, accompanied not only by the new guide but also by some Sabuaganas who had suddenly lost their fear of Comanches. One stuffed himself with so much of the Spaniards' food that he became violently ill, and his hosts feared the others would avenge his death if he succumbed. Fortunately for all, he survived. Nevertheless, the dent made in food supplies as a result of feeding guests, then and later, would adversely affect the journey.

A few days later the party met eighty well-mounted Sabuaganas on the east side of Grand Mesa. These Utes were from a village of about thirty tents, which, like the previous one, had "Laguna" (Timpanogots) visitors. The Sabuaganas turned out to be Indians with whom Andrés and his brother were expecting to trade, using goods they had smuggled despite the leaders' orders. When their enterprise was discovered, the padres were incensed. This was not the only unpleasant event at the camp, however. The Spaniards needed fresh horses, and much haggling was required before they were obtained, while the Utes made dire predictions about danger from Comanches if the journey continued northward.

Swapping white beads for dried bison meat was easier. Father Domínguez also enjoyed some success proclaiming a message of salvation to the Utes. When it was learned that the Timpanogots guide's Ute name meant "Red Deer," the priest lectured the Indians about the indiscretion of naming a human for a "brute." Meanwhile, Silvestre had become recalcitrant about proceeding farther because of the Comanches. Finally the Sabuaganas convinced him that he would have to go on because he had accepted gifts for doing the job.

In this Sabuagana camp Domínguez visited the tepee of a man who was in charge of the village and whom the padre addressed as the chief. The embarrassed Ute corrected Domínguez and pointed to a handsome young man who actually was a chief and, even more important, was the brother of a highly respected chief, Yamputzi. The village was preparing

at this very time to move to Yamputzi's camp. The padres were dismayed
to learn that even such high-ranking persons were guilty of polygamy.

The padres were delighted to leave this camp, which had policies
that contradicted their beliefs and had caused friction with their guides.
When they moved on, a young Timpanogots boy, who had begged to be
allowed to accompany the party, went with them. He was given the
name Joaquín and doubled up on a horse with one of the men. He
proved to be a devoted companion, accompanying the expedition all the
way to Utah and back to Santa Fe.

After departing from the Grand Mesa camp, the explorers observed
more Ute villages with small huts on Plateau Creek and met three Ute
women with a child who were drying berries. The women gave the men
chokecherries, gooseberries, squawberries, and piñon nuts. As the expedition traveled on, its members found three more camps of Sabuagana
Utes between the Colorado River and Douglas Pass. A half dozen Utes
visited one of the Spaniards' camps and said that five Utes had just
returned from Comanche territory, where they had intended to steal
horses, but the Comanches had left the country for the Arkansas River.

These were the last Utes seen in western Colorado, although in the
far northwestern corner of the state, near Dinosaur National Monument at the Green River, some Indians were known to be close by. Since
this was the junction where Ute and Comanche country met, the mys-
terious Indians alarmed Silvestre, who believed they were Comanches.
No contact was made, however. The only untoward event at this location occurred when Joaquín decided to race a horse across a field. His
steed, a strong one that would be missed, stepped in a hole, fell, and
broke its neck, but the remorseful lad was not hurt.

After fording the Green River, the expedition proceeded west across
the Uinta Basin, where the men saw tracks of horses and of people on
foot. Silvestre believed the horsemen were Comanches who were pursu-
ing Utes. The Spaniards passed near the confluence of the Uinta and
Duchesne Rivers, where one day the Northern Ute Tribe's headquarters
would be located. Beyond this point they saw smoke coming from the
camp of "Laguna" hunters, so Silvestre thought. At Trout Creek Joaquín
redeemed himself by catching two trout, each weighing more than two
pounds, with his bow and arrows. Silvestre commented that "Lagunas"
had lived on this river in the past and that fish were their main source of
food, but Comanches had been coming into the area and had frightened
the Utes away. Underscoring his point about Comanches, Silvestre quick-
ened his pace, although he did stop long enough to point out where
Utah Lake lay beyond the mountains and where many other Indians of

the "same language and type" lived southeast of the lake. Perhaps he was referring to the Sanpits Utes.

Approaching Utah Valley from the mountains, the party saw many smoke signals—sent by his own people, Silvestre said—and the signals were returned to indicate that the travelers were friendly. Meadows were burning, too, as if fires had been lit to obstruct the advance of the strangers. Meeting two Utes, the Spaniards gave each a yard of woolen goods and a piece of red ribbon with which to bedeck themselves to make a good impression when they arrived in camp. When Domínguez, Silvestre, Joaquín, and Andrés rode into the village ahead of the others, defenders appeared with weapons, but Silvestre spoke many assurances and the boy showed such pride in his companions that their reception turned welcoming.

Many Utes from other camps soon joined the gathering to share food and to smoke the tobacco offered by the Spaniards in their "king's camp" at the mouth of the Provo River. The gospel was preached to them, and when the guests were told that more padres would come to baptize them and that Spaniards would teach the Indians to farm and raise livestock, all were delighted.

Two chieftains who were not present at the first meeting arrived the next day with several elders and others, and the priests repeated the previous day's messages. The Spaniards were assured that they could have all the land they wanted. As a token of good faith they were given a skin, painted with figures in red ochre to portray the amounts of blood spilled by the clan's chiefs in warfare. The largest number of wounds belonged to the head chief, followed by two subchiefs and a war captain with fewer wounds. A crucifix was added to each figure at the behest of one of the members of the expedition, and the priests presented the chief with a *belduque*, white glass beads, and a hatchet. Eventually, the painted skin, apparently intended to be a kind of passport among other Utes, reached Santa Fe, where it was presented to the governor. The head chief was named Turunianchi, and the two subchiefs were Cuitzapunchi and Panchucuquibiran, meaning "Great Talker," who was, in fact, none other than Silvestre. He had gained considerable status by boasting of his service to the expedition. The war captain was Picuchi, brother of the head chieftain.

Since Silvestre was leaving the party here, another Ute, José María, became the guide. Having traded for a good supply of dried fish, the expedition's members departed with a reminder that the Utes expected some Spaniards to return in one year. For his part, Escalante, fully be-lieving that some Franciscans would come, gave a detailed description of the Utah Valley in his journal, where he said there was "sufficient irrigable land for two good settlements," good farmland and pastures, and abundant water. He mentioned the local waterfowl, beaver, and especially the abundant fish on which the "Fish-eaters" subsisted. He told how they also harvested seeds from wild plants and hunted rabbits and fowl but were prevented because of their fear of Comanches from hunting bison nearby to the northwest. He described the Timpanogots' primitive huts, their buckskin clothing, their basketry, and their beards, but significantly the Escalante journal did not mention having seen any horses in the Utah Valley. He explained that the name of these people was "Timpanogotzis" because of their lake, "Timpanogó."

As the expedition progressed south of Utah Lake, José María and Joaquín, who had insisted on coming along, escorted friendly visitors from nearby Ute camps. During the next two days a group of eight timid Indians and others were encountered. Some Indians wore only the skimpiest bits of buckskin to cover their nakedness. The full beards of some were mentioned.

On the Sevier River near Mills and Chicken Creeks, a region historically occupied by Pahvant Utes, a score of bearded Indians, covered with rabbit blankets and wearing polished bones in their noses, visited the "king's camp." Similar Utes appeared around Clear Lake and Pahvant Butte. They called themselves Tirangapui, "bearded Utes," and Escalante called them "Yutas Barbones," meaning the same. Like the Timpanogots, these Utes were friendly, even helping to find and bring in some of the expedition's horses that had strayed. The Indians listened attentively to the preaching of the gospel and welcomed the news that friars would come to these Utes as well as to those at Utah Lake. The departure of their visitors caused loud lamentations among the "Barbones."

Soon after the expedition crossed the divide west of Cove Fort and northwest of Beaver, José María abruptly departed without so much as a farewell. The Spaniards supposed that he might have been upset by witnessing a conflict between two members of the party or by the prospect of traveling farther from home. Other reasons one might suggest were that he knew he was leaving the territory of his own people or that he was more adept than the strangers at forecasting cold weather and snow, which arrived shortly.

In his journal Escalante noted that the bearded Utes, the "Lagunas" and "Barbones," were not met again south of the divide where the guide left them. He did mention seeing some very poor people, called "Yutas Cobardes," southwest of Beaver, and "Huascaris," who were even poorer, south of the Cobardes. Both of these groups were Southern Paiutes.

Without encountering Utes again, the Domínguez-Escalante expedition gave up their attempt to reach California and returned to Santa Fe by way of the Crossing of the Fathers. Miera later proposed to the provincial government in Chihuahua that some presidios and settlements should be created near Utah Lake and elsewhere in Utah, but nothing came of his suggestions or of the priests' promises to the Utes that missions would be established. The province had its hands full enough without trying to bring civilization and Christianity to the remote Ute country.

Indian raids continued to sap the strength of New Mexico's settlements, and hostilities among tribes vying for trade opportunities constantly disturbed the frontier. In 1775 and 1778 unlicensed trade was forbidden by Governor Pedro Fermin de Mendinueta in an effort to halt the dispersal of horses among Utes in exchange for captives, but the ban was widely ignored. When Juan Bautista de Anza arrived in 1779 as New Mexico's governor, he found goals such as creating a link between Santa Fe and California had to take second place to dealing with Indian troubles.

For instance, some Utes had joined forces with their former enemies, the Navajos, to attack Hopis, whom Spaniards were compelled to protect. Other Utes and Jicarilla Apaches were stirred up about raids by Comanches. During the summer of 1779 Comanches had attacked a Ute camp and stolen horses, although the horses were recovered and some Comanches were killed. When Anza mustered an army of 573 soldiers, settlers, and Pueblo Indians to pursue Comanches who had been raising havoc around the settlements, two hundred Utes and Jicarillas were happy to join when Anza passed through the San Luis Valley. On the heels of the Comanches, the force traveled into the Upper Arkansas Valley, through South Park, and past Pikes Peak before catching the quarry near present-day Pueblo, Colorado. The Comanches and their chief, Cuerno Verde, escaped south to the Greenhorn Valley, where they were soundly defeated and Cuerno Verde was killed. A few Utes fought in this battle, but others had suddenly departed at the Arkansas River without explanation or permission. As it turned out, the wayward band came upon a small Comanche village afterward and killed its nine families, including women and children, leaving alive one child who was taken captive. Further, the Utes made off with forty horses and the village's possessions.[22]

In the early 1780s a commander general of the Interior Province of New Spain reported that Anza had succeeded in making peace with "the valiant Ute and Jicarilla Appaches" during his tenure and was taking "care not to disturb the Navajo."[23] By offering to trade and bestowing gifts, the government in Santa Fe ensured that Utes would continue to assist in military campaigns against the Comanches. Utes even went far afield in 1785 to help in Spanish operations against Gila Apaches.[24]

Consequently, it was not surprising that Utes were offended when Anza met with their Comanche enemies in 1786 to negotiate a peace treaty and when he rewarded them with attractive trade agreements. The Muaches sent two captains, Moara and Pinto, to protest. Despite his cynical reaction, expressed privately, Anza acceded to the Utes' demands, which included the return of Ute leaders who were held captive by Comanches and an invitation to participate in a great trade fair, originally planned only for Comanches, at Pecos Pueblo in 1887.[25] The Spanish government presented everyone with gifts of corn, wheat, and sheep, as well as red cloth, tools, cooking pots, mirrors, bridles, tobacco, and baubles.[26]

Unsuccessful, though, were Ute demands that a village be built for them near Abiquiú like San Carlos, which the Spaniards were providing for Comanches on the plains. An uneasy balance existed after 1789 when the Spaniards and Utes agreed on a mutual defense treaty, with the understanding that the Utes would provide help when necessary against Navajos and Comanches. The following winter, Utes stayed at Santa Clara Pueblo, a few miles north of Santa Fe, without incident.[27]

In contrast, peace was far from guaranteed on the plains to the east where Comanches and Kiowas had joined in a formidable confederation. Utes who ventured south of the Arkansas River to hunt bison chanced skirmishes, as did their foes if they came into the foothills, but the alliance with the government in Santa Fe kept Utes as well as Jicarilla Apaches relatively peaceful around the settlements. In 1804 Muaches and Jicarillas were recruited to join a force against Navajos, who were devastated at Canyon de Chelly in the ensuing campaign. In view of the enduring enmity between most Eastern Utes and Navajos before and after this event, it seems unusual that Weenuches reportedly teamed up with Navajos to raid in northeastern Arizona in 1818.[28]

At the behest of their Spanish allies, Muaches traveled as spies to watch for interlopers in the lands of other tribes to the east and northeast. International affairs had again affected foreign claims in North America. First, France regained its territory from Spain, and, next, the United States purchased French Louisiana in 1803. Spain had no illusions about the goals of either the United States government or of adventurers of any nationality, so Muaches were sent to watch for suspicious travelers. When James Purcell of Kentucky visited South Park in 1803–1805, he was escorted to Santa Fe by Utes.

The progress of Lieutenant Zebulon Montgomery Pike's expedition in 1806–1807 was also duly reported to the governor in Santa Fe. In his report, published a few years after his journey, Pike noted that there were some Utes north of the Arkansas River in eastern Colorado. After entering the mountains, Pike traveled through South Park where he observed Indian camps—probably hunting camps that had been recently occupied—that stretched for several miles along the South Platte River. He saw evidence of hundreds of horses and many corn cobs but no Indians. Strangely, one very large site had a cross in its center.

When the Americans camped in the San Luis Valley in January and February 1807, they were on Spanish soil. John Robinson set forth from the camp to conduct a personal errand in Santa Fe, and he soon met two very shy Utes, armed with bows and arrows. They seem not to have been spies. Robinson induced them to guide him to Santa Fe by giving them some little gifts. Before setting out, the guides and Robinson stopped briefly in the Utes' camp, where their women were located.[29] While awaiting Robinson's return Pike saw fresh tracks, possibly left by two Spanish officers with two Ute scouts, about whom Pike would later learn. Robinson's arrival in the capital alerted the governor to send a large escort of dragoons and militia, led by a Ute scout, to bring Pike to Santa Fe, purportedly for his safety, on the pretext that Utes were about to attack the Americans.[30]

Meanwhile, intertribal hostilities continued. In Santa Fe Pike learned about an incident at Taos in 1806 between Utes and Comanches. As he recounted the event, about four hundred members of each tribe, it was said, had been lined up, ready to attack, when the heroic village administrator, the *alcalde*, rode between the two lines and prevented mayhem from occurring. Three years later about six hundred Muaches, who had been camped around San Juan Pueblo and Abiquiú with Utes from Utah, decided to go on a hunt with Jicarillas in the Pikes Peak region. They were attacked near the Arkansas River by Comanches, Kiowas, and Pawnees who killed the Ute leaders Mano Mocha, Delgadito, and El Albo. Their deaths assured future hostilities to avenge them.[31]

These tribes were not the Utes' only enemies on the plains, though. Since about 1800 Indian tribes, which had been gradually pushed from the northeast, were on the northern prairie. These tribes were Sioux, Arapahos, and Cheyennes, who pressed southward as far as the Arkansas River, while Comanches, Kiowas, and Pawnees ruled the plains south of the Arkansas. The Arapahos and Cheyennes did not hesitate to invade game-rich mountain valleys north of the Arkansas River's boundary and occasionally appeared in Ute country to the south as well. Anything that transpired north of the Arkansas was outside Spanish territory and thus did not meet military resistance.

In ensuing decades, Arapahos would prove to be the Northern Utes' fiercest enemies. As the nineteenth century progressed, many legendary battles took place. For instance, there is the often repeated story about the tragic drowning of Ute women and children in a windstorm on Grand Lake where they had taken refuge on a raft during a Ute-Arapaho fight. South Park, Middle Park, and the area around Steamboat Springs contain many tales of battles between Utes and Arapahos, and defensive stone breastworks are frequently found. In Utah stories are told of individuals who were killed by Arapahos as far south as Fish Lake.

It is important to note that the meeting of Utes and nineteenth-century Northern Plains tribes occurred relatively late in the story of the Núu-ci. Therefore, the influence of those plains people in altering Ute culture should not be exaggerated, as it has been on occasion. Although some of the newcomers' cultural traits were adopted, especially in postreservation times, Eastern Utes were experienced, mounted warriors, raiders, bison hunters, and traders long before 1800. They were using hide tepees and transporting them with horses while future Northern Plains Indians were still living far to the northeast.

Far more dramatic was the influence of Spanish colonists during two centuries of contact. When Mexico's independence ended the Spanish empire in North America in 1821, the once pedestrian Eastern Utes possessed huge herds of horses and new technology based on iron and steel, replacing in part at least Stone-Age technology. They roamed far, were aggressive, took part in an economy based on trade and raids, had become more reliant on group leaders, and had formed political alliances.

Still, they lived in temporary brush shelters or moveable tepees rather than in permanent dwellings. They still hunted and fought with bows, arrows, and spears more than with firearms. They still obtained most of their food, clothing, and remedies from nature's bounty rather than from agriculture. And they still performed the Bear Dance each year at the vernal equinox to win the favor of Bear in their endeavors.

The Circle of Life continued.

4
▼ ▼ ▼

Trappers, Traders, and Transition
(1810–1846)

Drastic change did not reach all Ute Indians simultaneously, although none escaped it eventually. By the early nineteenth century, change was reaching Western Utes, who were beginning to learn lessons through their contact with New Mexican colonists—lessons Eastern Utes had known for about two centuries. Primarily, Utes of Utah still relied on bands in west–central Colorado to act as middlemen for their occasional exchange of captive Shoshones, Gosiutes, and Paiutes for horses and goods, but the horses acquired were often eaten, as the arid climate and vegetation of the Great Basin could not support sizable herds of livestock, and food remained scarce.

Nevertheless, traders from New Mexico were making inroads, usually illegal ones. Residents around Abiquiú and Taos knew the Indian trails used by Rivera and the Domínguez-Escalante expedition, spoke Indian languages, and could move back and forth without close government surveillance, although a few enterprising men were arrested and brought before the *alcalde*, the administrative justice, in Santa Cruz in the 1780s and 1790s. An unlicensed pack train destined for Ute country in 1783, for instance, had taken corn, flour, tobacco, biscuits, and knives along with horses and mules, it was learned.[1] In 1805, after a seventy-year-old Ute *genízaro*, Manuel Mestas, had traveled to Utah Lake from Abiquiú to recover stolen horses and mules, he reported to the governor that Indians in Utah had been in contact with New Mexicans for years. Meanwhile, Sabuagana and Capote Utes regularly came to Abiquiú and the northern pueblos to trade.

About 1810, the government relaxed its sanctions, and trade with the Western Utes began to increase. A licensed expedition took place in

1813 when Mauricio Arze and Lagos Garcia of Abiquiú dealt with the Timpanogots, Pahvants, and Sanpits. The Sanpits insisted on bartering with hides plus Indian captives, both female and male, as they claimed they had done previously. When Arze and Lagos reportedly refused to accept the captives, the Utes began to kill the expedition's horses, thereby forcing the traders to accept the captives along with about a hundred tanned hides.[2]

In addition to traders, a few foreign trappers were also beginning to work their way north and northwest out of the New Mexican settlements. Some were guided by local Hispaños. Other trappers were coming into Spanish territory illegally from the north and east. With Mexico's independence in 1821, doors were opened wider to foreign traders and trappers, who came for beaver, otter, and other furs, ending the isolation of Utes, whether Eastern or Western. The population of frontier settlements like Abiquiú quickly tripled, and the price paid for captive children doubled.[3] With the Spanish military no longer available as an ally for mutual protection, Utes were on their own to fend off Indian foes and to retaliate with warfare. Settlers on the northern frontier also became more vulnerable to raiding by Indians, for the military force in Santa Fe was too small to oppose them, and the majority of people in outlying villages had no firearms with which to defend themselves.

Another change was the rapid increase of commerce as wagon trains crossed the Santa Fe Trail on the plains. Comanches and Kiowas were a constant threat to these caravans, and Muache Utes sometimes joined attacks on travelers.

By 1828 pack trains were crossing Ute country, en route between Santa Fe and California, on the old Ute trail that became known as the Old Spanish Trail. Increasing numbers of pack trains headed out from Abiquiú on the now familiar trail that followed the Chama River through southwestern Colorado to Moab, Utah, where it forded the Colorado River and proceeded to Green River, Utah, where it crossed the Green River. The route traversed the San Rafael Swell and reached a point east of Sevier, Utah, from which it headed southwest and west to California.

Utes and other tribes encountered along the trail received gifts such as tobacco in exchange for safe passage, but Indians at the eastern end of the trail, where opportunities for plunder were too rich to resist, badgered the pack trains.[4] The depletion of grass by grazing horses and mules and the appropriation of game and precious water farther along the trail were resented, so the capture of woolen goods and other articles from New Mexico or of herds of horses and mules from California was considered fair play by Indians whose territory the pack trains crossed.

The most famous Ute to loot travelers on the Old Spanish Trail was Walkara, also known as Walker or Wakara, meaning "yellow." He was a Timpanogots of imposing stature, more than six feet tall and of towering intelligence also. With his band of followers, most of whom appear to have been recruited from the Sanpits Band, Walkara halted traders and, later, emigrants on the portion of the trail between Utah and California to exact tolls in gifts, but he soon discovered that this source of wealth was minor when compared to the horses and mules that could be taken from missions and ranches in California and driven east. With horses worth five times in New Mexico what they were in California, this was a profitable business despite its hazards.

Walkara's activities, which began in the early 1830s when he was twenty to thirty years old, continued until after Utah's settlement by Mormons. During this time he became powerful enough to establish a confederacy of bands led by his brothers and half-brothers who lived in various bands. The names of these leaders—Sowiet (a half-brother), Arrapene, Sanpitch, Tabby, Grosepene, Ammon, Kanosh, and others of lesser fame—would become well-known to early settlers in Utah in the 1840s and following years.

So much has been written by popular authors about the exploits of Walkara and his cohorts that his story has become the stuff of legends. Walkara's most daring adventures took place after he had teamed up with mountain men Pegleg Smith and Jim Beckwourth. These rascals conceived a plan whereby more livestock made it across the arid desert instead of turning back to their own green pastures. The technique entailed taking fresh mares from Utah and leaving their colts behind. In California the mares were turned loose to lead a stampeding herd back to the foals. The most famous expedition involved an intricate strategy in which different groups of Utes simultaneously drove off choice herds from various sources they had pinpointed previously as ripe for the taking. The group was pursued, and a skirmish took place at California's Cajon Pass where Utes, including brothers of some of Pegleg's wives, were killed and some of the stolen horses were lost. However, Walkara's men captured their pursuers' mounts to augment the remaining herd and made it home with at least 2,000 horses and some fancy Spanish saddles.[5] Walkara increased his wealth additionally by raiding the Kaibab Band of Southern Paiutes for captives, whom he sold to New Mexicans and Navajos.[6]

If Walkara's adventures seem larger than life, so too do those of Thomas "Pegleg" Smith who, like other mountain men, reveled and often suffered in Ute country during the years of the fur trade. Pegleg earned his nickname by fashioning a wooden appendage to the stump of the leg he himself had sawed off after it was shattered by Arapaho arrows. While his wound healed he was cared for by Ute women, and like many other trappers he took multiple Indian wives—in his case Ute women.

Interaction between trappers and Utes was sometimes friendly and sometimes not, for much diversity existed in the customs, experiences, and dispositions of the various groups. For instance, some Northern Utes of Utah had contact with French-Canadian fur trappers in southern Wyoming about 1812 when, needing food, the trappers were able to trade for it. But when Manuel Lisa and other men employed by Auguste Chouteau and Jules DeMun of St. Louis entered the headwaters of the Arkansas River in 1813, most of the party was killed by unidentified Indians. In 1820 Dr. Edwin James of the Stephen H. Long expedition mentioned the presence of trappers in the vicinity of Manitou Springs, Colorado, who had been removing beads and other tokens Indians offered to spirits in the springs. The objects were then traded back to the Indians, according to a trapper named Bijeau—hardly a way to win friends if discovered. In 1822, in the headwaters of the Rio Grande, Utes stole two buffalo robes, lead, knives, and traps from Jacob Fowler's party and would have taken their horses, too, but were intercepted.[7]

These and other incidents reveal how widespread trappers' activities were as early as the 1820s. In 1822 Louis Vásquez was in the area of Great Salt Lake, which he decided was an extension of the Pacific Ocean. Others were trapping around the San Juan, Gunnison, and Green Rivers and in Middle Park by 1824–1825 when the Mexican government, to stem the influx of foreigners, banned trapping in its northern territory without official permission.

Indians were reacting unpredictably to the intruders who were depleting game and other resources. When Étienne Provost's party was near Great Salt Lake in 1824, Shoshones killed seven or eight men, but after wintering on the Green River at the mouth of the White River, Provost returned the next year and was able to trade with friendly Utes.[8] Provost established a camp at the mouth of the Timpanogos River and named it the Provo, phonetically after himself, in 1825.

That same year William Henry Ashley and a detachment of his fur company, coming down the Green in bull boats, saw that a huge encampment of Indians, living in conical brush shelters, had wintered at Brown's Hole. These were either Shoshones or Utes, perhaps the former.[9] At Desolation Canyon Ashley met friendly "Eutaws" and tried to buy seven horses from them to continue his journey over land. Ashley learned that a large number of the horses had been obtained from Timpanogots, who had many. Ashley, however, was able to get only two horses, and even those were relinquished reluctantly.

In his journal Ashley, who was not an average mountain man but an educated businessman and political figure, described the first Ute he met at this site as an individual of "great familiarity and Ease" who acted as if he had long mingled with white people. Ashley also said that the group as a whole was the finest he had encountered west of the Missouri River. They were wearing mountain sheep skins, buffalo robes, and shell ornaments, he noted. About half possessed English-made flintlocks, and the others were equipped with bows, arrow, and tomahawks.[10] Peter Skene Ogden's Hudson Bay Company men were in the area around Great Salt Lake at this time, and they also met friendly Utes who were ornamented with crosses.[11]

Jedediah Smith, who mapped a route through eastern Utah's Ute country to California, spoke highly of Utes he encountered at Utah Lake in 1826–1827. He noted their dignity, cleanliness, and honesty. Having received gifts of red ribbon, awls, knives, tobacco, and ammunition, the Timpanogots accepted Smith's presence in their area, as did Sanpits whom he met on the Sevier River. His partner, Daniel Potts, wrote that thirty-five large lodges made of bulrushes were present in the Utah Lake village, near which game consisted of a few bison, antelope, and mountain sheep but chiefly rabbits. Fish provided the main food source, but Smith observed that berries were gathered in Spanish Fork Canyon. Smith's Ute friends said other white men had been there the previous year but that they were starving and had returned to New Mexico.[12] By then a growing roster of fur trappers from Taos was contributing to changes in the Western Utes' possessions and, ultimately, in their lifestyle.

In 1825, north of the Uinta Mountains, Ashley held the first rendezvous for traders, trappers, and Indians who had joined in opportunities to trade. The rendezvous eliminated the need for trappers to journey to St. Louis, Santa Fe, and Taos and evolved into annual trade fairs, held in the summer. Most took place near the Uinta Mountains or in Green River country at Brown's Hole, although at least one was held in Colorado's San Luis Valley, a location that was abandoned to avoid the high tariffs imposed at nearby Taos.

The fairs offered a wealth of goods desired by native people—guns and ammunition, woolen blankets, knives and tobacco, vermilion and ornaments, traps, and whiskey. Trappers and Indians brought furs, hides, meat, horses, native women, and a colossal appetite for debauchery. Following a long cold winter setting traps in icy water, the trappers enjoyed a frenzy of recreation that often wiped out all their profits, while, besotted by whiskey, Indians accepted less than fair value in trading and sold their women as prostitutes.

Many mountain men who had eluded the refining influences of their own society "went Indian," as Western pulp literature put it. More than just adopting the survival techniques of native people, some trappers also acquired Indian women as companions and helpmates. This arrangement profited the women's Indian families, as the trappers gave their new relatives trinkets, guns, and alcohol. Less desirable were the white men's diseases passed on to natives who had no resistance to them. Ute wives performed much manual labor and were a definite asset to mountain men. The women dressed meat and gathered plant foods, cooked them, tanned buckskins, and made moccasins and shirts, all the while tending the children who were born into the marriage or who tagged along with their mothers from previous alliances.

Some well-known mountain men had such relationships with Ute women. Jim Bridger, who bought Jedediah Smith's trading post, which became known as Fort Bridger, had at least one Ute wife, as well as others from different tribes. The trapper Old Bill Williams is said to have had five Ute women at various times. Pegleg Smith, the horse thief, also seems to have had several Ute wives simultaneously. In contrast, Miles Goodyear settled down at his trading post at Ogden with a lovely Ute wife and raised a family.

With the advent of trading posts, year-round centers for meeting and trading arose. The first known post existed in 1828 at the confluence of the Whiterocks and Uinta Rivers in the heart of Uintah Ute territory, although it also attracted Shoshones. This was the Reed Post, sold four years later to Antoine Robidoux, who built a stronger stockade only a few yards away in 1837. His operation was called Fort Uintah or more often "Fort Winty." Fully equestrian by that time, Western Utes were able to take advantage of the opportunity to trade beaver pelts, buckskins, jerked meat, and captives to Robidoux. They camped around the post in large numbers, as did Shoshones, and spent their time in gambling, foot racing, horse racing, telling stories, and holding councils.

Earlier, Robidoux had established his first post, Fort Uncompahgre, in Colorado on the Gunnison River just below the mouth of the Uncompahgre River, in the heart of Tabeguache Ute territory. Although the date is not certain, this trading post appears to have been built around 1830.[13] Here Robidoux traded woolen blankets, cloth, ribbons, knives, rifles, powder, lead, kettles, mirrors, beads, tobacco, sugar, and other goods. His pack trains came in by way of the San Luis Valley and

Cochetopa Pass on the old Indian trail that had become known as a "trappers' trail," later occasionally called a northern branch of the Old Spanish Trail. Robidoux's route continued west and joined the main Santa Fe–California trail at the Green River crossing. An extension to the north reached Fort Winty and trapping country in northeast Utah.

Another illustrious mountain man, Antoine Leroux, described this alternate to the Old Spanish Trail as follows: "There is not much snow in this pass [Cochetopa], and people go through it all the winter; and when there is much snow on the mountains on the Abiquiu route (which is the Old Spanish Trail to California) the people of Taos go 'round this way and get into that trail in the forks of the Grand [Colorado] and Green Rivers."[14]

The design of the posts was typically a quadrangle surrounded by a tall log palisade enclosing crude log buildings with dirt floors and roofs. Trappers and their women lived inside, and Indians camped outside the palisade. Where Indian trails crossed the Green River at the mouth of the White, Kit Carson built a small fort of this type about a mile below the confluence during the winter of 1833–1834, but like so many other mountain men, Carson did not remain in any one place, including this one, for long.

As an example of the trappers' mobility and their encounters with Indians wherever they went, Carson had been in South Park where a party of Indians stole one of his horses and would have taken them all if he had not stopped them. He moved to a creek in the Upper Arkansas where his horses were run off, but they were recaptured and one Indian was killed. Carson then went to Middle Park to trap. By the fall of 1833 he was back in Taos, outfitting for his journey to northeastern Utah and Fort Winty where a brother of Antoine Robidoux's was employing a score or so of trappers and traders. It was then that Carson established his winter quarters near the mouth of the White River and, one would assume, did some trapping.[15]

As time went by, other trading posts came and went. In Brown's Hole a post called Fort Davy Crockett was in business near Vermillion Creek by 1837. Its one log building was visited in 1839 by German scientist Dr. F. Adolphus Wislizenus, who found its hungry occupants eating dog meat.[16] Nicknamed "Fort Misery," this poverty-stricken outpost was abandoned after only a few years, although a sizable rendezvous took place nearby.

In 1841 another post existed at the later site of Fort Duchesne, Utah, today's headquarters of the Northern Utes. The Duchesne River was named after a French trapper.

Although the abundance of beavers had greatly diminished and market prices for beaver pelts had dropped during the 1830s, Fort Uintah hung on in the early 1840s. Traveling with missionary Marcus Whitman in 1842, Rufus Sage described the place as he found it. The fort was on the right bank of the Uinta River, where horses and skins of beaver, otter, deer, mountain sheep, and elk were exchanged for guns, ammunition, knives, tobacco, beads, and other items. The skins, finished by Utes and Shoshones, drew Sage's admiration because of their large size, whiteness, and softness. One such skin might be purchased for eight to ten charges of ammunition or two to three awls, he noted, and would bring two dollars in Santa Fe. Because of the scarcity of bison in the surrounding area, Indians were living on small game, he observed.

During this visit, Robidoux's pack train came from Taos in October with a year's supply of goods. The train consisted of a guide with eight mules, each packed with 250 pounds. Horsemen rode at the rear of the train.[17]

Earlier another visitor, Reverend Joseph Williams, had been at Fort Uintah where he had waited for several days so he could accompany Robidoux and his pack train as they set off for New Mexico. Williams's description was more subjective. He expressed shock at the wicked conditions in the place, especially the deplorable business of men selling Indian women to one another. When the party finally got under way, taking women along with other goods to New Mexico, it was delayed for two days because two of Robidoux's female companions had escaped and a replacement had to be brought from the fort. Stopping at Fort Uncompahgre, Williams preached to an audience of French, Mexican, American, and Indian sinners.[18]

When John Charles Frémont's expedition passed Fort Uintah in June 1844, its time was running out. The beaver trade was nearly finished, and hundreds of Robidoux's horses and mules had frozen to death during his annual caravan to Missouri. The following year, while Robidoux was away, angry Utes—their emotions inflamed by alcohol—attacked the fort, killed the seven men there, captured the women, and burned the place down. According to lore regarding Fort Uncompahgre, it was at about this same time that Utes also killed the Mexican who was running Robidoux's post in Colorado and some trappers there and made away with the trade goods.[19] Historians debate whether that post was burned, however.

Thus ended the heyday of the fur trade in Utah, although Utes continued to join Shoshones in going to Fort Bridger in southwestern Wyoming. Angry about their loss of game and trade, they harassed the trappers who still operated in Western Ute country and in Shoshone territory to the north. The slave trade was still flourishing, however, with captives the principal commodity at Taos's trade fairs, so intertribal raiding took on more importance.

This discussion, which so far has focused on the fur trade in Utah, has neglected activities on Colorado's Front Range during the same period. With easier geographic access for traders and a shorter distance to supplies of Taos Lightning, activities there were even livelier than those in Utah. Bison along the margin of the plains further augmented the trade and perpetuated it a little longer.

The first post in this region was a crude outfit on the Arkansas River near the mouth of Hardscrabble Creek where William Bent and Ceran St. Vrain were trading by 1829. Bent's brother Charles freighted goods between St. Louis and the mountains, and in 1833 the two built their main place of business, Bent's Fort, on the plains, where some Utes visited. Smaller operations along the Front Range north of the Arkansas served trappers and Indians who brought in beaver pelts and buffalo robes. By locating on the north side of the river in United States territory, these operations eluded Mexican jurisdiction while still having proximity to Santa Fe and Taos, where the traders could buy and sell goods. This location also ensured a reasonably short haul for Taoseños when they conveyed kegs of whiskey to the trading posts.

Independent traders also sought a share in the business. About 1833 John Gantt at Fort Cass (at the later site of Pueblo) discovered that he could reap great economic benefits by providing his Indian customers with Taos Lightning before trading began. Up Hardscrabble Creek, south of Florence, Colorado, French-Canadian traders dared to establish Buzzard's Roost in Mexican territory. Not until 1842, when the beaver trade had faded, did George Simpson and Robert Fisher establish El Pueblo at the later site of Pueblo, with bison hides as the principal trade item. Another post, Mathew Kinkead's San Buenaventura, went into business on Hardscrabble Creek the following year.

All of these ventures attracted a motley assortment of Americans, Mexican men and women, Muache Utes, and Plains Indians, with liquor enlivening the scene and triggering quarrels. By 1840 the Utes' fiercest foes were Arapahos, Cheyenne, and Sioux, and encounters with them occurred near the trading posts as well as on trails that led through the Front Range. Both tribes frequently traveled the Hardscrabble route, as it connected the Arkansas River and the Wet Mountain Valley. In 1847 Utes were victorious in a battle with Arapahos at Kinkead's place. Mexicans from San Buenaventura took the part of the Arapahos, who lost the battle. The victorious Utes then went to San Buenaventura and demanded a victory feast, after which they left and never returned there to trade.[20]

By that time, although a few furs still came to the posts, bison had replaced beaver, and the small trading establishments had become places where former trappers loafed and Mexican farmers raised a little corn and livestock. Wagons, hauling loads too heavy for pack trains, occasionally traveled to the Utes on more accessible trails so the Utes did not have to come in to trade. One such expedition took place in 1846 when Alexander Barclay went through the Wet Mountain, San Luis, and Upper Arkansas Valleys, where he visited several Ute villages and did business. As the trade in buffalo robes moved farther east, some of the early traders took up farming and ranching along the Arkansas, in the Greenhorn area, and south into New Mexico, where they were still in contact with Muache Utes, friendly and otherwise.

As Muaches, along with Plains Indians, sought the wealth of goods and livestock that could be acquired from caravans on the Santa Fe Trail, the United States government attempted to bring charges against the culprits. In 1841 they were accused of making an attack on American citizens on the Canadian River.[21] Complaints also arose because Utes had raided wagon trains between Bent's Fort and Taos and intimidated others.[22] At Taos, outspoken Padre Antonio José Martínez, the foremost opponent of activities by American entrepreneurs in Mexican territory, wrote to his president that the reason Indians were involved in raids was so they could sell their booty for liquor at American trading posts.[23]

Such incidents appear to have been the work of different individuals and not the result of organized action. Although Martínez's accusations were true in many cases, most operations at Bent's Fort and at a post on Hardscrabble Creek belonging to Alexander Barclay and Joseph Doyle were exceptions, for the owners were relatively well educated. For his part, Charles Bent claimed in 1846 that he had maintained friendly relations with "Eutaws" when he had traded with them at the mouth of Fountain Creek.[24] Barclay's expedition to the Utes that same year had also been successful.[25] When Charles Town went from Taos to the San Luis Valley to trade in 1846, however, Utes stole his horses, and two years later Utes and Apaches killed Town and his companions who were packing furs east of Raton Pass.[26]

Much of the trouble in New Mexico, Colorado, and Utah in the 1840s resulted not only from too much alcohol but also from too little bison and other game. Utes were hungry. Heavy snow in the winter of

1844–1845 killed many bison along the Front Range and in Utah, where they were virtually eliminated. Along the eastern margin of the plains, vast quantities of bison bones and skulls were seen and mentioned by white travelers.[27] Although the loss hurt traders, it was crucial for Indians who depended on the animals for subsistence. Thereafter, Indians were forced to hunt farther east on the plains or to compete with each other in Colorado's mountain valleys where some bison still were found. Before the severe winter of 1844–1845, game had already been scarce in Utah. For example, in 1843, when Frémont's expedition passed through the area around Great Salt Lake, all they could shoot were gulls, and a horse had to be eaten. The following spring, though, game was slightly more available, for Frémont was able to purchase bison tails and beaver tails from friendly Utes south of Great Salt Lake. When he had passed Brown's Hole and was traveling in North Park and South Park, his men saw and killed bison every day.[28]

In increasing numbers, travelers were visiting Ute country, sometimes writing accounts that reflected personal biases about the native people they met. For instance, in describing his journeys in the Rocky Mountains in the early 1840s, Jesuit missionary P. J. De Smet mentioned that he had baptized several "Yam-pah" Utes, a satisfactory enough experience.[29] In contrast, when he also met "Sampeetches" Utes, some of whom he baptized, he considered them to be a timid, wretched group who lived in rocks and crevices and ate ants, grasshoppers, "insipid roots," and "nauseous seeds." He complained that they offered their infants to white people in exchange for trifles and that dead "Sampeetches" were thrown on burial piles with their best horses. Father DeSmet felt he would happily return to give these dreadful Utes religious instruction if the opportunity arose.[30]

Government-sponsored parties like those of Frémont that were working in Ute country in 1843, 1844, and 1845 provided more objective accounts. They may have had an advantage because they were accompanied by experienced frontiersmen such as Thomas "Broken Hand" Fitzpatrick and Kit Carson who knew the land and its people well. In 1844, after having been pestered by Paiutes, Frémont's men had misgivings when they met Walkara's mounted band, who were armed with rifles and were on their way to exact tribute from a Mexican caravan on the Old Spanish Trail. Keeping his dignity, Frémont traded blankets with Walkara, whose attitude toward the American explorer was that "You are a chief and I am one, too," according to Frémont's cartographer, Charles Preuss. The Utes were described as "robbers of a higher form."[31]

After crossing the Sevier River in a tule boat, Frémont went on to Utah Lake, where he learned that the normally abundant fish had migrated into steams where Utes could not catch them. Some dried fish was found, though, and a Ute acquaintance of the guide, Kit Carson, gave them a piece of delicious deer meat.

Another kind of dealing took place when, heading east from Utah Lake toward Robidoux's Fort Uintah, Utes sold a Paiute boy in his early teens to Carson for forty dollars. Carson joked that he planned to train him so he would be of some use, like stealing horses.[32] At the time of the purchase, the boy's diet consisted of raw meat and raw bone marrow. Later Carson's household included another Paiute named Juan.

In contrast to Frémont's pleasant reception, a small party was traveling east by way of the Yampa River, Gore Pass, and Middle Park that same year. With them was Major William Gilpin, who later became the first governor of Colorado Territory. Camping on a tributary of the Colorado River, the group was joined by Utes. Their manner was so suspicious that Gilpin feared he and his men might be harmed, although that did not happen.[33]

During these years, when contact with Americans was becoming more frequent, much of Ute territory lay within the jurisdiction of the Republic of Mexico. Mexico's land took in the plains south of the Arkansas River and the mountains west of the river's headwaters—the line extending north into southern Wyoming. For the Utes, these political boundaries were meaningless, as was the fact that after 1821 everyone born in Mexico's territory was supposed to live peacefully and recognize legal authority. Instead, raids on Mexican settlements and counterraids had escalated, and the government in Santa Fe lacked the means to deal with nomadic "barbarians," as they were called. Settlements on the northern frontier were under constant threat of attack. Volunteers who joined militias were generally armed only with bows and arrows, whereas Indians were obtaining guns illegally through trade.[34]

Despite these threats, thousands of livestock from northern settlements were grazed in the San Luis Valley—Ute territory—because of insufficient pasturage nearer their home. Losses of this stock to Indians were predictable. A few daring Mexicans who attempted to plant small fields of corn and wheat in the north were fortunate if they could return home in the fall with harvests and their lives.

To encourage colonists to expand their villages, New Mexican governors granted several large parcels of land to individuals and to groups of applicants. With these grants more villages gradually spread northwest into the Chama Valley's Tierra Amarilla and east around Cimarrón and Ocaté, but movement onto other grants, such as those in the San Luis Valley, were thwarted by Utes and Navajos who considered the land to be theirs.

New Mexico's Padre Martínez, a powerful figure in territorial politics, sent the governor a proposal that foreshadowed later United States policies for resolving the problem of roving bands of Utes. In addition to concerns for his parishioners' welfare, Martínez may have been troubled because his family had lost large numbers of sheep in one raid. He suggested that the way to stop the nomads' attacks on ranches and haciendas was to persuade them to settle down on farms, where, becoming civilized, they could cultivate the soil, raise animals, and learn useful skills.[35]

Contrary to derogatory remarks made by foreign entrepreneurs whom he had accused of usurping power and corrupting native people in New Mexico, Martínez was a well-educated man who put some of his proposals into practice.[36] For instance, when he established the first public school in New Mexico, Native Americans were accepted for instruction. Among the Utes who came under his influence were two brothers, Ouray and Quenche. Because of Ouray's importance in later Ute history, it is interesting to examine what is known about his early life.

Ouray was born in 1833, the year of a spectacular shower of Leonid meteors, at Abiquiú to a Tabeguache mother and a Jicarilla Apache father, Guera Murah. The father had a Spanish name, Salvador, suggesting that he might have been adopted earlier into a Spanish household or at least had been baptized. The parents sometimes are said to have married at Red River (Questa), where Ouray was allegedly baptized, too, but there is no supporting evidence in records of the Archdiocese of Santa Fe that such sacraments ever took place.

Ouray's name had various spellings, often appearing with the letter "l" in place of the letter "r," as in "Ulay," pronounced "oo-lay." Ouray said that this was simply the first sound he uttered and that it had no meaning. Popular writers say it meant "arrow," but the Ute word for arrow is *úu*.[37] Ouray's younger brother was Quenche, and in 1845 a half-sister, Susan, was born. There may have been two other younger brothers and a younger sister who died.

Ouray's parents lived with the Mexican community at Abiquiú, where they sold wild game to their neighbors, an acquaintance of the family, J. M. Manzanares, recalled in his late years.[38] Manzanares was just three years older than Ouray, and his recollections seem credible. Around 1843 the parents took Ouray and Quenche to a hacienda at Taos and left them there to work, most likely as *criados*, as involuntary laborers were called. If the normal rate of exchange prevailed, the hacienda owner paid one horse for each boy. It is believed that the hacienda was that of Padre Martínez's family because they owned the largest one at Taos. Typically, the boys would have herded sheep, gathered wood, and helped with various agricultural chores. They would have been baptized if they had not been previously, as this was a requirement for "adopting" servants into a household, and the boys would have attended mass in the padre's church. During the years of the Mexican Republic, there were no religious orders in New Mexico, and Martínez was the powerful leader of the province's secular priests at the time, so Ouray's and Quenche's lives would have been entwined with one of the most important figures in northern New Mexico.

Manzanares said it was Quenche, not Ouray, who attended Martínez's school. Although many biographies of Ouray have said he was well educated, there is no evidence that he could read or write, although he learned to write his name after he was twenty years old. Americans who knew him when he was a chief remarked about his great intelligence and his skill as a conversationalist instead. Quenche, on the other hand, could read, write, and play the fiddle, Manzanares reported.

As *criados,* the boys would have been permitted to leave the hacienda when they reached maturity at about age sixteen or seventeen, according to the law of the time, and Ouray did, in fact, return to Abiquiú in 1850. Quenche remained at Taos because he liked Mexicans better than Indians, so Manzanares claimed. Quenche was a lifelong bachelor who sold piñon wood around town, delivering it with his burros. At Abiquiú, meanwhile, Ouray worked for the prominent Martínez family—relatives of the Martínezes in Taos—and he also worked for Manzanares's grandfather. Well-versed in tending sheep and in local horticultural practices, Ouray planted grain and hoed for his employers, Manzanares said, noting that while Ouray was among the Hispaños he dressed in clothing like that of his Mexican neighbors. In later years, when Manzanares was living near Walsenburg, Ouray visited him from time to time, and the two remained friends.[39]

Because of these experiences in his youth, Ouray had acquired facility in Ute, Apache, and Spanish languages, as well as some knowledge of English, and he had observed the way Mexican and American people lived. He would have known many local men who were prominent in the years prior to and following the United States occupation of New Mexico, and he would have been aware of important current events around Taos and Abiquiú.

During the years when Ouray was in Taos, Navajos had stepped up their aggression on frontier settlements, and both Capote and Weenuche

Utes had aligned themselves with the Navajos.[40] This association led to trouble for the Utes in 1844 when Mexican authorities sent a militia to punish the Navajos, who had escaped, but the militia found a Ute party and killed some of its members. In protest, a large force of Ute warriors and six leaders went to Santa Fe to demand reparations. In Governor Mariano Martínez's office a scuffle broke out between the unsympathetic governor and the belligerent Ute leaders. Guards came to the rescue of the governor, who was defending himself with only a chair, and the Indians escaped into the street, where some were shot. Several who died were left unburied for days, while Santa Fe's preparations for an Independence Day celebration lost their luster.

The Utes fled from Santa Fe. As they headed for the safety of a remote camp, they killed people north of El Rito. Residents of northern villages abandoned their homes as a general uprising broke out throughout Ute territory.[41] In 1845 the army and volunteers moved north from Taos Pueblo into the San Luis Valley and the Upper Arkansas Valley, where Ute camps were destroyed. Volatile conditions continued for the next ten years.

Not only had Ute-Mexican relations broken down during the years of the Mexican Republic, but intertribal conflict had also escalated. Relationships between Utes and Jicarilla Apaches solidified, with intermarriage common, and Utes were friendly with the powerful Navajos at times.[42] In the meantime, enmity with Comanches, Kiowas, Arapahos, and Cheyennes intensified as a result of raids for horses and captives and competition for hunting territory and trade. One incident in 1834 involving stolen horses led to a major dispute that generated bad feeling between Utes and Shoshones for decades.

Utes' skill as strategists matched their courage, and a story told by a Ute much later exemplifies how their reputation spread among their enemies. Long ago, according to the story, Utes attacked Comanches in southern Colorado. For two or three days the Utes kept the foes cornered in a cave while a brave Ute would sneak up and shoot them, one at a time, with arrows. Finally, the Utes let the survivors escape from the cave, but they shot them too as they emerged, except for one man who was permitted to get away so "he could tell the story."[43]

During the early 1800s, rivalry between Arapaho-Cheyenne allies and Comanche-Kiowa allies deflected some of the combat away from Utes until a horrendous battle in the late 1830s killed so many of their people that the plains tribes sought peace with one another. In 1840 an enormous gathering of Arapahos, Cheyennes, Comanches, and Kiowas took place near Bent's Fort, and they made peace. The truce was acknowledged with a huge giveaway of horses and other possessions among the allies. Thereafter, these tribes joined forces against Pawnees to their east and Utes to their west.

The landscape of Colorado's mountains, passes, and valleys contains hundreds of sites that testify to battles fought by Utes and their enemies. Many stone fortifications, similar in appearance to game blinds, still remain on hills in Colorado's San Luis Valley; in South, Middle, and North Parks; in surrounding passes; and on the Front Range. One fortification near Granby that for years remained a local landmark was made of rocks and logs. It was said to have been used in a battle led by Standing Bear. In the past, local people collected large numbers of projectile points around such battle sites. Rock art depicted battle scenes in which Utes rode horseback and carried guns, bows, arrows, and spears. Earlier, much Ute rock art represented chiefly hunting scenes.

Early journals and reports of travelers mention a few fights that were observed. For instance, in 1844, when Frémont's expedition traveled through South Park, the group came upon Ute women wailing over the loss of leaders killed by Arapahos at a hunting camp. The Utes wanted Frémont's men to assist in the fight taking place nearby, but as cartographer Preuss recounted, "it was most advisable for us to remain neutral. Therefore, we hurried past as fast as possible."[44]

Stories about incidents such as a mighty confrontation at Steamboat Springs indicate that Arapahos came west across southern Wyoming and fought Utes in their northern territory, and there are tales about Utes and Southern Paiutes who were killed by Arapahos in Utah as far south as Fish Lake. Evidence of a battle between Utes and Arapahos remained for decades at a site near Carbondale on the Roaring Fork in west-central Colorado. Most of the countless contests occurred nearer to the plains, though. In general, Ute warriors succeeded in driving their enemies away. After the battle at Hardscrabble Creek, for example, the Arapahos and their Mexican aides who survived fled from the area.[45]

It is sometimes said that Utes were a peaceful tribe, a point of view perhaps attributable to Chief Ouray's efforts in the 1860s and 1870s to avoid trouble with Americans. Furthermore, pre-horse Utes, prior to the 1600s, would have had few hostile encounters with other tribes or even with other groups of Utes. History supports the fact, however, that they were ready to fight by the time of the Pueblo Revolt in 1680 and that they became increasingly warlike over the next 150 years. The Utes' reputation for courage and skill was reflected in the opinion of Arapahos, who themselves were among the fiercest of warriors but who said they preferred to fight Utes above all others because they were the bravest in battle, the hardest to kill.[46] Warfare took place for several reasons. Glory and honor were not the foremost objectives of Utes, who usually fought for more practical purposes. Raids and counterraids had goals of revenge or of stealing or retrieving captives, horses, food, and other goods. Such blows were struck rapidly to avoid retaliation, not to invite it.

Captives were not always taken in raids to be sold as slaves. Some were kept by an Indian group to augment its size and productivity. Such captives, often small children, were adopted into their captors' villages. A number of well-known figures in Ute history came as captives from other tribes. For example, Colorow began his career among the Utes as a young captive of Shoshone origins. Ouray's Apache father, Guera Murah, was taken into the Tabeguache Band when he was young. Chipeta, Ouray's Kiowa wife, was found as a small baby at a battle site where Utes had destroyed or run off the rest of her Kiowa people.

When Utes lost possessions or were killed by an enemy, those acts were avenged, but on the whole the tribe took a pragmatic approach to warfare and did not seek it to gain prestige. Illustrative is an incident in which Utes had killed a Kiowa and had taken his belongings, among which they discovered the Kiowa tribe's sacred Sun Dance doll, Tai-me. When the Utes realized what they had and the trouble that could result, they threw the doll away.[47]

Although many Utes possessed firearms before the end of the Mexican period and Frémont's party heard gunfire at the battle in South Park in 1844, bows and arrows remained the most common weapons in warfare. Even on horseback, a warrior could shoot a number of arrows with precision faster than he could reload and fire a gun. When metal became readily available, arrow points were often made of iron rather than stone. Some points were fashioned from barrel staves and other metal objects, but traders also supplied Indians with large quantities of manufactured metal points. Men still made their own bows and arrows or had a camp expert make them in exchange for meat or other desirable products. Coup sticks were not used by Utes, as counting coup was considered foolish. Scalping was done, however, because it had the practical purpose of proving that the enemy had been killed.[48]

Ute women had roles related to warfare. Most obvious was their responsibility for moving camps and providing food, but in addition women accompanied war parties, sang songs preceding a fight, and took part in looting camps and bodies and occasionally even in the fighting itself. Women also performed the Lame Dance to mimic hauling heavy loads of captured goods and the Scalp Dance to celebrate a victory.

When engagements were premeditated rather than accidental, warriors prepared by fasting and holding ceremonies, such as the sweat lodge. Medicine men sang songs, but they also participated in battles. The use of paint on faces, bodies, and parts in their hair was common in daily life but took on special importance in warfare. Plains-style war bonnets appeared in some Ute rock art in the 1800s.

Military societies of young men, so well-known among Plains Indian tribes, do not appear to have existed among all Ute bands. Western Ute Chief Tabby, one of Walkara's brothers, claimed that even the oldest Utes living in about 1880 could remember no soldier bands.[49] Southern Utes, however, are said to have adopted the practice of having Dog societies, as these military organizations were called. Members were young and unmarried, frequently orphans, who were supervised by older men. They lived outside the main camp, which they protected. Other functions included raiding and taking the dangerous rear position during retreats following encounters. After Utes were assigned to reservations, Dog companies gradually became singing groups and eventually ceased to exist.[50]

During the Mexican period a number of changes occurred in the lives of Ute Indians. Trading caravans came across the Santa Fe Trail, which connected the Rocky Mountain West with the United States, and travelers on the Old Spanish Trail, which connected New Mexico and California, traversed Ute country. On Ute land, trapping, trading, and bison hunting developed into business ventures in the hands of foreigners, with whom Utes exchanged horses, furs, hides, and women for alcohol, guns, metal goods, and numerous other articles. Mexican land grants and some expansion of settlement took place on Indian lands, although most colonists were disrupted by Utes and Navajos. A few missionaries, explorers, and tourists appeared and quickly disappeared. Warfare with Plains Indian tribes increased, and Utes became more aggressive toward anyone, including Mexican authorities, who interfered with the acquisition of necessities for survival.

By the mid-1840s Utes were angry, ready and willing to do whatever was needed to protect their land and their way of life from intruders, for more than land had been usurped. Game, wild plants, and sources of water were being lost, too. When the first thunderstorms rumbled in spring and Ute Indians held their Bear Dance to ensure success and survival through another year, more was at stake than ever before.

Bear Dance at Ouray Agency, Utah, 1891. Photo by Robert E. Waugh, clerk at the trading post; courtesy Colorado Springs Pioneers Museum.

Musicians at Southern Ute Bear Dance, 1898. During the Bear Dance musicians hold a notched rasp, a morache, against a resonator that mimics the growl of the bear when the rasp is rubbed with a stick or a bone. Courtesy Colorado Springs Pioneers Museum.

Ute tepees near Denver, 1874. These tepees show the type Ute Indians made from hide and the random placement of them in Ute camps. The tripod seen at left is keeping an Indian's saddle dry by holding it off the ground, but possessions hung on tripods also identified the lodge's owner. William Henry Jackson photo; courtesy Colorado Historical Society, neg. no. F-11313.

Big Joe's canvas tepee and brush shelter, Uintah Agency, Utah. Different types of dwellings often served a family. J. H. Crockwell photo; courtesy Colorado Springs Pioneers Museum.

Chief Antero's encampment on the eastern slope of the Wasatch Mountains boasted a two-level shade house, providing a lookout from which its occupant could watch activities. J. K. Hillers photo, 1873 or 1874; Smithsonian Office of Anthropology, neg. no. 1544; courtesy Utah Historical Society, all rights reserved.

Ute Indians adapted available materials in constructing their habitations. Many early wickiups consisted simply of poles covered with brush or canvas and leaned against a tree. A. F. Randall photo; courtesy Denver Public Library, Western History Collection.

Chief Walkara's portrait, painted by Solomon Carvalho, who traveled with the Frémont expedition in 1853–1854. Used by permission, Utah Historical Society, all rights reserved.

Ute Indians acquired horses in New Mexico in 1640. Horses then spread throughout Colorado and Utah and became the primary form of transportation into the twentieth century. This view is of Strong Left Hand's family on the Ute Mountain Ute Indian Reservation in 1915. S. Olop photo; courtesy Colorado Historical Society, neg. no. F-42539.

A photograph in the Uinta Basin in the early 1870s shows the domestic lifestyle of Ute Indians; it depicts a baby in a cradleboard, a child seated on a buffalo robe, and, perhaps most significant, corn drying in the background. J. K. Hillers photo, Smithsonian Office of Anthropology, no. 1452; courtesy Denver Public Library, Western History Collection.

Susan, sister of Ouray and Quenche. This photograph by William Henry Jackson has been incorrectly and crudely identified as "Chipeta—Ouray's Squaw." Courtesy Colorado Springs Pioneers Museum.

Brothers Ouray (left) and Quenche. Drawing by Janet Lange in *La Tour du Monde* (1868); courtesy Denver Public Library, Western History Collection.

Chipeta, photographed by William Henry Jackson in 1874 at the Los Pinos Indian Agency. Courtesy Robert G. Lewis, Esq., Collection.

Kanosh, chief of the Pahvant Ute Indians at Corn Creek and elder of the Church of Latter-day Saints. The word *kanosh* is also applied to the basketry water jugs used by Ute Indians. Used with permission, Utah Historical Society, all rights reserved.

Ration day at grist mill, Cimarrón, New Mexico, in the 1860s. Courtesy Museum of New Mexico, neg. no. 8957.

Ute Indians at Abiquiú Indian Agency in New Mexico. T. H. O'Sullivan photo, 1874; courtesy Museum of New Mexico, neg. no. 40221.

Shavano, Tabeguache war chief and medicine man, engaged in conflicts during the 1860s. He is seen wearing a peace medal he received during his visit to Washington with a delegation in the 1870s. William Henry Jackson photo; courtesy Denver Public Library, Western History Collection.

Black Hawk (Autenquer, Antonga), leader of an uprising in Utah in the 1860s. Used with permission, Utah Historical Society, all rights reserved.

Uintah Chief Tabby led Utah's Indians to the Uintah Valley Reservation in the late 1860s after resisting white control. Used with permission, Utah Historical Society, all rights reserved.

Chief Antero, dressed in typical buckskin apparel. J. K. Hillers photo, 1873 or 1874, Smithsonian Office of Anthropology, neg. no. 1486-b; courtesy Utah Historical Society, all rights reserved.

In 1868 a group of Ute and Jicarilla Apache Indians posed in Nicholas Brown's studio at Santa Fe. Those in the photo are, *left to right, seated,* Panteleon (Jicarilla), Piquitigon (Ute), Martine (Capote Ute), Corinea (Capote Ute chief), Timpeache (Ute), Isidro (Ute), Boy Chief (Ute); *standing,* Huero Munco (Jicarilla), Arny's son William, Subagent Henry Moore Davis, Vicente (Jicarilla), territorial official and Abiquiú Agent William F. M. Arny, Sobatar ("chief of Capote and Weeminuche Utes"), Curlwitche (Ute), Tomás Chacon (interpreter), Taputche (Ute, son of Sobatar), Pedro Gallegos (Ute). Nicholas Brown photo; courtesy Museum of New Mexico, neg. no. 45814.

Ute delegation in Washington, 1868, at negotiations for the Treaty of 1868. Those pictured are, *left to right,* Ankatosh, Piah, Suriap, Uriah M. Curtis (interpreter), Congressman George M. Chilcott, Sowwachwiche, Albert G. Boone, Governor A. C. Hunt, Nicaagat (Jack), Congressman Hiram P. Bennet, Agent Lafayette Head, Guero, Agent Daniel C. Oakes, Ouray ("chief of the Uncompahgre Utes"), Edward H. Kellogg (Bureau of Indian Affairs employee), Severo (chief of the Capote Utes), William G. Godfrey (Godfroy). Matthew Brady photo; courtesy Colorado Historical Society, neg. no. F-7809.

Group of Ute Indians in Washington, 1868. *Left to right,* Nicaagat (Jack), Piah, Chippen, and Suruipe. A. Z. Shindler photo, Smithsonian Office of Anthropology, neg. no. 1577;

Group of Ute Indians at White River Agency, 1872. *Standing, left to right,* Agent J. S. Littlefield, Tabuchakat, Pahant, Catz, Uriah M. Curtis (interpreter); *seated,* Wanzits (Antelope), Special Agent James B. Thompson, Honko. Courtesy Colorado Historical Society, neg. no. F-5809.

Ute Indians in Washington in 1872 during negotiations for the Brunot Agreement. *Front row, left to right,* Guero, Chipeta, Ouray, Piah; *middle row,* Uriah M. Curtis, James B. Thompson, Charles Adams, Otto Mears; *top row,* Curecanti (Washington), Susan, Nicaagat (Jack), Johnson (Canavish), John. Courtesy Colorado Historical Society, neg. no. 24385.

Ute Indians visiting Colorado Springs in the mid-1870s proudly display their weapons and finery. Colorow is seated on the right, and Shavano is standing, second from left. B. H. Gurnsey photo; courtesy Colorado Springs Pioneers Museum.

Pauvitz and Jane, who worked in the Meeker household at the White River Indian Agency and was believed by Agent Meeker to have carried gossip to her husband's allies. William Gunnison Chamberlain photo; courtesy Robert G. Lewis, Esq., Collection.

Chiefs Douglass (left) and Johnson were living at the White River Agency during the period leading up to the killing of Agent Nathan C. Meeker and agency employees and were among the women's captors. Courtesy Colorado Historical Society, neg. no. F-1209.

The adobe home (top center) of Chief Ouray and Chipeta in the Uncompahgre Valley was surrounded by several outbuildings. On the far left and right are storerooms and cellars. At the lower center and right are boarding rooms for Mexican employees. A carriage given to Ouray by Governor McCook stands near the fence. Courtesy Colorado Historical Society, neg. no. F-40196.

Los Pinos Ute Agency No. 2, better known as the Uncompahgre Agency. Barnhouse and Wheeler photo, 1877–1879; courtesy Colorado Historical Society, neg. no. F-7357.

Ute Indians in Washington, 1880, to give testimony and negotiate the removal from Colorado. *Upper, left to right,* Golota, Otto Mears, Severo, Shavano, Agent Henry Page, Jocknick, Ignacio, Secretary of the Interior Carl Schurtz, Woretziz, Ouray, Charles Adams, Chipeta; *lower,* Ojo Blanco, Agent William H. Berry, Tapooche, Jack, Tim Johnson, Henry Jim, Sowowick, Buckskin Charlie, Wass, William Burns, Alhandro. L. E. Walker photo, 1880; courtesy Robert G. Lewis, Esq., and The Colorado College Special Collections.

82

Uncompahgre Ute Indians crossing the Grand (Colorado) River during the removal from Colorado, September 1881. From Sidney Jocknick, *Early Days on the Western Slope of Colorado*; courtesy Colorado Historical Society, neg. no. F-5458.

In September 1882 this group of Southern Ute Indians traveled from Ignacio to Denver to appear at the first National Mining and Industrial Exposition at Exposition Hall. They were accompanied by Agent Warren Patten, *standing, fifth from right*, and by black interpreter John Taylor, an agency employee. Severo is standing at the rear, *fifth from left*. William Henry Jackson photo, 1882; historical research and photographic print, courtesy Robert G. Lewis, Esq.

5

▼ ▼ ▼

On a Collision Course
(1846–1858)

Even in Indian country, news could travel quickly to distant places. From Santa Fe to Abiquiú, Mexicans related the latest rumors and alarms, and from Abiquiú along the Spanish Trail reports spread to the Great Basin. Gossip flew from Taos up the Rio Grande through the San Luis Valley and the Gunnison and Uncompahgre Valleys to northeastern Utah, or from Taos across the Sangre de Cristos to the Cimarron and Arkansas Rivers. It did not take long for news of the United States Army invasion of the Province of Nuevo Mexico to reach Utes wherever they roamed. There was an abundance of interesting news to relay in 1846.

In August Brigadier General Stephen W. Kearny's Army of the West had marched down the Santa Fe Trail and into the provincial capital without firing a shot. One explanation for this easy triumph might have been that New Mexicans welcomed a well-organized army as a potential protector from relentless raids by nomadic Indians. It was hoped also that the United States government might be responsive to administrative needs, although not everyone was happy when Charles Bent, part owner of Bent's Fort and a prominent resident of Taos, was appointed territorial governor in September 1846.

By 1848, when the Mexican War in the Southwest ended with the Treaty of Guadalupe Hidalgo, dramatic changes had taken place. The effects of the army's presence were quickly felt. After establishing Fort Marcy at Santa Fe, Kearny quickly sent two companies to Abiquiú to set up a post to control Indians, especially Utes and Navajos who were considered to be causing the most trouble.

It was the army's job to assume authority in such matters because the Bureau of Indian Affairs had been established as an agency of the

Department of War in 1824. Consequently, Major William Gilpin was sent with a detachment to round up Utes for a parley. He succeeded in bringing in two groups who met in Santa Fe with General Kearny in September and with Colonel Alexander W. Doniphan in October. While some of these Utes were agreeing to be peaceful, others were stealing a herd of horses from the quartermaster's depot, though. The agreement made by sixty Utes with the colonel has been called the Doniphan Treaty.

Another interesting topic of conversation among Indians would have been the presence of 275 Mormon families who had detoured on their journey to Utah to spend the winter of 1846–1847 in makeshift cabins near El Pueblo on the Arkansas River, along with ailing volunteers who had been part of the Mormon Battalion of the United States Army. Utes would have heard, too, about the uprising at Taos in January 1847 when Governor Bent and several other unwelcome "foreigners" were murdered by Taos Pueblo Indians and their Mexican allies. And Utes would have learned that United States soldiers arrived at Taos and that the rebels came to grief.

Nevertheless, this information did not stop Muache Utes and Jicarilla Apaches from joining forces to commit depredations around Las Vegas, New Mexico, and elsewhere. Most outlying settlements were spared outright annihilation by the Indians, only because, as Englishman George F. Ruxton observed when he passed through Río Colorado (now Questa) in early 1847, the Indians tolerated the presence of peons "for the purpose of having at their command a stock of grain and a herd of mules and horses, which they made no scruple of helping themselves to, whenever they required a remount or a supply of farinaceous food."[1] Ruxton also noted that Utes and Arapahos in the area were constantly fighting over hunting rights. A reason behind such difficulties can be deduced from his comment that natural food sources were scarce. Ruxton said that no bison remained except in South Park and a hundred miles east of the mountains. Although he failed to see some additional locations in the mountains where remnants of bison herds still existed, his impressions revealed the unrest in the area and at least some of its causes.

When a party of twenty-one men led by Kit Carson passed down the San Luis Valley and through Río Colorado in early summer of 1848, their chronicler, Lieutenant George Brewerton, mentioned similar problems. First, they learned that Indians had attacked another party of travelers and taken their possessions. Later, about fifty miles north of Taos, the Carson party came upon a camp of about 150 Indians whose warlike intentions were obvious. Speaking Ute, Carson determined that these unfriendly Indians belonged to a tribe that did not understand the

Ute language. The warriors withdrew only when word came that a militia of two hundred volunteers was approaching on a punitive expedition.[2]

During the winter of 1847–1848, raids by Utes, Jicarillas, and Navajos had increased. Military detachments were sent to Taos and Las Vegas, and others were sent to punish raiders elsewhere. In July 1848 an extensive force, led by Major W. W. Reynolds and guided by the old trapper Bill Williams, pursued Jicarillas into the San Juan Mountains, where the Apache band was joined by Utes. In a fierce battle near Cumbres Pass, thirty-seven Indians and two soldiers were killed.[3] Williams, who had lived with Utes and had been their friend, was wounded in the arm.

A few months later, however, he was guiding John Charles Frémont's Fourth Expedition when it met disaster in snowbound mountains about seventy miles north of the Cumbres Pass battle site. In March 1849 Utes killed Williams and Dr. Benjamin Kern, another survivor of the ill-fated Frémont venture, when they were retrieving the expedition's abandoned equipment. Often, such murders were intended to avenge wrongs previously committed against Utes, and Williams's death fits this category. Not only had he taken part in the Cumbres Pass affair, but he had also betrayed Utes while on an errand with which he had been entrusted not long before. Utes had given Williams a large number of hides to trade at Taos, and he had used the proceeds to indulge in a drinking spree of monumental proportions. He had never dared to return as a companion of the cheated Indians.

Adding to the Utes' anger was a military campaign undertaken in March 1849 by Lieutenant J. H. Whittlesey. Finding a camp of fifty lodges north of Río Colorado, his men had attacked it and fought off other Indians who approached the scene. Some were killed, more were wounded, women and a chief's son were taken captive, the village with all its contents was destroyed, and a score of horses were killed or wounded.[4]

Other, more typical grievances stemmed from attempts by New Mexicans to expand their homes, livestock grazing, and farming lands farther into Indian country. During the years of Mexican authority, land grants had multiplied, on paper if not with actual colonization, until they took in almost all the land from Tierra Amarilla, northwest of Abiquiú, eastward far onto the plains. In the mountains land grants existed northward into the San Luis Valley. A large proportion of the grantees were opportunistic French Canadians and Americans with economic and political influence in Taos. Most early attempts to graze livestock and to farm lands in the San Luis Valley during the summer months were given up in the early 1840s because of Ute and Navajo hostilities.

By the mid-1840s, however, some of Taos's well-known figures, Lucien Maxwell and Kit Carson among them, were moving onto the western margin of Maxwell's two million acre grant. This was prairie land frequented by Muaches, Jicarillas, and Indians from Plains Indian tribes, all of whom disrupted this effort, too.

Despite attempts by the military to control the Indians, Utes remained free and far-flung, some reported as far afield as the Garden City, Kansas, area where presents were distributed to tribes that normally lived there. When Utes were invited to come to nearby Abiquiú to parley, however, they refused. The Muache leader Kaniache was arrested and placed in a room with some Mexicans who, as it happened, had been found with items belonging to Bill Williams and Dr. Kern. When he heard that he was going to be hanged, Kaniache escaped.

Undeterred, Utes continued their activities beyond the eastern foothills. In 1849 they attacked the settlement of "Bondrino" (probably Golondrinas), north of Las Vegas, and some Utes were killed by dragoons from Taos afterward. A band of Jicarillas and Utes attacked a wagon train led by James White near Point of Rocks on the Santa Fe Trail. They killed the men and took Mrs. White, her daughter, and a servant as captives. Soldiers from Las Vegas pursued them but found Mrs. White dead and the daughter gone.[5]

With the army's policing role well understood by Native Americans, improved relations were anticipated when the Bureau of Indian Affairs was transferred from the War Department to the Department of the Interior by an act of Congress in 1849. The bureau's territorial functions then became civil responsibilities. In December New Mexico Territory's governor and ex officio superintendent of Indian Affairs James S. Calhoun succeeded in negotiating a treaty with the Utes. Calhoun's document, usually considered the first treaty with Ute Indians, was signed with "x" marks by twenty-eight principal and subordinate chiefs, possibly Kaniache himself being the principal.

In the treaty the "Utah tribe of Indians" submitted to the jurisdiction of the United States government and agreed to peace with United States citizens and their allies. American and Mexican captives and property were to be delivered to authorities. People of the United States were to have free passage through Ute territory, and military posts and agencies, along with authorized trading posts, could be established there. "Relying confidently upon the justice and liberality of the United States," as the treaty read, the Utes agreed that the government would establish boundaries within which they would live, build stationary homes, cultivate the soil, and undertake "such other industrial pursuits as will best

promote their happiness and prosperity." In exchange for these concessions, the Utes were to receive donations, presents, and implements.[6] In
1851 funds were appropriated by Congress for such purposes, but no
reservation boundaries were established at this time.

The treaty expressed the well-established goals held at the time by
the United States government and iterated by Taos's Padre Martínez.
Those goals embodied the widely accepted concept that Native Americans should settle down peacefully on reservations where agriculture and
manual labor rather than raiding would provide their basic needs, with
the government distributing rations until the Indians became
self-supporting. Unfortunately, this policy overlooked the fact that Utes
were nomads who had hunted and foraged on the land for centuries and
who had neither the experience nor the desire to change their life ways.
Stealing livestock and food was a justifiable supplement to hunting and
gathering in the eyes of the Indians, who, with or without a treaty,
became increasingly antagonistic toward both the new Americans and
the Mexicans as they plowed and grazed livestock on Indian land and
usurped its timber and water resources.

Only a few days after the signing of the treaty, Utes killed seven
Mexicans in the Chama Valley and took their livestock, and Capotes
were trying to forge an alliance with Navajos to oppose the white intruders. Between 500 and 1,500 lodges of well-armed Utes were said to
be camped about sixty miles from Abiquiú. Muaches, who were camped
along the Culebra River in the San Luis Valley, also were testy.[7]

Despite such threats, people from New Mexico's settlements, where
water and arable land were insufficient for the ever increasing population, pressed north but with little success, exceptions being the new
plaza and placitas around Costilla. One of the rare individuals to be
treated hospitably by the Indians was Tata Atanasio Trujillo, who came
seasonally to the west side of the Rio Grande where he raised a few
crops. He spoke Ute, and his visitors gave him dried deer meat, deerskins, and other gifts.[8]

The early 1850s witnessed the births and deaths of settlements, but
as a result of the United States Army's strategy of creating several forts
and small posts throughout the territory to protect settlers, a few took
root. Between 1849 and 1851 a small detachment was posted in rented
quarters at Abiquiú. Although dragoons were located in quarters rented
from Lucien Maxwell at Rayado, near Cimarrón, in 1849 and 1850,
Apaches and Utes still managed to steal livestock only two miles from
the post. Pursued by military and volunteers, including Kit Carson, the
livestock was recovered, and five Indians were killed and scalped.[9]

Utes in that area considered themselves to be at war. To prevent powder, flints, and knives from falling into Indian hands, unlicensed traders were arrested.[10] Calhoun licensed others as traders, who were required to show inventories of their trade goods, though this process proved futile. Depredations continued around Las Vegas and over Raton Pass as far north as the Greenhorn area.[11] In 1852 Muaches were raiding along the St. Charles River east of El Pueblo. In the San Luis Valley in 1853, a legendary attack on the lower Culebra Creek was stemmed when a man wearing shining armor and riding a white horse miraculously appeared in the sky and frightened the Utes away, it was said. Some believed their savior was San Acacio, who became the patron saint of the village.

Intertribal hostilities also kept the region stirred up. Numerous skirmishes occurred along the western edge of the plains and in the mountains between Muaches and Jicarillas on one side and their Kiowa, Arapaho, and Comanche enemies on the other. A major battle between Utes and Arapahos also took place in 1849 at what became known as Battle Mountain near Red Cliff, Colorado. Another against Comanches and Kiowas in South Park lasted three days.[12]

The mission of New Mexico Territory's military and civilian organizations was to bring order to this tumultuous scene so American expansion could move ahead. To make his army more effective, in 1851 Colonel Edwin V. Sumner moved his men out of Fort Marcy at Santa Fe—"a sink of vice," as he called it—and established Fort Union about eighty miles to the east where he hoped it would be easier to protect the Santa Fe Trail and to strike quickly against Indians all along the plains' margin.

Serving as the Southwest's army supply depot, Fort Union also had a link to other forts throughout the region. Among nearly a dozen small outposts in New Mexico Territory were Cantonment Burgwin near Taos and Fort Massachusetts on Ute Creek at the foot of Blanca Peak in the San Luis Valley. Although the latter fort was well situated to control traffic on an Indian trail between the Rio Grande and the lower Arkansas River Valley, the location proved to be too far removed from settlements to be practicable, although its presence encouraged many new colonizers to come into the region. Another fort was proposed but not built at the confluence of the Animas River with the San Juan. The intention was to control Weenuches and Navajos who were collaborating on raids. A condition that encouraged such raiding was the increase of traffic westward following the opening of California's gold rush. An exception to this practice took place when a party herding thousands of sheep was helped by Capote Utes under Chief Tamuche, who helped the travelers cross the San Juan River.

Following the organization of the Territory of New Mexico, four agents were appointed to serve under the territory's superintendent of Indian Affairs. Agencies were created, although they got off to a lame start. New Mexico's first agency was located at Taos in 1850, but it soon closed because no money had been appropriated for it, although some Capotes received gifts at nearby Arroyo Hondo in 1852 and 1853.[13] The Taos Agency reopened in the winter of 1853–1854 with Kit Carson serving as agent for Taos and Picuris Pueblo Indians and also for Muache Utes and Jicarilla Apaches who frequented the area. Utes in this region became known as "Taos Utes."

Most agents elsewhere served for only a year or two, too brief a time to develop continuity or even expertise. The job was not easy, for an agent's time, aside from that spent issuing rations, was taken up with complaints about troubles between settlers and Indians, as a later agent at Abiquiú reported.[14] Carson was an exception, as he was agent longer than most—until 1861 when he resigned to serve in the Civil War. His inability to read and write was overcome by hiring a clerk who could handle paperwork and carry on business when Carson was away, as he often was. This former mountain man's ability stemmed from his knowing the Indians in his charge, their languages, and their territories firsthand.

An example of Carson's knowledge of Ute country is found in the Brewerton account of their journey from California to Taos in 1848, when Carson was carrying important dispatches, not the least of which was news of the discovery of gold at Sutter's Mill in California. On this trip, after they had passed through Mojave and Paiute territories, they came upon the first "Eutaws," who were camped near Little Salt Lake, west of Parowan, Utah. The Utes comprised four lodges belonging to "Wacarra" (Walkara) with his wives, children, and some followers. Walkara had taken up this position to exact his annual toll from a large trade caravan that was approaching on the Spanish Trail. Walkara's group was well armed, but they received Carson's party graciously and agreed to trade a fresh pony for Brewerton's footsore mount plus one of his two Mexican blankets. Brewerton added some observations about Walkara, who seemed "overbearing," especially in his table manners, for he ate more than his share of the Americans' scant food. Compared with other tribes farther west, however, these Utes seemed to Brewerton to be of a superior nature and were the "most powerful and warlike tribe" left on the continent, he commented.

From Walkara's camp Carson's party traveled northeast through Utah's high plateau country to Fish Lake, where they found Utes who gave them a piece of mountain sheep meat and a trout that had been caught with arrows. The Utes took gunpowder in exchange. The visitors soon discovered that they themselves could catch the abundant, spawning fish simply by clubbing them.

At the Green River the crossing was made difficult by high water. Rafts were built and loaded with saddles, clothing, rifles, and other items, many of which were soon lost in the river's current. Friendly Utes who appeared lent the wet, shivering troupe some buffalo robes to warm themselves and helped them swim their horses and mules across the river. From the Green the party continued east to the Colorado River, crossed it near Grand Junction, and followed the Gunnison River up past the abandoned site of Robidoux's Fort Uncompahgre. They entered the San Luis Valley by way of Cochetopa Pass, one of the Indians' most heavily used routes. It was in the southern part of this valley that Carson employed his linguistic skill, mentioned previously, to ascertain that a large group of hostile Indians were not Utes.[15]

Events in Utah were following a course much different from those in New Mexico, where contact with permanent Euro-American settlement had existed for more than two centuries. Until 1847 Utah had escaped colonization by white newcomers, but about 150 Mormons in the Pioneer Company arrived at Great Salt Lake in July of that year. At Fort Bridger, Jim Bridger had warned their leader, Brigham Young, about "bad Utes" around Utah Lake, as well as about the climate, which would make farming difficult. Nevertheless, the people of the Church of Jesus Christ of Latter-day Saints remained unconvinced, at least by his predictions about the Utes. Mormons believed American Indians belonged to one of the lost tribes of Israel, the Lamanites, and as such were likely to respond to kindness and proselytizing by the Saints. Despite their optimism, during the next two decades relations between Mormons and Indians in Utah were marked by violence as often as by friendship.

The first Utes the Mormons met were a friendly group of about twenty who wanted to trade. The second group was a party who visited Great Salt Lake during the winter and brought some captive children, whom the Utes threatened to kill if they were not purchased.[16]

Nothing could have prepared Utah's Indians for the wave of Mormons who soon descended upon their land without permission from the Indians. By the fall of 1848 5,000 had come to their self-proclaimed state of Deseret, a theocracy with the church's president, Brigham Young, as governor. The Mormon population grew to 11,000 by 1850. Within a few months of their arrival, the newcomers were plowing and planting the land with corn and wheat, channeling the water into irrigation ditches, cutting trees for buildings and firewood, putting livestock out to graze on the Utes' rapidly denuded horse pastures, gathering wild berries and nuts, and fishing and hunting game on which Utes had depended for centuries. Similar changes were happening in New Mexico but not with the explosive speed seen in Utah.

In September 1848, only a few months after Walkara had graciously received Kit Carson's party at Little Salt Lake, the Ute war chief and his half-brother Sowiet visited Great Salt Lake with hundreds of Utes and several hundred horses that were offered in trade. Walkara was reportedly delighted by the thriving scene he found, although he urged the Mormons in the future to trade farther south, in his own country. Walkara was still friendly toward whites in 1849 when he met William L. Manly and his companions as they were traveling to the California gold fields. In southern Wyoming this company of Missourians had made the ill-advised decision to float down the Green River, rather than continue overland, to avoid meeting Mormons, with whom they were on unfriendly terms. Manly emerged at the Uinta Basin, where he encountered Walkara and some of his band, after a harrowing adventure on and in the river. Still determined to continue by water, he was warned by Walkara against doing so because of the dangerous river. Walkara traded the Missourians two ponies for a coat, needles, and a few odds and ends in exchange for helping the travelers continue their journey by land. The Indians shared their meal of bobcat and rabbits with the white men, who learned that Utes wasted nothing, as they ate every part, including the intestines and stomach. Enjoying one another's company, Indians and whites danced together. When Manly's group departed and headed west across the basin, Walkara followed for awhile, noticed that they had taken the wrong fork in the trail, and caught up with them to set them on the correct path.[17]

Relations with the Mormons were breaking down, though. Two Utes, Kone and Blue-Shirt, killed some cattle that the Saints were grazing north of Utah Lake. A posse of about thirty-five Mormons then chased Utes into a canyon and killed five of them at what became known as Battle Creek.[18] Mormons were well aware that their relations with Utes were strained to the limit when, in early 1849, they established a stockade called Fort Utah with cannons for protection. Built on the Western Utes' finest land, the fort was at the future site of Provo. In April a Ute visited Fort Utah. He was wearing a white man's shirt, which the Mormons believed had been stolen, and they tried to retrieve it. In the ensuing struggle, the Ute was killed. Thrown into the river, the body was discovered by enraged Utes, who attacked the property of Mormons around Utah Lake and Salt Lake City. The Utes stole grain and corn and shot at anyone who exposed himself in order to hunt or to gather firewood.

By winter a militia of a hundred men was sent from Salt Lake City with orders to take no prisoners except women and children. In a battle near Fort Utah with the Utes, led by Big Elk, about seventy Ute casualties occurred, and Big Elk later died from his wounds. As the Indians retreated they were engaged repeatedly, and five more were killed. About thirty women and girls were taken as prisoners to Salt Lake City, where they soon became servants in Mormon homes. A delegation of Ute chiefs came to Utah Lake to parley. Among them were Walkara, the war chief; Sowiet, recognized as head civil chief of the Western Utes; their brother Tabby, a subchief; another brother Kanosh, the Pahvant chief; their cousin Anthro or Antero, an important Uintah chief with influence among Eastern Utes in Colorado; and others.[19]

Meanwhile, more than two hundred Mormons, along with their livestock and farm equipment, had moved into the Sanpete Valley, where Manti soon was founded. They brought measles, a scourge that decimated the Utes in the winter of 1849–1850. One victim was Chief Arrapene's daughter. Sanpits Utes continued to camp near Manti in 1850, hunting and fishing there. With the exception of those who had horses, permitting their owners to hunt in more remote places, the subsistence of these Utes was desperately poor. To increase their food supply, Walkara and Chief Sanpitch asked the Mormons to teach local Utes how to farm, but this occupation met with little enthusiasm among most of the band. When the Saints proselytized this band, they were equally unenthusiastic until Walkara and Arrapene took the lead, and more than a hundred Utes were baptized in Manti Creek. Defections soon indicated that their religious conversion was half-hearted.[20]

Evidence that native habits still prevailed became obvious in midsummer when Walkara and his band arrived in the Sanpete Valley with some Shoshone prisoners. A successful raid had just been completed against Walkara's special enemies who had been responsible for the death of the chief's father. For two weeks the Mormons of Manti were an unhappy audience for scalp dances, the wailing of the captive wives of the victims, and feasting.

When Utah became a territory of the United States in 1850, Brigham Young was appointed territorial governor and ex officio superintendent of Indian Affairs. Although Utes were regularly pasturing their horses on the sprouting wheat and corn of the Mormons, he urged settlers to avoid conflict. He advocated that it was cheaper to feed the hungry Indians, who often came to doors asking for food, than to fight them. Young appointed agents and two subagents for the Pauvan (Pahvant) and Uintah districts, with the latter serving Uintah Utes, Yampa Utes, and Shoshones. The Salt Lake City Agency was the headquarters, and other agency facilities were not built.

Fort Laramie, formerly a trading post in eastern Wyoming, had by then become an important military post, protecting travelers on routes to Oregon, California, and Utah and having oversight over Utes of northern Colorado as well as some other tribes. In 1851 thousands of Sioux, Cheyennes, Arapahos, and Crows were summoned to Fort Laramie to negotiate a peace treaty. Young ordered his Utah Utes to attend and made elaborate plans to send them in a carriage in disguise to avoid detection by their enemies. When only Chief Grosepene, his sister, and representatives of Sowiet, Walkara, and Wanship showed up, the journey was canceled.[21] Eventually, in 1852, Sowiet, Walkara, Antero, and around thirty lodges did grudgingly attend a council with Shoshones and agreed to peace. At this council the Utes also consented to allow settlements on their land and to give nine horses to the Shoshones as payment for some members of that tribe who had been killed by Utes.[22]

But all was not tranquil in Utah. Young accused Jim Bridger of furnishing Indians with guns at his fort and of fomenting bad feeling among them toward Mormons until, finally, Mormons burned Bridger's trading post. A trouble spot at this time was west of Utah Lake, where the fierce Tintics, a group of Utes led by Chief Tintic, were raiding.

Far to the south Chief Peteetneet's Utes were destroying crops around the new settlement of Parowan and were fighting with Piede Paiutes. Walkara was causing little trouble at home because he was busy raiding in lower California after spending the winter of 1853–1854 among the Navajos and Hopis.

Walkara's attention was about to turn to the Mormons, however. The most serious provocation was the curtailment of the slave trade. Sanctions against slave trading resulted from United States laws that forbade this activity in its territories. In 1852 the Utah legislature duly prohibited the common practice of trading in or possessing slaves. Those in households had been treated like indentured servants with the provision that they could choose freedom after twenty years. Now, euphemistically, they were to be "adopted" instead and clothed, fed, and sent to school. Nearly every household continued to benefit from this labor force, and Indians continued to threaten to kill captives unless they were "adopted." Chief Arrapene himself set an example by dashing out the brains of a captive child who had been refused.

With the 1852 prohibition traders could no longer enter Utah from New Mexico to engage in the time-honored slave trade with Utes. Pedro León of Abiquiú, who was found in Sanpete Valley in the company of 150 Yampa Utes, was arrested with his party of 28 Mexicans.[23] He was tried and fined, and the slave traffic between Utah and New Mexico ended in its customary form thereafter. This disruption of the economic livelihood of many Utes added to their animosity toward the Mormons.

A different kind of incident in 1853 fanned emotions into violence. A Ute family had come to a Mormon's cabin near Walkara's camp on Spring Creek, near Springville, to trade three fish for food. They were given three quarts of flour, an exchange the Utes felt was unsuitable. Two more Indians appeared, and one entered the cabin, where a scuffle took place. One Ute died, and two others were wounded. Although all too typical in the story of conflict between Utes and settlers, this event was notable in that it triggered the beginning of what has been called the Walker War.

This war consisted of a series of guerrilla-style raids led by Walkara and Arrapene over a period of several months. Their adversaries were a Mormon militia of more than seven hundred men, far outnumbering the Utes who were involved. During the war about a dozen white people and a great many more Utes died. The Indians would have been exterminated if Brigham Young had not urged restraint. Examples of the kind of violence attributed to Utes, on one hand, were the killing of a guard at Fort Payson by one of Arrapene's followers and the killing of men working at isolated mills and of others hauling crops in wagons to Salt Lake City. Retributions by Mormons, on the other hand, included six Indians suspected of stealing, who were captured, taken to town, and shot. Utes who sought protection in Mormon camps were killed. The final raid saw the burning of Allred's Settlement in the Sanpete Valley, where some buildings had been erected at a spring traditionally used by Utes. After the Walker War, Mormons claimed nearly $115,000 in damages from the federal government as payment for losses caused by the government's "wards," as American Indians were called.[24]

Not all Ute leaders had favored the war. Opposing it were Sowiet, Kanosh, Peteetneet, and others. In the spring of 1854 Brigham Young and Indian agent Garland Hurt, with Kanosh's assistance, arranged a council at Chicken Creek, where Walkara signed an agreement to stop the fighting. Having been brought low by hunger during the previous winter and by continued confrontations with Shoshones, his followers were ready for peace.

Several months later, in January 1855, near Meadow, Walkara died of natural causes at about age forty. Some say his death was caused by sorrow over the Utes' downfall. His burial was appropriate for a war chief with great power and wealth. His body was placed in a grave on the side of a mountain southeast of Fillmore, and with it were buried two of his wives, blankets, buckskins, and many other possessions. A dozen of his horses were killed and placed at the site. Two captive Piede (Paiute) children, a boy and a girl, were confined within a rock cairn atop the grave where they slowly died. In the early 1900s the grave was desecrated by a looter who removed the collectible articles.[25]

Walker's burial was exceptional among those of other prominent Ute leaders in the number of horses and the sacrifice of the two children. Utes were often buried in rock crevices or caves with many personal possessions to be used in the afterlife, and some items were given away as gifts. Other possessions, even the lodge, were destroyed. Burials took place at a sufficient distance from camp to keep away the spirit of the deceased, or the camp itself was moved. Persons of lower rank, especially women, were buried less ceremoniously, often in shallow graves, perhaps covered with rocks.[26] Occasionally, Ute bodies with their possessions were placed on platforms in trees. Women in mourning slashed their skin, wailed, cut their hair, darkened their faces with pitch and ashes, and wore old clothing. A number of so-called burial grounds have been found in Ute country, but it is believed that many of them mark sites of battles.

In 1853 other events involving contact with Utes were taking place in Utah. Three American surveying parties came in search of a central route to California across Ute country, and one of these—the tragic expedition of Captain John W. Gunnison—has been linked incorrectly to the Walker War. The others were those of Gwinn Harris Heap, who was traveling with Edward F. Beale, and of John Charles Frémont.

The Heap-Beale group passed through Utah in July without mishap. At the swollen Green River, they constructed a leather boat and made a safe crossing while Utes, some armed with rifles and others with bows and obsidian-tipped arrows, looked on without causing trouble. After the transit had been accomplished, the Indians cut up the leather boat for moccasin soles.

Two months later, in September, Gunnison's team of United States Topographical Engineers arrived at the same river and had another benign meeting with Utes camped on the west shore. The Utes came across to trade and pointed out to Gunnison's men the best place to cross. Continuing west, the Americans reached the Pahvant Valley about a month behind an emigrant company that had been headed for California on the north-south road through Utah. Despite warnings from local Mormons to use caution, the emigrants had expressed contempt for any Indians who might try to come near their camp. Unfortunately, some Pahvant Utes, led by war chief Moshoquop, did come to the emigrants' camp and asked for food and other items. Their request received an antagonistic response, and a scuffle followed, with Moshoquop's father, Mareer, being shot and killed before it ended.[27]

When Gunnison's party arrived in the same area, they naively assumed the Walker War was of no concern to them because Gunnison had enjoyed friendly relations with Indians in northern Utah on a previous journey. Now, in 1853, his expedition split into two groups, with Gunnison and seven others setting off to investigate Sevier Lake and its surrounding marshes. While encamped there, on the morning of October 26 one of the men fired a gun at a rabbit, and their presence thus was discovered by Moshoquop and his followers, who happened to be camped nearby. The Utes fell upon the American team and slaughtered all eight men. One of the dead was artist Richard Kern, brother of Dr. Benjamin Kern who had been with Frémont in 1848–1849 and who, with Bill Williams, had been killed by Utes in Colorado. Another was botanist Jacob Creutzfeldt, who also had accompanied Frémont's ill-fated expedition. Chief Kanosh later identified the culprits in the Gunnison episode and confirmed that their purpose had been to avenge the death of Moshoquop's father.[28] The deaths of the Gunnison party have sometimes been incorrectly included as part of the Walker War, bringing the tally of white victims in it to a score. Another misunderstanding about the Gunnison Massacre, as it is usually called, was that it was instigated by Mormons who resented the presence of surveyors, as well as other representatives of the federal government, in Utah.

A survey led by Frémont was the third to enter Utah in 1853, purposely late in the year, he said, to test the suitability of weather conditions for a railroad route. Without experiencing any trouble, he found a camp of a few hundred Utes before his Green River crossing, though a visit by Utes to his camp caused some nervousness. His trouble came from cold and snow in the Wasatch Mountains to the west, where one man died and others suffered acutely. Equipment was cached, and in the spring a Mexican who went to find it was killed by Utes.[29]

In the spring of 1854, because of the Gunnison deaths and the increasing antipathy between Mormons and non-Mormons, a troop of three hundred men under Colonel Edward J. Steptoe was sent to Utah, ostensibly to arrest the Utes responsible for the Gunnison episode. Kanosh, who had consistently been friendly to the Mormons, turned over six Utes, one of them a woman. It was generally felt that not all, if any, of these Utes were guilty, but three were tried. Their lawyer, A. W. Babbitt, was murdered, and feelings ran high, not only against Utes but increasingly between Mormons and non-Mormons, the "gentiles."

In September Agent Hurt, who was often at odds with Young, facilitated a peace council at Salt Lake City with about five hundred Utes, Shoshones, and Cumumbas. With so many Indians camping in the city, opportunities for trouble abounded. Outside Governor Young's office, armed Utes intimidated unarmed Shoshones with a display of war paint and war dances, but Chief Peteetneet succeeded in calming the atmosphere. A peace accord was negotiated, and the following day Hurt distributed presents. Former enemies in the Ute and Shoshone camps happily agreed to hunt bison together that winter on the White River.[30]

In December Hurt persuaded Arrapene to deed Ute land in Sanpete County to the Church of Jesus Christ of Latter-day Saints and to settle his band on a plot of about 2,000 acres where there was water to irrigate an Indian farm. Until his death, Arrapene henceforth was considered by Mormons to be the principal Ute chief in Utah. Chief Sowiet and seventy lodges of his followers vanished for two years, and with Walkara dead, the choice of Arrapene went unchallenged.[31]

Before and during these troubled times, Kanosh's band had been living in the Pahvant Valley and for several years had been raising a little corn on Upper Corn Creek, where the Mormon community of Kanosh was later located. In 1856 Agent Hurt expanded the Pahvants' farm at Corn Creek and created two others, one at Twelve Mile Creek in Sanpete County for the Sanpits Utes and the other at Spanish Fork in Utah County for the Timpanogots. Hurt intended that these three small parcels would become reservations where the Utes could become self-sufficient farmers. Despite his efforts, Mormons soon alleged that Hurt was arming the Utes to fight them. Adding to Hurt's frustration, no Utes other than Kanosh's group were inclined to farm. By late 1857 Hurt had built a few utilitarian buildings and a corral at the Twelve Mile farm, but Mormons were hired to perform work while the Indians went to the mountains to hunt and to forage for their traditional food.[32] In 1863 the Indian farm project was given up and the lands were sold.

Hand-in-hand with settlements, Mormons established missions to the Lamanites as colonists moved onto Indian lands. Hurt claimed the missionaries were little more than low-class scalawags and estranged himself by criticizing the short-lived Elk Mountain Mission. Located at the future site of Moab, this mission was established by forty-one Mormons who were sent out by Young in 1855. That summer, a stone fort, corral, and tilled fields appeared near the Spanish Trail's crossing of the Colorado River, and a few Elk Mountain Utes, the Seuvarits, were converted. In the fall, however, unconverted Indians killed three Mormons and drove livestock away to Sanpete County, thereby terminating the Elk Mountain Mission project. Brigham Young was shocked, because he claimed the Utes had asked to have a Mormon colony there. He blamed "young bloods" among the Utes for its failure.[33]

Writing to Washington for appropriations to assist his Indians, Hurt complained that they were starving because of Mormon intrusions on their land and loss of game, and he accused Young of using Indian moneys more to further the church's programs than to help the Indians. Moreover, Hurt claimed, Mormons were baptizing Utes and ordaining some as elders without proper instruction in Christianity.[34] The agent's accusations created so much ill feeling that he was chased out of Utah in 1857.

Meanwhile, Indians under Chief Tintic had again undertaken depredations that led to conflict with the Utah County militia. In this "Tintic War," a posse pursued Chief Tintic and another leader, Cottonlegs, without success. After Chief Arrapene sided with the Indians, livestock taken by Tintics was found in the hands of Sanpits Utes, but some had already passed through the Uinta Basin into buffalo country in northwest Colorado. A few Utes, including Washear (Squash Head), were arrested. While he was being held prisoner, Washear either committed suicide or was killed.[35]

To quell the turmoil in Utah, the United States Army, under Albert Sidney Johnston, marched across southern Wyoming in the summer of 1857. Before he reached his destination, Johnston's army was met by Utah's Nauvoo Legion and about four hundred Indian allies of the Mormons who burned Fort Bridger and destroyed some of the army's wagons. During the "Utah War," which did not include actual warfare, Hurt fled Utah and his Mormon enemies, and many fearful Mormons abandoned their homes to seek protection in larger towns such as Provo. Hysteria reached a climax in the fall when a Mormon militia and Paiute Indians together slaughtered an emigrant party at Mountain Meadows in far southwestern Utah. Although it has been said that Brigham Young was removed as superintendent of Indian Affairs because of the troubles in Utah Territory, the title and functions of the superintendents in both Utah and New Mexico Territories were, in fact, separated administratively from those of the governors in 1857.

During this first tumultuous period in Utah, New Mexico Territory was moving relentlessly toward its own crisis, which struck in 1854 and 1855. Essentially, the causes were the same—expansion of settlements on traditional Ute lands, depletion of natural resources, plowing and irrigating fields to raise crops, grazing livestock on sparse grassland, hunger, disease, and fear and anger on both sides. In New Mexico, where liquor was readily available, it added fuel to the fires.

Hunger was most prevalent near settlements. In the fall of 1853 about forty starving women and children were seen stripping bark from pine and aspen trees in the foothills of the San Luis Valley.[36] Had it been spring, they might have merely been gathering the sweet sap or the nutritious inner bark, a favorite treat, or if someone had been sick they might have been collecting medicine from the trees' inner layer. Because the region was experiencing a drought in the early 1850s, berries and piñon nuts were probably in short supply, so the people were probably eating bark instead. Perhaps the same drought had driven Utah's Indians to extreme measures.

Indians continued to hunt and raid for their sustenance as much as was possible. Bison were gone from lower elevations, although the Heap-Beale expedition mentioned seeing fresh signs of bison at Cochetopa Pass, and Heap's account of the journey claimed that Mexicans still came to this pass to trade for buckskins and buffalo robes. He came upon one Ute woman staggering along a trail under the weight of two packs of buffalo robes. Presumably to supplement game in the San Luis Valley, Utes were also seen herding a large number of "tame" goats that had come from the settlements. Other Utes were chasing wild horses in the valley. These Indians were friendly. Heap was able to trade with the Utes, giving them tobacco, ammunition, and "lucifer matches" in exchange for dried meat. He showed the Indians how to light and use the matches, which were a wonderful novelty. A negative note was sounded, however, when he mentioned that five Americans and some Mexicans had been killed earlier that year in the same area while herding sheep to California.

Near the site of Fort Uncompahgre, where Beale and some others of the expedition camped, they were visited by Utes who insisted that the Americans come to their own village about ten miles away. There Beale observed that these prosperous Indians had hundreds of horses and goats. In the lodge of a very old chief, the visitors were served fat deer meat and boiled corn on wooden platters and cornmeal boiled in goats' milk with a piece of elk fat for flavoring. Beale, who had been on short rations for two weeks, claimed he wolfed down "half a bushel of this delicious atole." Clearly, these Utes, although they lived far from settlements, were living quite well in their traditional manner, if not as grandly as Beale felt. Invited to hunt with the Utes, the Americans bagged a "wild cat" and some antelope and deer. They traded for many buckskins and enjoyed watching two groups compete with one another in horse races.[37]

When Captain Gunnison's team had crossed Colorado, their experiences were less pleasant. In the Cebolla Valley near the Gunnison River, they were surrounded by Utes who were threatening in manner and who demanded—not requested—gifts. Referring to the Walker War, they said they were at war with Mormons and had killed many. In the Uncompahgre Valley, although the Americans were treated to a dance, the atmosphere turned unfriendly when the Utes recognized Gunnison's guide, Antoine Leroux, who had killed a Ute Indian at a prior time. With great diplomacy Leroux now managed to avert trouble, but the guard was increased that night, and everyone spent a sleepless night. In the morning Gunnison smoked with the chief and was given permission to cross the band's territory, but he was warned about "bad Indians" beyond the mountains.[38] Farther west, Gunnison was able to trade with Utes for some horses, regardless of this warning. It has sometimes been suggested that Leroux's presence was a factor in the massacre of the Gunnison party at Sevier Lake, but this seems to be untrue for he had left the expedition at Green River to fulfill a previous assignment as a guide with a different party.

Frémont also met many Utes in Colorado. About two hundred came into one of his camps and were happy to trade a pony to the explorer's artist, Solomon Carvallo, for an old coat, knives, a piece of red cloth, vermilion, and other items. Curious about his daguerreotypes, they spoiled one while handling it. At the crossing of the Green River in arid Utah, the Americans concluded there was a scarcity of food for Utes, who were subsisting on grass seeds.[39]

Not surprisingly, Indians resented the destruction of native vegetation and game, and a traveler in the mid-1850s undoubtedly raised their ire. This man was Sir George Gore, who came on a safari with a retinue of fifty servants and companions, an equal number of hounds, six ox-drawn wagons, and a carriage. For three years the "sportsman" slaughtered game in Colorado and Wyoming, proving that some parts of the unsettled West still contained abundant wildlife.

In New Mexico Territory, as temporary and more permanent trespassers on Ute land bred bad feelings, Fort Union and its satellite posts were slight deterrents to conflicts. In 1853 dragoons' horses were run off by Chief Tamoooche (Tamuche?), and many mules were taken from Ocate Creek, north of Fort Union.[40] Conforming to prevailing Indian Bureau theories about how to deal with the Indian problem, David Meriwether, governor and ex officio superintendent of Indian Affairs in New Mexico, persuaded 250 Utes to try farming on the Pecos River, but the experiment did not last long, and they returned to raiding with their Jicarilla friends. In 1854 families from Abiquiú moved onto the site of an old Indian camp on the Conejos River in the San Luis Valley. Raids there became frequent because the nearest fort, Fort Massachusetts, was fifty miles away—too distant for a quick response. Lafayette Head, one of the leaders in the settlers' stockaded village, called Guadalupe, won a reputation as a courageous man by defending his neighbors during raids. A veteran of the Army of the West, he had opened a store at Abiquiú in 1852 and was subagent there in 1854, distributing rations to Capotes and Jicarillas. That previous association, though, did nothing to protect the new village at Guadalupe from raids. Nevertheless, he became agent at Conejos, across the river from Guadalupe, when an agency was established there in 1860.[41]

In 1854 thousands of head of livestock were taken from the east side of the San Luis Valley, where troops chased Utes across Mosca Pass. Raiders struck from Río Colorado and Ocate Creek to Las Vegas and were pursued north across Raton Pass. Agent Carson reported to Governor Meriwether that dragoons had been sent to Culebra, where cattle had been killed and horses stolen by a "Utah and his sons," whom he described as "outcasts and vagabonds" in contrast to other Utes. In October Meriwether and Carson met with the Muache chiefs who were involved in some of the trouble and gave each a woolen coat to win their friendship. Soon afterward, while camping in the San Luis Valley, the recipients of the coats began to die from smallpox, and the coats were blamed for this curse. As the disease spread, Utes and Jicarillas who were with them prepared to go to war. At Costilla they drove off almost all livestock and killed some settlers.

In December of the same year, 1854, a massacre at El Pueblo occurred. About fifty Muaches and Jicarillas, led by Tierra Blanca and Guero, respectively, were on the Arkansas River. The day before Christmas they came to El Pueblo, where seventeen Mexican men, women, and children still lived in crude adobe huts inside the fort. Apparently in a friendly mood, Tierra Blanca challenged one of the Mexicans, Benito Sandoval, to a shooting match. Afterward, Sandoval invited the Indians into the fort for a drink or two of Taos Lightning. While the Mexicans enjoyed their jugs of Christmas cheer, their guests held back until, at a signal from Tierra Blanca, they attacked the drunk Mexicans, all of whom were killed with the exception of Sandoval's two young boys and a woman, Chipita Miera. These three were taken captive. Three or four Indians also died. Chipita Miera was later killed and scalped "because she cried too much."[42]

Within two days Indians also struck at the mouth of the St. Charles River east of El Pueblo. They withdrew to the Wet Mountain Valley to celebrate their victory, but in January, their number having grown to about 180, they attacked a Huerfano River settlement. With a military force guided by Carson in pursuit, that spring Utes raided San Luis Valley settlements, killing men and driving off livestock at Costilla while frightened people fled from their homes and hid in shrubs. When Kaniache led his Utes on a raid at Guadalupe, though, Lafayette Head and the village men met the attackers east of town and battled for half a day until Kaniache was wounded and his Muaches retreated.[43] It has been said that Ouray and some Tabeguaches not only assisted Guadalupe's defenders but also wounded Kaniache, but the story cannot be proved.

Hostilities at El Pueblo and in other portions of northern New Mexico led the army to undertake punitive expeditions to subdue Utes and their Jicarilla cohorts in New Mexico Territory. In March 1855 Colonel Thomas T. Fauntleroy came to Fort Massachusetts from Fort Union to organize a major campaign in which the army regulars and six companies of volunteers vigorously pursued Indians. Giving no quarter, the military chased Muaches and Jicarillas over Cochetopa, Poncha, and Mosca Passes and through the Grape Creek area (near present-day Cañon City). Among the several engagements that took place, a noteworthy one occurred in the Salida area where forty Utes were killed and much livestock was recovered.

By July the Indians were ready for peace negotiations.[44] These were held in the summer and fall of 1855 with Governor Meriwether at Abiquiú and were attended by both Muache and Capote Utes, as well as Jicarilla Apaches. Muaches agreed to accept a reservation of a thousand square miles on the west side of the Rio Grande, north of La Jara Creek, an area Carson said they had occupied for the previous thirty years.[45] The Capotes agreed to 2,000 square miles north of the San Juan River and east of the Animas River, while the Jicarillas were to receive 160,000 acres. Congress never ratified these agreements, chiefly because of annuities that had been promised. All of the Indians ignored the assigned boundaries. Capotes, together with Weenuches, continued to occupy land farther west around Sleeping Ute Mountain, called the Datils at the time, and southward as far as New Mexico's Río Puerco, where raiding took place in cooperation with Navajos.

Around settlements where natural resources were depleted, Indians continued to need food. When Utes and Jicarillas appeared at Taos and Abiquiú in the late 1850s for rations, Carson was sympathetic, for, as he commented, they were forced to travel so far for them that their horses were worn out on the journey.[46] The locations for distribution also brought Indians into towns, even to Carson's own door in Taos, for the agency office was located at his home after the first year. Previously it had been adjacent to the plaza in Taos, no more suitable as a place for gathering Indians. At Taos, liquor was a constant source of trouble, as Indians could quickly trade their rations for alcohol or for money with which to buy it in local stores.

Hostilities continued. In 1857 Carson reported to the commissioner of Indians Affairs that Utes had stolen livestock at Río Colorado and Culebra Creek. They also remained at war with Indians from the plains who came into Ute territory. A battle with Kiowas took place at about this time east of Guadalupe at El Cerrito de Los Kiowas, where Utes killed about sixty Kiowas and claimed a decisive victory. In the same year Kaniache and twenty-seven Muaches attacked a party of Arapahos accompanying Charley Autobees's load of grain east of El Pueblo. Both Autobees and Kaniache were wounded, and several Utes were killed in the skirmish.[47] Utes roamed farther east, and one was killed near Fort Lyon in 1859. A three-day battle between Utes and their Arapaho-Cheyenne foes took place west of Salida during the same period. To end this costly strife, in 1858 more than a thousand Muaches and Tabeguaches who were assembled in the San Luis Valley indicated their willingness to make peace with their enemies from the plains, but the appearance of Cheyennes and Kiowas in Ute country abruptly ended that plan.[48] In the meantime, relations also broke down between Muaches and Jicarillas.

Trouble was brewing between Capote-Jicarilla allies and Navajos. In a Navajo attack on Utes near Abiquiú in 1856, three Ute leaders were killed, and much livestock was stolen. In 1858 a raid led by Chief Temuche (Tamooche?) against Navajos at Canyon de Chelly in northeast Arizona was so bitter that the Navajos immortalized it with rock art. The victorious Capotes and Jicarillas made off with twenty-one Navajo girls and several dozen horses. Temuche later brought gifts to the Navajos to assure them that he intended to be peaceful in the future.

With Utes scattered over such a vast region, it was impossible for agents to keep track of them except when they came into an agency.

Capotes came primarily to Abiquiú, but a few also appeared at Taos. By 1856 several hundred Tabeguaches under Chief Augkapowerbran began to arrive at both places to collect presents.[49] Calling this band the largest, numbering a thousand or more, Carson recommended that a separate agency be set up in their own country, for they had to travel a couple hundred miles to reach existing agencies, but none was provided.[50] Some distributions were made near the headwaters of the Chama River, closer to both Tabeguache and Weenuche territory. The difficulty in providing rations for Utes who appeared at unpredictable intervals can be appreciated when one considers that there were also eight or nine hundred Capotes and about six or seven hundred Muaches at this time.[51] When Albert H. Pfeiffer became agent at Abiquiú in 1858, he was annoyed by Indians who simply helped themselves to sheep as he was attempting to divide them properly among recipients and by those who made themselves at home, sitting around on the floor of his office.[52]

It is believed that Ouray, who lived at Abiquiú, was first engaged as an interpreter around this time. Ouray was married to a Ute, Black Mare, whose subsequent death or other fate is unknown. By her, Ouray fathered a boy, Cotoan (also called Pahlone), in about 1857. He and Black Mare may have had a girl, too. In 1859 Ouray married a beautiful Kiowa girl, Chipeta, then about sixteen years old. Like other Kiowas, she was taller, slimmer, and of fairer complexion than many Numic people. Ouray and Chipeta's relationship over the next twenty-one years was renowned for its closeness, but they had no children, although it appears that Ouray fathered other children during this period.

In the late 1850s Muaches and Jicarillas, who had usually frequented Carson's Taos Agency, were finding another center of activity. Lucien Maxwell had begun to build up his ranch and the town of Cimarrón. He got a contract to feed his Indian neighbors and was soon distributing rations to them at his ranch. He allowed these Indian groups, who often camped nearby at Ute Park, to hunt on his enormous grant, and in return they provided a buffer between his settlement and belligerent tribes from the plains.

By 1858 the United States military presence in New Mexico and Utah Territories was becoming more conspicuous and effective. A new Fort Garland replaced nearby Fort Massachusetts; Camp Floyd, later called Fort Crittenden, was built near Salt Lake City; and old Fort Bridger was rebuilt as a military post in southwest Wyoming. Observing the movement of troops through their country, Utes had various responses. When Captain Randolph B. Marcy came through Colorado's Rockies in late 1857, he met Indians who resented this military intrusion in their country, but when Colonel William Wing Loring marched from Camp Floyd to Fort Union in 1858, he met a large number of Tabeguaches who were friendly. Led by Chief Kachoompeeache, they camped with his party after they had ascertained that they would be welcome. Later, though, near the Culebra settlements, more than a hundred Utes in war paint came into Loring's camp, but, as it turned out, they were hunting Arapahos, not the United States Army, and trouble was averted.[53]

Only a dozen years had passed since Kearny's Army of the West had occupied New Mexico, eleven years since Mormons arrived in Utah, and the changes that took place in Ute country during that short time were irreversible. Bear, for whom the Utes danced in the springtime, and all the wild creatures that survived were retreating into the remote vastness, from which they would not return.

6
▾ ▾ ▾

Sherman's Solution: Freeze and Starve
(1859–1867)

Persistent waves of newcomers had washed into New Mexico and Utah since 1846–1847. They continued to arrive throughout the 1850s, with Utes gradually losing ground to white intrusions. This pattern continued in Utah in the later 1850s, while a tidal wave was bearing down on the Eastern Ute country that became Colorado.

Utah's experiment with Indian farms was meeting with little success except at Corn Creek, where some Pahvants had already had some experience as farmers for several years. Chief Kanosh, a moderating influence there, was baptized by Mormons in 1858 and later became an elder in the Church of Jesus Christ of Latter-day Saints. In 1859 a Mormon settlement was begun on Lower Corn Creek and apparently met no resistance. In contrast to Corn Creek, so little food was produced at the Spanish Fork and Twelve Mile Farms that Timpanogots and Sanpits Indians would have starved if Mormons had not provided food during the winters of the decade's closing years, especially since, with government funds unavailable, other provisions were not to be had.

After Agent Hurt fled for his life in 1857, Jacob Forney had served briefly as agent but was soon run out of office on grounds of mismanagement. During Forney's short tenure the Utes were caught up in the tension that still existed as a result of the Mormon War. In late 1858 Chief Arrapene was planning to lead five hundred warriors against the United States Army, it was claimed, but when military detachments arrived to put down the anticipated uprising, the Indians and their chiefs—Sanpitch, Peteetneet, and Tintic—had scattered, stealing cattle, wheat, farm implements, and a wagon from Mormons as they headed south. They also killed two white men on the road. Arrapene and Kanosh managed to restore a tentative peace, however.[1] Following this incident, Arrapene left for Hopi country to trade with Hopis and Navajos, as Walkara had so often done before, and Peteetneet showed his friendship by occasionally paying peaceful visits at Payson.[2]

Growth of settlements continued in Utah in the following two or three years of relative peace. Colonization expanded southward as far as Panguitch and Circleville, although some settlers erected stockades, such as those at Fort Wilden (later Cove Fort) and Payson, to protect residents and travelers. As it had in Colorado Territory, the Pony Express came and went, replaced by telegraph lines, stagecoaches, and freight companies. Cattlemen brought in livestock from Texas and dammed the Sevier River to provide water for their animals. Utah's population of 40,000 in 1860 was growing steadily.

Far to the east in New Mexico, meanwhile, Muaches were concentrating on the margin of the plains east of the Sangre de Cristo Mountains. A magnet in this region was Lucien Maxwell's home at Cimarrón, where rations were distributed. Another was the watered-down liquor, called Indian whiskey, sold by itinerant traders in the vicinity. In addition, a limited amount of hunting still lured Utes to the plains to supplement food obtained in raids on settlements and on supply trains along the Santa Fe Trail. During the winter of 1858–1859 a large number of Utes led by Chief Kaniache pitched tepees near Wagon Mound and were joined by Jicarilla Apaches and more Utes until a detachment from Fort Union broke up the encampment.[3] The Utes' old Comanche enemies were also in the area, and they stirred everyone up by stealing a hundred Ute horses at Ocate Creek.[4]

In the mountains in 1858, the army improved its position for keeping an eye on Indians in the San Luis Valley by moving the troops at Fort Massachusetts to the new Fort Garland, only a few miles away. That same year, more than a thousand Tabeguaches and Capotes were located in the valley. These were nearly half the estimated total of the two bands in both Colorado and northern New Mexico. (In the 1850s there were twelve to fifteen hundred Tabeguaches and eight hundred Capotes, while about six hundred Muaches roamed to the east.)

The lands of the Eastern Utes were about to change forever. In the fall of 1858 gold was discovered at Cherry Creek, today's Denver, and in the following year thousands of gold seekers swarmed into the mountains west of the original discovery. Mining camps and towns sprang up. By 1860 diggings and supply points were filled with nearly 35,000 people, their arrival usually unwelcome among the Utes. When prospectors crossed the range from Gregory Diggings (Central City) into South Park's

Tarryall area in 1859, Tabeguaches killed four or five men, and later in the year several more, along with their horses, died in South Park.

In contrast, the thousands of prospectors who swarmed into the upper reaches of the Arkansas River in 1860 found the Utes sometimes friendly, although when gold hunters tried to follow an old Ute trail across the Continental Divide into the Gunnison country, they were killed. Usually, Indians were merely considered to be "pests," asking for food or making off with a few articles that were lying around, maybe an ax or some laundry hung out to dry on bushes and rocks. It was paltry repayment for the Ute land that was being trampled, staked, and gouged; for the crystalline streams that were being diverted, sluiced, and turned into mud; for the forests being chopped down for timber and firewood and the air that was filled with smoke; for the fish and game that were being killed; for the desecration of Mother Earth.

Trouble between Utes and their Indian foes continued, meanwhile. Denverites and prospectors witnessed numerous skirmishes and their aftermath between Utes and their Arapaho enemies because Denver was located on favorite Ute and Arapaho campsites. Members of these tribes passed through the area often as they traveled back and forth between mountains and plains—sometimes to hunt, sometimes to fight, often both. In a battle in South Park, Utes captured a woman from Arapaho Chief Left Hand's family, an event sure to bring reprisal.[5] In May 1860 Arapahos held a scalp dance at Denver to celebrate the killing of four Utes and the capture of about fifty horses in South Park. A Ute boy who had been taken captive was purchased by a Bostonian and taken to New England like a curiosity.[6] One of the biggest conflicts took place near Garo in South Park. Others occurred around Cañon City.

In the next year or two Denver's *Rocky Mountain News* reported a number of incidents throughout the mountains between Utes and Arapahos, with forays especially common when Indians traveled in and out of South Park by way of Platte Canyon. In a surprise attack by Chief Left Hand's band, six Utes were killed and thirty horses were captured, but Left Hand's adopted son also died. A month later Arapahos predictably came into Denver with five female Utes, three babies, and six scalps. Utes then came to Denver and killed the son of Little Raven, an Arapaho chief.

Susan (Shosheen), the sister of Ouray, was captured during this period of constant strife. According to legend, she was about to be burned at the stake when she was rescued. In 1863 Agent Simeon Whiteley restored her to Utes in northwestern Colorado, but that same year, while Ouray and other Tabeguache hunters were on the plains, Ouray's little boy, Cotoan (Pahlone), was captured. Although Sioux, Cheyennes, or Kiowas have been named as the child's captors, it seems most likely that they were Arapahos. The event has variously been said to have occurred around Fort Lupton or the Upper Republican River.

Farther south and east, raids and counterraids continued between Plains Indians and Ute and Jicarilla Apache allies. In 1862 the latter raided Cheyennes near Fort Lyon in eastern Colorado and stole about 80 horses. During these intertribal conflicts, white people along Colorado's Front Range were not safe from depredations. In the spring of 1861 Utes ran off about 125 horses belonging to some latter-day trappers in the La Porte area. Pursued into North Park, the Indians were overtaken and, except for one whose ears were cut off, were killed.

In New Mexico the effects of the mining excitement were felt more slowly than in Colorado, but it was only a matter of time before gold fever infected the white population in the southern territory, too, but intertribal conflict was occupying most of the Indians' attention. In 1859, for instance, Agent Albert H. Pfeiffer at Abiquiú reported that he was raising a company of volunteers because war had broken out again between Utes and Navajos, and "Pah Utes" had killed the son of a Navajo leader. Pfeiffer complained that his home was filled with Utes who had gathered there.[7]

As they had been for generations, Weenuche Utes, Paiutes, and Navajos in northwestern New Mexico and the Four Corners region remained a volatile mix, although some alliances existed. In the late 1850s Paiutes and Weenuches had started coming into the Abiquiú Agency for presents and thus were adding to the agency's customary visitors, the Capotes, while Muaches and Tabeguaches also were there occasionally. Without identifying the band, Pfeiffer reported in the late 1850s that Utes and their Apache allies had returned from a campaign against Navajos with twenty-one small girls and fifty horses. Confirming that the slave trade was still conducted through customary channels, Pfeiffer said he expected many Mexicans to join the Utes and Apaches who had come in.[8]

Despite such distractions, Abiquiú and its agent were becoming involved in the mining excitement. Soon after J. N. Macomb's United States Topographical Engineers traveled through the Chama River Valley in the summer of 1859, en route to Pagosa Springs and points west, a group of prospectors followed. They included Agent Pfeiffer. The next year he and other opportunists, led by Charles Baker, organized the Pagosa Town Association and the Abiquiú, Pagosa, and Baker City Road Company to the Animas River to profit from the mining boom they expected in the San Juans. They even proposed moving the Indian agency there, with Pfeiffer as its agent.

During the summer prospectors in the San Juans had met a few friendly Navajos and Utes, but such a reception did not last long. Baker led a large party of mineral seekers into the heart of the mountain range that winter, but the prospectors broke up in the spring, largely out of fear of hostilities. One of the men had been forced to trade a large supply of provisions against his will.[9] Utes succeeded in bartering four Navajo children who left with the prospectors. One was adopted by Pfeiffer, another by a German family in New Mexico, and two by a Denver resident. Later the fledgling town of Animas City, just north of the present Durango, was burned by the Indians as evidence of their displeasure about the presence of white people.

Territorial changes soon brought new conditions for the Utes. The gold rush prompted Congress to authorize the establishment of the Territory of Colorado in 1860 and its organization the next year. After the creation of New Mexico and Utah Territories ten years earlier, Ute lands north and east of the Arkansas River headwaters had remained in the jurisdiction of the federal government, although without overseers present. New Mexico's jurisdiction extended north to the Arkansas, and Utah's theoretically reached east as far as the Continental Divide, but the mountain Utes in what became Colorado Territory had enjoyed a virtual absence of government interference. The inclusion of eastern Colorado in Kansas Territory in 1854 had brought no change.

In the mid-1850s the San Luis Valley, the upper Rio Grande Valley, the Chama Valley, and the Front Range north and south of Raton Pass were still the only areas where Ute-white contact could be expected with any frequency, whereas the mountains of southwest, central, and north-central Colorado remained undisturbed. In Utah Territory, which originally crossed the future political border with Colorado, many Eastern Utes had been within the jurisdiction of Salt Lake City's Indian agency and thus had commanded Utah's attention from time to time prior to the establishment of the Territory of Colorado, but Utes who roamed down the Colorado River to the La Sal Mountains (Elk Mountains) or across the Green River into the Uinta Basin still had an abundance of wilderness into which they could vanish eastward. Weenuches in the Four Corners area also enjoyed vast wilderness refuges where no white people would aggravate them.

With the creation of Colorado Territory and its western boundary, these Indians and their associates in Utah were arbitrarily placed in separate jurisdictions that ignored extended kinship and friendships. In

1861 William Gilpin was appointed territorial governor and ex officio superintendent of Indian Affairs in Colorado, with oversight of the Ute Indian Agency at Conejos. Lafayette Head had been appointed agent in 1860. The new agency soon attracted many Tabeguaches, although the Utes actually assigned there were Muaches. In 1860 about 2,000 Utes came to Conejos, a development New Mexico Superintendent J. L. Collins claimed was resulting from the fact that Tabeguaches were at war with tribes on the plains and, consequently, were increasingly on the move.[10]

Collins also pointed out that duties and expenses at the Abiquiú Agency had been strained because of the Capote-Navajo war. No mention was made of evidence that the time and energy of the agent there were also strained because his attention was divided between his job and his personal business interests. In the meantime, depredations by Navajos were causing so much trouble that in 1860 the commander of the army's Department of New Mexico, Colonel Thomas T. Fauntleroy, organized a campaign against them and recruited Utes to accompany the military force. In the fall a detachment of soldiers from Fort Garland also was sent out.[11]

The story of individual agencies reveals how the real needs of the Indians often were secondary. At Conejos, for example, in 1860 Head's annual salary was set at $520 "more or less" and was increased to $750 the following year, an above-average per capita income in the United States at the time. An "interpreter sometimes" was allotted $170 and $250 in 1860 and 1861, respectively. The Utes protested that the interpreter, probably a local villager, could not speak their language, although he presumably spoke Spanish, the Utes' second language. At the same time Head initially received only a thousand dollars for supplies, which did not last long. The kind of goods made available by a superintendency helps explain why the Indians were still hungry, for an invoice from a Boston firm to New Mexico's superintendency in April 1860 itemized 258 blue frocks, trimmed in red, at six dollars each to be supplied to that territory's Apache, Navajo, and Ute Indians. Capotes were to receive sixteen of these costumes, and "Mohuches" and "Tabihwaches" combined would get thirty-seven.[12]

Head reported 5,000 Utes at his agency in 1861 and claimed that 8,000 lived in the San Luis Valley, an impossible figure. Game was gone, and the Indians would starve without supplies, he warned.[13] Head might have been inflating his estimates to get more money for provisions, possibly even as graft. Head, his business partners, and neighbors in Conejos owned stores and a flour mill, from which both Fort Garland

and the agency were procuring provisions. At Fort Garland Utes complained about the quality of the rations they received at the agency, saying the food was moldy, wormy, and too scant for their needs. Nevertheless, when Head was accused of buying goods on credit, Governor Gilpin defended him as an efficient and competent officer, as well as a Republican and friend of the administration.

Information about Head's personal life at Conejos helps to explain the role he played there. Head had lived in New Mexico's and Colorado's Spanish-speaking communities, spoke fluent Spanish, and had adopted their social and religious customs as his own. He easily assumed political leadership in territorial legislatures. He had established himself as a trader and special agent at Abiquiú before he moved to the San Luis Valley with his Spanish-speaking neighbors, so he was personally acquainted with some of the Utes who visited Conejos. His home and, at times, the village of Conejos were called "Fort Head." His wife, a forceful and well-to-do Spanish woman from Santa Fe, ruled the domestic household with the assistance of Navajo and Ute Indian servants, whom, Head insisted when he was criticized for their presence, she had adopted for humanitarian reasons. When Head's widowed sister, Eliza Head Downing of Illinois, visited Conejos in 1863, however, she was so disturbed by the plight of one Navajo girl who was whipped by her male bosses by day and locked up by night that Eliza helped the girl escape from her captivity, an episode that abruptly terminated Eliza's visit. Her impulse to liberate a slave can be understood because her son had died recently in the Union Army.

Although most military action during the Civil War took place far from Colorado Territory, which was aligned with the Union, repercussions from the war were felt by Native Americans because funds for rations became scarcer. Also, Confederate sympathizers enticed the Utes' enemies among Plains tribes to make trouble along transportation routes, whereas, along with the Pueblo people and Jicarilla Apaches, Utes have sometimes been called "Union Indians" because they did not cooperate with the Southern cause.

Such generalizations about the activities of tribal groups can be misleading. For example, in Utah, where Indians had shown no affection for the United States Army, Utes attacked troops, plundered supplies, and killed some soldiers near Spanish Fork as they were departing from Camp Floyd to take up duties at the Civil War front. Two hundred men had to be deployed to rescue their comrades, and Camp Douglas was soon established near Salt Lake City to protect the mails and to maintain peace in Utah.

In New Mexico, Confederates from Texas brought the war to the Utes' doorstep by capturing Santa Fe. Although they were soon defeated at Glorieta Pass and were sent south, the Confederates had seized supplies at the Indian agency's headquarters as well as public funds when they entered Santa Fe. Another effect felt by New Mexico's Indians was the departure of two of their agents, Kit Carson and Albert Pfeiffer, who resigned to serve with New Mexico volunteers in the Union cause. With the departure of Carson, northern New Mexico lost a man who had provided a steady hand in Indian affairs and who had maintained the trust and friendship of many, if not all, Utes. On one occasion the powerful Kaniache had prevented another Muache, Blanco, from killing Carson at the agent's doorstep. With Carson's departure the Taos Agency stopped serving Muaches and Jicarillas, who were now to report to a new agency at Maxwell's ranch at Cimarrón with William F. M. Arny as their agent.

For twenty dollars annually, the federal government leased 1,280 acres of Maxwell's land on Ponil Creek for the agency for a period of twenty years. Maxwell profited by selling beef and flour to both the agency and Fort Union. Following federal policy, Arny intended to make his Indians self-sufficient farmers, a hope that was not fulfilled, and he erected several adobe buildings, one of which served as a council room and schoolhouse.

Whenever Native Americans congregated around white settlements, diseases spread, and smallpox soon struck the Indians gathered at this agency. Several died, although Fort Union sent vaccine in an attempt to curb the epidemic.[14] (Elsewhere, when such diseases afflicted them, Indians resorted to their own remedies, as when a woman with smallpox was dipped into an icy stream one winter in the San Luis Valley. Her skin peeled off, and she recovered, living the remainder of her life in the home of a Spanish-speaking settler.[15] A more common but less effective treatment was an application of pine sap to the pustules.)

In his efforts to bring the scattered Indians of northern and western Colorado Territory under control, in 1861 Governor Gilpin established an agency in Middle Park for the Utes of northern Colorado and appointed a special agent, Harvey M. Vaile, who was sent to find his charges. Some normally roamed around Middle Park but were scattered far afield. They needed to be brought under governments supervision, for Middle Park was gaining the attention of the territory's entrepreneurs. In 1861 *Rocky Mountain News* editor William Byers set his sights on a favorite Ute spring and campsite, Hot Sulphur Springs, as a future resort he wanted to develop. To facilitate a route between Denver and Salt Lake

City, the Overland Stage Company also wanted a road built across the mountains through Middle Park. In 1861 E. L. Berthoud surveyed the route over the pass that would later bear his name and through Middle Park. Although Berthoud Pass was not a heavily used Indian trail, with Rollins Pass being traversed instead, the Utes resisted these intrusions into their territory and attempted to block the building of the road when construction began.

Accompanying Berthoud to Utah on his survey, Agent Vaile located no Utes until he found about 800 lodges, or 3,000 persons, at Provo. He reported that these were Indians from the Colorado River–Green River area under "Chief White-eye" (Antero). At Salt Lake City he saw a thousand Elk Mountain Utes (Seuvarits), all well-armed and possessing fine horses. Vaile went on to describe the great circuits these Utes made each year from the Colorado River to the White and Yampa Rivers and even into southern Wyoming to hunt. Furthermore, they made southerly journeys to trade with Navajos and Mexicans, he said.[16] He gave no specific accounting of Utes who frequented Middle Park, although Vaile must have learned that the Grand River Utes and the bands of northwestern Colorado did, indeed, roam into the headwaters of the Colorado River, as did Tabeguaches.

With a little information gained in Utah, Vaile set up his agency at Hot Sulphur Springs the following year. With a remarkable absence of good judgment, the superintendency also placed a band of the Utes' foremost enemies, the Arapahos, under the care of this agency—a situation that was soon corrected, fortunately. In 1863 Vaile was replaced by Simeon Whiteley as agent for the Middle Park Utes, the Yamparika-Uintahs of northern Colorado, and the Grand Rivers of west-central Colorado, with Uriah M. Curtis as assistant and interpreter. Curtis had previous experience with Muaches and thus was at least acquainted with Utes and their language. When Whiteley sent Curtis to locate the Utes assigned to his agency prior to a treaty council at Conejos in 1863, the Utes were again found visiting Utah's Utes, this time at Spanish Fork. Curtis reported that their numbers were smaller than they had been previously as a result of disease. He also said they were ready to settle down on farms with some cattle.

The Utes told Curtis that they had recently been making raids on Overland Stage Company stations in southern Wyoming.[17] Attacks on the stations were, in fact, a common problem, the offenders sometimes being Uintahs from northwestern Colorado and northeastern Utah and sometimes far-ranging Tabeguaches.[18] During the early spring and summer of 1863, Utes stole rifles, revolvers, clothing, harnesses, and especially horses from the stations.[19] The Utes were chased by soldiers from Fort Halleck and by Colonel John M. Chivington's First Colorado Infantry, eager for action after a victory over Confederates at Glorieta the previous year.

Elsewhere, Colorado's Ute lands were under increasing pressure as agriculture joined mining and commerce in attracting emigrants. The 1862 Homestead Act encouraged farmers and ranchers to join the movement to the West, where Indian lands were considered public lands. The greatest impact by homesteaders took place at the end of the Civil War, but as homesteaders began to take up land in areas such as the Upper Arkansas Valley—sometimes on traditional Ute campsites—the reception was often unpleasant, and some settlers were ordered off their chosen properties. Colorow emerged as the least hospitable Ute host. Ouray, however, who often camped just west of Buena Vista, was amicable, and one group of Utes in that area even helped some new arrivals cross the Arkansas River.

When John Evans replaced William Gilpin as Colorado's territorial governor and superintendent responsible for Indian Affairs, he vigorously addressed the growing problems resulting from white intrusions into Indian country by trying to establish reservations. He urged that Colorado's Indians, both on the plains and in the mountains, be moved to reservations in accordance with policies in place elsewhere in the West at the time. The only alternative seemed to be a war to exterminate unfriendly Indians, so the federal government sought treaties with the various Western tribes, and several were negotiated in 1863. Colorado Territory's delegate to Congress, Hiram P. Bennet, agreed with this policy, and in New Mexico the Indian agent at Cimarrón believed his Indians should be placed on remote reservations, far from opportunities to raid local livestock and to buy liquor. Before he went to fight with the Civil War volunteers, Carson had made the same argument at Taos.

In an effort to impress Utes with the power of the United States and the futility of resisting its plans, Agent Head escorted a delegation of thirteen Indians, representing all the bands and including Ouray and Tabeguache war chief Shavano, to Washington in February 1863. The journey was revealing. It included a ride on a train east of the Mississippi River, a visit to New York City, and a circus performance there. The Utes saw the enormous white population in the East, its military power, and the technology and luxuries of nineteenth-century America. Ouray was convinced that it was hopeless to hold back the westward migration. Nevertheless, back on the High Plains the entourage was reminded that some things had not changed, as Plains Indians near Julesburg threatened to attack the travelers. Trouble was averted only by the presence of their cavalry escort.[20]

In October of that year Evans made arrangements for the council at Conejos to negotiate a treaty with the Eastern Ute bands. In preparation for the council Head's secretary, W. G. Godfroy, went to Denver to procure enough supplies to feed thousands of Indians who were expected to be present, along with six companies of troops from Fort Union. Ten wagons, each drawn by three yoke of oxen, headed for Conejos with their loads, but one rolled down a hillside en route, spilling a precious cargo of the Indians' favorite commodity—sugar.

Attending the council were Evans, New Mexico Superintendent of Indian Affairs Michael Steck, President Lincoln's secretary John Nicolay, and Agents Head and Whiteley. Not all invited Utes arrived. Whiteley's Utes who were in Utah, where Curtis had found them, chose not to go to Conejos. Most Muaches also refused to come. Some Capotes and Weenuches started for Conejos but changed their minds on the way, so only a few actually joined the 1,500 Tabeguaches who did attend. In the end, one Capote chief and three Muache chiefs arrived, but because of these small numbers Muaches were not included as negotiators.

The agreement reached at Conejos has been called the "Treaty With the Utah-Tabeguache Band, 1863," or the Treaty of 1864 because it was amended and confirmed by Congress in the latter year. By its terms, the Tabeguaches agreed to relinquish all Ute lands east of the Continental Divide plus Middle Park. In effect, the Tabeguaches gave up all claims to Ute lands in Colorado that already had been occupied by towns, mines, and homesteaders. The northern border of Tabeguache land was to be the Colorado and Roaring Fork Rivers, the southern portion roughly taking in the Gunnison and Uncompahgre Rivers and their watersheds. Military posts, roads, railroads, and mines would be permitted within the reservation. Nothing explicitly prevented the Utes from moving about on nonreservation land. "Mohuaches" would be allowed to settle on the same reservation if they so chose, and the secretary of the interior soon paved the way for this possibility by assigning New Mexico's Muaches to Colorado's superintendency.

In exchange for their concessions, the reservation Utes would receive annually $10,000 in goods and $10,000 in provisions for a period of ten years. They would also get five American stallions for breeding stock, up to 150 head of cattle, and a thousand sheep annually for five years, as well as a blacksmith who could repair firearms and the farm equipment the Utes were expected to use. Ten Utes—including "U-ray, or Arrow," and "Colorado" (Colorow)—signed with an "x." The promised goods were supposed to be payment for lands taken from the Utes. In fact, Euro-Americans only begrudgingly acknowledged Indian sovereignty and land claims. They believed Native Americans were at best nuisances and at worse "savages" deserving punishment, not presents. Although the Tabeguache Treaty was ratified, Congress, strapped by the costs of the Civil War, did not immediately provide moneys for the promised annuities, rations, and livestock, and funds were in arrears for years.

Ouray's influence was growing at the time of the negotiations at Conejos, but events over the next four years would prove that he was far from being chief of all the Utes, not even of all the Tabeguaches. If, as some historians have said, he was the interpreter at the council, no evidence exists for this claim either, for the names of three Hispanic men appeared on the document as interpreters.[21]

Many Utes did not recognize the agreement made by Ouray and the others at Conejos. Although Muaches were permitted to join the Tabeguaches on their reservation, the Muaches continued to appear at Cimarrón instead, along with their Apache allies, while Whiteley's charges continued to roam through Middle Park and to come to the agency there. These northern Utes resented the fact that Tabeguaches had given this area away in the treaty agreement. In July 1864 Secretary of the Interior J. P. Usher, at the request of Evans and Steck, granted permission for Capotes and "Pah Utes" (presumably meaning Weenuches) to remain under the New Mexico superintendency. Lacking a firm grasp of the Utes' thoughts or even of their identity, Evans tried to put a good spin on things by explaining to Indian Commissioner William P. Dole that some Utes had not attended the council at Conejos because of fears of retaliation for recent depredations in the San Luis Valley. The governor also assured the commissioner that a similar treaty could be worked out with the reluctant Capotes and "Pahutes" as soon as they agreed to settle in the San Juan River area.[22]

Muaches had reason to feel independent. They were in the unique position of having had the military come to them to solicit help against Ute enemies, the Navajos. This tribe and some Utes, especially Capotes, had been engaged in conflicts continually during the late 1850s, and by 1858 New Mexico Territory Governor Abraham Rencher reported to United States Secretary of State Lewis Cass in Washington that attempts to reconcile the two groups had failed. Governor Rencher described Utes as "the most warlike and formidable of any of our Indian tribes. Their weapons are rifles, which they use with great skill and success."[23]

Regardless of that assessment, Navajos had killed a Muache chief, Benito, in 1863, an incident that called for retaliation. Furthermore, Navajos were causing much trouble for United States forces during the Civil War years. When Brigadier General James H. Carleton ordered Colonel Christopher Carson to take to the field against the Navajos in 1863, Carson was given authority to employ one hundred Utes to act as auxiliaries. Carleton recommended them because "Utes are very brave, and fine shots, fine trailers, and uncommonly energetic in the field." He believed they would be of more service than twice as many troops.[24]

This was not the first time the idea of using Utes against Navajos had arisen, as is shown by Fauntleroy's recruitment of Utes in 1860. In that campaign the Utes did not require pay as soldiers but only provisions. Now, in 1863, Muaches responded to the opportunity, whereas Capotes at Abiquiú who also hoped to be recruited were disappointed. The Muaches received firearms, clothing, and provisions for the expedition, along with permission to take livestock as reimbursement for their service as scouts. Contrary to some written accounts, Carson did not give Utes permission to take human captives. By the end of the summer of 1863, Utes had accumulated so many sheep that some departed for home with their booty, but Utes still participated in later phases of the campaign. Several thousand Navajos were rounded up and marched to Bosque Redondo on what has been called the "Long Walk."[25]

The roundup did not terminate contact and conflict between Utes and Navajos, though, for hundreds of Navajos escaped Carson's net and took refuge in areas of the lower San Juan, Navajo Mountain, Little Colorado, and Blue Mountains. They occasionally appeared in Monument Valley, where Utes stole their horses and engaged them in skirmishes. Members of both tribes were killed in these encounters, so traditional enmities remained alive, although, as is frequently the case with generalizations about Ute Indians, there were exceptions. In 1866, when Capotes, Weenuches, and Mexicans collaborated in a raid on Navajos, Weenuche Chief Cabeza Blanca (Cabeza Blanco) protested because he had friends among these Navajos. It has been said incorrectly that Capotes killed Cabeza Blanca because of his defection.

Having satisfactorily performed their role during the Navajo campaign, Muaches again received a call from Carson to participate in his campaign against Comanches and Kiowas in the fall of 1864. With encouragement of Confederate interests in Texas, these Southern Plains Indians had severely hampered traffic on the Santa Fe Trail south of the Arkansas River, and Northern Plains Indians were doing serious damage on routes north of the river. Again, Utes were a logical choice, as animosity between them and Plains Indians had never ceased. In the spring of 1864 Cheyennes and Arapahos had made off with around fifty Ute ponies, and when they were recaptured near Fort Lyon four Utes died in the skirmish. Later in the summer, when Evans heard a rumor that about four hundred Utes were planning to go on the warpath against Arapahos, Cheyennes, and Sioux, the governor reportedly commented that the Utes should not be stopped, for it would save the government much trouble if one group of Indians killed off another.[26] As it turned out, the Utes did not save the government its trouble by carrying out the campaign, and instead the First Regiment of Colorado Volunteers under Colonel John M. Chivington massacred hundreds of Cheyennes and Arapahos at Sand Creek in late November.

In November 1864 Carson's campaign on the Southern Plains was under way. Seventy-five Muaches under Kaniache and Jicarilla Apaches came to Maxwell's ranch, where the United States Army supplied them with rations, clothing, blankets, and firearms. Accompanying Carson's 336 troops southeast through a blizzard into the Texas Panhandle, the scouts located two camps of Comanches and Kiowas whose lookouts already knew about the army's approach and enjoyed taunting the soldiers. Near the abandoned trading post of Adobe Walls in the Texas Panhandle, where a large village consisting of about 150 lodges was located, an engagement took place on November 25. Greatly outnumbered, Carson's men held off the enemy by firing two howitzers at them. The village was burned, and the troops escaped in the dark of night. The Utes killed some Kiowa women in the village and made away with the horse herd. Sixty of the enemy and one Ute died at Adobe Walls, and three Utes were wounded.[27] (This fight is called the First Battle of Adobe Walls to distinguish it from a second, better-known fight ten years later that did not involve Ute Indians.)

Such mercenary activities, endorsed by the federal government, ran counter to its goal of getting the Indians to settle down peacefully on reservations and to become farmers. Instead, the Ute Indians continued their aggressions around settlements and on outlying farms and ranches. Game was scarce, and promised rations were not forthcoming. During the winter of 1864–1865, when heavy snow killed the Utes' flocks of sheep and goats as well as wild game, residents of Cañon City were alarmed by Indians who entered their homes and demanded food. A clergyman on a pastoral call drove away intruders at his hostess's home by swinging an ax at them. At Colorado City, on the west side of what was later Colorado Springs, Tabeguaches frightened local people into giving them several sacks of flour. When Utes wanted more, the citizens were rescued by the arrival of Agent Head with ninety-five sacks of flour. In northern New Mexico some rations were distributed at Tierra Amarilla, but they were not enough to satisfy Indians who came there.

Utes in the Four Corners region remained troublesome, and General Carleton urged that a military post be established in San Juan country to control them. One obvious explanation for this unrest may have been the presence of miners who were killing game in the San Juans. Another would have been attempts to curtail the slave trade, an effort that was only partly successful. Lincoln's Emancipation Proclamation and the Civil War had not halted the slave trade in New Mexico and southern Colorado, where it continued in the 1860s. In the San Luis Valley many captives were brought in by Utes and Mexicans despite protests by Fort Garland's commander to his superior.[28] New Mexico's Bishop Jean B. Lamy estimated that there were perhaps two or three thousand captives in his territory alone.[29] After the war had ended, President Andrew Johnson issued a special proclamation directed against Indian slavery and thereby ended the opportunities for Indians and Mexicans to sell captives, a decision that was not popular.

In the mid-1860s Utes were restless nearly everywhere in Colorado Territory and for a variety of reasons, in addition to the end of the slave trade, and the concurrent Black Hawk War in Utah may have fanned flames in Colorado. In the spring of 1865 several Utes fought with Hispanic ranchers in the Huerfano Valley area over possession of a powder horn. One of the ranchers was killed, and his sons, seeking revenge, killed three Utes, including Colorow's brother-in-law.[30] Ouray went to Fort Garland and stated that the Utes had been at fault in the original fight, but Shavano beat up a Spanish-speaking man who was present.[31] After this episode, Shavano and Colorow appear to have become leaders in a faction of angry Tabeguaches over whom Ouray had little control. Governor Evans sent presents to the victims' families in an effort to restore peace, but fearing more trouble between the two ethnic groups, Agent Head wanted to move the distribution of rations to a location at a distance from Conejos.

The chosen site was closer to Denver than to most Ute Indians. In the fall, Evans selected South Park's Salt Works as the distribution point for Tabeguaches, who received several hundred sheep, but he suggested that a better solution would be to move the agency to the Uncompahgre Valley. Empire, at the eastern approach to Berthoud Pass, was the distribution point for large numbers of sheep for Utes attached to the Middle Park Agency. The choice of Empire also underscores the fact that the Indians' needs were secondary to other considerations, for Utes from northwestern or west-central Colorado might have to travel two hundred miles or more to reach the site, which would remain their distribution point for the next two years. Empire also had the disadvantage of bringing miners and Utes together in one place, although the white onlookers considered the Indian dances, performed during long waits when goods were slow in arriving, to be good entertainment. The Middle Park Utes, whose agent was now Daniel C. Oakes, a cousin of Congressman Bennet, also received provisions in Denver in 1866 before they left for their winter camps.[32]

In the meantime, tensions between Utes and Hispanic residents of southern Colorado and northern New Mexico continued to be bitter for two more years. More Spanish-speaking ranchers had moved into the area of the Apishipa, Purgatoire, and Huerfano Rivers by the mid-1860s, and construction of a wagon road over Raton Pass in 1865 brought increased travel through this portion of the Front Range. From Cimarrón north to the Huerfano and south to Fort Union, Ute activities increased along this route. In the summer of 1865 there were about four hundred Muaches near the Spanish Peaks, fifteen lodges near the Purgatoire, and another fifteen on the Apishipa. Livestock began to disappear, but when settlers asked for military protection, none arrived.[33] Traveling with his family, Maxwell was stopped on the road by Utes, but he managed to persuade them to refrain from causing harm.

After a hungry winter, with resentment and impatience mounting, Ute Indians became even more troublesome in 1866. Around the Huerfano Valley and Trinidad, depredations were committed by Muaches, Tabeguaches, and Jicarilla Apaches. Shavano's Tabeguaches raided the Huerfano, where some ranchers were reportedly killed, and Kaniache's Muaches were raiding on the Purgatoire. As a result of these incidents, cavalry troops from Fort Union and from Maxwell's ranch moved to the newly established Cantonment Stevens near the Spanish Peaks that summer. Aided by local volunteers, the soldiers engaged Kaniache's Utes in a fight in October. Defeated, the Utes went to Fort Garland to surrender, although settlers continued to be harassed in the Cuchara and Huerfano Valleys.

During 1866 Cimarrón residents were also uneasy when Muache Utes and Jicarilla Apaches assembled there to get rations. In 1864 Maxwell had built a large new home, well-known for the gambling that took place there. That same year he constructed a stone grist mill to produce the flour he had contracted to supply to Indians and to Fort Union, and he also raised beef cattle for them. A hub of activity, Cimarrón gained a notorious reputation for debauchery with gambling, women, and cheap liquor in abundance, all of which encouraged frequent alarms and bad blood among inebriated Indians, Hispaños, and Anglos.

Meanwhile, incompetent and corrupt agents who followed Arny's tenure, combined with the government's failure to send promised supplies, kept the agency's affairs in turmoil. When money did not arrive to pay Maxwell for the food he had contracted to provide, he was forced to feed the Indians at his own expense to maintain a modicum of peace. He did so until 1865, when he stopped issuing the beef. As a result of this decision, in 1866 Maxwell and his family were forced to move into the grist mill for their safety while awaiting the arrival of troops from Fort Union and two companies of volunteers.[34] Carleton at Fort Union then began to send food from military supplies.

When New Mexico Superintendent of Indian Affairs A. B. Norton inspected conditions at the Cimarrón Agency in the summer of 1866, he heard complaints about the absence of distributions the preceding year, and he authorized $500 a month for Maxwell to feed the ragged, hungry Indians.[35] They were to receive half a pound of meat and half a pound of flour per capita per day. When Indian Commissioner D. N. Cooley in Washington learned of this unilateral decision, he criticized Norton for his actions because the federal government wanted to force the Indians to become self-sufficient. It could also have been argued that the Muaches at Cimarrón had not been the responsibility of New Mexico's superintendency since 1864, although the Jicarilla Apaches were still under Santa Fe's charge.

The deteriorating condition of New Mexico's Indians was described by the aging Padre Antonio José Martínez of Taos in a reply to a questionnaire he received from Washington in 1865. He cited intemperance, prostitution, and diseases "arising therefrom" and stated that "drinking of spirituous liquors" was injurious to the Indians' health and was causing many diseases. The solutions, as he saw them, were:

> to induce the Indians to temperance, to live in healthy and permanent places, to build good houses, till the land, plant corn, raise cattle, and adapt themselves to other industries; and now and then the men will go hunting, using the game for food, and the skins to make shoes— always owning a place to live in with their families; prohibit the sale of ardent spirits; encourage them to peace and good will towards other nations with which they are at war; give them the idea that there is a God, Author, Creator, and Preserver of us all.[36]

Martínez's statements echoed the most idealistic theories underlying the policies of the federal government, which in 1866 were solving nothing, however.

The military detachment remained at Cimarrón, camped on Maxwell's land, for the next two years, and their presence prevented some trouble, especially the violence that might otherwise have accompanied the arrival of miners in the area. Ute Park, only seventeen miles west of Cimarrón, had long been a favorite camping ground of the Indians. Through this wide valley passed well-used trails from Taos and Red River to Cimarrón. In 1866, when copper was discovered northwest of Ute Park, prospectors poured through the valley and added to the Indians' justifiable complaints. Gold discoveries later added to the rush.

In August trouble erupted again between Utes and their Hispanic neighbors when a party of Indians killed three sheep north of Fort Union. Kaniache's son had been shot and killed as he tried to catch another sheep from the same flock. Pursued by a dozen warriors, the young Mexican herder who had resisted the theft fled for his life to Fort Union. He was tried at Mora, although Utes demanded in vain that he should be surrendered to them for justice.

In retaliation for the death of his son, Kaniache led an attack near Trinidad that fall, for the principle of an eye for an eye did not necessarily mean vengeance had to be exacted from the original offender. After the fight at Trinidad, Kaniache tried to enlist Ouray and his Tabeguaches to help in raids on the Huerfano, but instead Ouray went to Fort Garland to report to Brevet Brigadier General Kit Carson, who in 1866 had become commandant at the fort. At the time Fort Garland had only about sixty men to defend the installation when Kaniache's Muaches joined Ouray's Tabeguaches there and the Indian encampment swelled to about a thousand. Adding to the tension was the discovery of a Tabeguache boy's body near the fort, and it was believed he had been killed by a white civilian in the neighborhood. Carson feared all-out warfare.

Lieutenant General William Tecumseh Sherman was traveling in the West at this time to appraise its Indian problems and to recommend solutions to them. In the Territory of Colorado the arrogant general already had concluded that most of the hysteria was resulting from exaggerated claims by white settlers about depredations. His party, accompanied by Colorado Territorial Governor and Indian Superintendent Alexander Cummings, arrived at the fort, and a council was begun. Because of the tense environment at the fort, the council soon adjourned to a pleasant cottonwood grove at the Big Bend of the Rio Grande, the future site of East Alamosa. When Sherman tried to convince the attending Utes that they needed to settle down on their reservation, Ouray, as spokesman, refused to concur. Sherman gave up and announced the best way to deal with the Indians: "They will have to freeze and starve a little more, I reckon, before they will listen to common sense."[37]

By winter the Utes were indeed cold and hungry but still unrepentant. Carson reported to Cummings that Tabeguaches were complaining about unfulfilled promises of provisions and that Muaches were continuing their rebellion.[38] During this winter of 1866–1867 about a thousand Tabeguaches under Shavano and Colorow camped on Fountain Creek, just south of the Garden of the Gods in Colorado City, and survived on flour demanded from the town's residents.[39]

In May 1867, after Kaniache and his followers had conducted raids on the Huerfano and killed three men, Ouray sent the Tabeguache Chief Shavano to bring the Muache Chief Kaniache to Fort Garland.[40] It must be assumed that Ouray still had no authority of his own but was acting as a liaison for Carson.

Utes in northwestern New Mexico also continued to engage in fighting. In August 1866 Superintendent Norton had protested that the Indians around Abiquiú and Tierra Amarilla should receive provisions, but in November Abiquiú's special agent, Jesus M. S. Baca, complained that he had to give the Utes beef and cornmeal from his own supplies. The Indians, he reported, were coming almost daily for ammunition, which he doled out in small quantities. In his letter Baca also noted that "Caneache" and other Muaches had passed through two days earlier on their way to join Capotes in an expedition into Navajo country.[41]

Only days later volunteers manned a new post, Camp Plummer, near Tierra Amarilla and Los Ojos. The camp's purpose was "to keep peace among unruly Indians" who might cause trouble for settlers, increasing numbers of whom had moved up the Chama Valley in the early 1860s.[42] Another reason for the military post was to protect traffic on the road to the San Juans. In 1867, when a company of regular troops arrived, Camp Plummer was renamed Fort Lowell. Rations had been distributed in this vicinity in 1863, and now, in hopes of keeping Utes farther away from the more populated portions of the lower Chama Valley, in 1872 the Abiquiú Agency moved to Tierra Amarilla. The agency's former name was retained.

Similar problems were occurring in Middle Park. At Hot Sulphur Springs in 1866, Agent Oakes and Superintendent Cummings held a council with Uintah, Yamparika, and Grand River Utes to persuade the Indians to allow the construction of a stage road between Denver and Salt Lake City. This central route through Colorado passed not only through Middle Park but also through the western portions of Ute territory. Much of the trouble could be eliminated if these Utes would move from the "government's land" to the reservation delineated by the 1863 Tabeguache Treaty, it was argued. Not surprisingly, the Utes chose not to give up their hunting grounds, but they did make concessions regarding the road and agreed to a Treaty of Amity, which was not ratified. Cummings's authority was weakened by the knowledge that he was widely suspected of unethical dealings in handling supplies.

Despite the Utes' refusal to remove themselves from Middle Park, William Byers had built a cabin at Hot Sulphur Springs, and settlers were coming into the area. Conflicts began to occur as natural resources were exploited by the newcomers, although when Bayard Taylor made a pleasure trip through Middle Park in 1866, he wrote that the Indians he met there were friendly.

Another site of contact and conflict with white people in northern Colorado was Hahns Peak, north of Steamboat Springs, where prospectors arrived in 1865. More miners came the next year. Utes attacked their camp in 1866 and took a few miners prisoner, but, after killing their pack animals and stealing their possessions, the Indians released the captives.

Following the severe winter of 1866–1867, Antero, Nevava, and Nevava's brother Douglass (Quinkent) visited Denver to argue for permission to hunt in Middle Park. This delegation is noteworthy because it shows the ties between important Utes from western Colorado and Utah. Nevava was from northwestern Colorado. He may have been a Tabeguache who took some followers and split from that band following the Conejos treaty. His brother Douglass, who later figured prominently in events at the White River Agency at Meeker, Colorado, was said to be chief of twenty-one lodges of "Salt Lake Utes," though, perhaps meaning that he was known to have come to Utah's agency at Salt Lake City and became enrolled there. Antero, sometimes called a Uintah and sometimes a Grand River leader, would reappear on the Uintah Reservation in 1873.[43]

Tabeguaches also went to Denver and demanded better food, for they complained that the rations they were receiving at Conejos were unfit for consumption. By then, A. C. Hunt had replaced Cummings as governor and superintendent. In a letter to Commissioner N. G. Taylor in May 1867, Hunt requested $20,000 to purchase cattle and sheep that had not been delivered to fulfill the terms of the 1863 treaty, and he urged that wheat be bought to replace the rice Cummings had unwisely purchased. Most of the rice, for which Utes had no use, was still in a warehouse in Golden.[44] A month later, Denver's citizenry was agitated about the presence of five hundred Utes, but Hunt still had no money to buy provisions and Washington had no intention of sending it.

In Utah, unrest was growing as the white population doubled. Technically, Utah's Indians were supposed to have gone to the Uinta Basin. In 1860 Brigham Young ordered a survey of the basin, and when it was determined that the basin was a valueless waste, unfit for Mormon farms and towns but suitable for nomadic Indian hunters, he proposed a reservation there. President Abraham Lincoln issued a proclamation creating the reservation in 1861, but Congress took no immediate action, and the Indians demonstrated no inclination to relocate to the basin.

By this time new settlements were spreading southward as far as Panguitch and Circleville. Some sites had stockades like Fort Wilden's (later the location of Cove Fort) to protect travelers and residents, but by the mid-1860s geographical expansion ceased when Indian hostilities increased. Chief Peteeneet, who had maintained sporadic peaceful relations with Mormons, died in 1861, and Tabby became chief. In the spring of 1863 he led successful skirmishes against Camp Douglas's cavalry, and, thus encouraged, Black Hawk (Autenquer, Antonga), a Timpanogots Ute, summoned a council of Ute bands at Spanish Fork. This council was convened in response to Congress's authorization that year of the sale of Utah's Indian farms and the demand that all of Utah's Indians, including the Utes, move to the Uinta Basin. Parianuche and Yamparika Utes attended Black Hawk's council at Spanish Fork, where Uriah Curtis found them when he came to summon them to the council in 1863 at Conejos in Colorado. They refused to go.[45]

When the Spanish Fork council ended, Utah's Utes undertook a series of raids, and in 1864 Chief Tabby led warriors in a battle at Spanish Fork. Adding to the uproar, smallpox devastated Indians in the Gunnison, Utah, area during the winter of 1864–1865, and the Utes believed white people had deliberately sent the disease to destroy them. Among the victims was Chief Arrapene.

In 1865 Utah Superintendent Oliver H. Irish and Brigham Young called a council at Spanish Fork to negotiate a treaty whereby the Utes would agree to cede their land, including the three farms, and move to the reservation. In exchange for their land, the Indians were promised annuities for several decades. The treaty council was attended by several headmen, among them Pahvant Chief Kanosh, who declared that Sowiet was "the father of all Utes."[46] Although this gave Sowiet the respect due him as an elder and a civil leader, it could have resulted from a white negotiator's impossible demand that one chief, not many, should speak for Utah's Utes.

The Spanish Fork Treaty of 1865 was not ratified by Congress, but the federal government promptly took action to extinguish Ute land titles and those of other Utah tribes as well. In the fall of 1865 another treaty council with Utah's Southern Paiute bands took place with the same results.[47] Only a few Utes began to move after being told that only those who went to the reservation would receive annuity goods, which, in fact, were not forthcoming. By the terms of the treaty, Paiutes were also to go to the Uinta Basin, but they refused because they said they were afraid to live with Utes who always had taken Paiute children as captives. Paiutes never went to the Uintah Valley Reservation, nor did Gosiutes for the same alleged reason.

The Spanish Fork council and its treaty precipitated an outbreak of raids and skirmishes among Utes that has been called the Black Hawk War, which lasted from 1865 to 1867. Although the uprising had broader causes, its immediate provocation was an incident at Manti in 1865. Arrapene's son appeared at a Mormon meeting there and demanded restitution for the death of his father. John Lowry, a Mormon who had a reputation for being friendly with his Sanpits neighbors, pulled the Indian from his horse and beat him, in self-defense he said. The next day the Utes killed a Mormon.[48]

Two years of violence and thefts of livestock followed, with Black Hawk as the leader of warriors who were primarily but not exclusively Sanpits and Seuvarits Utes. A few Paiutes and Navajos also joined in the attacks. During the Black Hawk War about two dozen settlements were temporarily abandoned, and new fortifications, such as Fort Deseret and Cove Fort, were built at others. Countless head of livestock were run off to distant places such as the Bookcliffs and southern Colorado. Action was concentrated chiefly in Sanpete and Sevier Counties, but it moved as far north as Wasatch County's Heber City, where raids took place after a Mormon killed a Ute. To halt acts of revenge and counterrevenge that were multiplying there, Brigham Young sent Heber City's Mormon participants to Lower Corn Creek, where they joined refugees from the hard-hit Panguitch area. Kanosh's peaceful band, which was living at Upper Corn Creek, seemed to have no objection to this invasion by Mormons only a few miles downstream, and, in fact, eighty-five Utes were baptized in the warm springs at Lower Corn Creek in May 1867.[49]

During the war a major encounter took place in Salina Canyon, where a militia blocked the escape of Utes with hundreds of stolen horses. Another dramatic event occurred near Circleville, where an encampment of Utes was captured and taken to a makeshift prison. All the adult prisoners were then killed.[50] When they were not fighting, some of Black Hawk's followers retreated to the Fremont River region. Ute women, children, and elderly people from the area sought refuge in the rugged country around Capitol Reef and Canyonlands.[51]

By the end of the Black Hawk War, about fifty Mormons and at least as many Indians had died. Mormons claimed the war had cost them one and a half million dollars. The Utes lost some important leaders. Chief Sanpitch was killed in 1866, and Black Hawk received wounds in 1867 from which he later died. After Black Hawk was forced to quit, the uprising came to a virtual end, although some skirmishes took place over the next five years.

Superintendent F. H. Head had fields plowed for Kanosh's peaceful band at Upper Corn Creek, where they were farming and were sometimes working for their Mormon neighbors at Lower Corn Creek. Ironically, in 1867 Brigham Young ordered the Mormons to move upstream to the Utes' better land. Upper Corn Creek was then renamed Kanosh. The Indians at Upper Corn Creek apparently did not balk overtly at being displaced by their Mormon brethren, but within a year or two Kanosh took his band for a while to the Uintah Valley Reservation.

The major portion of Black Hawk's uprising had coincided with Ute hostilities in northern New Mexico and Colorado. Moreover, both outbreaks were part of widespread Indian resistance throughout the West to increasing expansion onto Indian lands after the Civil War and the military actions that were part of the United States' Indian War. The period was one of desperation for the Utes and other American Indians of the West, and emotionalism was rampant on all sides.

Human nature being what it is, violence directed at one enemy fanned enthusiasm for bloodshed among a variety of targets. For instance, when photographer William Henry Jackson passed through Fort Bridger in 1866–1867, he found Utes preparing to go "give the Mormons hell" in Sanpete country, but he also noted others who were about to join with a United States military force to fight the Sioux, old antagonists of the Utes from the plains.[52] In December Sioux warriors under Red Cloud had wiped out Captain William J. Fetterman and his eighty men, and troops were on the move. A few Utes also were ready to go.

Meanwhile, a slow migration of Utes was going to the Uinta Basin. Regardless of whether they had historically been members of the Uintah Band, they and others who followed were later called Uintah Indians and were assigned to the Uintah Valley Agency. Needing sustenance but having none, the early arrivals appealed to their first special agent, F.

Kinney, but he had received nothing with which to feed them. The next year a new special agent, Thomas Carter, arrived with flour, supplies, and seventy head of cattle, as well as employees to plow acreage and build irrigation ditches.[53] Suffering from his wounds and sick with tuberculosis, Black Hawk visited the reservation in 1867 but chose not to stay. (He died that same year on a mountain near the Utah Valley, once his homeland, and was buried nearby in a respectful manner with some of his possessions. In the early twentieth century his grave was looted, and his body was removed. For several decades his remains rested in a museum in Salt Lake City, but in response to public protest and to the Native American Graves Protection and Repatriation Act of 1990, they have been reinterred at Spring Lake.)

After Black Hawk's death and the end of the uprising that had continued with occasional raids, Tabby led most of Utah's Utes to the Uinta Basin to begin their lives as reservation Indians. Sherman's solution had proved effective, and many Utes throughout Utah, Colorado, and New Mexico were being frozen and starved into submission.

Still, across the steppes, hills, and mountains, the sound of drums called the Utes to remain connected to Earth, their universe, wherever they were scattered. Bear stirred in his cave, far beyond the confusion and grief, calling on the Núu-ci to survive.

7

▼ ▼ ▼

Attempts to Create Reservations
(1868–1874)

The year 1868 was a milestone in the federal government's program to move Ute Indians to reservations. Setting aside designated lands and even getting some bands to approve of them did not mean the new arrangements would be embraced, however.

Regardless of whether the people accepted the notion that they were expected to live on reservations, the government established agencies on them, and some Utes assigned to them were henceforth usually called by the names of their agencies instead of by band names. For instance, those assigned to the Uintah Valley Agency became known as Uintahs regardless of their previous band affiliations. Another way of differentiating Utes arose, as those amenable to the reservations and regulations were considered "good Indians," whereas those who lived according to their own inclinations—roaming off of the reservations and occasionally getting into trouble—were called "renegades." There were many "renegades" in Utah, Colorado, and New Mexico.

In the 1860s the only Ute reservation was Utah's Uintah Valley Reservation until the Treaty of 1868 created one piece of land in Colorado, the Consolidated Ute Reservation, for all the Ute Indians then in Colorado and New Mexico. Attending negotiations for this treaty was a delegation, accompanied by Territorial Governor Alexander Cameron Hunt and Kit Carson, who went to Washington in February. Having resigned from military service the year before because of ill health, Carson had recently been appointed Colorado's superintendent of Indian Affairs. (He would, in fact, die in May 1868 shortly after his return to Colorado.) The Treaty of 1868 has sometimes been called the "Kit Carson Treaty" because of this popular figure's involvement.

As had the 1863 delegation, the group in 1868 enjoyed a dazzling
sightseeing trip. After traveling north to Cheyenne by stage, delegates
boarded the Union Pacific to head east. Following the treaty negotiations they were treated to a tour of Philadelphia, New York, Boston, and
Niagara Falls. A highlight was a visit to the armory at Springfield, Massachusetts, where each guest received a rifle.

Among the better-known Utes who signed the treaty with a mark
were the Tabeguaches Ouray and Guero, the Muaches Kaniache and
Ankatosh, the Yampa Nicaagat (Jack), the Grand River Piah (Black-Tail
Deer), and the Capote Suviap. In August and September 1868 several
headmen of the seven bands signed the treaty as amended by the United
State Senate.[1] The powerful Nevava, who died in 1868, did not sign
either document.[2]

By terms of the treaty concluded in March 1868, Colorado's Consolidated Ute Reservation took in most of the territory's Western Slope,
nearly twenty million acres. Boundaries ran west from the 107th meridian to the Colorado-Utah territorial boundary and from the Colorado–
New Mexico border north to a line fifteen miles north of the 40th parallel. Later, the northern boundary was moved south a few miles. Straight

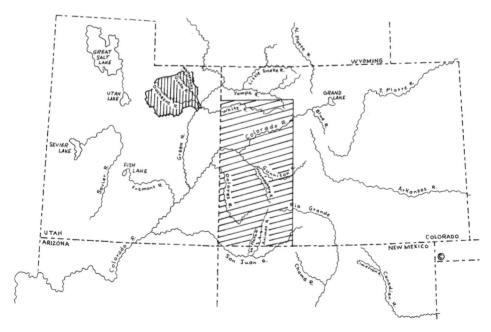

Utah's Uintah Valley Reservation and Colorado's Consolidated Ute Reservation, 1868.

lines marked off the reservation without regard for natural watersheds or customary uses of land and resources. The 107th meridian runs roughly through a point about ten miles west of today's Aspen, through Gunnison, and through Pagosa Springs. Excluded were the important intermontane basins—North Park, Middle Park, South Park, and the San Luis Valley—as well as the Yampa Valley.

In exchange for ceding other traditional lands, the Utes were told they would receive total annuities valued at $60,000 over the next thirty years, a cow and five sheep for each family, farm implements, schools, other buildings, a sawmill, and agency employees. Individuals could select tracts of land to farm. A major point was that non-Indians other than employees and authorized individuals were not to be allowed to pass through, settle on, or reside within the reservation. The two agencies of the reservation were to be located "on the Rio de los Pinos" and on the White River, to serve, respectively, the "Tabeguache, Muache, Weeminuche, and Capote bands" and the "Grand River, Yampa, and Uintah bands."

President Andrew Johnson gave each Ute delegate a silver peace medal, a symbol that had designated rank and honored "good Indians" since George Washington's presidency. When subsequent Ute delegations went to Washington, participants continued to receive medals, which appear in contemporary photographs of many individuals. At the 1868 meeting Johnson appointed Ouray chief spokesman for all of Colorado's Utes.

The treaty soon caused dissension among the Indians. Capotes and Weenuches who met with William Arny at Pagosa Springs during the summer insisted that the only reservation they might approve would have to extend north and west to the Colorado and Green Rivers. Meanwhile, Ouray denied that any treaty had been signed in the Washington hotel where the meeting was held.[3] He claimed the signatures of Kaniache and Ankatosh were forged. Perhaps his protests were intended to appease other Utes, or perhaps he was fabricating the situation in self-defense. Nevertheless, the treaty was proclaimed in November 1868, and the reservation and its agencies were accomplished, on paper at least.

Although the "Los Pinos" to which the Conejos Agency was to move, according to the treaty, might well have been the Los Pinos River near Conejos, the agency had moved by 1868 to the fledgling community of Saguache, about sixty-five miles north of Conejos, a desirable distance from the numerous small settlements in the southern San Luis Valley. Ambitious merchants, farmers, and ranchers moved to the new location in hopes of benefiting from the Indian trade. Lafayette Head's alcoholic clerk, William Godfroy, was in Saguache in 1867 and was filling some of the functions of agent.[4] Many Utes began to gather in the area to trade buckskins for wheat, flour, and corn at local farms.

Among Saguache's energetic settlers was Otto Mears, a Russian immigrant whose apprenticeship in America had included fighting Apaches and Navajos as a member of the California Volunteers, milling and merchandising at Conejos, and learning the Ute language. In 1867 he began his career as a road builder by hacking a toll road north to the Upper Arkansas Valley. A pragmatist, Mears missed no opportunity to advance his enterprises and ambitions, even giving voters groceries from his store to influence county elections, and he quickly became closely involved with Utes as a trader, interpreter, and special commissioner and through any other means of profit that came his way, as we shall see.

Another pioneer at Saguache was John Lawrence, whose contribution to the history of Ute Indians includes a candid journal and letters to newspapers wherein he recorded the comings and goings of his neighbors and visiting Indians. For instance, Lawrence reported "Uray's" denial at Godfroy's place of any treaty, as well as other local gossip, such as a story about Sheriff James Fullerton who, Lawrence reported, bought Sapinero's niece for a horse and a cart in 1868.[5]

As governor and superintendent, Hunt optimistically believed not only that Utes should and could become stock growers and farmers but also that the consolidated reservation would eliminate problems created by contact with settlements in Colorado and New Mexico.[6] Appropriations for buildings, equipment, livestock, and rations, however, attracted opportunistic officials and entrepreneurs who could benefit from appointments and contracts. Mears was only one of the local people who took advantage of such opportunities at Saguache and wherever agencies existed.

On a national scale, scandal and corruption were common in this era. When President Ulysses S. Grant took office in 1869, it was the beginning of an eight-year administration renowned for its exploitation of the spoils system. The effects of this political corruption were felt in Colorado when Grant abruptly removed Hunt and appointed a fellow Civil War general, Edward M. McCook, as Colorado territorial governor and ex officio superintendent of Indian Affairs. McCook knew nothing about Colorado or its Indians, but he had a keen eye for chances to make profits for himself and his sycophants and to give jobs to family members.

In the summer of 1869 Second Lieutenant Calvin T. Speer became temporary agent of what was then called the Southern Ute Agency, later the Los Pinos Agency. Military personnel at the time were being assigned as agents, while reformers in Washington were organizing a new method for selecting them. The location of Speer's agency lay over Cochetopa Pass in an open valley on a previously unnamed creek, about fifty miles northwest of Saguache. The site actually was a short distance east of the reservation boundary and a very long way from lands occupied by Muache, Capote, and Weenuche Utes. It was more than a hundred miles from any existing Los Pinos River, so to meet the stipulations of the Treaty of 1868 the stream was christened Los Pinos Creek. To no avail, former agent Lafayette Head wrote to Governor McCook protesting that there was no Los Pinos Creek near the agency site, and in January 1870 the Santa Fe *New Mexican* complained that with this trick the "Colorado Clique in Washington" had stolen the agency's business away from New Mexico. Former Governor Hunt's hopes of turning Utes into farmers were also largely dashed because the site's elevation was too high and cold for an adequate growing season.

The Utes staged a frightening reception for Speer and his party and the materials he was bringing to build the agency and its sawmill. Mrs. Godfroy, who was part Indian, had gone along as interpreter. Eight hundred Utes in war paint blocked the party's way, galloped forward, and so frightened Mrs. Godfroy that she fainted. The warriors then claimed that the party was a joke, but Speer reported that the Utes did not want him to enter the reservation until Ouray and others were assured that Speer was bringing annuities.[7] Chief Uncanarcs, whose name does not appear on the treaty documents, was the principal opposition leader.

Speer quickly built a schoolhouse forty by twenty feet in size with a cupola topped by a flag staff. Other structures surrounding a small square included houses for the agent, the farmer, a blacksmith, and a carpenter, as well as workshops. A log house for Ouray and Chipeta was erected close by. A corral, stables, and sawmill completed the structures. The Utes soon had a racetrack, which today is flooded by a small reservoir, while a ranch presently overlies the agency site. Either prior to or during the agency's existence, Indians who gathered nearby peeled bark from many trees in the area for food or medicine, and they built low rock structures that may have been used as hunting blinds or defense works. (Remnants of similar stone circles, large enough to hold up to three or four men, are found in many places in Colorado, such as near Colorado Springs and Saguache, where pickets could keep watch on white settlers, soldiers, enemy Indians, or game.[8])

Aware that contractors could make good profits when the agency was established, Mears applied for and obtained contracts to supply beef and other foodstuffs, which farmers in the San Luis Valley raised and sold in large quantities. On one occasion he had fifty unbranded cows held back and proved they had "died" by branding the same number of old hides.[9] A herd of cattle and more than a thousand sheep were delivered to the agency's cow camp at Gunnison, but John Lawrence described another four hundred head, which the Utes refused, as "the poorest, scrubiest and ordinariest Texas cattle that ever passed through the territory." Furthermore, the bid had specifically excluded Texas cattle. One of McCook's relatives by marriage provided the stock, and McCook made a profit of over $23,000 on this one deal.[10]

Some Utes' attitude toward both the reservation and Ouray's appointment as chief became evident early in the agency's life. In 1869 both Uncanarcs and Ouray were at the agency with a total of 120 lodges. The next year, after Uncanarcs was forced out, only thirty lodges remained under Ouray, Guero, Shavano, and Jim. During the next two years Ouray's cabin was burned and had to be replaced. As reimbursement for his lost possessions Ouray received $400 from the government. In future years he was forced to protect his authority by killing at least five Utes, one attacker being Sapinero, Chipeta's brother or more likely her step-brother.

In the often told story of Sapinero's attempt on Ouray's life, around 1872 or 1873 a plot was hatched by six Utes who had been drinking. All but Sapinero abandoned the plan, and Ouray was saved in the nick of time by a warning from the blacksmith. Ouray seized Sapinero and would have killed him with a knife if Chipeta had not rushed in to restrain Ouray.[11] Interestingly, after this incident the hot-blooded Sapinero continued to serve as a leader of the band when Ouray was absent.

After more than a year as temporary agent, Lieutenant Speer was relieved in the autumn of 1870 by a Unitarian clergyman, Jabez Nelson Trask, a remarkably ill-suited, eccentric Bostonian. It should be pointed out in sympathy that the recent death of Trask's wife had delayed his arrival. When he did assume his post after walking from Denver in an unusual getup that featured green sunglasses and a wide-brimmed beaver hat, he judged his agency's physical condition as deplorable and his Ute Indians' as no better. Lawrence's daily accounts describe unhappy Utes coming to Saguache to complain about their equally unhappy agent, who sought peace by shutting himself up in his house. On one occasion a disgruntled former employee beat up the hapless agent. In his one brief report to the commissioner of Indian Affairs, besides brimming over with self-righteous disgust with the agency, the livestock, and the Indians, Trask seemed especially upset because he had been unable to begin any missionary work under existing conditions.

Soon after Trask's arrival, a group of Utes asked Lawrence to write to President Grant and Governor McCook about their unsuitable agent, and in response a Captain Jocknick was sent to investigate. He blamed much of the dissension on the Indians. Sidney Jocknick, thought to be the captain's son, also went to the Los Pinos Agency and stayed on as a cook and hand for the next few years. He wrote rather inaccurate but nevertheless useful firsthand descriptions of the agency in his book *Early Days on the Western Slope of Colorado*.[12]

When the puritanical Trask departed less that a year after his arrival, the agency's bank account contained $25,000 that the agent had chosen not to use to purchase provisions. It is impossible to explain this situation unless Trask felt his naughty Utes had not earned their distributions.

How a man such as Trask happened to be appointed warrants an explanation. Disturbed by graft and corruption within the Indian Office, reformers in the East advocated the Peace Policy that was initiated by Grant's Department of the Interior in 1869, an effort to clean up corruption. The program had begun in 1867 with congressional authorization of a Board of Indian Commissioners to advise the Bureau of Indian Affairs and to share in oversight of expenditures with the Secretary of the Interior. Accordingly, the commissioner of Indian Affairs appointed nine nonsalaried members to the new board. They were wealthy Eastern philanthropists and Protestant churchgoers.

Their goal—to civilize Native Americans by making them self-supporting farmers and Christians—was going to take longer to achieve. Its philosophy was based on a mixture of benevolent humanitarianism and the conviction that the dominant agrarian culture was superior to anything indigenous peoples possessed. The "savages" were to be acculturated without regard for inherent differences in the accumulated experiences, memories, and habits of the two races. Native Americans of all tribes were to be taught the blessings of peace and education on reservations, with farming rather than nomadic hunting and gathering as the basis of their economy.

The Board of Indian Commissioners parceled out the Indian agencies to various Christian denominations, some of which had some experience conducting missions. The Utes of Colorado and New Mexico had never been the recipients of missionary programs, although Mormons had proselytized and assisted Utah's Indians. The board assigned Utes near Maxwell's ranch at the base of the "Rattoon Mountains" first to the

Congregational Church and then to Presbyterians. Utah's Utes and the White River Agency were also supposed to have Presbyterian agents, as were Utes on the San Juan River who were lumped with Navajos, Hopis, and Pimas. With no experience working with agencies or American Indians, Unitarians were given the Los Pinos Agency.

Trask was the Unitarians' nominee. His replacement, a brother-in-law of Governor McCook, was a German, Karl Adam Schwanbeck, who went by the name General Charles Adams. He had acquired the rank of general in the territorial militia and had completed a very brief stint as agent at White River. An able man, Adams's chief drawback was that he was a Catholic, not a Unitarian as his application stated, so he was removed when this fact came to light, but not before he had won the friendship of Ouray, the chief's partisans, and contractor Otto Mears.

Regardless of who the agents were, a difficulty with operating Colorado's agencies was that neither wandering Utes nor trespassing whites respected the boundaries of the reservation. Many attractions, such as a desire to hunt in time-honored places, enticed the Utes to roam. The large parks, especially South Park, attracted them because some bison could still be found there.

Moreover, distributions of rations took place off the reservation. For example, after a flour mill was built on Chalk Creek near Nathrop in 1868, hundreds camped close to one of their favorite hot springs at the base of Mount Princeton. Goods were issued to a large number at Poncha Springs, where tense interactions between the Indians and local people took place. The Utes wanted the newcomers to leave. When game was scarce and Utes were killing cattle near Cañon City, flour was given out there as well.

Trading posts, such as Castello's at Fairplay and Florissant or Hartsel's near a hot spring, drew Indians, and well-worn trails led Utes to Denver and other Front Range towns, as well as to the plains to hunt and fight. Colorow and his followers enjoyed sojourns, especially around Denver, where they camped at a cave southwest of the growing town. Settlers on the streams between Denver and Colorado Springs became accustomed to having Indians come to their doors to ask for biscuits, for which Colorow's appetite was legendary. White River Utes came all the way to Colorado Springs as well. Chief Washington and his followers, with forty or fifty lodges, spent the winter of 1872–1873 there. Utes led by Piah camped south of Deer Trail, and the *Rocky Mountain News* reported that he was married on Cherry Creek in 1873.[13] The newspaper mentioned incidents in locations as far-flung as Hugo, Cuchara, and even Rawlins, Wyoming.

Encounters with Plains Indians tribes still occurred frequently. Utes fought Cheyennes and Arapahos in South Park in 1868, and two years later Utes drove Sioux out of the Upper Arkansas Valley. A disturbing report indicated that Colorow had killed a white person east of Mosca Pass, and in 1871 a woman in the same area said a Ute had shot at her through a window after she refused to give him food.

Because so many Utes were coming to Denver, a special agency was established there in 1871. The agent was another of McCook's brothers-in-law, James B. Thompson. Despite negative implications regarding nepotism and the spoils system, Thompson, like Adams, generally got along with his Indians. Ouray struck up a friendship with Thompson, and the chief and Chipeta were entertained in the agent's home. Thompson claimed to have taught Ouray to write his name and praised his intelligence and comportment.[14] Unfortunately, however, issuing annuities at Denver attracted more Indians—as many as a thousand at a

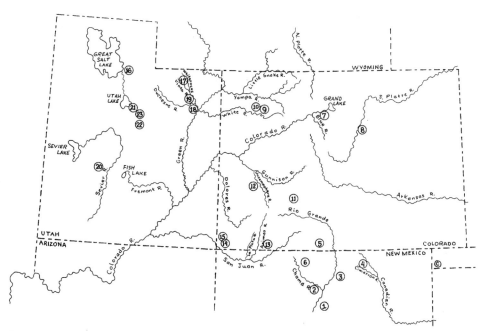

Locations of Ute agencies and subagencies: 1. Santa Fe, 2. Abiquiú, 3. Taos, 4. Cimarrón, 5. Conejos, 6. Tierra Amarilla, 7. Middle Park, 8. Denver, 9. White River #1, 10. White River #2, 11. Los Pinos #1, 12. Los Pinos #2 (Uncompahgre), 13. Ignacio, 14. Navajo Springs, 15. Towaoc, 16. Salt Lake City, 17. Whiterocks, 18. Ouray, 19. Fort Duchesne. *Locations of Indian farms:* 20. Corn Creek, 21. Spanish Fork, 22. Twelve Mile Creek, 23. Thistle Valley.

time—and the availability of liquor there led to degrading episodes on the streets.

White River Utes, often more independent and excitable than Tabeguaches, were given an agency near the future site of Meeker, where it was supposed they would be far from opportunities for trouble. The first agency was located in Simpson Park, southeast of the mouth of Coal Creek. With rapid turnover, the first agent, A. J. Beck, was followed by Charles Adams and others until the Presbyterians sent John S. Littlefield, who managed to stay for three years, until 1874. The Utes assigned to his agency wandered far and wide, sometimes but not always because game was scarce in their own country. In early 1868 a hundred lodges, led by Nevava, hunted bison on the plains after being forced to beg for food in Middle Park during the previous year. Resentment toward the new treaty also impelled a few belligerent White River Utes to travel as far south as Hardscrabble Creek, near Cañon City, where Governor Hunt reported that they stole cattle and threatened to kill Ouray.[15]

White tourists and surveyors were entering the White Rivers' traditional but off-reservation lands. Eight hundred Utes accepted the presence of Schuyler Colfax's party at Hot Sulphur Springs in Middle Park in 1868, when newspaperman Samuel Bowles, traveling with Colfax, mentioned that friendly Ute women exchanged wild raspberries for biscuits and honey and that the men and boys who gathered around the tourists' evening campfire stole nothing. Enjoying this friendly reception, Bowles recorded the condition of the Indians he saw. He wrote about the prevalence of arthritis and respiratory and digestive illnesses, and he described taking ailing horses into the hot springs for their cure. He saw tents made of "cloth" (canvas) and the mixture of buckskin and white men's clothing the people were wearing.[16]

Major John Wesley Powell was also in Middle Park the same summer as he prepared for his first survey of the Green-Colorado River country. With his wife and survey team, he camped during the winter of 1868–1869 at Powell Park, a favorite Ute campsite near Meeker where Agent Nathan Meeker would relocate the White River Agency a few years later. A student of the tribes of the Great Basin, as well as of geography and geology, Powell kept busy making notes about the Numic language and ethnology, and he taught a little English to Douglass, whose village was nearby.

In 1870 anger toward Euro-Americans increased after the first pan-Indian Ghost Dance took place among the Northern Paiutes and others in Idaho. Yamparikas, Uintahs, and some Tabeguaches who attended taught the dance to their people, although it did not capture a large following until a revival occurred two decades later.[17] An interpretation of the first dance was that it was an evocation of dead Native Americans to return to destroy the white people. Perhaps inspired by this rite, belligerent Utes burned a blacksmith shop at Hot Sulphur Springs in 1870, and in following years Utes attempted to evict visitors from the resort and demanded gifts. Piah refused to go to the reservation and, with his band of about thirty-five lodges, chose to camp around Denver. His White River friends, who also preferred Denver to the reservation, included Washington, Antelope, and Jack, all of whom figured prominently in later events at White River.[18]

A growing aggravation was the number of ranches with cattle grazing on the Utes' old hunting grounds, not only in Middle Park but also to the north in Brown's Park and the Little Snake River Range. With livestock came rustlers who were often identified, correctly or incorrectly, as Indian raiders, and Hispanic cowhands sold liquor to the Indians. Agent Littlefield seems to have made little effort to impede the travels of his Utes and the mischief that ensued. Far off the reservation to the northeast in North Park, miners were chased out by Piah, John (Jack), and sixty or seventy Ute warriors in 1870, according to the Laramie (Wyoming) *Daily Sentinel*. Claiming the resources were theirs, the Utes took a small amount of gold dust and about a hundred beaver pelts from nearby trappers. To the south near Aspen, where prospectors were entering the Crystal River area, which was highly prized by the Ute Indians, Colorow and his men burned a cabin and ran the prospectors off in 1872.[19] The angry Colorow also went to North Park in 1876 to kill miners, an event that drew soldiers from Laramie.[20]

In 1873, as conflicts with Plains Indians continued, Douglass took his warriors north to fight Arapahos, and Piah went east to the Little Republican River and fought other Arapahos. Piah's party returned to Denver with several scalps and held a three-day Scalp Dance in the middle of the city, with the cooperation of Uriah Curtis, over the objections of Agent Thompson and the mayor. The next year Sioux and Cheyenne victims offered up their scalps for another dance at Sloan's Lake in Denver.[21] The White River Utes continued to have little regard for their reservation's boundaries and the location of their agency, as William Henry Jackson noticed when he was in Middle Park in 1874. He found about two hundred Utes at Grand Lake preparing to go to the White River Agency for their annuities, and he saw several other lodges on the Blue River, from which Utes were going to the Los Pinos Agency for the same purpose.[22]

Although New Mexico Territory's Ute Indians were supposed to have moved to Colorado after the Treaty of 1863, they continued to show no inclination to go. Muaches also refused to recognize the terms of the Treaty of 1868 and continued to congregate at Cimarrón along with their Jicarilla Apache friends. All of the Indians vanished when Colonel S. F. Tappan went to talk with them in June 1868, though.[23] Fort Union had been purchasing food from Maxwell for the Indians and provided some oversight, but a decision was made in 1869 to halt the issuance of rations in an effort to force the Muaches to go to Colorado. The plan did not work. It only provoked depredations on the area's livestock, and Fort Union again stepped in to furnish food and blankets to prevent Indians in the area from starving and freezing. When alcoholic agent Erasmus B. Dennison was replaced by Charles F. Roedel, a Presbyterian mission board choice, no supplies of any kind were on hand for distribution to the Indians. Fort Union manned a post at Cimarrón, and a semblance of order was maintained.

In the fall of 1868 some Cimarrón Indians were again recruited as auxiliaries to assist the United States military in a campaign against Plains Indian tribes. One hundred and fifty "generally fine-looking" Utes accompanied two companies of cavalry to Fort Bascom. Although some accounts charged that the Utes deserted after drawing their supplies, a later report explained that the Indians had simply taken a route of their own choosing.[24]

That winter, Muaches avoided Cimarrón because of a report of smallpox there, while Ouray and a couple hundred Tabeguache hunters, undeterred by the new treaty, spent several weeks near Trinidad, Colorado, where Muaches also tended to congregate. In the spring of 1869 the son of either Kaniache or Curecanti was killed near Trinidad in a fight with a mixed group of Plains Indians.[25] (Confusion about these two Muache men is common because they were twins. According to the usual practice, one twin infant was abandoned—in this case Curecanti—but he survived in the care of other Indians and later rejoined the band. Both men were in Denver in the early 1870s, where misidentifications occurred.)

The sale of Lucien Maxwell's ranch, first to Denver businessmen and then to British investors, in 1870 came as a shock to the Indians who had enjoyed unhampered access for camping and hunting on the huge grant. Insisting that the land was theirs, they refused to leave.[26]

The Cimarrón Agency had no funds for purchasing provisions, and instead of reporting to the Abiquiú Agency as instructed, the Indians remained, hunting on the plains and engaging in occasional fights with the tribes there. A jail was built at Cimarrón to incarcerate any Indians who loitered after dark, but the sale of liquor—especially by people from Rayado—created ongoing problems among people of both races in Cimarrón.

Some Muaches continued to travel north from New Mexico. On New Years Day 1872, a group appeared in Colorado Springs where they saw the new Denver and Rio Grande Railway and a hotel that had opened there before they continued on to Denver. On a trip the next year to the Cuchara area in Colorado, however, depredations and a rape took place. This episode brought Ouray and Charles Adams with troops from Fort Garland to rein in Kaniache's group. The Muache chief refused to acknowledge Ouray's authority, and instead of going to the Los Pinos Agency as ordered he and his band went on a drunken spree, killing cattle and running their ponies through planted fields. The behavior of this once-respected leader eventually led the normally tolerant agent, James Thompson, to order Kaniache to stay out of Denver.

By late 1873 Muaches were again receiving rations at Cimarrón when Agent Thomas D. Dolan negotiated an agreement with the band to move to the San Juan River area in the southern portion of the Consolidated Ute Reservation in Colorado Territory. A Southern Ute Agency was to be established there, with Capotes, Weenuches, and Muaches attached to it.[27] At the same time, the Jicarillas agreed to be located on an adjoining reservation in New Mexico that would be administered by the Southern Ute Agency. Dolan succeeded in getting three Muaches—not including Kaniache—and six Jicarillas to put their marks on the agreements, and he distributed provisions, presents, and annuity goods to the Indians who had gathered for the proceedings. Technically, these and subsequent documents were called agreements rather than treaties because in 1871 the United States Senate had ordered that treaties were no longer to be negotiated with Indian tribes, which were henceforth not to be recognized as sovereign nations. Regardless, the agreements had no immediate effect because the Indians still refused to move.

The list of items Dolan presented at the "treaty" council gives a glimpse of what an agent might find in his warehouse. Besides 2,630 pounds of fresh beef and 5,260 pounds of "shorts" (?), he gave out 4 pounds of coffee, 20 pounds of sugar, 105 pounds of tobacco, and miscellaneous goods including 310 blankets, a little more than 80 yards of blue cloth, 710 yards of blue drilling, 40 yards of canvas, 500 yards of calico, 20 yards of manta (New Mexico's hand-woven woolen goods), 2 pairs of drawers, 5 pairs of pants, 6 hats, 5 overcoats, 226 shirts, a pair of shoes, a mirror, almost a pound of thread, 3 papers of needles, 24 bunches of corn shucks, 142 butcher knives, 2 coffee pots, 1 camp kettle, 34 frying pans, 36 hatchets, 5 boxes of caps, 2 pounds of lead, and 9 pounds of powder.

In 1874 the recalcitrant Cimarrón Indians were supposed to be transferred to the Abiquiú Agency, but a special agent, A. G. Irvine, was assigned to Cimarrón instead. The Muaches and Jicarillas remained.

The Indians in the upper Chama River area continued to consist of Capotes, Weenuches, and Jicarilla Apaches. The Utes there were sometimes peaceful and sometimes not. They were displeased with the Treaty of 1868, but in 1869 their alcoholic agent benignly reported that they appeared to be agreeable, and only one case of "drunkardness" was known.[28] Some of the Utes were keeping goats and even consuming goat milk, he reported.

When William F. M. Arny set out in 1870 as a special agent to conduct a survey of New Mexico's Indians, he provided more specific information about these Ute bands. He found 286 Capotes who followed Sobotar as their leader and another 79 who followed Chaves, the latter a renegade group that was stealing livestock. Another Capote, Cornea, had gone to the Los Pinos Agency to receive a distribution, but the others refused to go there and were complaining because rations had not been issued in the Chama Valley. Other complaints pertained to miners who were on their reservation and to increased travel on the wagon road. Sobotar told Arny that his Capotes intended to drive the miners out.[29]

Conditions deteriorated from the time of Arny's visit, and in 1872 rumors were flying that Indians around Tierra Amarilla were planning to go to war. This alarm was sounded when Sobotar and his followers went to Utah and stole some horses. Agent John S. Armstrong sent a messenger with orders to restore the horses, but Sobotar refused to give them up. The Presbyterian Armstrong, another in a seemingly long list of agents with a penchant for liquor, may have overreacted, for he requested that troops come to Tierra Amarilla. At a meeting with Sobotar and about thirty of his men, the cavalry commander demanded that both the stolen property and the culprits be surrendered. Instead, after the meeting Sobotar's Utes and some allies armed themselves, and shots were exchanged briefly. Sobotar's warriors galloped away to the mountains, and cavalry reinforcements were sent to Tierra Amarilla.[30]

After this incident Armstrong and his agency were moved from Abiquiú to Tierra Amarilla to lessen chances of trouble around settlements in the lower Chama River Valley. Officially retaining the name Abiquiú Agency, the headquarters moved into buildings abandoned by

Fort Lowell in 1869. Later that year Armstrong issued a large quantity of goods at Tierra Amarilla, thereby helping to restore peaceful relations.

The list of items issued is worth comparing with those available at Cimarrón a few months later. At Tierra Amarilla the "Capota" and "Wemenutche" Utes received 36,450 pounds of beef, 300 blankets, approximately 366 pounds of tobacco, 150 awls, 60 pounds of brass wire, 200 butcher knives, 60 fanegas of corn (a fanega is a Spanish measure equaling about a bushel), 200 pounds of sugar, 241 pounds of coffee, almost 53 yards of blue cloth, 57 camp kettles, 204 tin cups, 150 frying pans, 33 pounds of harness leather, 56 hatchets, 180 hats, 2,000 yards of manta (handwoven woolen goods), 6 fanegas of salt, 108 sheep, 21-plus caps "per C," 325 pounds of lead, and 236 pounds of powder.[31]

As had the Muaches at Cimarrón, in late 1873 the Capote Utes agreed to move to the proposed Southern Ute Reservation, but no immediate change occurred. In 1874 settlers were still complaining about depredations, and Capotes protested about intrusions by miners on their land. The commissioner of Indian Affairs sent a letter emphasizing the agreements that had been made and clearly defining the boundaries of the future Southern Ute Reservation, which were to include the strip, fifteen miles from north to south, in southernmost Colorado Territory beginning where the San Juan River crossed the New Mexico–Colorado border and extending west to the Navajos' reservation.[32] The strip would be occupied exclusively by Muaches, Capotes, and Weenuches, according to the commissioner.

In the late 1860s the region west of the Chama River and north of the San Juan River was still used primarily by Weenuche Utes, whose numbers, contemporaries estimated, ranged anywhere from 485 to 1,500; Abiquiú Agent Lieutenant J. B. Hanson reported 650 in 1871, which is probably the most accurate figure. They roamed west into southeastern Utah and overlapped with the less numerous San Juan Southern Paiute Band in that region. To the south the Weenuches traded with Navajos, exchanging buckskins and furs for blankets—a commerce that ensured friendship among at least some members of the tribes. Weenuches also traveled on occasion to Abiquiú and later to Tierra Amarilla to receive distributions of goods. In rare instances members of the band went as far east as Cimarrón to trade with Muaches for buffalo robes. McCook reported to the commissioner of Indian Affairs that Weenuches were hostile toward the Tabeguaches, and like the other southern bands, they had been opposed to moving to the reservation delineated by the Treaty of 1868.

When Arny made his survey in 1870, he reported finding many Weenuches under Cabezon, Powarit, and Cabeza Blanco on the La Plata River, where they were growing food and possessed large herds of horses, sheep, and goats. He also found Ignacio with fifty-six warriors west of the Animas River who told Arny they would sell their lands in the San Juan Mountains if an agency were provided on the Los Pinos River, as promised in 1868. The river referred to by Weenuches would have been the stream in today's Archuleta County, not the one in Conejos County or the one where the Los Pinos Agency had been located. Otherwise, they would accept an agency in the "Sheberitche Utah Indian Country," meaning the region of the La Sal Mountains around Moab or the Blue Mountains near Monticello. Ignacio's people wanted sheep and goats in exchange for the mining lands.[33]

In his report Arny explained a problem associated with inducing Weenuches to move to the same reservation as Muaches. The Weenuches were led by several head men with three principal leaders—Persechopa, Ignacio, and Savillo in order of rank. Savillo was actually a Muache, a brother of Kaniache. Ignacio killed Savillo, predictably leading to animosity and mistrust among Muaches. Savillo and Manuel, a Ute, had attacked a Navajo camp, killed a man and a woman in it, and made off with several horses and a large herd of sheep and goats. In retaliation the Navajos had stolen several of Ignacio's horses, as well as many others from settlers near Abiquiú.[34] Ignacio then killed Savillo.

Strains between Weenuches and others were also reflected in an unusual incident in 1873 in the midst of negotiations with Felix Brunot to sell the mining country in the Consolidated Ute Reservation. Independently, Ignacio made a private agreement with one Captain John Moss. In exchange for a hundred horses and many blankets, Moss was granted the right to farm and mine on thirty-six square miles on the upper La Plata River, where Moss located Parrott City.

Weenuches and Capotes sometimes cooperated in raids on Navajo livestock, but in 1871 an episode had repercussions extending beyond the frequent Ute-Navajo conflicts. Navajo Agent James Miller reported that in an attempt to steal Navajo horses, Utes "belonging to the Abiquiú Agency now living near the San Juan River" on the Navajos' reservation had wounded a Navajo. Miller noted that this incident occurred at the location where these tribes customarily met to trade peaceably, but to prevent further trouble the trade should be stopped, and the Utes should be sent to their reservation. The following year, as Miller, an agency trader, and a physician for the Navajos, John Menaul, camped on the San Juan River, two Utes were seen firing on the camp. Miller was killed, and five ponies were stolen. When crimes were committed by members or a member of a tribe, federal government policy mandated that it was the duty of the chief to turn over the guilty party or parties or to exact punishment, and Ouray, as chief, was duly ordered to do so in this case. In 1873 Ouray's Utes killed one of Miller's murderers, who belonged to a Ute-Paiute renegade group.[35]

As Weenuches continued to have contact with both Navajos and Southern Paiutes in the Four Corners region—a triumvirate that still exists today—Utes intermingled and intermarried with both groups, especially the Paiutes. Weenuches brought goods to trade for Navajo goods around Montezuma Creek, Bluff, and Blue Mountain in Utah.[36]

Additional glimpses of Utes in the Four Corners came from photographer William Henry Jackson in the early fall of 1874. He observed an Indian trail that had been used recently by about a hundred Indians with horses and goats, and at Yellow Jacket Canyon he saw a Weenuche trading party heading south with furs to trade with Navajos. In the country north of Sleeping Ute Mountain he came upon a nearly dry spring that had been excavated to a depth of three or four feet to create an "insignificant" source of water that was "oozing away," and in Montezuma Canyon he discovered that Weenuches were able to grow corn without irrigation. When Jackson's party approached the wickiup village of Poco Narraguinip, the Ute headman hospitably fed the explorers from the precious supply of boiled green corn. The next day, when Jackson's pack animals trampled the cornfield and angered the Indians, Jackson's party departed hastily.[37]

In the meantime, Territorial Governor McCook, his political backers, miners, and would-be settlers had little sympathy for the Utes. McCook contended that it was impossible for him "to comprehend the reasons which induced the Colorado officials and the General Government to enter into a treaty [in 1868] setting apart one third of the whole area of Colorado for the exclusive use and occupation of the Ute nation," whose members he described as "indolent savages."[38] He contrasted the 12,800 acres each head of a Ute family—an "aboriginal vagrant"— enjoyed with the 160 acres a white homesteader could obtain. McCook's protest, of course, ignored the rights of Indians, the "aboriginal vagrants" to whom all of the land had once belonged.

Trespassers took matters into their own hands while McCook fumed. As former agent Albert Pfeiffer, Charles Baker, and their partners had foreseen a decade earlier, rich minerals in the San Juans were luring miners onto Indian lands. An additional intrusion from New Mexico by Spanish-speaking settlers took place in the lower country. The settlers were farming and ranching along the San Juan River and its tributaries, and the Weenuches wanted them to leave. The persistence of such miners and settlers can be explained, if not excused, by population pressure, the loss of inheritance, scarcity of land and water, economic failure elsewhere, or simply a lust for adventure. In the view of those who pressed for the right for a new chance in this vast open country, the Indians had far more land than they needed, but the Indians had always moved through large amounts of land to hunt and to collect food in their traditional way, which they were not inclined to give up.

It was such pressures as these that got Los Pinos Agent Trask in trouble. He maintained a strict interpretation of the law as it applied to the Ute reservation, and his attitude contributed to his abrupt replacement by McCook's brother-in-law, Adams. In 1871, when Ouray wanted troops sent to the southern portion of the reservation because of illegal entries there, Trask wrote to Washington for advice. He was told to warn the miners to leave. Trask then wrote to Adnah French, a leader among the Silverton-Howardsville trespassers, and told him and others to depart. In early 1872 a long, sarcastic reply came, signed "Indignantly, Adnah French," who insisted that the miners were there with the permission of the Indians and of civil and military authorities and that no one would be leaving without orders from the government. Meanwhile, Governor McCook was again protesting about the size of the reservation, and the territorial legislature sent a memorial to President Grant asking him to reduce the reserve's size or at least to allow miners to enter it.[39]

Only Trask was surprised, then, in June 1872 when Charles Adams rode in a buggy across Cochetopa Pass to assume the agent's post. (By then the industrious Otto Mears had replaced the old trail with a road to connect his mercantile enterprises at Saguache and Los Pinos and to serve his mail contract to Los Pinos.) By July Adams had brought Ouray and ten other Utes to Denver for a meeting to plan a general council for negotiating an agreement to sell the part of the reservation that contained the valuable mines. In August Governor McCook, Arny from New Mexico, Felix R. Brunot, and two other members of the Board of Indian Commissioners, along with its secretary, joined about 1,500 Ute Indians at the agency to discuss a cession of the mining lands. Others who attended were the commandant of Fort Garland, former agent Head, Special Agent Thompson, interpreters, and assorted interested citizens, including Mears. Representatives of all Ute bands were present with the conspicuous exceptions of Muache Chief Kaniache and of all Weenuches. The issue at hand involved a sale, not a treaty, inasmuch as Congress had abolished Indians' sovereignty and treaty rights in 1871. Brunot, a wealthy commissioner from Pennsylvania, was simultaneously trying to inveigle Shoshones to give up part of their Wind River Reservation, as he succeeded in doing in 1874 when Shoshone Chief Washakie was promised an annual stipend of $500.

At the four-day council at Los Pinos in 1872, Ouray flatly asserted that the Utes did not wish to sell any of their land and that it was the government's responsibility to remove intruders.[40] Clearly, some persuasion would be needed, so in November Adams, Thompson, and the ubiquitous Mears escorted a few Tabeguache and White River Utes to Washington. The party included Ouray, Chipeta (on her first visit to the capital), Sapinero, Guero, Piah, Washington, Ouray's sister Susan, her husband Johnson (Cavanish), and Jack. They visited with President Grant and Mrs. Grant in the White House and with officials of the Indian Office. The beautiful Chipeta easily won the admiration of all. The excursion lasted three months, during which time the travelers took in the sights of Baltimore, Philadelphia, the zoo in New York's Central Park, and Boston.

When Brunot again came west in the spring of 1873, Adams and Ouray went to Cheyenne to meet him and convinced him of the importance of locating Ouray's long-lost son, Pahlone, as a means of earning the chief's support. Eventually, an intensive search for the boy produced a young man called Friday, who was living with Southern Arapahos. He was later brought to Washington to meet Ouray and insulted the chief by denying any Ute ancestry. Eventually, Friday did agree to come to Colorado, but he died on the way.[41] Meanwhile, another general council was scheduled at Los Pinos Agency for August.

Before the August 1873 council was scheduled, a Miners' Cooperative and Protective Association had organized. Consequently, when the secretary of the interior asked the War Department to send troops to southwestern Colorado to evict miners by June 1, the miners had a united voice, and with it they promised to use gunfire to resist expulsion. Territorial Governor Samuel H. Elbert, who had replaced McCook, backed down. Orders for troops were withdrawn, the date for the miners' departure was postponed, and 3,000 more miners rushed in and filed claims in the San Juans during the summer.

At Los Pinos Agency a crowd of 2,000 Utes, about 300 white people, officials, cooks, servants, clerks, and a regiment from Fort Garland assembled and waited for Brunot, who had been delayed not only by his search for Pahlone but also by negotiations with Crow Indians.[42] This time, civilians without credentials were excluded. By the time Brunot arrived, many in the crowd had been at Los Pinos for nearly six weeks, and some Utes had left. After considerable argument among the Indians, Mears suggested that Ouray be promised an annual stipend of $1,000 for as long as he was chief and the Utes remained peaceful. Ouray capitulated, and the agreement for the cession was signed on September 13.

Some Utes believed that in the Brunot Agreement they were ceding only the mining claims, where no houses would be built. Instead, they relinquished title to the heartland of the San Juan Mountains, roughly a sixty-by-ninety-mile piece of land, nearly a quarter of the reservation in 1868. The ceded portion began fifteen miles north of the New Mexico–Colorado border, ran to a point ten miles north of the 38th parallel, and then east to the eastern boundary of the reservation. This left the narrow strip on the south, along the Colorado–New Mexico border, for the Southern Ute Reservation for Muaches, Capotes, and Weenuches. The Muaches and Capotes agreed to this arrangement within a few weeks in separate negotiations, which have been discussed earlier in this chapter. Also excluded from the cession was any part of the Uncompahgre Valley. The agreed price for this sale of land by the Utes was a half million dollars, the annual interest on which (twenty-five thousand dollars) was to be paid annually by the federal government to the Consolidated Ute bands: the Tabeguaches, Muaches, Capotes, Weenuches, Yampas, Grand Rivers, and Uintahs of Colorado.[43]

Trouble soon arose in the Uncompahgre Valley. Ouray had dictated a long letter to Brunot to be sent to Governor Elbert explaining the importance of excluding the valley, where he and his band had customarily wintered and raised crops and livestock. The letter said in part:

> Perhaps some of the people will not like it because we do not wish to sell our valley and farming lands, but we think we have good reasons for not doing so. We expect to occupy them ourselves before long for farming and stock raising. About eighty of our tribe are now raising corn and wheat, and we know not how soon we shall have to depend on ourselves for our bread. We do not want to sell our valley and farming lands for another reason. We know if we should the whites would go on them, build their cabins and drive in their stock, which would of course stray upon our lands, and then the whites themselves would crowd upon us till there would be trouble. . . . We feel it would be better for all parties for a mountain range to be between us. We are perfectly willing to sell our mountain lands, and hope the miners will find heaps of gold and silver.[44]

Instead, a survey in 1874 included in the cession a strip near the present towns of Ouray and Ridgway, a parcel at the south end of the

Uncompahgre Valley that was highly prized by the Utes because of its sacred hot springs. It is believed that Ouray may have had an adobe cabin at the spring. As a result of this error, deliberate or not, miners and land promoters quickly poured in before a small notch was withdrawn and added to the southern end of the reservation. Called the Four-Mile Strip, the notch was ceded by the Utes in 1878 because of persistent trespassers at a price of $10,000, which was not paid until several generations later.

After the San Juan Cession was signed, Utes again went to the nation's capital with Adams and Mears. During this visit Ouray met Friday (Pahlone) face-to-face for the first time in a decade. The sojourn also produced some legends, true or not, that white society enjoyed circulating for years with condescending chuckles. One tale had the Utes visiting the White House in swallow-tail coats and trousers with the seats cut out. Another story had Grant asking, "What is the greatest thing, Chief Ouray, you have seen in our civilization?" and Ouray responding, "Little children working."[45]

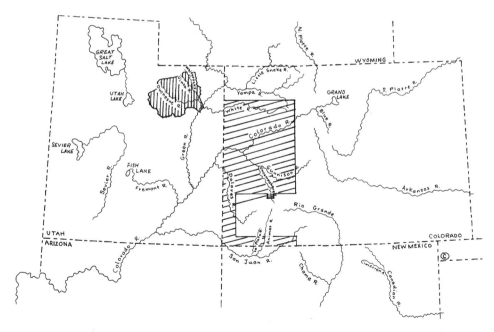

Reservations following the Brunot Agreement of 1873 and the San Juan Cession. The Four-Mile Strip, a small notch in the Uncompahgre Valley that contained some of the Utes' choice hot springs, was restored to the reservation but was later ceded.

Back in Colorado Territory, as Mears forged his toll roads into the exploding San Juan mines, Grant removed Elbert to make way again for McCook as governor. Elbert had originally been installed because of protests in Colorado about corruption in territorial affairs. Grant's spoils system had won after all.

The winter of 1874 witnessed an anomalous incident that has lingered long in Colorado lore. In late January a score of hungry prospectors, traveling east from Utah, came into the Uncompahgre Valley where Chief Ouray, wintering there as usual, recommended that they remain until spring. He allowed them to camp at a cabin near his farm. After a three-week rest, five of the prospectors started out for Saguache by way of the agency cow camp at Gunnison and the Los Pinos Agency, but they became lost en route. Agent Adams sent a rescue party with supplies. Although a few followed Ouray's advice and waited in the Uncompahgre Valley, another five prospectors left, taking a short but snowy route through the headwaters of the Lake Fork of the Gunnison. When the leader of the group, Alferd (or Alfred) Packer, appeared alone at the agency in March and announced that his companions had perished, he appeared remarkably well fed, as indeed he was because he had cannibalized his late companions. Utes and agency employees investigated, and Adams assisted in Packer's subsequent arrest.

This episode brought much public attention not only to Packer but also to the agency and Adams, and Unitarians noticed that a person who was not from their denomination was the agent at Los Pinos. Adams was thereupon replaced by the Reverend Henry F. Bond. At many agencies an agent's wife became the schoolteacher, as Mrs. Adams had, with an annual salary of $1,000, and Mrs. Bond took over the post. Virtually no Ute children attended school, however, because most parents refused to send them. Nevertheless, the federal government's goal of civilizing the "savages" required that schools be built and operated on all agencies.

A glimpse of life at Los Pinos Agency in the summer of 1874 is found in accounts of photographer Jackson and journalist Ernest Ingersoll, who was traveling with Jackson at the time. The accounts also reveal the lengths to which a photographer would go to capture images of cooperative subjects like Ouray, Chipeta, and Piah and uncooperative ones like Shavano, Guero, and most of the other Utes at the agency. When foiled in their attempts to photograph unwilling people, the visitors instead wrote descriptions of distribution day, for which about seventy lodges had gathered. The Indians camped a few miles east of the agency in an open area where Los Pinos and Cochetopa Creeks join and came into the agency for the distribution. Women took turns drawing rations, but when livestock was turned loose the men gave chase on their ponies and shot them. The women then rushed out to cut off their share of the meat. The agency was described as consisting of about a dozen log buildings and the agent's building, which was built of lumber. Ouray's little house was very modestly furnished. The chief was said to have ordinarily worn a broadcloth suit, but he donned his fine buckskin attire for the portrait Jackson made.

In an effort to learn what the visitors were doing and when they would be leaving, Ouray sent an emissary, Billy, to call at Jackson's camp. Jackson said he would be moving on the next day. A government survey team was also camped nearby, and objections were voiced about their presence on Indian land, too.[46] Billy is an individual warranting mention, for he bears a striking resemblance to Ouray in photographs that frequently are misidentified as the chief himself. It seems safe to speculate that Billy might have been Ouray's son. His mature appearance in photographs suggests that he was born in the 1850s. Another interesting individual at the agency was Piah, whom Ingersoll said was Ouray's brother-in-law. Piah's documented presence at Los Pinos Agency, Middle Park, Denver's special agency, and White River underscores the fluid familial and band relations that continued to be typical of the Ute tribe as it moved from place to place.

During the early years of the Uintah Valley Reservation in Utah, conditions for the Western Ute bands were no more stable and homogeneous than they had been among the Eastern Utes in New Mexico and Colorado since 1868. The boundaries of Utah's reservation were vague, but generally they were delineated by the watershed of the Uinta Basin, west of the Green River. Although Utah Utes were not included in the Treaty of 1868, a peace treaty was agreed to in Utah's Strawberry Valley that same year. After that council many people followed Chief Tabby onto the two million-acre reservation to live, but not everyone came and not everyone stayed.

After the Black Hawk War ended in 1867, Seuvarits (Elk Mountain Utes) continued occasional raids around the upper Sevier River. The band roamed from the La Sals westward through Castle Valley and the San Rafael Swell country until 1873 when, decimated by disease, most of the survivors settled on the reservation. Fish Lake Utes resisted removal from their favorite haunts and never went to the Uinta Basin. Kanosh's Pahvant Utes did go to the basin in 1868 but returned to Corn Creek annually to hunt and to gather wild foods, even raising a few crops and begging from the Mormons who had taken over their farm at Kanosh. In 1872, however, Kanosh's people returned and stayed at Corn

Creek.[47] The Mormon community gave the Utes land at a spring just north of Corn Creek in 1875 in exchange for their campsite close to the town of Kanosh. People from the two groups appear to have gotten along reasonably well, although a few scuffles occurred and the townspeople were not above playing unkind practical jokes, as when the local blacksmith burned the hands of an unsuspecting Indian with a hot wagon tire.

Chief Kanosh's personal history entails the story of a Ute who was exceptionally friendly with Mormons, beginning with his baptism in 1858. Like many other Utes and his Mormon neighbors, Kanosh had multiple wives. The first three met tragic deaths. The first was killed by Indians after she became insane. The second, a beauty, murdered the third in a fit of jealousy, and the second was starved to death as punishment. The fourth was Sally, an Indian servant (like many, called a "tame" Indian) raised as a Mormon in the home of one of Brigham Young's brothers-in-law. After she married Kanosh she lived in a log cabin at Kanosh, where she sorely missed the refinements of the house in Salt Lake City. She participated in church activities such as the Relief Society, and Kanosh was ordained an elder in 1876.

When Kanosh visited Washington in 1872 with Antero, Tabby, and other Western Utes, he received the customary peace medal. Because large patches of his skin lost their pigmentation, Kanosh's detractors liked to blame his conversion to the Church of Latter-day Saints and his friendship with the Mormons. Sally died in 1879 and Kanosh in 1881 or 1884. He received a proper church funeral.[48] Since he had no children, those who later bore his name were descendants of an adopted child, of admirers who adopted his name, or of people who lived at Kanosh.

Other groups of Utah's Utes chose not to go to the Uintah Valley Reservation or to leave it. Some went to Thistle Valley, where Brigham Young sent Mormons to help them farm, with much success. One of their missionaries, Mormon V. Selman, remained at Thistle Valley as a teacher for more than two decades, and during that service he compiled a dictionary of the Ute language. With Mormon aid, some Utes acquired their own farms.

In the 1870s White River Utes led by Douglass were also at Thistle Valley. Another seventy-five Sanpits stayed in the Sanpete Valley where they, too, acquired some land with Mormon assistance. Off-reservation Fish Lake Utes, intermixed with Southern Paiutes, later received some allotments from public land around Koosharem, and some went to Kanosh. Still other Utes who were supposed to be on the Uintah Valley Reservation chose instead to join White River Utes in Colorado.

Administration of the Uintah Valley Reservation got off to an uncertain start. Several agents came and went during the initial five years. Beginning in 1866, the first agents had few Indians, fewer supplies, and no established agency headquarters. Pardon Dodds, a Mormon, arrived in 1868 and, following the advice of Chief Antero, selected Whiterocks as the agency site. The next year George W. Graffam came as agent, but he disliked everything about the situation and soon departed. The *Salt Lake Herald* reported in July 1870 that Tabeguache Utes had attacked the agency on July 18 and burned its buildings. One employee escaped, but another was missing. The Indians claimed that white people, wishing to cause trouble, were the culprits. The incident recalls the burning of Robidoux's Fort Winty only a generation earlier at almost the same location.

In 1871 a Presbyterian agent, John J. Critchlow, came to Whiterocks, and his wife and children later joined him. Mrs. Critchlow became the first teacher in the log schoolhouse erected at Whiterocks in 1874. Critchlow remained for twelve years and was able to establish a fair degree of authority, as well as getting a number of Utes to maintain small farm plots as Dodds had done previously. But all was not tranquil. Some of the Utes threatened to kill a saddlemaker, David Jones, because he was a Mormon, and Mormon traders Pardon Dodds and George Basor were giving Critchlow a difficult time because he purchased materials from gentile merchants.[49] Critchlow, in turn, complained about the caliber of his employees.

Critchlow also fretted because the agency's Ute Indians failed to stay on the reservation and others were coming from Colorado to collect rations. The Utes were doing what they had often done elsewhere, traveling to as many distribution points as possible in all three territories, regardless of agency affiliation. When Critchlow refused to make distributions to the White Rivers, his Uintahs insisted that he should do so because the visitors were friends. Similarly, Tabby and his followers went to the White River Agency.[50]

Traveling back and forth across reservation boundaries, Douglass appeared at Whiterocks in 1872 and became a particular thorn in Critchlow's side. Douglass belittled the Utes who were farming, saying Indians were not supposed to do such work. He encouraged some Uintah Valley Reservation Indians to come with him to Sanpete County, where a gathering was taking place that summer. The council was attended by Uintahs, White Rivers, Capotes, Elk Mountain Utes, and Paiutes and may actually have included Weenuches.[51]

When White River Agent John S. Littlefield received word of these goings on, he blamed the vagrancy on an epidemic of "lung disease" that had infected about a fourth of his eight hundred White River Utes in the spring of 1872. Littlefield explained that the Utes had decided to go to Navajo country to recover. After Littlefield received a telegram from Salt Lake City about his wandering Indians, he went to Utah and found them, still ailing, at Provo. Some died on this journey. He asked the various Colorado Utes whom he met in Utah that summer to send delegates to Brunot's upcoming council at the Los Pinos Agency, but they refused to go.[52]

When John Wesley Powell and George W. Ingalls were preparing a report about Utah and Nevada in 1873, they gathered information about Utes, including those who were off the reservation. On the Uintah Valley Reservation, they reported there were 556 Utes, with Tabby recognized as chief of them all. Antero was chief of the "U-in-tats" group, composed of 194 persons. There were 144 Seuvarits on the reservation, these being band members who had survived the recent epidemic, the report said. Prior to 1873, Powell and Ingalls reported, Seuvarits had occasionally come to the agency to collect rations but had not remained. Only thirty-six Sanpits and forty-nine Timpanogots were on the reservation in 1873, and there were three other very small groups, possibly extended families. At Corn Creek there were 134 Pahvants.[53]

Powell had prior experience in the Uinta Basin. When his party came down the Green River in 1869, they had come to Pardon Dodds's agency to obtain provisions, forward mail, and set up an astronomical station. On that occasion Powell met several Indians who proudly showed him the plots of wheat, vegetables, and melons they were cultivating. After this trip Powell took a Northern Ute boy, Richard Komas, to Washington. A handsome young man, Richard attended school in Pennsylvania from 1870 to 1874 and was an interpreter when Utah Utes came to Washington in 1872. He died in 1875.

Powell's 1873 expedition also yielded a fine photographic record of Native Americans in the region. Although they were posed, most of the images have special value because the photographer, John K. Hillers, refrained from dressing his subjects with clothing and props that were inappropriate for the tribe and the period, as did many of a growing number of studio photographers.

What the images failed to show were the disruptive conditions taking place among the Ute Indians of three territories between 1868 and the mid-1870s. Further, the images could not suggest the cataclysm that would strike the Utes in the following half decade. Photographs did not foresee it. Bear himself could not prevent it.

Ute Indians gathered for distribution of rations at an unknown location. The log building refutes the possibility that the scene is the Navajo Springs Subagency, for buildings there were adobe. Courtesy Denver Public Library, Western History Collection.

Ute Indians seen here were playing a game, possibly the popular monte, and were probably gambling. The scene is identified on the photograph as Indiuta, Utah. J. E. Birch photo; courtesy Colorado Historical Society, neg. no. F-37590.

These Southern Ute women and children posed at their agency with traditional water jugs (*kanosh*) in the foreground, although they possessed cotton garments and canvas tents, which were very common by the late 1800s. Buckwalter photo; courtesy Colorado Historical Society, neg. no. F-25713.

Ignacio, chief of the Weenuche Utes and police captain. Courtesy Colorado Springs Pioneers Museum.

The Ouray Boarding School at Randlett, Utah. The children's hair has been cut, and they are dressed in the school's uniforms. (Uniforms varied from school to school.) Used with permission, Utah Historical Society, all rights reserved.

Protesting the opening of the Uintah and Ouray Ute Indian Reservation, these delegates went to Washington in 1905. *Front row, left to right,* Appah and Arrike; *middle row,* Ungacochoop (Red Cap), Kachootch (David Copperfield), Charlie Chavanaux, Witchito; *back row,* Wallace Stark, Charley Mack, John Duncan, Suckive, unknown, Boco White, unknown. Delancey Gill photo, Smithsonian Office of Anthropology; courtesy Utah Historical Society, all rights reserved.

A small group of the many Northern Ute Indians who left the Uintah and Ouray Ute Indian Reservation in 1906 to go to South Dakota. *Left to right*, Willie Willie, Arapo, Dewey (child), Duchesne George, Slim Jim, and Chief Red Cap. Used with permission, Utah Historical Society, all rights reserved.

Northern Ute Indians in South Dakota, 1907. *Left to right*, Chuponas, Apona, Pompy, Rainbow. C. C. McBride photo, 1907; Robert G. Lewis, Esq., Collection.

In 1894 Chief Severo (center) posed for photographs at the Broadmoor Casino near Colorado Springs, where he and others entertained spectators with a mock battle. Courtesy Colorado Springs Pioneers Museum.

When Chipeta came to Colorado Springs with other Ute Indians for a festival in 1911, she called at the home of Mrs. Charles Adams. Courtesy Colorado Springs Pioneers Museum.

In 1912 Southern Ute Indians, led by Chief Buckskin Charlie, rode down the Ute Trail in Ute Pass, west of Manitou Springs, Colorado, at the time of its dedication and marking by community leaders. Courtesy The Colorado College Special Collections.

In 1913 the town of Ouray, Colorado, whose citizens had been eager to drive out the Utes only a generation earlier, paraded Chipeta and her traveling companions through town. Courtesy Colorado Historical Society, neg. no. F-32357.

Ration day at Navajo Springs Subagency. S. F. Stacher photo, 1908: courtesy Colorado Historical Society, neg. no. F-39622.

Navajo Springs Subagency, which served Weenuche Ute Indians from 1906 until 1918. The subagency was about two miles south of Towaoc, which replaced it as the agency. Sleeping Ute Mountain is in the background. Charles Goodman photo; courtesy Colorado Historical Society, neg. no. F-30234.

Weenuche Ute women playing shinny near Navajo Springs Subagency in 1908. The game, popular with many Native American tribes, was similar to field hockey. One game might last for several hours, and wagers on the outcome were common. S. F. Stacher photo, 1908; courtesy Colorado Historical Society, neg. no. F-1614.

Sun Dance enclosure at Ignacio in 1960. Courtesy Colorado Historical Society, neg. no. F-30366.

After the conflict of 1915 in Utah's San Juan County, Ute prisoners were transported on the Denver and Rio Grande from Thompson to Salt Lake City. They were escorted by a government agent, a United States marshal, the superintendent of the railroad, and General M. Scott. The four Utes are, *left to right*, Polk, Jess Posey, Posey, and Tse-ne-gat. Used with permission, Utah Historical Society, all rights reserved.

Chipeta, left, enjoyed traveling by train from the Uintah and Ouray Reservation to Ignacio, where she visited her old friend Buckskin Charlie, chief of the Southern Ute Tribe, and his wife Emma. Courtesy Archives, University of Colorado at Boulder Libraries.

Emma Naylor Buck and the famous Chief Buckskin Charlie, in late years. His Indian name was Sapiah, also Peah or Piah, which is easily confused with the name of the Northern Ute, Piah. Emma was the best-known of the chief's wives. Courtesy Fort Lewis College, Center of Southwest Studies.

Watermelon feast at Ignacio. Numerous festivals of various kinds, including baby shows and especially agricultural fairs, were held on Ute reservations beginning in the early 1900s. Courtesy Fort Lewis College, Center of Southwest Studies.

The Towaoc Boarding School served both Ute and Navajo children. Later, the Ute Mountain Ute Agency used the buildings. Courtesy Colorado Historical Society, neg. no. F-39611.

The Southern Ute Boarding School at Ignacio had large dormitories as well as other school buildings. The Southern Ute Indians' tribal offices now occupy some of them. Courtesy Colorado Historical Society, neg. no. F-1612.

Pupils at boarding schools, like the one at Ignacio, spent time in activities like raising onions in addition to learning the "three Rs." Courtesy Denver Public Library, Western History Collection.

8

▼ ▼ ▼

Beating Plowshares into Swords
(1875–1881)

For Colorado's Ute Indians, the second half of the 1870s was marked by confusion, frustration, anger, and tragedy. Utah's Utes were adjusting to life in the Uintah Valley, as were Tabeguaches in the Uncompahgre Valley. Muaches and Capotes, reluctant for so long to take up a permanent home on a reservation in Colorado, were finally accepting the necessity of yielding to pressure. They began to move out of northern New Mexico. Many Weenuches continued to be more independent and roamed in the Four Corners area.

In late 1874 Agent S. A. Russell was notified that Tierra Amarilla would continue with a "special agent, no doubt you," while another special agent, A. G. Irvine, would take care of Cimarrón. Services provided by the subagencies were limited, however. Toward the end of 1875 Irvine's Indians, numbering about six or seven hundred Utes and Jicarilla Apaches, augmented by other Indians who came from time to time, were destitute. Irvine was giving them inferior and scant rations. Flour was moldy and maggot-infested, and meat was spoiled. On one occasion the recipients threw the meat in Irvine's face. He drew his gun, and an exchange of fire ensued in which a Ute-Jicarilla named Barela was killed. Once again the military intervened by sending troops and provisions.

Such difficulties caused about two hundred Muaches to temporarily join White River Utes during the summer of 1875. A related problem was the constant flow of alcohol at Cimarrón. A Spanish-speaking woman was taken to court seventeen times for trafficking in liquor, it was said, but legal actions were no more than temporary inconveniences.[1]

The agency at Cimarrón was officially closed in late 1876, the agent's salary was terminated, and the buildings that had been leased on the land grant for years were supposed to be vacated. A Presbyterian agent assigned by the Pueblo Agency at Santa Fe continued some distributions, though, because the Indians were surviving otherwise only by hunting, fishing, stealing what they could, and peeling bark from trees. The final days of operations at Cimarrón finally came in July 1878, and Muaches at last began their trek to the Southern Ute Agency, while Jicarilla Apaches, contrary to previous agreements, were assigned to Abiquiú.

Like Cimarrón, the agency at Tierra Amarilla had been placed under New Mexico's Pueblo Agency at Santa Fe in 1876 by default and had limited resources.[2] Complaints by Ute Indians who still gathered around Tierra Amarilla abounded. They objected to settlers on Ute land, to a toll road across it to Cañon Largo and the San Juan mines, and to the quality of flour and beef from Thomas D. Burns's ranch and store. Toll road construction did not cease, but black troopers—"buffalo soldiers" of the Ninth Cavalry—arrived to try to control settlers and miners, and Indian Commissioner E. A. Hayt ordered that samples of ten percent of all sacks of flour be inspected by agents. Inferior material was to be replaced with goods from suspect contractors, such as Burns and Zadoc Staab in New Mexico. In his effort to wipe out graft, Hayt even required that inferior samples be sent to Washington for scrutiny.[3]

Feisty Utes were still committing depredations in the Tierra Amarilla area and were traveling to multiple distribution points to draw more rations. To control this abuse, the Bureau of Indians Affairs had instituted ration tickets to ensure full issues were made to legitimate families at all agencies, but those coming to Tierra Amarilla refused to accept and use the tickets.[4]

Of the three southern bands, Weenuches were the only ones raising some of their own crops at this time. Cabezon's group, along with some Navajos who farmed on shares, was growing food along the La Plata River in New Mexico, south of the Southern Ute Reservation boundary, but during a Ute hunting trip in 1878 two white homesteaders had taken over the fields. When five companies of troops came in, the situation was resolved when Cabezon agreed to move upstream after the corn was harvested.

To keep the peace in southwestern Colorado and northwestern New Mexico, a post was established on a military reserve at Pagosa Springs in October 1878. Until 1876, when white people built temporary cabins there, Utes had enjoyed sole possession of these popular hot springs for years, for rival claims by Navajos had been decisively put aside long ago by Albert Pfeiffer in a legendary hand-to-hand duel on behalf of his Ute friends. The new military post was called Camp Lewis, although the name was changed to Fort Lewis within a few weeks.[5] Black troops of the Ninth Cavalry were posted here, and a military road was constructed across the San Juan Mountains to provide shorter access than the customary Chama Valley route from Fort Garland to Fort Lewis. (In the 1880s this fort would move to the La Plata River.)

Ironically, at the very time when Muaches were finally arriving at the Southern Ute Reservation in August 1878, Congress complicated matters by passing two bills calling for the removal of the Southern Ute and Tabeguache Bands to the White River portion of the reservation. A commission was soon on its way to Fort Lewis to meet with the southern bands. This astonishing proposal, impossible to justify, can be ascribed to Colorado's incessant push to remove Utes from increasing amounts of land, as well as to railroad builders' determination to exploit mining country. Among the commissioners who met with Utes was an officer of the Denver and Rio Grande Railway, William Sharpless Jackson, husband of Helen Hunt Jackson, an outspoken advocate of the Indian reform movement. Regardless, her husband's railroad was destined to cut through the Southern Utes' reservation in 1881.

The 1878 commission met with Ignacio, Aguillar, and Severo, representatives of the three Southern Ute bands, and they all opposed a move to White River, as did the Tabeguaches. At first an agreement, not consummated, was made to delete the southernmost portion of the reservation, lying south of the 38th parallel, in exchange for the headwaters of streams that flowed from the high mountains on the north and northeast down into the existing Southern Ute Reservation. The matter of ceding the southern portion and subsequently moving to White River was theoretically resolved in November 1878 when a document to that effect was signed with marks by thirty-four Yampa and Grand River Utes, ninety-one Muaches, sixty-one Capotes, sixty-three "Weeminuches," and twenty-three Tabeguaches—but not Ouray. Congress approved the removal in March 1879, but it was not put into effect.[6]

The Southern Ute agency was located briefly at Arboles, but Agent Henry Page reported in 1878 that the agency's first two buildings on the Los Pinos River had been erected in 1877 and that after supplies and annuities arrived in early 1878, 358 Utes and 44 Navajos came to receive them. The arrival of a small detachment of cavalry to investigate depredations irritated the Indians, and their "bad spirit" toward the amount of rations soon led the agent to fear for his safety. Page also reported that herds of cattle belonging to white people were pouring onto the reservation and eating all the grass.

In hopes of preventing trouble on the reservation, Page created a twenty-man, uniformed police force made up of representatives of the three bands. Congress had authorized Indian police in 1878, and within a decade forces existed on nearly all of America's Western reservations. An incentive to join was the pay, five dollars a month for privates and eight dollars for officers. Members were issued badges and uniforms, although the latter were often worn haphazardly. To avoid conflict with white people, Indian police on the Southern Ute Reservation, as elsewhere, dealt only with their own people, and local law enforcement in neighboring white jurisdictions had no authority on reservations. Indian courts also were established.

Despite these accomplishments Page described his Utes as "blanket Indians," living in tepees and brush huts. He reported that they spoke no English but some Spanish. They had some sheep and goats, the latter used for milk as well as meat, but the only cattle were a hundred head belonging to Cabezon on the La Plata River. Of the reservation's more than 864,000 acres, only three percent consisted of irrigable bottom land along streams.[7]

Although he gave a larger count in 1879, Page reported in 1880 that there were 197 Capotes, 254 Muaches, and 356 Weenuches. Muaches were roaming, and many Weenuches, who had never gotten along well with other Southern Utes, were staying in the western part of the reservation, he said.

Troublesome encounters between Weenuches and cattle ranchers, who were arriving in southwestern Colorado and southeastern Utah in the late 1870s, were predictable, although it is impossible to say whether all participating Indians were Weenuches or Southern Paiutes of the San Juan Band. The early white people in Colorado's Mancos River area and Paradox Valley and in Utah's Blue Mountains and La Sal country were vulnerable to attack. A team of Hayden's Geological and Geographical Survey had a taste in 1875 while they were working near the La Sal Mountains. The workers were fired upon by Indians with muzzle loaders, which, luckily for the surveyors, the Indians did not handle with skill. The team was able to escape to the Mancos River and from there to Parrott City. Ouray blamed Paiutes, whereas others blamed Weenuches for this incident.

A year or so later two brothers, George and Silas Green, who were living in the old ruins of the Elk Mountain Mission, were killed near the future town of Moab. The Greens had been running a few head of cattle, as were two prospectors, a mulatto named William Granstaff and a French-Canadian. The latter pair got along with the

Indians by trading whiskey to them until 1881, when they were forced to leave.

In 1879 around Lone Cone, near Norwood, Colorado, while Fred Mayall was trailing cattle, Utes beat him up, made him eat grass, and killed some cows to convince him that he should depart. Strays on the Uncompahgre Plateau were also killed and left to rot, and gardens were destroyed. An exchange of fire between cowboys and Weenuches took place on the La Plata River, and by 1879 ranchers were beginning to worry that the Utes might kill all their strays, which were overrunning the reservation.[8]

Whereas Southern Ute bands had avoided moving onto their reservation until the late 1870s, Tabeguache Utes were somewhat more inclined to recognize their reservation and were even possessive toward it when intruders entered their land. For example, a Ute sheep owner, Catz, resented the toll roads Otto Mears and others had built as soon as the Brunot Agreement was signed. Catz burned their bridges, and only the presence of troops prevented violence on the Four-Mile Strip near Ridgway.[9] Off the reservation, too, Lake City's population complained about vandalism on their property and in their gardens.

Until the Denver Special Agency closed in late 1875, it continued to draw many Ute visitors, lured especially by the availability of liquor. Many of these Utes were from the "Pi-ah band" from Middle Park, as Agent James Thompson referred to them. After being humiliated when Governor McCook kicked him down a flight of stairs, Colorow came into Denver less often. This quarrelsome Indian, who once had hurled Governor Cummings against an office wall, was now concentrating on rural settlers.

Although Tabeguaches roamed widely and camped off their reservation, most maintained fairly good relations with people in the San Luis Valley, South Park, and the area west of Pikes Peak, where ranch families often kept barrels of apples to offer their visitors. In exchange for their kindness, Utes frequently left a freshly killed deer for their hosts, but several homes had an interior room without windows, just in case.

One incident turned ugly in the winter of 1874–1875 when several hundred Tabeguache and White River Utes including Ouray, Shavano, Antelope (Wanzits), and Tabernash camped near James Castello's popular trading post at Florissant. While they were there, J. Pleasant Marksbery came to the store on a horse the Utes believed had been stolen from Antelope, although Marksbery protested that he had purchased it from someone who had bought it the previous spring. The Utes removed Marksbery's saddle and bridle and took the horse to their camp. Marksbery and Shavano then got into a scuffle. Marksbery later went to the Ute camp with a paper he claimed was from Agent Thompson ordering the Utes to release the contested horse. Marksbery departed with it, but he was followed and shot, allegedly by Tabernash, a White River Ute. Ouray surrendered Tabernash to authorities when ordered to do so, but the case did not go to court.[10]

These Utes were in Florissant at a time when they might have been expected to be in their winter camps, but Ouray and others had recently returned from their latest trip to Washington and, one might assume, they were holding a council. There was much to tell about the tour of Eastern cities, for this time art galleries and the theater in New York had been included, but the big issue in the visit to Washington had been the question about who should make decisions concerning the use of annuities—a moot point because the federal government had been delinquent with moneys owed for lands ceded by the Utes. With superintendents no longer in the picture, agents had become directly responsible to commissioners of Indian Affairs and were relatively independent at their agencies. The final, unwelcome conclusion in Washington was that agents rather than Indians should continue to make decisions about how annuities were used.

The agents, some of whom were competent and honest and some of whom were not, had many responsibilities. Following the Brunot Agreement the Reverend Bond at Los Pinos Agency had a new task, that of moving his agency from its original site northwest of Saguache to the Uncompahgre Valley. Horses, cattle, sheep, wagons, the sawmill, and other equipment had to travel many miles over some difficult terrain, and the transfer was not completed until late 1875. A few items were auctioned off, and buildings were abandoned.[11] Mears unaccountably lost some supply wagons and oxen that had been left in the valley of the Cimarron, east of the Uncompahgre Valley, in the winter of 1875–1876, and it was rumored that some of the government herd from the cow camp at Gunnison eluded the roundup and became the foundation of a few pioneer ranches. Bond, however, was blamed for the shortages of livestock and for other losses, and he was replaced as agent. The Utes' relations with his successor, Major W. D. Wheeler, a former military man and a Unitarian, were more harmonious, but a few Utes avoided the agency and were still farming in the Gunnison area in 1878.

The new agency was eleven miles south of Montrose on the west side of the Uncompahgre River, at the present community of Colona. The agency was officially called the Los Pinos Agency, although it was often referred to as the Uncompahgre Agency and Indians attached to it were usually known as Uncompahgre Ute Indians. The old Los Pinos Post Office continued to operate until 1879 at its former location, and a new Uncompahgre Post Office was established with Otto Mears holding the mail contract and hiring men to carry the mail, sometimes by dog sled in winter but more typically by mule train. One of his toll roads to the mining country ran directly past the agency, conveniently enough. (The problem with post office names was compounded when yet another was named Los Pinos. This one was at a crossing of the Los Pinos River in southwestern Colorado near Bayfield.)

In the Uncompahgre Valley the agency soon had several adobe build-ings to serve as an office and as homes for the agent, carpenter, and physician, and the sawmill was in operation again. Most employees bunked in one large building and ate in a common dining hall. Smoking and chatting, Utes habitually hung around the agency regardless of whether goods were being issued. The cow camp was a few miles north of the agency, where, following Ouray's recommendation, livestock was no longer turned loose for a chase on distribution day but instead was corralled and dispatched in an orderly manner. An irrigation ditch was ready to deliver water to the agency and to Ute farms even before the new loca-tion was completely set up, although in all of southwestern Colorado at the time only twenty or thirty Utes were raising a few crops of corn, beans, squash, and melons. More gardens soon appeared in the Uncompahgre Valley.

Ouray's home was eight miles north of the agency at an excellent spring near the present site of the Ute Museum operated by the Colo-rado Historical Society. Long before Ouray's birth, the Domínguez-Escalante expedition had camped here and noted the location's merits. Ouray's first small adobe cabin, in which he and Chipeta had wintered for several years, was replaced with a larger four-room adobe house with a flat roof in the style of countless Hispanic homes he had seen in northern New Mexico and southern Colorado. (The flat roof later was replaced by a pitched one.) In fact, Spanish-speaking laborers built Ouray's house at government expense. Near the dwelling were store-rooms, vegetable cellars, and log and frame outbuildings that served as living quarters for his Mexican employees who cared for the livestock and crops. Ouray had a corral, wagons, and a carriage, which was a gift from Governor McCook.

Within two or three years the chief, who was showing his people what they might accomplish, had nearly a hundred acres of bottom land fenced and planted to vegetables and grain, but his pride was his herd of several hundred beautiful horses, some acclaimed racers. Ouray's greatest wealth, however, was in sheep, totaling about 40,000 head, for he had begun to accumulate flocks before his band moved to the new agency. Luis Montoya of Del Norte took care of the sheep business on shares, with an Indian runner facilitating communication with Ouray who inspected the sheep occasionally.[12] Montoya became a major sheepman in his own right, perhaps thanks to this start.

Gradually, the home of Ouray and Chipeta acquired the furnishings and manner that won praise from their white visitors. Although less lavish than many urban homes, it had luxuries such as carpets, curtains, iron beds, rocking chairs, and a handsome desk, the upper portion of which was a cupboard housing Ouray's guns. Ouray had callings cards, cigars, and wines to offer his guests, although he was a teetotaler himself. Chipeta managed her domestic responsibilities efficiently with the help of adopted "wards" who lived on the property, some returning to their families after becoming homesick.[13] Unable to read or write more than his name, Ouray was assisted by a Spanish-speaking secretary, Mariano. Completing the image of a man who was integrated into the white man's culture, Ouray became a Methodist about 1878, it is often said, although no verification of formal reception or frequent attendance in any Christian church has been found.

Ouray achieved much success, but he lacked one essential—good health. The chief had visited Dr. J. F. Lewis in Cañon City in 1876 and had been diagnosed by him as a victim of nephritis, a chronic kidney disease also known as Bright's Disease.[14] Despite prescriptions filled by Cañon City's druggist, C. W. Talbot, Ouray likely suffered from swelling, pain, nausea, and fatigue during the final years of his life.

Ouray had detractors, but he possessed absolute authority as chief. He had gained his power by distinguishing himself as a hunter, a courageous fighter, an orator, and a person of high intelligence, any of which qualities typically earned Native Americans respect as leaders. Powerfully built, if not tall, Ouray was agile in physical combat, and his intellectual agility paralleled the physical. Some resentment lingered, though, about his appointment by the federal government as chief of all Utes instead of recognition coming solely from his own band or group.

Ouray's accumulation of possessions caused jealousy, no doubt, but compromises with the government led to greater discontent. His advocacy of the white man's schools was one such issue. Hot Stuff, a young man who had been sent away to Pennsylvania's Carlisle Indian School, returned from his unhappy experience there with a fierce desire to kill the chief. Chipeta observed the would-be assassin as he rode through the brush, and Ouray saved his own life by shooting Hot Stuff through the neck.[15] In his memoir *Pioneering in the San Juan,* the Reverend George M. Darley, a pastor in the mining region, told another story about the way Ouray dealt with troublemakers. A Weenuche named Succett created so much trouble whenever he visited the Uncompahgre Valley, even threatening Ouray's life, that the chief let it be known that if Succett ever returned he would be killed. Succett failed to heed the warning and was killed by Osepa under Ouray's orders.[16]

Another strong leader of the Uncompahgre Utes was the war chief and medicine man Shavano. In early years he had often camped a short distance west of Ouray's wintering place. This fine location, called Shavano Valley, shows archaeological evidence of having been popular with many native peoples for centuries. Following some rebellious raiding along the Front Range during the late 1860s, Shavano seems to have accepted the futility of aggression, and in the 1870s he settled on a piece of land in the Uncompahgre Valley near Billy's Creek. Like Ouray, he obtained the assistance of Hispanic laborers and planted a garden and apple trees at his cabin.[17]

The war chief's domestic life belies the continuing agitation in the valley caused by trespassers. Many were crude riffraff bent on taking advantage of the Indians, whom they despised. Miners around Ouray and Dallas and trespassers on the Four-Mile Strip caused problems. A pair of scalawags from the San Luis Valley, Avelino Muniz and Agapito Alleres, set up shop near Ridgway where they illegally sold liquor and firearms. When they made an unfair deal with an Indian in a horse trade, the victim threatened their lives. Muniz killed the Ute and fled into the mountains.[18]

Because illegal traders continued to be the source of much trouble, the agent called for troops to run them out but then changed his mind and told the soldiers to leave when outright warfare seemed possible. This vacillating agent, J. B. Abbott, had arrived from New Hampshire in January 1878 and quickly found much to be unhappy about. In a letter to his brother he complained about his health, about Colorado's cold weather, and about too much responsibility for too little pay, but he nobly asserted that he would prefer to return to New Hampshire rather than to defraud "the poor, miserable wards under my care" as other agents had done.[19] Only a few headmen and Ouray seemed at all intelligent to this New Englander.

Complaints, especially about preceding agents, were common, as their replacements seemed to boost their own reputations by denigrating others, although unquestionably many assertions were true. Abbott had better things to worry about when he began to fear for his life, for his "wards" were demanding more goods than his warehouse contained. The agent again sent for troops, and Otto Mears, the agency's contractor, came to the rescue by delivering two hundred sacks of flour over the Lake Fork and Ouray Toll Road.[20] By the end of the year Abbott was gone, replaced briefly by Leverett Kelley.

Such difficulties played into the hands of Colorado's promoters and politicians, who believed the presence of any Indians, good or bad, was an obstacle to progress. During the 1860s, when Colorado was still a territory with a comparatively small population in need of federal assistance, the prospect of statehood had gained too little support to make it an accomplished fact. By early 1876, though, statehood was on the immediate horizon, and the territorial legislature sent a memorial to Congress calling for the removal of all Utes to Indian Territory in Oklahoma, a fate the Utes dreaded and that Ouray had been able to avert with his compromises.[21] Many Plains Indians had already been forced into Indian Territory, and a military campaign was under way to move any Indians who remained on the Northern Plains. When every man in Lieutenant Colonel George Armstrong Custer's battalion of the Seventh Cavalry was killed in the Battle of the Little Bighorn on June 25, 1876, only a few weeks before Colorado advanced to full-fledged statehood, the clamor to remove all Indians in the West, including Utes, increased.

Advocates of removal conveniently overlooked the role White River Utes had played in the campaign against the Plains Indians in 1876. These tribes were still time-honored enemies of Utes, regardless of similar abuses they suffered as a result of the white migration. When Shoshones, Bannocks, and Crows were allowed to become auxiliaries in the campaign against Sioux and Cheyennes on the Northern Plains in 1876, Utes also wished to join up. In April Uriah Curtis asked permission to enlist three companies of Utes, who, he argued, could inflict more damage with their knowledge of the land and their own style of fighting than could 5,000 troops.

After Custer's defeat thirty-five Utes were permitted to join General George Crook's campaign. Although the *Rocky Mountain News* reported that they had deserted, they, in fact, arrived on August 1, 1876.[22] The best-known of the volunteers was Jack, also called John, Ute John, and Captain Jack. A headstrong, courageous fighter, Jack seemed to become cockier during his service with the army. Soldiers found him entertaining at first. For instance, when dozens of Sioux remains were discovered in tree branches at the Canyon of the Rosebud, Utes and Shoshones overcame any superstitious fear they might have and began knocking down bundles of bones to retrieve trophies such as bows, arrows, and revolvers. Jack boasted that he would be protected because he had been baptized by Mormons many times when he lived with them, and he dared to attack one special bundle that looked like bad medicine to the other Indians. To everyone's amusement, Jack released bones that contained a large nest of scattering field mice.

As the campaign progressed, discontent arose among warriors who felt insulted because they were ordered to travel with the pack train. Some then left, but Jack was determined to "stick it out to the last," and his strong will earned him admiration from soldiers who had previously belittled him. About 250 Utes, Bannocks, and Shoshones were still participating in the campaign in December.[23]

In the ongoing struggles in Colorado, Jack was not the only White River Ute who was determined to stick it out to the end. With few illusions about what their future held, Utes led by Piah and Colorow had taken up the cudgel, especially against settlers in Middle Park, still a favorite hunting ground, for Utes never conceded that they had surrendered their hunting and fishing rights on relinquished lands. In 1875 more than three hundred settlers, afraid of wandering Utes, requested that a military post be set up in Middle Park, but after a cavalry unit looked over the situation it was decided that none was needed. The Indians became more threatening the next year because they were receiving no provisions at White River and also because increased numbers of cattle were competing with game in Middle Park's meadows. When William Byers prohibited Indians from using their old Hot Sulphur Springs, Colorow and Piah became even testier, and Douglass warned that his Indians were ready to go to war.

In 1877 the legislature reiterated the need for a military post in Middle Park. The cavalry again made a reconnaissance, and this time the captain suggested that Egeria Park, south of Steamboat Springs, would be a better location because ranchers were moving into that area as well. Colorow and Piah were furious when they found the big Medicine Springs at Steamboat Springs being fenced off. Still no military post appeared.

The discovery of enormous quantities of silver and the development of mines at Leadville, meanwhile, were luring hordes of prospectors to the headwaters of the Arkansas River and across the Continental Divide, often onto the Ute reservation. Miners staked out claims and settled on the Roaring Fork River, the Crystal River, and even the Flattops in 1878 and 1879. Piah, Colorow, Jack, Washington, and others were busy driving the trespassers out, but Frederick W. Pitkin, a mining man and governor-elect, warned that the Ute lands would be acquired by force if necessary.

By now, even remote Brown's Park was becoming the home of ranchers, some of whom established friendly relations with Indians. For instance, when the Bassett family's daughter Ann was born in 1878 and her mother had no milk, a Ute woman camping nearby with her people became the infant's wet nurse until the Bassetts could obtain a milk cow. The families remained friends for years, and Utes continued to hunt and camp in Brown's Park.[24] This remote area was a popular hangout for a motley mix of outlaws, rustlers, Shoshones, Utes, and eventually some honest ranchers. After Denver's special agency closed, James Thompson with his family took up a ranch in 1876 at Hayden in the Yampa Valley. For the first three years at least, he maintained friendly relations with Ute Indians, many of whom he had known for a long time.

By 1878 the breaking point at White River had been reached. Annuity goods were being held at Rawlins, Wyoming, through the winter of 1877–1878 because the Union Pacific's freight bill had not been paid, and the White River Utes were suffering from hunger and cold. Not surprisingly, they were traveling far and wide to obtain food, blankets, and other necessities. Their agent, the Reverend Edward F. Danforth, previously had written reports that were unusually benign compared to those from most agencies. He had defended the innocence of his Utes when they were accused of thefts and other infractions. Now he complained to Commissioner of Indian Affairs Hayt about the missing supplies, while the Union Pacific agent, in turn, accused Danforth of failing to collect goods that were being stored in Rawlins. Eventually, the blame was laid on a bankrupt freighter but not before false rumors circulated about Danforth's supposedly selling supplies and using wagons for his own profit. He resigned during the winter of 1878–1879.[25]

A few months elapsed before Danforth's successor arrived. In mid-June, a month after the agent came to White River, a shipment was delivered. The new agent who succeeded in obtaining the goods was Nathan C. Meeker, temporarily enjoying the favor of his White River Ute Indians as a result of this achievement. Born in Ohio, Meeker had been educated at the church-affiliated Oberlin College, noted for producing idealists and reformers, and he later worked as a journalist for the New York *Tribune*. He went to Colorado to organize a cooperative agricultural community named for Nathan Meeker's New York editor, Horace Greeley, and edited a newspaper there. When Meeker was in his sixties financial problems at Greeley caused him to need income to support his family. Therefore, he applied for and received an appointment as Indian agent at the White River Agency.

His wife, Arvilla, who was older than he, and one of his daughters, Josephine, followed him to White River in July, and several agency employees also came from Greeley. His age and his thatch of white hair earned him the nickname "Father Meeker." With his theoretical and practical knowledge of agriculture, Meeker believed he could turn his Utes into civilized, self-sufficient farmers, the goal long promoted by the Bureau of Indian Affairs, but he soon encountered hurdles. The agency's climate, with its temperature extremes and short growing season, made agriculture chancy. Only a little farming had been attempted previously at the agency, although farther south, in the warmer Grand Valley of the Colorado River, a few Ute Indians had raised crops of corn, melons, and potatoes and had a few head of cattle.

Within a few weeks after his arrival, Meeker, recognizing that the agency was poorly situated for laying out irrigation ditches and raising crops, decided it should be moved downstream a short distance to Powell Park, where more irrigable land existed. Unfortunately, the Utes pastured hundreds of horses and enjoyed a race track there. Nevertheless, during his first summer Meeker had started irrigation ditches.

By fall, forty acres had been plowed at Powell Park, and some buildings had been moved there from the old agency. Most work was done by employees, but a few Utes earned cash wages for manual labor by digging ditches and doing other tasks. To Meeker's displeasure, many left the reservation during the summer to hunt instead of remaining to irrigate and cultivate the crops they had helped to plant. They returned only when it was time to claim their share of the harvest. Meeker also complained that the Utes did not care for tending the government cattle or its twenty milk cows.

Factions were beginning to develop as Indians grouped around different leaders at White River. The villages of Douglass and Ouray's brother-in-law Johnson were located in Powell Park, as they had been previously. Meeker's decisions regarding farming had a direct impact on these people and their land. Antelope and Jack, whose reputation as a warrior had steadily increased, remained at the former agency site unless they were roaming, as they often were.

Trouble among White River Utes escalated during the summer of 1878. Among the off-reservation wanderers were Piah, Jack, and Washington, who in August traveled east of Denver to hunt. Near Cheyenne Wells, trouble erupted. One story claimed that when a rustler stole a horse near Cheyenne Wells, the Utes were believed to have taken it, and when its owner, Joe McLane, pursued them, they killed him. McLane's brother Louis told another version. He said the horse had returned to the ranch with a blood-stained saddle but no rider, and Indians wearing Joe's clothing were soon seen. In either case, chased by a posse and a detachment of troops from Fort Wallace, the Utes hurried back to Middle Park. About forty Utes camped in the park in a pasture belonging to William S. Cozens who, brandishing a rifle, ran them off. They moved a short distance to Johnson Turner's Junction Ranch, a stage station later known as Tabernash. The Utes began cutting harnesses on horses and tearing down fences while the women set up tepees in a meadow. Turner summoned a posse from Hot Sulphur Springs, and in a charge against the posse Tabernash was killed.[26]

The Ute belief in vengeance for the loss of one of their own had not changed through the centuries, and Tabernash's death was no exception despite his unflattering reputation for drinking sprees and stealing cattle. From Junction Ranch the Utes hurried away toward the west but stopped near the mouth of the Blue River to claim their victim, Abraham Elliott, a rancher who had previously enjoyed friendly relations with Utes. Elliott's family was so terrified that they hid in their house for a day until the Utes were well on their way across the Flattops to the reservation.[27]

Later in 1878 a group of White River Utes attended a council at Hot Sulphur Springs and agreed to make amends for their rampages that year by returning horses they had stolen. Among those signing with their marks were Douglass, Jack, Colorow, Washington, and Johnson.

Thanks to Arvilla and Josephine, Meeker's domestic life was tranquil compared to his frustrating relations in dealing with Utes. A happy young woman, Josephine taught school for about a half-dozen Ute children, who seemed as fond of her as she was of them. She and Arvilla cooked meals that were often enjoyed by Utes who visited with the agent and his family in their house. Also helping with household chores was Jane (Red Jacket), the wife of Pauvitz, a son of the late chief Nevava and brother of both Antelope and Douglass. Jane understood a fair amount of English, which she had learned at Fort Bridger, and Meeker soon suspected that Jane was carrying unpleasant gossip about him to her people and thereby contributing to their growing discontent with him.

Several times in 1878, Jack and others went to the Uncompahgre Valley to express complaints about Meeker to Ouray. They asked Ouray to have Los Pinos Agent Abbott send letters to Washington on the chief's behalf, asking to have Meeker replaced as White River agent. Perhaps feeling the problems were not within his province, Abbott did not write the letters. Although Meeker needed all available support, he quickly lost much hope of forming friendships with contractors, who, he charged, were selling inferior flour to the agency. He reported it was "black flour" that made the children sick and, following the rules stipulated by Hayt, he sent samples of the flour to Washington.[28]

When farming was not occupying his time and attention, Meeker was able to indulge his other talent, writing. He expressed doubts in his 1878 report that most Indians could ever be induced to work, and he quoted Douglass as saying, "White man work; Indian no work but hunt." Meeker also said that Douglass had ordered a young tribal member to disobey the agent's orders to help a merchant by driving his team. During the winter Meeker busied himself with writing an article that expressed his opinions about the character of Colorado's Ute Indians, whose cultural development he compared unfavorably with that of the Ancestral Puebloan and Fremont peoples. He criticized the Utes, "whose constructive and inventive faculties have never been exercised." Along with their many other shortcomings, he cited health problems that resulted from "excessive sexual indulgence" and pontificated that, combined with "a deficiency of the religious and moral sentiments," the result was "a race without ambition." As a first solution, hardly a novel one, he proposed teaching Utes "to work and to live in a fixed home."[29]

Meeker's impatience and intolerance could not have escaped the notice of Indians around the agency, and the frequent communications to officials and newspapers became a matter of great concern to the White River Utes. The tone of the contents alone was suspicious, but another issue was the fact that he was constantly writing specifically about them, an act that violated the taboos of superstitious Indians.

During the bone-dry summer of 1879, White River Utes became increasingly angry and more ferociously determined to save their old way of life, which clearly meant running settlers off the land that had once belonged to the Ute people. With a severe drought in progress, forest fires broke out and spread throughout the mountains of central and northern Colorado. Rightly or wrongly, the conflagrations were blamed on Ute Indians, whereas the Utes insisted careless miners and railroad tie cutters were causing them. A federal law halting the logging of living trees might also have induced woodcutters and the collieries, which supplied smelters, to transform at least some healthy forests into dead stands by means of fire that then got out of hand. In such a dry year lightning probably ignited some as well. Nevertheless, in July Governor Pitkin complained to Commissioner Hayt about off-reservation Utes who were allegedly destroying forests and game in Middle Park and North Park and were even burning houses.

Already well aware in June 1879 that White River Utes were roaming and getting into trouble, Meeker requested troops to help keep them on the reservation. He wanted a trading post on the reservation as well, for he believed the Utes would then have less reason to leave and that he could control the traffic in liquor. Troops began to patrol north and east of the reservation although not on it, and Meeker did not get his proposed trading post. Lawless elements and stores outside the reservation boundaries continued to offer not only firearms and ammunition needed for hunting but also whiskey, a dangerous combination. A number of trading posts in the Yampa Valley and southern Wyoming were magnets for the roving White River Utes, who often visited Peck's place on the Yampa River west of Hayden, the Morgan brothers on the upper Yampa, Baggs on the Little Snake, and, especially, Perkins on the Little Snake.[30]

A long letter written by Mrs. Albert Smart of Hayden to family members back East provides an eyewitness account of events in the summer of 1879, beginning in July. She and Mrs. James Thompson were alone with their children on their ranches, separated by about fifteen miles. Fires began to break out nearby, and Mrs. Smart wrote to Agent Meeker about them. He sent Douglass and another Ute to bring his Indians back to the reservation, but fires continued in the Yampa Valley and elsewhere. The Thompsons left the area, but the Smarts stayed, with Albert fulfilling jobs he had contracted to do for other ranchers around Steamboat Springs. "Old Yarmint" (Yarmony) came by and felt sorry for Mrs. Smart, who was alone with her brood and sick. Next, she fell off a ladder, suffered a miscarriage, and became quite ill.

Indians camped close by, and from them she learned that five hundred black troopers were patrolling Middle Park and that the Utes were very angry about their presence because black soldiers were an "insult" to them. (The patrols in 1878 and 1879 were detachments of buffalo soldiers of the Ninth Cavalry, sent out from Fort Garland and Fort Lewis at Pagosa Springs.) The Utes burned two vacated houses near the Smarts' ranch and left for the reservation. In September Major Thomas T. Thornburgh was in the area with four companies from Wyoming. He assured Albert Smart that it was unnecessary for his family to move because if trouble arose 2,000 troops would be on hand within five days.

The major's confidence proved unjustified. On September 28, Mrs. Smart wrote, an agency employee stopped at the ranch overnight. He was on his way to summon Captain F. S. Dodge's Company D, then patrolling in Middle Park, back to the Yampa Valley where they had been located earlier. The man had met Jack, Colorow, and a few other

Utes on the road, and although they had let him pass, they warned him that the agent was going to be killed. Within only a day or two another man (possibly the army scout Joe Rankin) rode into the ranch and reported that Major Thornburgh had died in a battle with Utes and that the Smarts should leave, as they promptly did. They went to Hot Sulphur Springs, where Mrs. Smart wrote her letter to family members. She died a few weeks later.[31] Although Mrs. Smart's memory may have been affected by stress, her account seems reasonably accurate. It is interesting that she did not mention a fire at Thompsons' home, which several stories have claimed destroyed his property but which Charles Adams, a responsible source, later denied.

As other episodes occurred during the summer, not only close to the reservation but also as far away as North Park, residents panicked. The cavalry responded to calls for protection, and James Pinkham built a blockhouse at Pinkhamton for his neighbors' protection.

At the agency the contest of wills was reaching its climax. A leading figure was Johnson, who had fallen out with Ouray in an argument over stolen horses that Johnson refused to return, and Ouray had shot a bullet into Johnson's arm, breaking it. Although Johnson was very proud of his many fine horses, he showed some willingness to farm and had planted some potatoes. Aware of Johnson's influence as a good example, Meeker had a house built for him and his wife Susan (Ouray's sister) at the agency, but the Ute tricked Meeker into having some horses broken for him. Supposedly, they were for use with a farm wagon, but instead he was racing them. Meeker was furious when he discovered the ruse.

By late summer Meeker had reason to fear for his agency's safety. Seeking advice and assistance, he traveled to Denver and Rawlins, and he sent several letters and telegrams to Governor Pitkin, Commissioner Hayt, other officials, and the military. A party of Utes—including Jack, Piah, and Sowerick—also went to Denver in August in an attempt to prevent trouble by having Meeker replaced but to no avail. Still determined that his Utes were going to become farmers, like it or not, in early September the stiff-necked Meeker instructed his agency employees to continue plowing, fencing, and building irrigation ditches in Powell Park, with some of the work being done on Johnson's horse pasture. Further angering the Utes, Meeker contended, as Jane reported, that the land belonged to the federal government, not to the Indians. James Thompson later commented that Meeker's approach was responsible for the tragedy that later befell him, his agency, and, to a lesser extent, Thompson, too.[32]

One day in September, while Shadrach Price was plowing as Meeker had ordered him to do, Johnson's son Tim fired at the worker, although he was not injured. To keep the peace, Meeker reported to Commissioner Hayt that he agreed to stop plowing, to remove a corral, and to give the Utes a well and stoves. A few days later Johnson went to the agent's house, and a quarrel broke out between the two. When Meeker forced Johnson out of the building, Johnson hurled the agent against a hitch rail so violently that the old man's arm was hurt. Only intervention by agency employees prevented further injury. Thoroughly frightened now and fearing for his own life and for the safety of others, Meeker urgently repeated his requests for military protection at the agency. Until then, no troops had entered the reservation.

The Utes told a different version of events, especially regarding the reason Meeker summoned troops. In the 1930s the son of a Ute named Steve Birch, who had been at White River, said some Indians were meeting in a tent when the agency farmer came and told them they were going to be sent to Utah. Therefore, no rations were to be issued, and soldiers had been ordered to come to move them.[33] Historians agree, however, that it was Meeker's appeal for help, not escort duty to Utah, that finally brought Major Thornburgh and his four companies of the Fourth Cavalry from Fort Fred Steele in Wyoming.

When a few White River Utes, led by Jack and Sowerick and accompanied by an Uncompahgre called Unc (Unca Sam), encountered Thornburgh's troops near Peck's trading post, the soldiers were asked about their destination and purpose. Thornburgh thought the Indians seemed friendly, but about halfway between the Yampa River and Milk Creek, where Thornburgh camped on September 27, he was visited by two Utes—Colorow and Henry Jim—and an agency employee who delivered a message from Meeker telling Thornburgh that Indians at the agency had learned about his approach and were greatly disturbed. Meeker said that only Thornburgh and five soldiers should proceed to the agency. Instead, the column continued on, disregarding the fact that if soldiers entered the reservation, the Utes would consider that a state of war existed.

War dances kept people at the agency awake all through the night of September 28. On September 29, 1879, northeast of Yellowjacket Pass at Milk Creek, the boundary of the reservation, Indians led by Jack and Colorow fired on the moving column from surrounding hills and ridges. The strategy of the Utes was not unusual in successful Indian warfare, regardless of the public's later assessment that an ambush had somehow been an unworthy military tactic. Thornburgh was one of the first men killed, and his troops took refuge within a breastwork of wagons and dead mounts where the Utes kept them pinned down for six days. Joe Rankin, the scout, galloped on horseback to Rawlins, Wyoming, 160 miles away, to sound the alarm. During the siege at Milk Creek Captain Dodge's Company D of the Ninth Cavalry arrived and, unable to execute a rescue, joined the others within the breastwork.

On October 5 Colonel Wesley Merritt and five companies from Wyoming appeared, and the Battle of Milk Creek ended with the Utes raising a white flag. Thornburgh and ten other soldiers and thirty-seven Indian warriors, including one of Johnson's sons, had died. The fighting was halted so abruptly because Ouray and other chiefs had sent the Utes at Milk Creek an order to quit. Hoping to recruit more warriors among Uncompahgre and Southern Utes, six White River Utes had raced south with information about the battle, and upon receiving the news Sapinero and an employee of the Los Pinos (Uncompahgre) Agency were sent with the message to stop fighting.

At the White River Agency Colonel Merritt found a gruesome scene, for Nathan Meeker, nine employees, and an itinerant peddler who had the misfortune to be in the area had been killed and mutilated on September 29, immediately after the start of the battle at Milk Creek. Arvilla and Josie Meeker, Flora Ellen Price, and her two small children were gone. Led by Douglass, their captors took them south across the Colorado River to the northern end of Grand Mesa, where they camped on Plateau Creek at today's Mesa, Colorado. To ensure the safety of the captives, Merritt ordered the troops who were following them to halt and to stop fighting the Utes they met. Interventions by Susan, who restrained her husband, and kindness by Persune, who was infatuated with Josie, helped to keep the women from being killed, although once safely out of harm's way they told of physical abuses.

A fictitious tale about the release of the captives developed following publication of a poem entitled "The Queen of the Utes," penned by Denver newspaperman Eugene Field and read at a press convention in 1882. Field described "Queen Chipeta" galloping on horseback over rivers and mountains to rescue the captives. An excellent horsewoman, she may have ridden to relay news to Ouray, who was hunting in the mountains when the trouble commenced, but she did not go to Grand Mesa. Rather, Charles Adams was appointed special agent to locate the captives and to effect their release. He went to the Uncompahgre Valley, learned where Douglass's camp was located, and hurried to it with Shavano and several other Indians and white men. They reached the camp on October 21, met with Douglass and others, and persuaded them to give up the women and children. At Plateau Creek the women denied that they had been molested, but later, safely away from their captors, they told a much different story. From Plateau Creek they traveled back to the Uncompahgre Valley, where the women found comfort and hospitality in Chipeta's home. From there they traveled to the railroad terminal at Alamosa.[34]

Hysteria gripped Colorado as word of the events at Milk Creek and the White River Agency became public, and in reaction people demanded that Indian affairs be turned over to the War Department because a widespread uprising was expected momentarily. For their protection, miners at Red Cliff built a log fort, and those at Aspen who had not instantly fled to Leadville holed up in a fortified cabin. Many in the San Juans headed for Saguache as rumors flew that Howardsville or perhaps both places had been destroyed. Animas City, which had been rebuilt after Indians burned it in the 1860s, was falsely reported to have been leveled again. Supposedly, Lake City was surrounded and a huge encampment of Utes was lying in wait north of Cochetopa Pass.

Governor Pitkin mustered three state militias. Throughout the fall and winter volunteers and regular troops at a temporary Camp Rose on Cochetopa Pass watched for attackers who never appeared. No Ute, however innocent, was safe anywhere. Ouray reported that two of his relatives, while trapping beaver, were killed by militia members or prospectors.[35]

Troops proceeded to Colorado from all directions. Colonel Merritt's original army was quickly joined by more companies from Wyoming. They set up a camp at the future site of the town of Meeker where they established a post, buildings of which can still be seen adjacent to the town park. General Edward Hatch, commander of the Ninth Cavalry, and 450 men marched north from New Mexico to Fort Lewis and thence to Animas City, where a camp remained until January 1880 when the men were relieved by troops from Fort Gibson in Indian Territory. Others came from Fort Wingate in New Mexico, and Brevet Brigadier General Ranald S. Mackenzie, the hero of Palo Duro Canyon in Texas in 1874 and of a victorious assault on Dull Knife's Cheyenne Camp in 1876, was on his way to Fort Garland with six companies from Fort Clark in Texas.

Little chance remained, then, for the imagined destruction of Colorado by Ute Indians. Many White River Utes had scattered. Ouray had ordered Uncompahgres to stay in their camps, and most Southern Utes were doing the same, although some Weenuches, led by Ignacio, had gone to meet the troops from Fort Wingate and a few others had fled to southeastern Utah to avoid bloodshed. The opportunistic citizens of Animas City, for whom General Hatch expressed much contempt, were busy making money off of the soldiers and promoting the arrival of a railroad to boost the future economy.[36]

Secretary of the Interior Carl Schurz appointed a special commission composed of General Hatch as head, Adams, and Ouray. The group convened at the Los Pinos (Uncompahgre) Agency in November and December 1879. With his physical condition worsening, Ouray was not present at all sessions, and when he did come to the meetings from his ranch, he had to be helped from his carriage. Representatives of the Uncompahgre Utes included Ouray and Shavano. Alhambra was present for the Southern Utes. About twenty-five Utes testified. Henry Jim acted as interpreter, and fifty Utes served as policemen. Predictably, Otto Mears also came to the Uncompahgre Valley.

The fight at Milk Creek was not an issue before the commission. Thus, figures such as Jack and Colorow, who had been engaged in the battle, were not suspects in the main business, which was to determine who had murdered Meeker and the others at the agency and to bring them to trial. The list of suspects included twelve Utes whom the women had pinpointed as the likely participants in the deaths and ten others. Douglass, who had held Arvilla Meeker as his personal captive, was foremost among those considered to be guilty of complicity, but the brothers Antelope and Pauvitz were thought then and later to have been Meeker's actual killers, although they were never tried and convicted.

The commission heard testimony from Douglass, Johnson, Colorow, Sowerick, and other White River Utes. When the commission was about to consider the accounts by the two Meeker women and Flora Ellen Price, the Utes balked, and Ouray objected that the testimony of women was unsuitable in such proceedings and should not be heard. He became angry and declared that Adams was no longer his friend. Ouray also said it was impossible to try only a few Utes because all White Rivers were involved. When Hatch threatened to send the army after the suspected murderers, nevertheless, and Adams still wanted to question the twelve suspects, Colorow and others drew their knives in a symbolic gesture of protest, and all but Douglass promptly vanished. Ouray demanded that any trial should be held in Washington where the Utes had their only true friend, Carl Schurz.[37] Ouray, who had come to the first commission sessions attired in city clothes, wore only buckskin garments after the commission broke down.

In contrast to the harsh criticism many writers a century later leveled at Nathan Meeker, his contemporaries elevated him to the status of a martyr, "one of the best-hearted men that ever set foot in Colorado." His mistake lay in threatening his Indians without having military backup nearby, it was argued.[38] Angry citizens and newspapers took up the cry "The Utes Must Go," and there was no question that they would indeed leave Colorado. Powerful Senator Henry M. Teller, a friend of mining interests, threw his support behind the Utes' antagonists in Washington.

To resolve the matters of trying and punishing the guilty parties and of deciding where Colorado's Utes should be sent, hearings were ordered in Washington. In late 1879, during a winter of unusually heavy snow and bitter cold, the ailing Ouray, Chipeta, eight other Utes, and Agent W. H. Berry left the Uncompahgre Valley on horseback to begin their journey to the East Coast. By January 7, 1880, they had reached Alamosa, Colorado, where they hurriedly boarded a train as a mob threatened to lynch them. At Pueblo, where they changed trains for Denver, several hundred jeering people threw rocks, lumps of coal, and sticks at them and struck Sowerick with a club. With angry crowds meeting their train at every station, the Indians could not get off to eat, and Chipeta suffered from motion sickness. Thus, they arrived in the nation's capital dirty and disheveled, but they recovered shortly at their hotel and donned new clothing from a local store.

Secretary of the Interior Schurz, a reformer who had fought to clean up the Bureau of Indian Affairs, proved sympathetic to the Utes. He was at odds with Senator Teller, bureaucrats, and prevailing public opinion that called for removal to the reservation.[39] On January 15 testimony by numerous government officials, citizens, military personnel, Josephine Meeker, and Ute Indians began, but little new information was added to the findings of the earlier special commission.[40]

It was decided that all twelve Ute culprits must appear before the commission, so on January 24 Charles Adams departed with Jack, Unca Sam, and three other White River Utes to bring those who were absent.[41] By late February Adams was back with some but not all of the suspects. Douglass had started for Washington with the group, but at Fort Leavenworth Adams had turned him in to be imprisoned. Agent Page, meanwhile, had brought four Southern Ute leaders to legitimize any decisions related to the subject of reservations.

During the hiatus Ouray, Chipeta, and others shopped for clothing, visited such sights as Mount Vernon and the Carlisle Indian School, and had their pictures taken. Ouray received medical attention and heard a dire prognostication concerning his kidney disease and his life expectancy, but he also shopped for silver tableware and bought a baby carriage (perhaps for Mears's infant daughter). Ouray and Chipeta dined at the White House and were frequent guests in the home of Secretary Schurz, where a crystal chandelier caught the chief's eye. Ironically, he wanted to know how he might purchase one for his home in the Uncompahgre Valley. At most public appearances Ouray and Chipeta wore splendid garments of beaded buckskin and doeskin, with a small medicine bag on each shoulder of Ouray's shirt. Nevertheless, when Chipeta testified before the House Committee on Indian Affairs, the press described in detail her elegant costume of the latest Eastern fashion.

Chipeta's testimony revealed her staunch loyalty to her people, as she reported the little she admitted to knowing—that Meeker had "talked bad" and that the captives appeared to be "all right" when they were at her home. Governor Pitkin, however, testified that when Jack visited him in Denver in 1878, the Ute had asserted that Ouray had "played out" the Utes, meaning he had betrayed them just as all white men, the United States president, and Agent Meeker had "played out." Senator Teller vociferously denounced the reform policies of President Rutherford B. Hayes and Secretary Schurz and thereby contributed to Hayes's ouster and, consequently, to Schurz's as well in the next election.[42]

On March 6, 1880, nine Ute Indians—Ouray, Shavano, Ignacio, Alhandro, Veratzis, Golota, Jocknick, Wass, and Sowerick—signed an agreement that was passed, as amended, by Congress on June 15. The terms provided that White River Utes would move to Utah and settle on farms within the Uintah Reservation. Although they had not participated in the events at White River except as Ouray's messengers and the captives' rescuers, the Uncompahgre Utes were to move to allotted "agricultural lands on Grand [Colorado] River, near the mouth of the Gunnison River, in Colorado, if a sufficient quantity of agricultural land shall be found there; if not there upon such unoccupied agricultural lands as may be found in that vicinity and in the Territory of Utah." The Southern Utes, so recently settled on their own reservation and in no way involved at White River, were to move to allotted farms on unoccupied land on the La Plata River in Colorado or, if not possible there, along the same river in New Mexico. Approval by three-fourths of the bands' adult males was required by October 15, 1880, to effect the agreement. A five-member commission was to negotiate the approval and to locate appropriate land for the Uncompahgre and Southern Utes. Upon their removal the Uncompahgre Utes and White River Utes were to receive annuities from a $50,000 trust, and compensation was to be paid to the captives and the families of the victims at the agency from White River annuities for a period of twenty years.[43]

Members appointed to the commission were former Commissioner of Indian Affairs George W. Manypenny; Alfred B. Meacham of Washington, D.C.; John J. Russell of the Department of the Interior; a mining man from Kentucky, John B. Bowman; and Colorado's Otto Mears. They began work in June when, with Manypenny and Meacham absent, Russell, Mears, and Bowman went to the confluence of the Gunnison and Colorado Rivers and decided there was inadequate agricultural land for the Uncompahgres. When the two absent commissioners objected, Bowman knocked Meacham down during an argument and was replaced on the commission by Judge Thomas McMorris of Colorado Springs. Mears and Agent Berry, five Uncompahgre Utes including Shavano and Sapinero, and a large cavalry escort next went to Utah and selected a site at the junction of the Duchesne and Green Rivers, south and southeast of the Uintah Reservation. Although some irrigable bottom land existed there, much surrounding terrain was a badlands of alkali, sand, and gravel.

When the commissioners visited the La Plata River, they found a good part of the land already occupied, so the Southern Utes were allowed to remain on their existing reservation. The Southern bands were to receive no compensation for the land given up by Uncompahgre and White River Utes because, when they had previously accepted the Southern Ute Reservation, the Muaches, Capotes, and Weenuches had relinquished rights to the rest of the Consolidated Ute Reservation in Colorado.

In June 1880 visitors to Ouray's farm found him ill in bed with the agency's physician attending him. Few Southern and Uncompahgre Ute men had signed the agreement, so, in a valiant attempt to persuade them to do so, in August the mortally ill Ouray rode across the mountains from the Uncompahgre Valley to the Southern Ute Reservation with Chipeta and several Ute men as companions. Camping near the agency, Ouray managed to attend one meeting but was otherwise too ill to leave his bed in his tepee. He was visited by numerous Ute medicine men, the Southern Ute Agency's physician, his own agency's physician who made a swift trip on horseback when summoned, and a doctor from Animas City, but the renowned chief died on August 24 at the age of forty-seven. Although the physician from Animas City contended that the cause of death was an untreated hernia and some others charged that the chief's Ute enemies had poisoned him, Ouray died from the chronic Bright's Disease that had afflicted him for years, as the agency physicians stated.

Many have castigated Ouray for cooperating with the government and especially for agreeing to the removal of the Uncompahgre Utes from Colorado when they had not participated in the events at White River. His failure to resist the overwhelming encroachment of civilization may best be understood through an often-repeated statement he reputedly made at the time of treaty negotiations in 1868: "Agreements the Indian makes with the government are like the agreement a buffalo makes with the hunter after it has been pierced by many arrows. All it can do is lie down and give in."

Immediately after Ouray's death, Chipeta and a few Ute men took his body to a secret place in the rocks a few miles south of the agency and buried him with the possessions he had brought from the Uncompahgre Valley. Five horses were sacrificed nearby.[44] In a frequently repeated anecdote, Chipeta gave away some gold coins Ouray had in his belongings and threw the remainder in the river in a gesture of disgust toward white people, but her acts might have been part of the ritual giveaway and destruction of goods that traditionally followed a death. She later sent the beaded shirt Ouray had worn at the negotiations in Washington, along with a few other items, to Secretary Schurz as an expression of friendship. (The shirt was eventually given to the state museum near Montrose, Colorado, and is exhibited there.)

Kaniache, the Muache chief who had once possessed a great deal of power and who had resisted Ouray's dominance, was struck by lightning on the Southern Ute Reservation soon after Ouray's death. The Southern Utes regarded this incident as an omen and signed the agreement. Uncompahgres still refused to do so until Otto Mears gave each man two dollars in exchange for his mark on the document. Outraged by this bribery, Manypenny filed charges. In 1882, after Hayes and Schurz had left office, President James Garfield's new secretary of the interior, Samuel Kirkwood, heard the charges and concluded that Mears was not guilty of any crime because he had used his own, rather than government, funds. In fact, Kirkwood commended Mears for his accomplishment.

Never again was there a head chief over the Utes. Although it is often said that Ouray designated Buckskin Charlie, a Muache, to be chief of the Southern Utes, records make it clear that the government considered Ignacio, the Weenuche, the principal figure among Southern Utes during the next several years. He received more gratuities than anyone else, including Buckskin Charlie. Six feet two inches tall, this towering man compelled respect not only with his physical presence but also with his courage, for he is said to have killed twelve people in retaliation for the death of his father.

During the spring of 1880 General Mackenzie had moved several hundred troops of the Twenty-Third Infantry and the Ninth Cavalry from Fort Garland to the Uncompahgre Valley, where the Cantonment on the Uncompahgre, as it was called until 1886 when it became Fort Crawford, was established on the west side of the river, four miles north of the agency. During the movement of troops Mackenzie was aggravated by the fact that Mears was charging tolls even to the army, with the amount depending on the road's condition in a given section. Mackenzie threatened to tear down one of the gates, but Mears warned him to pay up or he would face trouble in high places.

En route to the new post, the army passed the old agency near Cochetopa Pass, where a few houses, a store, and a hotel of sorts remained.[45] In the Uncompahgre Valley as many as 1,700 men lived in tents and occupied themselves with restraining hundreds of white people who hoped to soon stake claims. The troops traded coffee, sugar, and other goods to Indians who came to the cantonment.[46] Most of the troops returned to Fort Garland during the winter and returned in the spring of 1880 when permanent structures were in place, but a small post remained on Cochetopa Pass at Camp Rose throughout the winter.

Trouble still erupted sporadically throughout Colorado. One of the most alarming incidents occurred on September 29, 1880, when four drunken Utes went into a freighters' camp on Blue Mesa between Gunnison and the Uncompahgre country and asked for food. They were refused. As they left a young freighter, A. D. Jackson, shot and killed Johnson Shavano, the son of Chief Shavano. The freighters quickly moved to Captain Cline's ranch at Cimarron, Colorado, where some troops were camping. Utes, assembled by Shavano, alerted William H. Berry, their agent. Some commissioners had come to the agency with money for the Uncompahgre Utes, and they accompanied Berry to Cimarron to arrest the freighters. With a military escort, the group set off for Gunnison with the freighters, but en route about sixty Utes captured Jackson and killed him.[47] Emotional residents of rough-and-ready communities such as Gunnison and Del Norte accused Berry, Cline, and even the commissioners of complicity. Vigilantes organized, and the men blamed for helping the Utes went into hiding. Although the Indians, the agent, and the commissioners were indicted, they were never brought to trial, and Berry was again serving as agent when the Uncompahgre Utes moved to Utah.

To offer a better military presence, Fort Lewis moved from Pagosa Springs to the La Plata River, midway across the Southern Ute Reservation. Although a few troops remained at Pagosa Springs until 1882, most went to the La Plata River during the winter of 1880–1881 and established a cantonment on the east bank.[48] The new fort was built on both sides of the river, about five miles south of Hesperus, Colorado, in 1882, and a battalion of infantry from New Mexico arrived. Otto Mears quickly built a road to the fort and charged tolls to army wagons as well as other traffic, so most travelers used a nearby route to circumvent the tolls.

In northern Colorado settlers were edgy, and military detachments patrolled Middle Park throughout 1880 and 1881, for Utes still roamed in the area. Of the eight hundred White River Utes, nearly a fourth eluded deportation to Utah in the summer of 1881.[49] Those who did go were encouraged by the news that annuities awaited them at Whiterocks, although, in fact, after victims' payments were deducted, each Ute received only about eleven dollars.

Despite frequent travels back and forth in northwestern Colorado and northeastern Utah for generations, and despite some blood ties with the Uintahs, attachment to the old territory, its hunting grounds, and the spirits of ancestors who had lived and died there ran deep. It was said that bitter Grand River Utes departing from the Roaring Fork and Crystal River region left a curse on the land for those who inherited it.

The White River Utes were also deterred by the glum reception extended by the Uintahs, who had no voice in the agreement made by Colorado Utes in Washington and who were receiving no monetary compensation for sharing their reservation with an equal number of White River Utes. Some Uintahs left the reservation for a time. Agent Critchlow at Whiterocks deplored the additional work and the factionalism the new arrivals created. For instance, he complained that he was now unable to get any of his Uintah Indians to serve as police chief.[50]

Resolution of the Uncompahgre Utes' move took even longer. Getting Ouray's people to gather their belongings, especially their roving livestock, and to leave their beautiful mountains was a difficult business. Uncompahgres protested that they had not been involved in the White River affair. They disliked the land to which they were assigned. Some had crops they had been tending. The highly esteemed Chipeta added her voice to the laments, for she did not wish to leave her good farm and house with its fine furnishings. The government's $700, which Otto Mears eventually delivered to her as payment for the property in accord with the 1880 agreement, were small reimbursement for the farm's worth. When Ouray and Chipeta's valuable personal belongings were sold at auction to local scavengers for a pittance, David Day, editor of Ouray's *Solid Muldoon*, complained that "an explanation is in order."[51]

Such opportunists, devoid of conscience, abounded not only on the fringes of the reservation but also within its boundaries before the

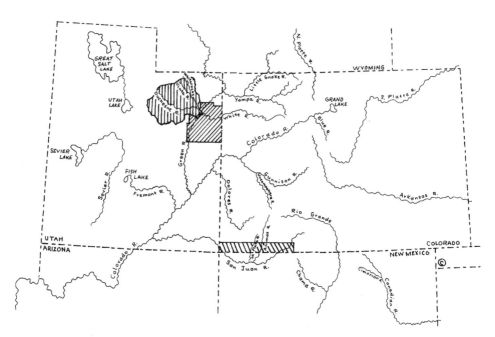

Utah's Uintah and Ouray Reservations and Colorado's Southern Ute Reservation, following the removal of White River and Uncompahgre Utes. The Ouray Reservation was created in 1882 as the home of the Uncompahgre Ute Indians who were removed from Colorado. The two Utah reservations were consolidated as the Uintah and Ouray Ute Indian Reservation in 1886.

Uncompahgres vacated it. Reservation jumpers had already gone to Hotchkiss, Olathe, and the Uncompahgre Valley in hopes of getting the best claims, and the army tried vainly to hold back trespassers.

In late August 1881 the commissioners said it was time for the move to begin, and Mackenzie gave the order to start, but a few more days elapsed before his troops had the reluctant Indians rounded up in a camp north of Montrose. The Indians were still pleading for more time to gather livestock, hunt, and harvest wild berries for their winter's food supply but to no avail. Finally, with his troops surrounding the Ute camp, Mackenzie threatened that he would use force if necessary, and the sad cavalcade started down the Gunnison River at dawn on September 1. There were nearly fifteen hundred Uncompahgres, a few groups of truant White Rivers including Colorow's followers, ponies and travois, thousands of sheep and goats, and hundreds of wagons loaded with food and belongings, accompanied by a military escort. They crossed the Colorado River by way of an arroyo at Grand Junction on large, flat ferries and left behind the band's homeland of five hundred years. The trek through arid hills and down Evacuation Creek to Utah was surely as heartbreaking as the Cherokees' Trail of Tears or the Navajos' Long Walk. Excluding stragglers, they arrived at their destination on September 13, having accomplished the two hundred-mile journey in less than two weeks.

Immediately on their heels, the Uncompahgre and Gunnison River country was staked by settlers. Towns like Montrose, Glenwood Springs, and Grand Junction were swiftly laid out, and a year later the Denver and Rio Grande Railway laid its rails through the Gunnison River Valley to the Grand Valley at Grand Junction, the burgeoning town where there had been insufficient land for Utes, or so the commissioners had claimed. Mackenzie, who drew the miserable assignment of making the Uncompahgre's land safe for so-called civilization, left the Uncompahgre Valley for New Mexico with six companies of the Fourth Cavalry on September 7, 1881. Without receiving the star he coveted for his shoulder (it went to General Miles), he resigned the next year and died in a mental hospital in 1889.

Chief Tabby of the Uintah Utes told his own version of what had happened. He said that "Shinnob," the Creator, hated white people and had gone to war against them. He filled several large bags with dirt and rocks and sticks, and when Shinnob's brother, the Devil, opened it, all the different tribes rushed out and fell upon the white people.[52]

The Utes had fought as Bear does when he is cornered, and in the struggle everyone had received terrible wounds, whether physical or spiritual. Pierced by many arrows, Bear turned and lumbered away. And no one knew whether he had gone away to die in a secret hiding place or whether he had survived.

9

▼ ▼ ▼

The Unraveling Begins
(1882–1895)

The exiled and transplanted Ute Indians quickly dispelled any illusions about their docility. In September 1881, soon after arriving at the confluence of the Green and Duchesne Rivers where Commissioner Otto Mears had contracted with the government to put up a few temporary structures to serve as an agency, Mears visited the Uncompahgres to inspect the work and to pay Chipeta $700 for her home and farm on the Uncompahgre River. Blaming Mears for his band's removal to Utah and for cheating Chipeta, Cohoe (McCook) tried to kill the busy little man.[1] Mears escaped and shortly thereafter resigned as commissioner to concentrate on his toll roads and railroad construction through lands vacated by Utes in southwestern Colorado.

The influence of Chipeta's extended family remained strong among the Uncompahgre Utes in Utah. When Agent William Berry took a delegation to Washington in the spring of 1881, Sapinero, McCook, and Piah, all of whom have been called her brothers, accompanied the delegation, and Sapinero was designated the Uncompahgre's chief by government officials.

Located on the west side of the Green River at the mouth of the Duchesne River, an agency named Ouray was immediately established. The agency had military protection during its first few months. Personnel of the Sixth Infantry encamped directly across the Green River beginning September 17.[2] Undiplomatically called Fort Thornburgh to honor the major killed at Milk Creek, the post relocated a year later to Ashley Creek because the Uncompahgres objected to its presence. At its new site the fort offered more protection to the budding Mormon town of Vernal and could keep a better watch on the Uintahs and White Rivers at Whiterocks. In 1884 Fort Thornburgh closed.

William Berry, who had last served at the Los Pinos Agency in the Uncompahgre Valley, continued at the Ouray Agency until June 1882 and oversaw the beginnings of the Uncompahgres' new reservation. On January 5, 1882, an executive order of the president created the Ouray Reservation. It consisted of about two million acres on both sides of the Green River and was nearly equal in size to the Uintah Reservation. The two reservations were connected by a narrow strip along the Duchesne and Uinta Rivers. Much of the Uncompahgres' land was a desolate waste within the East Tavaputs Plateau, the Indians' "Land of the Sun," east of the Green River. Except for arable bottom land along the rivers, the reservation was ill suited to farming and foraging, with scant land for grazing.

When J. F. Minniss arrived as agent in 1882, he found a shabby agency, cold in winter and hot in summer, on a low point above a sink where streams joined. The agent soon had the routines of a frontier outpost in place. A trading post opened, irrigation ditches were dug, and the people seemed to be settling in as best they could.

The Uintah Valley Agency at Whiterocks, however, was having difficulties. Some White River Utes had never arrived and were getting into trouble back in Colorado. For example, some of the Utes robbed a pair of travelers on the Flattops, causing alarm. When other stragglers came to the agency, they stayed only long enough to receive their meager annuities and rations and quickly departed.[3] In 1882 the agent could account for only 275 White River Utes.[4]

A series of tragedies struck the leaders of the White Rivers. One of the most prominent members of the band, Jack, along with three other Utes, had gone to Wyoming instead of to the reservation and had found a job as a teamster. The men were soon believed to have stolen some horses, and Fort Washakie's commander ordered their arrest. Attempting to escape, Jack shot a trooper and hid in his tent. The troops fired a howitzer directly into the tepee and killed Jack.[5]

Douglass also met a tragic end. In 1881, a year after his imprisonment at Fort Leavenworth ended because a report declared him insane, he appeared at Whiterocks brandishing a spear and a rifle. When he pointed the gun at Agent Critchlow, an Indian policeman named Tom pulled Douglass from his horse, although another policeman refused to help. A report about the incident corroborated the claim that Douglass was insane.[6] Fortunately for the agency, Douglass left without causing further trouble.

Douglass was an alcoholic, and he continued to drink heavily. In late 1882 he came to the trading post again and gave a "talk." For many Native American tribes a talk was much more than a mere discussion or chat, and proper protocol was required of listeners, even if the delivery went on for hours. As Douglass, a White River chief, was giving his talk, a Ute named Pont, possibly a member of the rival Uintah Band, interrupted him. Douglass hit Pont on the head and was arrested by Tim Johnson, a White River policeman, whom Douglass then threatened to kill. Douglass was not charged because it was concluded that the assault on Pont was justified.

Within a few months Douglass moved his lodge away from the agency and caused no further trouble until 1884 or 1885 when, according to one story, as he was returning to the reservation after a drinking binge in western Colorado, he again threatened Pont, who then killed him. Another version holds that Douglass was about to kill a white trader who purportedly had stolen ten dollars from him, and Pont killed Douglass to stop him. Whatever the correct facts, the tribal court tried Pont and condemned him to death by shooting to deter others from violence.

Many other incidents kept the Whiterocks agents and the police force busy. Sometimes the police themselves caused affronts by refusing to wear their uniforms properly or by being insolent toward an agent. Alcohol was the cause of many episodes, as when a general melee broke out after a police captain got drunk and began waving a sword around. When the ensuing brawl ended, the jail was full.

Critchlow had been in charge at Whiterocks since 1872, an unusually long tenure for an Indian agent. Among his agency's achievements were a few farms where Indians raised crops and owned livestock. With assistance from the Presbyterian Board of Home Missions, a school had operated intermittently. Its teachers included the agent's wife, his sister-in-law, and lastly a missionary teacher sent from back East, but classes never met for a full year. Feeding and caring for the few pupils who attended made the project difficult, Critchlow explained. By 1883 Critchlow was gone from Whiterocks, along with church-nominated agents elsewhere.

With a new administration in Washington, the faltering Peace Policy was terminated in the early 1880s, and with its demise the practice of assigning the nation's various Indian agencies to religious denominations ended. Although the mission programs of many denominations had made contributions, as by sending a teacher to Whiterocks, considerable inefficiency as well as fraud had existed in the Indian agencies, it was charged. Meanwhile, the Board of Indian Commissioners had gradually devolved into a group of ineffective squabblers, and the Peace Policy was pronounced a failure. With the end of the Peace Policy, church-nominated agents like Critchlow left the service.

In 1881, with the appointment of Henry M. Teller as secretary of the interior, other changes had occurred. As a United States senator, Teller had strongly advocated removing the Ute Indians from Colorado, and now, recognizing the inequity of moving the White Rivers onto the Uintah Reservation without compensating the Uintah occupants, he found a new way to inflict punishment on the White Rivers. In 1882 he directed that the Uintah Utes should begin to receive annuities and that the money would be withdrawn from the already small annuities the White Rivers were receiving.[7] This decision increased the factionalism that already existed on the reservation.

At the Ouray Agency other incidents might have caused trouble. For instance, a natural disaster occurred in 1883 when flooding destroyed farms and drowned livestock.[8] Despite the setback, on the other hand, the Uncompahgres seemed to become more cooperative. For instance, they philosophically accepted the news that during the past winter one of their members, Maromot, had been found dead in southern Colorado. They said he was a bad Indian who should have been killed long before and there was no need for Southern Ute Agent Warren Patten to take any action.[9]

Despite the upheavals in their lives, most Uncompahgres led quiet lives. They liked to sit around the agency—talking, playing Spanish monte, and smoking hand-rolled cigarettes.[10] Typically, the men wore calico shirts with buckskin leggings, moccasins, and a Navajo blanket, and their hair was parted, braided, and finished off with a headband rather than a hat. When official agency business had to be transacted, Utes Billy and Ueliandro acted as interpreters. Near the agency were a handful of one- or two-room wooden houses for agency employees and for Utes who agreed to farm, but the majority of people preferred to live in tepees, brush wickiups, or canvas tents instead of in the drafty buildings through which cold wind blew in winter and dust blew in summer. Chipeta received one of these houses in exchange for her former snug, well-furnished adobe home, but she preferred her tepee in the summer camp where her family group herded sheep.

An educated adventurer, Arthur C. Moulton, kept a journal that gives a picture of life at Ouray. First as manager of the store at Fort Thornburgh across the Green River and next as the hired storekeeper at Ouray when the soldiers left, Moulton witnessed crowds of Utes coming to the agency for rations each Saturday. The practice of turning cattle loose within the corral and letting the bucks shoot them still prevailed, Moulton reported. The women raced to reach a dead steer first and to bash its skull with a hatchet to secure the brain for tanning skins. Within a half hour the women had all the meat cut up, and quiet descended on the agency.[11]

The Utes also came to the store to trade tanned deerskins, muskrat and beaver pelts, ornaments, and occasionally Navajo blankets. When annuities were distributed each April, two-thirds was quickly spent at the store, Moulton estimated. Some of the rest was lost gambling before the day was out. The total amount of annuities was about $17,000 to be divided among about 1,255 Uncompahgres, so the per capita share was obviously not large. The money was in silver coins, which the agent traveled to Denver to get from a bank—a two-week trip because the nearest railroad was at Price, Utah.[12]

The 1885 Ute census provides much useful information. For example, for the populations on the two Utah reservations, the census counted 1,255 Uncompahgres, 508 Uintahs, and 514 White Rivers. These numbers reveal that about 300 Uintahs, 300 White Rivers, and nearly as many Uncompahgres were absent or uncounted.[13] On the list are Shavano (spelled "Shavanaux"), his wife Chito, and six children, the youngest ten months old. Also on the list are the names of Chipeta, enrolled as number 486; her husband, Accummooquats, enrolled as number 485; and their six wards—all boys—ranging in age from fifteen down to five and named Danas-cuno, Sevito, Guadaloupe, Jose La Cross, John Pito, and Francisco. Also listed were Cohoe (McCook), Sap-po-vo-na-ro (Sapinero), and Piah.

An interesting sidelight relates to an often repeated account that first appeared in the Denver *Republican* on April 1, 1883. The paper reported sarcastically, implying that it was unseemly for the widow of the great Ouray to have remarried, that Chipeta had a new husband, a Ute called "Toomuchagut." The census corrected this unfortunate joke. His name was also spelled Com-mo-qu-ueech. Her husband lived only a few years, during which time they traveled with Colorow's group.

In 1886 a tragedy befell the Uncompahgres when Shavano died. Moulton was still at Ouray, and he wrote a reliable firsthand account of Shavano's death. Like any medicine man, Chief Shavano was vulnerable to the hard rules of his role, which earned him confidence or distrust depending on the outcome of his treatments. When a medicine man failed to produce the desired results, he was believed to be evil, a witch, and he was ostracized or, worse, punished by death. That was Shavano's fate after he treated Pano's child, who died.

Moulton was in the store one busy Saturday when, as Shavano was entering the store, Pano placed his gun against the chief's back and shot him. Firing back toward the store, Pano then rode his horse up the rise to the "plaza," where Shavano's son Charlie lived. Not knowing that his father had been shot but hearing gunfire and seeing the fleeing Pano, Charlie shot Pano and killed him. A crowd of Indians tied Pano's rope around his neck and, with the other end attached to his saddle, led the horse, dragging the body, to the Duchesne River and threw Pano into it. The horse was shot and thrown in as well. Shavano was carried to the agency's doctor, who had been too frightened to go to the scene of the shooting, but some Utes refused to let him treat Shavano. They applied mud poultices to the wound and chanted while the agency's white population sought refuge in the store, as Antelope, who was visiting at Ouray, advised them to do. On the third night Shavano died. Thereafter, a long-standing feud existed between the families of Shavano and Pano.[14]

In 1886 administrative changes occurred, and Utah's Utes were controlled with a firmer hand. In 1886 the Uintah Valley and Ouray Reservations were consolidated as the Uintah and Ouray Ute Indian Reservation, with the two existing agencies becoming subagencies with a clerk in charge of each. Fort DuChesne (soon spelled Fort Duchesne) was established on August 23 on the west side of the Uinta River, eight miles above its confluence with the Duchesne River and midway between the two agencies.[15] The fort's commander was superintendent over the two agencies. Serving at the fort were two companies of black buffalo soldiers of the Ninth Cavalry and four white companies of the Twenty-First Infantry. Beginning in 1892 only black troops, with white officers as was customary, served at Fort Duchesne.

The Utes' displeasure at any military presence on their reservation was evident before the first troops, the infantry, had even arrived. Word leaked out that about three hundred Utes were planning to ambush the troops, so they averted conflict by digging trenches and remaining in them until the black cavalry arrived to reinforce them.[16] Once in place, though, the presence of the fort helped agency personnel to feel more secure than they had previously. For instance, in 1886 the Whiterocks agent had been so intimidated by White River Utes, who were angry about deductions from their annuities to pay the Meeker victims, that he took the money from all three bands. The Utes, in turn, discovered unexpected benefits from the military presence. When buffalo soldiers were assigned to string a telegraph line to Price, the Utes removed the poles and wire for their own use.

Although the army was supposed to control Utes in the area, the military failed to deter the nomadic tendencies of the Indians, who were still making annual hunting trips off the reservation. Colorow, now a permanent member of the Uncompahgre group, and his followers did so regularly. In 1885 the Meeker *Herald* complained that Colorow had been wandering through the White and Yampa Valleys, Garfield County, and Routt County and that range land had been burned. Although no one can be certain as to why Utes were burning the range in 1885, doing so was a normal way for Indians to improve the land's productivity, as white ranchers and wildlife managers eventually have learned. Many other attractions besides hunting were found outside the reservation—stores at Vernal, Rangely, and Meeker, for instance; liquor; sights to see in Grand Junction; and railroad trains. Once a popular resort with Ute Indians, Glenwood Springs was becoming a popular spa, and Indians still came annually to enjoy the hot springs and a special vapor cave where they had constructed a hut for steam baths. Providing another source of recreation, local cowboys liked to enter horse races with the Utes. Chipeta joined in some of these outings with Colorow's party.

It was impossible for the Núu-ci to give up in less than a generation the customs of centuries, the seasonal migrations, hunting, fishing, and harvesting berries, roots, and nuts for their winter needs. The Utes insisted that they had never agreed to relinquish their hunting rights on the lands they had vacated. Unfortunately, when the Indians were afield it was tempting to kill a steer or to steal a few horses from the increasing numbers white people brought to the former Indian lands. Such large numbers of Indians went out on the forays that the residents of towns, where streets were sometimes crowded with Utes, became alarmed, and those who lost livestock were becoming increasingly angry. The killing of large quantities of game also aroused settlers who were subject to game laws passed in 1877 and 1883. The laws mandated a closed season and limited the numbers of certain animals that could be taken, although the laws were consistently ignored by white poachers as well as Indians.

The summer of 1887 witnessed several incidents, accounts of which are frequently contradictory and confusing. In one episode Utes, who had been making what proved to be their last visit to Glenwood Springs, were believed to have stolen horses near Rifle, and the sheriff of Garfield County chased an Indian party out of that area. At Rangely a similar incident ended with a Ute named Augustine being shot and killed. On the headwaters of the White River a large amount of game was being killed. The meat was being dried, and hides were being tanned when Garfield County's sheriff and a posse came to the camp and broke up the venture. Cowboys or posse members also crudely heckled and frightened Indian women who were harvesting berries near Meeker.

With emotions on both sides rising, local residents requested that Governor Alva Adams send the state militia, and he responded by dis-

patching an excessively large force by train in August. This often-ridi-
culed campaign was called the Colorow War. As Colorow's people headed
toward their reservation in Utah for safety, the militia found them west
of Rangely, where a skirmish took place. Two soldiers and eight Utes
died, and several other Indians, including Colorow, were wounded. As
the Utes escaped to the reservation, a detachment of the Ninth Cavalry
stationed itself at the eastern boundary to prevent an invasion by the
Colorado militia, which was giving chase.[17] In their flight the Utes lost
the horses, sheep, and goats they had taken to Colorado and their entire
harvest of dried meat, skins, and berries. Colorow died in late 1888 as a
consequence of his injuries. (For unknown reasons, Piah is said to have
committed suicide in 1888, also.)

As ensuing years proved, such incidents did not convert the Utes to
staying at home and surviving solely on agency rations. Beginning in
1891 Colorado had wardens and deputies to protect game and fish, and
in northwestern Colorado these men were kept busy trying to control
the large quantities of game being killed and shipped out by white hunters to markets through Rawlins, Wyoming. The wardens also tried to
halt big game hunts by Indians, as game laws restricted hunters to having only one deer, elk, and antelope in their possession. In the fall of
1895 Uintah Utes reportedly killed a large number of deer, many of
them does. When a warden with a posse approached an Indian camp at
Lily Park in 1897, the law enforcement team found that most hunters
were gone, and the women and old men were alone. The posse tried to
arrest an elderly man, but the women sprang to his defense and a fight
erupted. The hunters returned and joined the fray. By the time the
battle ended, five men and three women lay dead. Fleeing down the
Yampa, the Utes killed a member of the posse before reaching safety on
the reservation.

Although Fort Duchesne was taking on a semblance of civilization,
with a stockade and a canal carrying water to young shade trees and
gardens, Ute life failed to change noticeably. Navajos visited the Utes
once a year to trade their blankets for tanned skins. Water Melon Jane,
daughter of the Meekers' one-time servant Jane, made enough moccasins and buckskin shirts to allow her to trade with her neighbors. Troops
had hauled logs from the mountains to build small cabins for the Utes,
along with the fort's buildings, but many Indians refused to live in them
and instead sheltered ponies in them during bad weather.[18] Although
the government gave them wagons and harnesses for farming, some Utes
said they had difficulty breaking their horses to such work and preferred
to race them. The agencies had physicians, but the Indians usually relied

on their own medicine men or folk remedies. Still balking at the presence of the military, Utes fired on two companies of infantry and sent them scurrying back to Fort Duchesne when they marched into the Strawberry Valley on reconnaissance.[19]

Alcohol was not a new problem but an increasing one. A basic ingredient of military life everywhere, liquor became more readily available in the area after Fort Duchesne was established. A draw near the fort became known as Bottle Hollow because soldiers tossed aside their empty bottles there. Nearby, a notorious parcel of land, the Duchesne Strip, where drinking, prostitution, and gambling were engaged in openly, came into being after trespassers, who were common on the reservation, found gilsonite, or asphalt, a tarlike hydrocarbon containing petroleum, east of Fort Duchesne. By an act of Congress in May 1888, 7,000 acres containing gilsonite were excluded from the reservation and sold by the Utes for twenty dollars per acre. This triangular piece of land became known as the no-holds-barred Duchesne Strip where Indians, soldiers, wayfarers, and outlaws like Butch Cassidy's Hole-in-the-Wall Gang enjoyed the debauchery.

Numbed by revelry on the Duchesne Strip, some patrons might have overlooked the import of a far-reaching piece of legislation passed in Washington in 1887. The Dawes Act, or the General Allotment Act of 1887, provided for the division of the nation's Indian lands into allotments that would belong to tribal members in severalty. The parcels were to entail 160 acres for male heads of families, 80 acres for single male adults, and 40 acres for male minors. Native Americans who owned their own land would become citizens of the United States although without the franchise to vote, according to the act. Lands remaining after allotment would become part of the public domain, open to the filing of claims. Besides opening vast acreage to the land-hungry public and to mining, timber, and agriculture interests, the General Allotment Act was intended to transform dependent Indians into self-supporting, assimilated citizens, long the goal of reformers and the Bureau of Indian Affairs. Before this breakup of Indian lands could occur, however, congressional acts applying to specific tribes were required, and these laws were not passed immediately. Meanwhile, the Utes of Utah and Colorado would continue to live on their reservations as before.

Another tool of assimilation was education, although agency schools required by the government had achieved little success among Utes for several reasons. Many Utes families lived in scattered locations and traveled around seasonally, and access to day schools was difficult if not impossible. Another problem was language, for few Utes spoke English and virtually none of the agency teachers spoke the Ute language. Also, when a few parents were induced to bring their children to the schools, they were exposed to diseases such as measles to which the Indians had no immunity. Finally, most parents refused to send their children to schools in which Ute ways were unappreciated and denigrated. Indian names were replaced with inappropriate English names, often borrowed from literature, and the Utes retaliated by giving white people unflatter-ing Indian names that were not understood by the recipients.

Although Agent Critchlow's school at Whiterocks had held classes sporadically and the Ouray Agency had opened a school in 1885, results were discouraging. Critchlow had decided early on that "the highest and best results can only be served by an industrial boarding-school where the pupils of both sexes can be brought under the constant supervision of the teacher, and kept from the demoralizing influences of the lodges."[20] Whiterocks got its Uintah Boarding School, operated by the govern-ment, in 1885. The pupils were required to wear American-style uni-forms and to cut their hair, adding to the foreign nature of the experi-ence. Although enrollment was not high in the early years, the physical plant expanded in 1892 when several large buildings were added.

Despite such tragedies as the deaths of seventeen of the school's sixty-five pupils as the result of a measles epidemic in 1901, the Uintah Boarding School survived until 1952, when public schools took over educating the area's Ute children. A second boarding school, serving Uncompahgre children, opened in 1892 four miles from Fort Duchesne at Randlett, a town named for Major James Randlett of the Ninth Cav-alry, superintendent for the reservation. The Ouray Boarding School, as it was called, soon boasted three brick buildings. The school closed in 1905, and its boarding pupils next attended the Whiterocks school.[21] The Ouray Boarding School's buildings were then given to the state to use for a day school.

Along with such local institutions, the Bureau of Indian Affairs also created boarding schools away from reservations and from the influ-ences of Indian families and customs. At these schools pupils from dif-ferent tribes received vocational training along with standard academic classes. The Bureau of Indian Affairs modeled the institutions on the Carlisle Indian School. When Ute delegations went to Washington, tours of Indian schools were part of the itinerary in the hope that the visitors would appreciate the advantages of education. Hampton Insti-tute was on the agenda when Utes from the Ouray Agency went to the capital in 1883. A little closer to home was the Haskell Training School (later Haskell Institute) at Lawrence, Kansas, where a few Utes eventually attended. When the Teller Institute opened in Grand Junction in 1886, a small percentage of its students were Ute. By 1900 three hundred Indians from various tribes were attending Teller Institute, but the school closed in 1911.[22]

There were a few other hints of future assimilation. To encourage and enable agricultural projects, in 1890 the government constructed three canals with Indian labor to bring water from the Uinta, Duchesne, and Dry Fork Rivers, and some Ute farmers began to use the water to grow hay and gardens.[23] The Indians were expected to help construct the ditches, and moneys for the tribe's trust fund paid for them.

Missionaries also encouraged assimilation. Although church-nominated agents had left the reservations, the influence of religious groups grew in the 1890s as missionary projects were organized. On the Uintah and Ouray Reservation the Episcopal Church opened a mission at Randlett in 1893, and chapels were established at Randlett and, later, Whiterocks that still serve their neighborhoods. At Randlett the Episcopal missionaries also operated a hospital, and the staff was held in high esteem by the Uncompahgres.

Despite such programs, many Utah Utes were determined to preserve their Native American identity. Nativism was taking hold on the reservation, encouraged by the messianic revelation of a Paiute in Nevada, Wovoka (Jack Wilson). Wovoka inspired the renewal of the Ghost Dance as a means of bringing harmony and revitalization to Indian people. In early 1889 Utes sent delegates to Nevada, and during the year 1,600 Indians from several tribes went to learn Wovoka's teachings and to learn the dance.

The rapid spread of the pan-Indian Ghost Dance caused hysteria among white people and the federal government. Basically, the dance was a round dance, but at Wounded Knee the Sioux Indians adopted a special dance shirt they claimed made them invulnerable to bullets—by implication, a threat to white people. Opposition culminated at Wounded Knee in 1890 with troops coming in and scores of Sioux being killed. Elsewhere, the dance, with its transformational emphasis, continued, although attempts were made to suppress it. The dance brought cohesiveness to Ute Indians in northeastern Utah and southwestern Colorado, where it was adopted by Uintah, Uncompahgre, and Weenuche Utes. Uncompahgres were said to have danced the Ghost Dance on Saturdays after rations were distributed at Ouray.[24] If that is true, the observance was a distinct departure from the more typical practice of holding a three- or five-day Ghost Dance once every three months or so.

At least a third of the Northern Utes were off the Uintah and Ouray Reservation around 1890, so their condition is impossible to assess. It is known, however, that Utah's Fish Lake Utes and Paiutes, who had never gone to the reservation, were not faring well. In 1889 their rights were sold to the Fremont Irrigation Company for nine horses, one steer, five hundred pounds of flour, and a suit of clothes, and they went to live in the Koosharem area.

In Colorado developments among Southern Utes differed from those of the Northern Utes in many ways. Southern Utes had remained peaceful during the uprising at White River, but orderliness on their reservation must be attributed in part to the gratuities paid to Indians who helped maintain peace there. In accord with Section 8 of the 1880 agreement made in Washington, the secretary of the interior in April 1881 approved gratuities totaling $1,200 for Southern Ute leaders and $800 for Los Pinos (Uncompahgre) Utes. In that year $200 was paid to Ignacio and $100 each to Alhandro, Mariano, Red Jacket, Aquila, and Buckskin Charlie.

As the decade progressed, the lists of names submitted by agents to receive gratuities grew to include policemen, farmers, those who sent their children to school, and those who were generally well behaved and a good influence. The lowest gratuity was $20. Ignacio's name consistently appeared at the top of the lists, where he is shown to have received $125 to $150 annually after 1881, more than other leaders received.[25] This fact reveals that the Weenuche chief Ignacio, not the Muache chief Buckskin Charlie, was the principal leader of all Southern Ute Indians until the Weenuche Utes went their own way and the Muache and Capote Bands alone comprised the reorganized Southern Ute Tribe.

In the years following 1880 an important influence was the rapid change resulting from increased pressures in the area contiguous to the Southern Ute Reservation. The Denver and Rio Grande's narrow-gauge railroad tracks, delayed for only a few weeks at Arboles at the reservation's boundary in 1880, were laid rapidly through the reservation in 1881 without permission from the Utes, the secretary of the interior, or Congress. The line reached its terminus, Durango, two miles south of the original town of Animas City, in July, and a railroad station called Ignacio was located only about a mile from the Southern Ute Agency on the Los Pinos River. As a concession to the railroad's presence on Ute land, Indians were allowed to ride on the train to nearby Durango without charge.

Trespassers had already been invading Southern Ute lands, but after the Uncompahgre Utes were sent to Utah and their former portion of the reservation was declared public land on July 28, 1882, population pressures increased on the northern and eastern boundaries of the Southern Utes' reservation. Although the reservation contained about a million acres, its long, narrow shape almost invited intrusion. Along the southern border in New Mexico were many Spanish-speaking people who had long associated with Ute Indians. Some Hispaños were living within the reservation or were grazing sheep there, and efforts were made to remove them. Others were enjoying a lively traffic in whiskey among the railroad's construction crews and trainmen, as well as among the Indians in the area. The liquor business thrived in towns like Arboles, Allison, Ignacio, Pagosa Springs, and Durango, and bootleggers plied their trade along the railroad grade.[26]

Along the borders of the western half of the reservation, where the population was less dense, the livestock of English-speaking ranchers encroached. Beginning in 1877 settlers had come into McElmo Canyon, the San Juan River area, and the south flank of Utah's La Sal Mountains. Large livestock operations soon began to use southeastern Utah's and southwestern Colorado's open range, where, with the best water holes fenced off for their own use, the ranchers established virtually private domains. The Kansas and New Mexico Land and Cattle Company (better known as the Carlisle Cattle Company) was the largest outfit, taking in the country east of the Blue Mountains. The LC Ranch was using the upper end of Montezuma Canyon.

The impact of thousands of cattle, as well as the Indians' own sheep, on the fragile vegetation of the Four Corners region was a serious problem, for Utes still relied on native species of plants for high-bulk foods, medicines, materials for baskets, cradleboards, ceremonial objects, fuel for warmth and cooking, construction materials for shelters, and forage for their livestock. Bark, inner bark, seeds, fruit, pollen, twigs, and roots continued to be used, as in earlier times. Water was precious. Grasses and other herbaceous plants were of utmost importance to the Utes and their livestock, and the huge herds belonging to ranchers were destroying them.

On lands to the west and north of the Southern Ute Reservation roamed Weenuche Utes, Paiutes, and Navajos, most of whom were herding livestock, usually sheep and lesser numbers of goats. These Indians were called renegades because they refused to remain on any reservation. Well-known names among the Ute "renegades" were the Weenuches Johnny Benow, Narraguinip (Poco), and Mancos Jim. Off-reservation Indians were suspected whenever horses and cattle disappeared.

In June 1881 cowboy Dick May and four other men were killed—by Utes, it was said—near Paiute Springs, an important water hole close to

Ucolo on the Utah-Colorado border. Posses formed, and troops came from Fort Lewis on the La Plata River. An engagement took place east of Moab at Pinhook Draw, where an estimated ten to fourteen white men and approximately half as many Indians fought. Narraguinip was involved in the conflict. Reports also circulated that a few days earlier Indians had severely beaten two men between Durango and Bloomfield, New Mexico.[27]

At Mancos, where settlement began in 1880, the people built a fortress for protection in response to these episodes. Incidents continued. Mancos Jim was a leader in a fight with cowboys over a horse Indians had apparently stolen on Montezuma Creek in 1884, and once again troops from Fort Lewis came to the cowboys' rescue. At least three Utes and two white men died in a shoot-out at White Canyon in the canyonlands country in this engagement.

With Utes, Paiutes, and Navajos all traveling through the Four Corners area, it often was impossible to identify which members of which tribe were responsible for actions. The Navajo agent complained about Ute trespassers on the Navajos' reservation, and the Ute agent protested that Utes were losing natural resources to livestock that belonged to wayward Navajos. Confusing rumors made it impossible to prove irrefutably who did what in some instances. It was never determined whether Utes, who were accused of the crime, killed two prospectors in Arizona's Monument Valley in 1883 or whether the murderers were Navajos. Also, it was difficult to assess accurate blame for losses when the area's ranchers made claims against the federal government, which was supposed to be responsible for crimes by its "wards." Between 1881 and 1884 such losses resulted in thousands of dollars in claims for restitution.[28] In contrast to persistent troubles with ranchers, the Indians of the three tribes— Ute, Navajo, and Southern Paiute—who roamed around Bluff, Utah, were able to come in to trade and got along reasonably well with the Mormons in that community.

There was no question about who was responsible for two incidents in 1885 in southwestern Colorado, though. Hundreds of permanent settlers were coming into the area around present-day Cortez and were beginning to divert water for farms and ranches. Among the newcomers were the Genthners who took up land near Totton's Lake in an area frequently traveled by Weenuches, who liked to stop at a neighboring store. One day in 1885 they robbed the store, went to the Genthner home, set it ablaze, and killed Mr. Genthner. Although she had been wounded by an arrow, Mrs. Genthner escaped with her six children.

In the Dolores River area at Beaver Creek that same year, cowboys killed all but one member of a village of Utes who were hunting off their reservation with permission from Agent Stollsteimer. The only survivor, a woman, escaped and reported the murders to other Utes. They avenged the deaths by killing several white people, and a detachment was sent out from Fort Lewis to ensure the settlers' safety.[29]

Besides traveling around the Four Corners region, some Weenuches liked to visit to the north. For instance, twenty-eight families of Southern Utes went without permission to the Ouray Agency in November 1881 to see their displaced Uncompahgre friends. Others traveled back and forth between the reservations with passes issued by their agents, who usually allowed a month's absence.[30]

This disinclination to remain submissively on the reservation added fuel to unquenched fires to remove the Southern Utes from Colorado. Teller, once again a United States senator following the 1884 election, introduced a bill in 1885 to remove the Southern Utes to Utah. In an 1885 census the population of the three Southern Ute bands totaled 983, slightly more than half being Weenuches and the remainder being approximately evenly divided between Muaches and Capotes.[31] The Utes would have had a significant impact, then, on San Juan County, Utah, if Teller's bill had succeeded. Ranchers and townspeople in Utah vigorously protested the move, and the bill failed. Utah continued to protest when subsequent attempts were made to relocate Southern Utes to San Juan County.

In 1885 Christian Stollsteimer was the Southern Ute agent, the reservation's fourth in rapid succession. Because of the political turbulence at the time and the fact that he was not a typical career employee of the Bureau of Indian Affairs, Stollsteimer is an interesting figure. He was a German immigrant who lived in Saguache during the time when the first Los Pinos Agency was nearby. He was well acquainted with other early pioneers, including Otto Mears, and when Stollsteimer took up a ranch west of Del Norte in the late 1870s, his close neighbor and business associate was Albert Pfeiffer, formerly an agent at Abiquiú. Both men ran sheep in the Pagosa Springs area and on the Southern Ute Reservation with the permission of Ouray and Ignacio, they said.[32] Pfeiffer died in 1881, and Stollsteimer moved to Dyke, southwest of Pagosa Springs. He became the agent at Ignacio in 1885, lived in Durango, and conducted business there while commuting to the agency. His wife was a Hispanic, a foster child of Antoine Robidoux, so it was natural for Stollsteimer to maintain friendly relations with Spanish-speaking people who, like him, had livestock on the reservation. He opposed the local

Anglo segment that was seeking to remove Hispaños and Utes so they could take over the range for their own use. Sympathetic to the Indians' need to hunt off the reservation for sustenance, he cooperated by granting passes to "good Indians," among whom he was a popular agent.

Chief Ignacio was one of the "good Indians" at the time, despite the independence he had shown prior to 1881. He was setting an example for other Southern Utes by serving as the police captain, living in a small cabin, and digging an irrigation ditch to his field from the Florida River. Three of the sixteen Southern Ute children who went off to the new Albuquerque Indian School were his. Sadly, water failed to flow through the ditch, and, worse, his children died in an epidemic at the school. Grieving and fed up, he cut his hair and in late 1885 reported to Agent Stollsteimer that he and his Weenuches wished to move to Utah.

Recognizing that the long, narrow strip of reservation land was impossible to protect from white intrusion. the agent took the Weenuche Ignacio, the Muache Buckskin Charlie, and the Capote Tapuche to Washington in 1886. The three agreed that all Southern Utes were ready to leave Colorado. In the following months a proposal was made in Washington for relocation either to the Uintah and Ouray Reservation, where Buckskin Charlie's followers wanted to go, or to southeastern Utah's San Juan County.

With nothing resolved by the spring of 1887, when yet another bill was pending for removal of the Utes, an exodus of Weenuches from the reservation began soon after they had received their per capita annuities. In addition to Ignacio's enrolled Utes, about thirty unenrolled Indians belonging to the families of Santiago Largo, Red Jacket, and Hatch also departed, because they feared being arrested for depredations, Stollsteimer reported.[33] Only a few weeks earlier, in a report to the War Department, the agent had identified the Southern Utes' peaceable leaders as Ignacio, Buckskin Charlie, Tapuche, Severo, Aquila, Talian, and Quarto, and he had named Red Jacket and Mariano as "obstinate" and Cavero Blanco as "mean."[34] With the Weenuche departure to Utah, Stollsteimer could no longer count on Ignacio's influence to help control his Weenuches and maintain harmony on the reservation.

San Juan County's invasion by Utes was unwelcome, not surprisingly. People there had hopes of growth and prosperity. Monticello and Blanding were just coming into existence in 1887. Accordingly, Congress made a new proposal, this time to move the Utes to Montana. Some of the Utes liked the idea, but nothing came of it.[35] The Weenuches began to straggle back to Colorado from San Juan County, although they stayed away from the agency and instead remained in the far western part of the reservation. Meanwhile, like a never-ending chorus, citizens in southwestern Colorado were complaining to the commander at Fort Lewis that Utes were tearing down fences, allowing sheep to graze off the reservation, stealing, poaching, and frightening the citizenry, especially in McElmo Canyon. A detachment was sent to lend protection.[36]

While the Weenuches had appeared to be vacating the land south of Mancos and moving to Utah, trespassers assumed they might as well take advantage of their opportunity. Among the white interlopers were the Wetherills, who had livestock ranging in Mancos Canyon on the reservation. In December 1888 one Wetherill son and his brother-in-law were herding cattle there when they came upon the Anasazi ruins of Mesa Verde. Their "discovery," although not the first, opened new opportunities for the Wetherills who were soon leading scientists, tourists, and looters to the antiquities on Ute land. A generation would pass before Mesa Verde was adequately protected and the complications that followed the Wetherills' "discovery" were resolved.

This picture of unsettled conditions is counterbalanced by a few efforts toward stability. Several Hispanic people dug ditches and farmed reservation land on shares with Ute friends and relatives, to everyone's advantage.[37] Agent Stollsteimer had Hispanic workers build small houses for the Utes, although few elected to occupy them, and agency buildings were going up. In 1886 the secretary of the interior authorized a day school at the Southern Ute Agency, and a teacher was sent. The school operated until 1890, although the number of students rarely exceeded ten and measles defeated the school's success.[38]

Although Stollsteimer managed the reservation's business with a fair degree of empathy, he balked when he learned he was also supposed to supervise Jicarilla Apaches. In 1887 the Apaches were assigned to a subagency at Dulce, New Mexico, on land adjacent to that of the Southern Utes. Stollsteimer left the same year amid accusations of dishonesty in business dealings related to contracts for goods and services, the sale of rations for his own profit, and the use of false vouchers. George Bartholomew replaced Stollsteimer as agent not only for the Utes but also for the Jicarillas. The subagency's business was conducted from temporary shacks beside the railroad tracks in New Mexico until 1891 when jurisdiction over Jicarilla Apaches was consolidated with New Mexico's Pueblo Agency.[39]

During the 1880s the Bureau of Indian Affairs and its employees, reformers, politicians, the public, and the Southern Utes seemed to exist in five disparate worlds. As the bureau bumbled along, citizens from Aztec, New Mexico, to Durango, Colorado, and westward trumpeted their belief that Indians were in the way of development of the best land for timber and lumber, the best land for irrigation, the best land for grazing, and the best land for settlement. Finally, in 1890 Congress introduced another bill to relocate the Southern Utes to southeastern Utah. The proposed reservation would have included all of San Juan County north of the San Juan River, from the Colorado River on the west to the state line on the east. The campaign for removal produced a good deal of support among Coloradans, and leaflets were printed and disseminated to sway the unconvinced. Some of this propaganda revealed profound racial bias, and at a hearing for the bill a statement from the agent was read, asserting that in southwest Colorado most people felt "that the Indians are not human."[40]

The Indian Rights Association simply and accurately reduced the white people's motivation to greed, but the association's winning argument was that the proposed new site in Utah had insufficient water for agriculture so the Indians, who were supposed to become farmers, should not be placed there. Meanwhile, ranchers and others in San Juan County, Utah, passionately protested the creation of a reservation in their domain. The Utes once again moved onto the disputed lands with their livestock without waiting for a decision from Washington. And once again, the bill failed.

The Indian Rights Association's position that the best outcome for Ute Indians would be farming and assimilation was basically the philosophy of the Bureau of Indian Affairs, although most bureau employees in the field seemed to understand that Utes were not inclined to farm and were more likely to succeed as livestock owners. In fact, by 1893 the Southern Utes still had only thirty-two to thirty-four farms.[41] Agent David Day reported that Weenuches were nomadic "blanket Indians" who owned livestock, primarily herds of sheep. The Weenuches owned up to three-fourths of the livestock on the reservation. A count of livestock owned by all Southern Utes showed that they had three times as many sheep as horses, in comparison to which they had few cattle, only about three or four per capita. Members of the Muache and Capote Bands showed a greater inclination than the Weenuches to stay in one area, but evidence of assimilation was still minimal, and adaptations were superficial, such as wearing calico instead of buckskin shirts or living in tepees covered with canvas instead of hides.

The Reverend A. J. Rodriguez, a Hispanic missionary who encouraged both education and religious conversion at the Southern Ute Agency, arrived in the 1890s. He worked tirelessly, but his efforts were resisted. Most Spanish-speaking people in the area were Catholic, not Presbyterian as was Rodriguez, and the Utes were friends—sometimes spouses or children—of the Spanish-speaking Catholics. Nevertheless, the missionary opened a small school that operated until 1920, and he won a small number of converts, including some important ones such as the Capote Chief Severo and Julian Buck, son of the Muache chief Buckskin Charlie.

Although problems in and around the Southern Ute Reservation were far from permanently resolved, the War Department deactivated Fort Lewis in 1891. The buildings were converted for use as a boarding school for Ute Indians, with sixteen children in attendance in its first year, 1892. That same year buildings were burned by the enrollees. The next year two pupils died and three went blind, probably from trachoma, an eye infection that was common among the Indians, and the parents removed their children. The school later reopened, and by 1895 the enrollment had grown to 183, of whom seventy-one were Navajos and the others Ute. The curriculum emphasized vocational training, with the students learning to milk cows, dig ditches, grow vegetables, and stitch garments and linens on sewing machines.[42]

In 1894 affairs came to a head. Congress decided that Colorado's Utes should not be moved to Utah or anywhere else and that those who were already in Utah were to return. Most of those in Utah did leave but only after the governor and troops arrived to prod them out of San Juan County. Seventy to a hundred "renegades" remained, intermingling with a somewhat smaller number of Paiutes and Navajos. Among the Ute leaders in Utah were Johnny Benow, Mancos Jim, Posey (a Paiute-Ute), and others who figure later in the Ute story.

In early 1895 Congress passed the Hunter Act, which imposed on Southern Ute Indians the provisions of the General Allotment Act of 1887. By its terms, following approval by three-fourths of the Southern Utes, the Indians were to select their parcels of land on the existing Southern Ute Reservation with the remainder of the reservation land being returned to the public domain, where it would be open to filing by the public. Even the best 180-acre parcels of arid and semiarid land in southwestern Colorado would be inadequate to support a family, much less so the 80- and 40-acre plots available to single and/or minor males. It was well-known in Washington that within three or four generations of dividing and subdividing the parcels, the Utes would be virtually landless. Nevertheless, 153 of the Southern Utes' 301 adult males agreed to allotment.

This total did not meet the three-fourths required for approval, but it did represent nearly all Muaches and Capotes. Because most who did not agree were Weenuches, the government decided to divide the reservation, with Muaches and Capotes receiving the eastern, allotted portion and the Weenuches the western, unallotted end. Thus by 1896, 371 Muache and Capote adults and minors had received allotments totaling 72,811 acres, with a much larger amount of the eastern portion—523,079 acres—becoming part of the public domain.[43] By presidential proclamation in 1899, the public domain portion in the eastern end of the reservation was opened to filing under homestead laws, desert land laws, and timber and stone laws.

Having refused to agree to allotment, Ignacio and his Weenuche followers now had land that took in the southwestern corner of Colorado—a tract that ran fifteen miles from north to south and about fifty miles from east to west—plus almost all of six adjacent townships in New Mexico.[44] This unallotted tribal land encompassed part of Sleeping

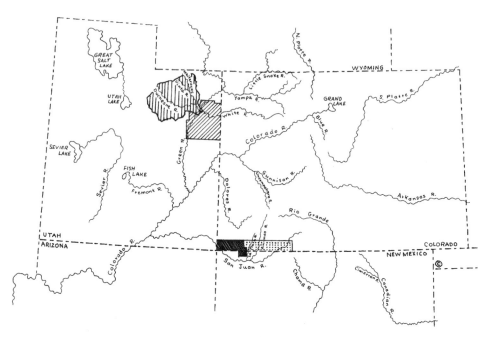

The eastern portion of the Consolidated (Southern) Ute Reservation was allotted for Muache and Capote Utes in 1895, as indicated by the dotted area. The Weenuche Utes, who did not agree to allotment, were given the western portion and a small amount of land in New Mexico.

Ute Mountain and later, with some changes, became the Ute Mountain Ute Reservation.

Through these years, as many-pronged assaults were made on their lands and customs, the Utes survived, although the final outcome was in doubt. The Bear Dance continued, but it often seemed to many dancers that Bear might not be listening to the drum, the growler, the singing. Perhaps Bear had died after all.

10

▼ ▼ ▼

Disorder and Chaos
(1896–1915)

In the half century since the United States Army of the West had marched into New Mexico in the 1840s, Ute life had been irrevocably disrupted by newcomers whose goals and culture were utterly different from those of the Indians. The Ute people had escaped the brutality of a massacre like that by the military of Cheyennes at Sand Creek in Colorado or extermination like that by miners and settlers of Yakis in California. The territories Utes had occupied, the resources they had depended on, their relationships with other bands of their own tribe, the traditions, and the long linear story that told the Núu-ci who they were had become a tangled skein, however.

After the passage of the General Allotment Act in 1887, it was only a matter of time until the lands of the Southern Ute Reservation and the Uintah and Ouray Reservation would become an archipelago of tiny islands of privately held allotments in a sea of public domain and white settlements. In southern Colorado, when the Muaches and Capotes had accepted allotments the Weenuches had successfully resisted that fate, but the Northern Utes were unable to muster the same kind of unity needed to avoid allotment of their reservation.

The government's first step in Utah was to survey the reservation in 1895. It determined first that insufficient arable land existed on the Uncompahgres' two-million-acre portion of the reservation for the allotments that would be needed. Consequently, it was proposed that the Uncompahgres should pay $1.25 each for 232 more allotments in the Uintah portion to make up a total of 315 parcels.[1] In protest, an Uncompahgre delegation went to Washington in 1897, and the Uintahs and White Rivers went the next year. Deep snow in the winter of 1897–

1898 caused the survey work to halt. With interests wanting to develop gilsonite on the reservation, further delays resulted until 1902, when Congress passed legislation to place the unallotted lands of the Uintah and Ouray Reservation in the public domain, thereby opening it to settlement and other purposes. A period for filing claims would follow.

Allotment continued to be unacceptable to many Utes, and a majority of those on the Uintah and Ouray Reservation never approved allotment, as required by law. The parcels consisted of eighty acres of irrigable land for families and forty acres for single Utes. If any eligible Indian refused to make a selection, a commission did so for him, as happened in the majority of instances. Allotments for Uncompahgres were mainly on the lower Duchesne River and, to a lesser extent, along the lower White River, east of the Green, but the latter parcels were disallowed. Thus, much of the reservation east of the Green River, with its oil and gilsonite resources, was declared public domain. Future leasing of mineral rights there, which developed into a major industry, consequently became possible with no economic benefit to the Utes. Allotments for Uintah and White River Utes were located chiefly around Whiterocks, with some others in the upper Duchesne River area on Lake Fork Creek. After the allotments had been made, totaling 103,265 acres, only a few Indians stayed on them.

White River Utes particularly resisted the allotment process and chose not to stay on their pieces of land. They had never stopped going off the reservation to hunt, although Colorado's game wardens had pressured Fort Duchesne to stop such activities. In the fall of 1898 troops did succeed in returning a hunting party to the reservation, but others eluded the net and continued to hunt around Lily Park and Brown's Hole. Differences of opinion about who was actually guilty of poaching prevented resolution of the problem. When an army officer reported in December 1898 that he believed white poachers were guilty of killing game, the warden replied that he had never heard of a white man killing game illegally.[2] Impasses of this sort continued for the next few years.

In addition to the Utes' desire to return to familiar habits and territory, food preferences and a healthy diet encouraged them to go on hunting trips. For centuries Ute Indians had depended on lean game, fish, and wild plant foods, but rations typically distributed at agencies included ten pounds each of beef, navy beans, and flour; two pounds each of sugar, coffee, lard, and salt pork; and a half pound of salt.[3] This shift to a diet high in fat and carbohydrates—especially the dearly loved sugar—is believed to have contributed to the diabetes, hypertension, and obesity that have become common health problems among Utes. Some of these ills might have been avoided with a traditional Ute diet.

Rations, on which the Utes had become dependent, were not always available after allotments were made. The Utes were expected to raise their food on their own land as they adopted white ways and became self-sufficient. To further encourage independence, by 1902 Agent H. P. Myton was denying rations to Utes who still wore the blanket, refused to cut their hair, or kept their children out of school. Unhappiness over allotments and Myton's stern policies might be reasons for a significant drop in the number of Utes enrolled on the reservation that year. The 1900 census counted 470 Uintahs, 383 White Rivers (19 of whom were at the Ouray Agency), and 846 Uncompahgres for a total of 1,699.[4] By 1903 the total was only 1,470. Although Agent W. A. Mercer began to pay parents to send their children to school, the census figures had dropped to 1,336 in 1904.[5]

Disease could have contributed to this decline, and addiction to alcohol was common, as were its consequences. The "pest hole," as one agent called the Duchesne Strip, was encouraging drunkenness, which was held somewhat at bay when purveyors of illegal liquor to Indians were sent from the Strip to a penitentiary in 1899. Other causes of death included infectious diseases. Schoolchildren suffered from both measles and chicken pox in 1901, when seven students died at Whiterocks and another four at Randlett. A diphtheria epidemic struck the reservation the following year and was stemmed only by the arrival of a doctor from Denver with vaccine. Influenza, pneumonia, and tuberculosis were common killers among all ages. The problem of locating a suitable place for burials was partially solved when Episcopal missionaries introduced a new mortuary practice by locating a cemetery at Randlett. At Whiterocks the traditional burying ground had scaffolds erected over the graves, among which the Utes' sheep wandered.

The chief cause of the population decline, however, was probably triggered by Indians who shunned the agency. Trouble was so prevalent at the turn of the century that detachments of the Ninth Cavalry were often on patrol. In December 1900 guards prevented the burning of property at Whiterocks, and one of the Indians involved, Black Hawk, was arrested.[6] In January 1903, when Agent Myton departed—to no one's regret—a Ute named Horsely chased him and threatened to kill him. Chief Sowerick with a group of White River followers "flew the coop for Pine Ridge" on September 7, 1903, according to the diary of trooper H. G. Clark, and cavalrymen chased them for nearly two weeks without overtaking them.[7]

The prospect of opening the reservation was the major issue in the discontent. Boomers kept up steady pressure, and not all of them were future settlers. In 1898 the Raven Mining Company and the secretary of the interior had signed a mining lease that permitted prospecting on 200,000 acres of gilsonite land on the reservation south of the Strawberry River, although the project stalled during the allotment fight.[8] Next, there was exciting news in 1902 when Denver's David Moffat was organizing the Denver, Northwestern, and Pacific Railroad with plans to extend rails all the way to gilsonite mines on the Duchesne Strip. A town and post office, named Moffat, appeared on the Strip, but after the railroad proved unable to build to Utah, the name of Moffat was replaced by that of Gusher.

Although some mining operations took place in the Gusher area, long-term gilsonite development became a reality neither on the Raven land nor on the Strip but around a large area of mining leases centered on the Black Diamond Vein at Evacuation Creek near the Utah-Colorado state line. Initially, loads of gilsonite from the region were carried through the reservation on a wagon road built by the army between Fort Duchesne and Price in the 1880s. Another wagon road was also constructed from the mines to Vernal, with a bridge called Ignatio crossing over the White River. A Green River ferry crossing was labeled Alhandra, and between Ouray and Bonanza a location on the road was called Chipeta. The shortest route for hauling large quantities of freight to and from a railroad lay across Baxter Pass to Mack, Colorado, west of Grand Junction, and so the narrow-gauge Uintah Railway was built south from the mines and was in service by 1905.[9]

Along the route of the railroad south of Baxter Pass was a point called Atchee, named for a friendly relative of Chipeta, whereas Lake McAndrew was named for a railroad superintendent who had been a government herder on the reservation. Dragon quickly became a popular place for visits by Chipeta and other Utes who in summer camped and grazed their sheep and goats in the Bitter Creek area. This land rose from alkali flats and dry brushland into forest-covered mountains about 9,000 feet in elevation. The upper reaches of Bitter Creek bore a faint but welcome resemblance to the Tabeguache homeland in Colorado. Its watershed and timber were prized by Utes, and the tarry gilsonite was useful for sealing their water jugs.

Whether for the natural resources or agricultural land, white interests sought as much acreage on the Uintah and Ouray Reservation as they could take. From 1,010,000 acres lopped from the reservation, in 1905 President Theodore Roosevelt created the Uinta Forest Reserve, later the Uinta National Forest. He also set aside land for homesites, towns, and reclamation projects. When the process was complete in 1909, the once four-million-acre reservation consisted of a patchwork of 360,000 acres, with about a third of this amount designated as allotments. After this restructuring the Utes in Utah were officially called the Confederated Bands of Utes in Utah, administered by a superintendent, as also the tribal members in Colorado officially became the Confederated Bands of Utes in Colorado after the restructuring of their reservation.

In 1905 land in the public domain was thrown open to homesteaders following a registration process. A lottery drawing lured thousands of hopeful people to Provo in August of that year, and future ranchers and farmers thronged onto the land to stake their homesteads. Suddenly, new settlements sprang up—Roosevelt a few miles west of Fort Duchesne, Myton at a Duchesne River crossing formerly called simply "the Bridge," and several other small communities. The overwhelmed and resentful Indians sent a delegation to Washington to protest, and the garrison at Fort Duchesne was increased with additional cavalry and infantry companies.[10]

Angered by the injustices, in 1906 White River Utes decided to leave the region en masse. They believed their only hope lay in going to live on the High Plains where there were fewer whites, and an exodus began with the objective of joining either Crow or Sioux Indians there. Led by Red Cap, Appah, and others including Tim Johnson, several hundred men, women, and children set out. Red Cap held special authority, because he was a son of Nevava, as were Douglass, Antelope, Jack, and Pauvits—all important players in White River Ute affairs when they lived in Colorado. Red Cap had headed the delegation to Washington in 1905. Tim Johnson, along with Eggleston (or Engleston, a Sioux), had been an agitator on the Uintah Reservation when seventy-five to ninety White Rivers and six or seven Uintahs had tried without success to organize a rebellion there in 1905.[11]

When the emigrants left Utah, they took fifty head of cattle, pack horses, wagons loaded with supplies, and about eight hundred ponies. First, they went to their old hunting grounds in northwestern Colorado where they split into several units, and from there it appears they planned to travel to the Bighorn country in Wyoming. As some progressed through Rawlins, Douglas, and Gillette, they purchased ammunition and flour at local stores, but nervous residents publicly accused the Indians of being insolent thieves. Although they were also charged with destroying vast amounts of game, the Utes, in fact, hunted only enough deer and rabbits for their food. The Utes argued that they had as much right as anyone to hunt and to travel wherever they pleased, because, as allottees, they were now citizens. This belief proved to be an illusion, for in 1907 Congress postponed their citizenship.

Confronted by six companies of the army's cavalry, 432 Utes agreed to go to Belle Fourche in South Dakota and from there to Fort Meade, where they remained for eight months. Others traveled to the Pine Ridge Indian Reservation, where neither the agent nor the Sioux welcomed their guests. By October a ragged group led by Tim Johnson had retreated to Rock Springs in southern Wyoming. Johnson sent a telegram to Fort Duchesne to report that his people needed aid, for they were out of provisions, the children were sick, a woman had frozen to death, and twenty-one horses had died.

Johnson's group returned to their reservation from that point, but the main contingent at Fort Meade held out. At a council it was agreed that they could move to the Cheyenne River Indian Reservation in northern South Dakota, where they were permitted to lease four townships of land. Still unable to provide for themselves, by the fall of 1907 the Utes were being pressed hard by authorities to sell their ponies, put their children in the Indian boarding school at Rapid City, and take laborers' jobs with the railroad. A few did accept this resolution, but only temporarily.

Violence seemed possible on the Cheyenne River Reservation during the winter of 1907–1908, and troops were ordered to the agency at Thunder River to maintain order. Humanitarians took up the cause of the Utes' plight, over the protestations of South Dakota's governor who resented having to send secondhand clothing and other goods to his state's uninvited guests. Meanwhile, the Utes were reaching the conclusion that they might be better off in their own homes in Utah. Thus in June 1908, under military escort, 225 Utes left Thunder Butte and went to Rapid City, where they met 369 others ready to travel to Utah.[12]

Any hopes that prospects had improved on the Uintah and Ouray Reservation during the absence of the White River Utes were quickly destroyed when it was learned that the most important natural resource— water—was under attack. Irrigation is essential for agriculture almost everywhere in the American West, and Utah is no exception. If Native Americans were to become self-sufficient farmers, they would need water. To be able to farm and ranch in the Heber Valley, Mormons had illegally been diverting water from the reservation's Strawberry River for some time. After the passage of the Newlands Act in 1902, the new Bureau of Reclamation promptly began to construct the Strawberry Reservoir on land long favored and owned by Ute Indians until it was taken for the reservoir by right of eminent domain. The reservoir was to divert water by way of a tunnel through the Wasatch Range to the Utah Valley where Mormons were farming around Utah Lake and where many Ute Indians had lived until they were removed to the Uinta Basin. The water stored in the reservoir and diverted to the Utah Valley would naturally have flowed east through the Uinta Basin, where it was needed on Indian lands.

For the Indians a few small irrigation systems were in place on the reservation as early as the 1880s, the largest being the Uintah Number One Canal, built in 1883 a mile below the mouth of the Uinta River. Utes had quickly settled there. From upriver on the Duchesne eleven ditches had been built, but they were irrigating only 3,000 acres of reservation land, much less than the original capacity.

In 1900 the United States Indian Irrigation Service was created to assist Indian tribes with developing water resources, and in 1906 the Uintah Indian Irrigation Project began under the wing of this organization. A project office was established at Whiterocks. Construction proceeded, primarily with Mormon contractors and laborers but also with a few Utes. Ultimately, less than three percent of the money paid for labor went to Utes, although the cost of the project, which came to about $665,000, was paid with moneys from the sale of reservation lands. Diversions, legal and illegal, from the Uintah Indian Irrigation Project reduced the amount of irrigated Indian acreage to 11,000 acres out of a total of nearly 88,000 acres served by ditches.[13]

For years, the Indian Irrigation Service continued to construct and maintain the water delivery system and to assess Utes for the water, regardless of whether they were farming. Although Western states' water doctrine requires that water be put to beneficial use to protect prior use rights, a United States Supreme Court decision in 1908, in a case involving the Blackfoot Tribe, confirmed that prior rights of the tribe were valid—with or without beneficial use—by virtue of the fact that the availability of natural resources was implicit for fulfilling the purpose of a reservation. Since this court decision in *Winters v. United States,* Native American tribes have owned reserved water rights. Having the rights and having the water were—and still are—two different things, however, as the Indians soon learned. Furthermore, those served by the water system were assessed, but many Indians were unable to pay. As unpaid accounts accumulated, water rights and land were lost.

Chipeta's strong character was still apparent in 1916, when she was about seventy years old and blind. She dictated a letter that year to

Commissioner of Indian Affairs Cato Sells concerning the frustrations she and her Uncompahgre Utes had experienced when they tried, in good faith, to create farms. She began by pointing out the federal government's failure to replace her valuable Colorado land with irrigated land in Utah. She continued:

> Some of my people were allotted on the bottoms of the Duchesne River, and they built for themselves an irrigation ditch and irrigated their land and built good homes there, but since the big canals have been constructed and much of the water is used at points above these lands, the ditch that my people constructed is a 'high-water' ditch and has water only during the floods of June. Consequently these people have been forced to abandon the homes that they built for themselves. . . . We have lands, it is true, but without water these lands are of no value.[14]

Agent Kneale, who helped Chipeta with her letter, wrote to Commissioner Sells that Chipeta had done much to keep her people orderly, and he felt she deserved to be rewarded. The commissioner suggested furniture for her home, but the agent responded that he thought this gift would be unsuitable, so two shawls were sent to her instead. Chipeta, in turn, sent Sells a horse blanket. Of course, what was needed was water, not shawls. Some reimbursements were eventually paid for the losses of resources, but Ute Indians on the Uintah and Ouray Reservation waited nearly twenty-five years before they received money for the loss of land that became the Uinta National Forest. The payment was one million dollars, about a dollar an acre. No reimbursement was paid for the loss of water.

An unintended result of the irrigation project draining the Uinta River was that Fort Duchesne found itself waterless, and it has been said that this situation caused the fort to deactivate. True or not, in the autumn of 1912 the troops went to Dragon, boarded the Uintah Railway, and left what little remained of the Uintah and Ouray Reservation.[15] The army buildings were occupied by the agency in 1912, and the two subagencies at Whiterocks and Ouray were closed, although the privately owned trading posts remained.

Without a military presence to restrain them, Ute hunters continued to go periodically to northwestern Colorado and southern Wyoming, and residents there continued to complain to wardens about game that was being killed. In 1914 it was rumored that eight hundred Indians were hunting illegally on Douglas Creek, south of Rangely. About one hundred of the Indians were rounded up by civilian law enforcers, since army personnel were gone, and sent back to Utah.[16]

A reminder of Fort Duchesne's heyday lingered in a store belonging to Wong Sing, a Chinese immigrant who came to America in 1889 and moved to Fort Duchesne in the early 1890s. At first he did laundry for the soldiers, and then he added a restaurant and a store on the Strip. His establishment was a fixture until his death in 1934. This honest man was trusted and loved by his Ute neighbors.

When Utes came to the trading posts, they often bartered their craftwork, which by the late 1800s featured excellent beadwork. With Utes increasingly sedentary on the reservations the women had more opportunity to perfect this decorative craft, although it is believed Utes learned it from Arapaho Indians earlier in the century. The highest level was reached among Utes around 1900. Favoring light green, light blue, and yellow seed beads, Ute women adorned cradleboards, pony trappings, buckskin and doeskin garments, moccasins, belts, cuffs, gloves, armbands, leggings, and hatbands with beadwork, primarily in geometric patterns but later with floral designs, too. Most of the apparel decorated with beadwork was intended for use in dances and other ceremonies. Functional beaded bags of numerous kinds were also popular—coin purses, awl and strike-a-light (match) containers, ration ticket bags, medicine and tobacco pouches, pipe bags, knife scabbards, and so on.[17]

Chipeta was considered an expert at beadwork. Even when her eyesight was growing dim because of cataracts, she continued to do the work with the assistance of children who handed her the colors she requested. She loved children and made them toys, including a small doll in a miniature cradleboard she gave to a friend at Dragon. It eventually passed to a museum.

A digression is needed to describe Chipeta's years in Utah. A friendly person who responded to kindness from white people, she became affiliated with the Episcopal mission church at Randlett near her home on the Duchesne River. She also came to Dragon from her summer camp in the Bitter Creek area, and her group seems to have established another campsite closer to the mining town, where she and her people enjoyed watching the activity around the railroad, the hotel, the schools, homes, and store that had grown up there. Chipeta had made several trips to Washington on various railroads, and now she could board the cars of the Uintah Railway to travel around Colorado. From Dragon she could go to Mack, board the Denver and Rio Grande to Grand Junction, and continue to Montrose and points south on Otto Mears's Rio Grande Southern to Durango, where the Denver and Rio Grande connected to Ignacio. One can only imagine how she felt about seeing railroad tracks built through her farm south of Montrose. She rode in parades at Delta and Ouray, stayed in Ouray's best hotel, and visited Buckskin Charlie at Ignacio. Accompanying a group of Southern Utes to a festival in Colorado Springs in 1911, she called on her old friend, Mrs. Charles Adams.

Chipeta's clouded eyes are evident in photographs from these jaunts. She went to Grand Junction for cataract surgery, but her vision continued to deteriorate. In Dragon Mrs. W. G. King, who was the recipient of the doll in the cradleboard and who, earlier, had been a nurse with the Bureau of Indian Affairs, treated Chipeta's eyes with hot packs and eye drops in 1912 and 1913. The two women became trusted friends.[18]

Chipeta also had help from wards, who had been in her household as early as the time in the Uncompahgre Valley and who had been listed in the 1885 census, as previously mentioned. In the mid-1890s there were four wards—Lunpeta, John Peta, Francisco, and Jose La Cross. Three Ute boys were listed on the rolls with her in 1908.[19] Until they reached maturity, the boys probably herded sheep and goats. She also provided for those in need of help, as when she cared for a captive white boy, Stephen Stridiron, until he was returned to his family.[20] After she became blind, she was assisted by both the young people and her family members, and she had a rope strung between her tepee and the nearby brush so she could take care of her personal needs.

Chipeta is an outstanding example of the Tabeguache or Uncompahgre Band, not because of her worldly achievements and rewards but because of her ability to live a peaceful existence under highly frustrating conditions. Many others in her band also lived harmoniously in difficult times and gradually progressed in a new way of life that was not of their choosing but that was the way things were and clearly were going to be. The same observations can be made about the Southern Utes in Colorado, where Buckskin Charlie and Severo were peaceful examples for their Muache and Capote peoples.

In Colorado, schools were beginning to have some success in the process of assimilation, and education continued to be a foremost goal of the Bureau of Indian Affairs. The Ignacio Boarding School opened in 1902, and two years later it had seventy students. The school was soon filled to capacity. The enrollment at Ignacio undoubtedly affected that at Fort Lewis and contributed to the latter's closure.

The Bureau of Indian Affairs' other guiding objective, to make farmers out of Native Americans, was enjoying limited success, but in contrast to the Utah Indians at the turn of the century, allotted Southern Utes were becoming more experienced at farming. Buckskin Charlie's allotment was usually singled out as a model, and about half of the allottees on the reservation were raising crops, particularly alfalfa and oats.[21] Associations with their Hispanic neighbors, whose lifestyle was agricultural, encouraged Ute farming. Moreover, the marriage of Ute women to Spanish-speaking men occasionally resulted in increased amounts of farmland under irrigation, as several of these men worked on shares with their wives' relatives.[22]

Other processes, however, eroded the success of Ute farmers. The most deleterious influence was the influx of people taking up land when the public domain area, consisting of former reservation land, was thrown open in 1899. A land rush by boomers from Oklahoma took place, with Arboles the starting point for the race to stake claims. Bayfield was a jumping-off point for crowds seeking land on the Los Pinos River and the Florida Mesa.[23] The newcomers were competitors for scant water resources, as were Mormons in Utah.

Although Indian allotments, which were held in trust, could not originally be sold, the holders could lease them, as often occurred. After 1907, if allottees were declared "incompetent" because of old age or illness or if allottees died, their parcels could be alienated and sold. Hispanic and white purchasers acquired many farms in this manner on the Southern Ute Reservation, as well as on the Uintah and Ouray Reservation. A unique situation was the sale of the land that became the townsite of Ignacio in 1910. John Taylor, a black interpreter for the Utes who had lived among them for several years and married several of the women, inherited Allotment Number One from a stepson, Henry Green, in 1909 and quickly sold it to the town promoters for five dollars.[24]

As elsewhere, easily accessible alcohol continued to be a major cause of trouble on the reservations. Sundays at Ignacio were days of revelry, despite the arrival of the Catholic Church in 1903, because Fabian Martinez had arrived from Antonito that same year to build a race track on the hill above town.[25] With liquor and gambling uncontrolled on the hill, Fabian Martinez instantly had many more faithful followers than the church did.

Authorities considered traditional dances to be another evil influence because of the crowds they drew and the drinking and sexual promiscuity that often accompanied them. Equally important to many white people was their belief that Indian dances represented unacceptable heathen spirituality. In the case of the Ghost Dance, subversion also was suspected. The Sun Dance was deemed a gruesome, primitive dance rather than a transforming one. In 1906, when Commissioner of Indian Affairs Francis Leupp was discouraging Indian dances, Southern Ute Superintendent Burton Custer reported that even the Bear Dance had been discontinued during the past few years, but he did not give suppression as the reason. Instead, he boasted that the Utes were too busy tilling their fields in the spring.[26] By the second decade of the 1900s the commissioner of Indians Affairs was forbidding dances outright, although such repression seems to have inspired the Utes to continue them more faithfully.

Within limits, pageantry was officially permitted. Southern Utes marched in Theodore Roosevelt's inaugural parade in 1905, and Buckskin Charlie and Severo, with some of their followers, were soon taking part in other public appearances, where spectators enjoyed the colorful processions with full regalia and Indian villages that exhibited traditional ways. Although it has been said that Southern Utes participated in Buffalo Bill's Wild West shows, support for this claim has not been found. Southern Utes did take part in other so-called Wild West exhibitions, including an Elks Lodge reunion in Denver and a sesquicentennial celebration in Boulder, Colorado. The Utes were in demand in Colorado Springs, where they appeared in 1911 at a fair—when Chipeta accompanied them—and in 1912 when they participated in a procession at the marking of the Ute Trail in Ute Pass, west of Manitou Springs. Severo and his handsome family previously went to the posh Broadmoor suburb and posed for photographs. Each Ute who attended such affairs received five dollars in addition to travel expenses as an inducement to come.

During this same period, agricultural fairs were introduced. Long popular in America's agrarian society, similar fairs at Ignacio provided opportunities to exhibit crops—especially watermelons if photographs are an accurate representation—and crafts. Large crowds attended. The superintendent and his employees encouraged Indians to take part in the fairs and discouraged most activities such as dances and celebrations off the reservation that might compete.

With farming taking hold on the eastern end of the reservation, it was decided injudiciously that the Utes no longer needed rations. In 1911 the Utes received a large reimbursement for timber and mineral lands taken from reservations, not directly as cash to individuals but as a credit held in trust by the government. With more money in trust funds although not in the pockets of the Indians, rations were cut off the next year, but humanitarians raised an outcry that resulted in restoration.

The Capote Band's Chief Severo died in 1913 at the age of about sixty-nine. His death left his counterpart, the Muache Band's Buckskin Charlie, as the principal chief at Ignacio until his death in 1936, when he was ninety-five and blind. Because Buckskin Charlie served as leader into relatively modern times, he is the most familiar of the Southern Ute chiefs, although his personal history is not well-known. He is said to have been born to an Apache mother and a Muache father, but the location of his birth is variously reported as Colorado Springs' Garden of the Gods, the Cimarrón area in New Mexico, and southwestern Colorado near Navajo Springs, close to Towaoc. Severo was a Muache who married a Capote and became a member of that band.

Following a path much different from that of the Muaches and Capotes on the eastern end of the Southern Ute Reservation, the Weenuches on the western portion remained independent and mobile, grazing livestock and resisting change for the most part. A Colorado Historical Society marker near Cortez relates a legend that says these Utes believed their Sleeping Ute Mountain—the most prominent landmark in Colorado's Four Corners area—was a god who, angered by the Indians, had put the rain clouds in his pockets and had lain down to sleep. Since then, clouds that occasionally hover over the mountain have slipped from him only momentarily. One day the Sleeping Ute will reawaken, the legend forecasts, to fight the Utes' enemies.

Abetting the Weenuches' independence was the absence of a resident agent. A subagency attached to the Southern Ute Agency was established in 1897 at a small source of water called Navajo Springs, a couple miles south of the present Towaoc. The superintendent of the Fort Lewis Indian School, more than forty miles away, was supposed to oversee the subagency. A few adobe buildings at Navajo Springs housed an employee and supplies, but the location was ill chosen for both the subagency and farming because water was scarce except in springtime or when flash floods occurred. In 1897 Congress appropriated $150,000 to buy water rights from the Montezuma Canal Company, without results, and in 1902 Congress authorized the secretary of the interior to construct a canal for irrigation, but the project was not built.[27]

As a result, Ute agriculture did not flourish, but the handmaiden of assimilation—education—was faring somewhat better. Children from the western portion of the Southern Ute Reservation were expected to go to the boarding school at Fort Lewis, not a desirable option for Weenuches. Fort Lewis's enrollment peaked at four hundred, largely Navajos with fewer Southern Ute pupils and only a few Weenuches. Attendance dwindled at Fort Lewis with the opening of other schools, until it closed in 1910 and was turned over to the state of Colorado to operate as a junior college specializing in agriculture, mechanics, and home economics. (In the 1950s that school closed and Fort Lewis College opened with a four-year program at Durango. The college offers free tuition to Native American students and has attracted many Ute Indians.)

With Chief Ignacio's encouragement in earlier years, Weenuches were not entirely averse to education, as shown by their attendance at schools closer to home. Beginning in 1897 the Presbyterian Women's Home Mission Board operated a mission program at Cortez that provided not only nursing care for Indian women but also a school, which soon boasted an intermittent enrollment of twenty-five children. The school closed when a government school opened at the Navajo Springs Subagency in 1906.[28] S. F. Stacher, who was employed at Navajo Springs from 1906 until 1909, was in charge of opening the school, and his wife was its teacher.

Chief Ignacio, who lived in a government-built two-room house a half mile from Navajo Springs, was encouraging not only schooling but farming as well. He had not forsaken tradition, though, including the Ute love of horses. When Indians gathered for distributions of rations at Navajo Springs, horse races were held, and Ignacio's pony, Joe, usually won.[29]

Ignacio's influence on the Weenuches' portion of the reservation did not go unchallenged. The band split into two factions composed of those who followed him and those who followed Mariano, labeled earlier as a stubborn individual, and Redrock, another reactionary who wanted nothing to do with new ways and assimilation. Instead of settling down, these rebels spent their time traveling to visit friends on the eastern reservation, on Utah's Uncompahgre reservation, and around Utah's Blue Mountains.

Relations between Utes on the two portions of the reservation appear to have been cool but civil for the most part. When two off-reservation Utes were killed in 1895 near the Dolores River by Paiutes, including Jimmie Hatch, the Weenuches did not become involved. Severo came from Ignacio and helped capture Hatch, who was sent to the state penitentiary with a death sentence. Severo received an official letter of gratitude and a ribbon from the federal government, but he was denied the cash he requested so he could go to Cañon City to witness the execution.[30]

Rations were distributed biweekly at Navajo Springs. The policy was to issue beef each time until its distribution was changed to once a month, with salt pork being substituted on the intervening ration day. This deterioration in the quality of rations was compensated for, it is supposed, with mutton from the Utes' flocks.

A fair amount of discussion and negotiation at Navajo Springs surrounded the proposed creation of Mesa Verde National Park, occupying

50,000 acres partly on public domain land and partly on Weenuche land. The latter contained the most important archaeological sites. As digging, looting, and desecration of Anasazi ruins by private parties and scientific expeditions accelerated in the late 1880s and the 1890s, a movement grew to protect the treasures. Led by Virginia McClurg of Colorado Springs, club women organized the Colorado Cliff Dwellers Association and pressed for the establishment of the national park. As the drive for the park's creation was under way, in 1901 members of the organization negotiated a ten-year lease with the Weenuches. The lease allowed not only protection of the ruins but also the development of a road and a few other amenities for visitors after the national park was created in 1906.

With the lease about to expire in 1911, it became important to acquire the park land that still belonged to the Utes, so some hardy club women from Durango made a trip to Navajo Springs to negotiate with the Utes for this cession. The meeting was unsuccessful, for the ladies were frightened by inebriated Indians who were holding a noisy dance, while those Utes who did attend as negotiators were difficult to reason with, the ladies complained. A second trip by the determined women proved more productive.[31] The Weenuches turned out to be better negotiators than they appeared, for in exchange for the 14,520 acres they ceded they received 20,160 acres. They retained land containing antiquities outside the southern boundary of the national park. (Today, the Ute Mountain Tribal Park protects these ruins and conducts public tours on Ute land. The last chief, Jack House, left an acclaimed legacy of his paintings on rocks within the park.) The land Weenuches received in exchange for what they ceded included the northern end of their sacred Sleeping Ute Mountain and acreage west to the Utah state line in an irregularly shaped parcel.

Most attempts by the Weenuches to improve their economic lot met with disappointment. For instance, they purchased several thousand head of cattle around 1913, but half of the herd soon died on the barren land.[32] In 1913 the still progressive eighty-five-year-old Chief Ignacio died, and one of his followers, John Miller, became his successor, despite an initial contest with more reactionary members. Miller proved to be a conservative leader, as was his successor, Jack House.

In 1914 the subagency at Navajo Springs closed and moved to a new hillside location at Towaoc, two miles north of the former site. Removed from the danger of flash floods and dust storms, the new site still lacked sufficient water, which had to be hauled from Cortez. In 1915 the Ute Mountain Ute Tribe was officially created, and the name was given to its reservation and to its agency at Towaoc, although administratively the latter was still considered a subagency of the agency at Ignacio. (The name Towaoc means "just fine.")

The Ute Mountain Ute Tribe's members were the Weenuches, but not the entire band belonged formally to the tribe. Some members of the band had not been enrolled in the Southern Ute books and continued to lead separate lives off the reservation, especially in Utah's San Juan County. Departures to Utah in the 1880s and 1890s, when some Weenuches remained in Utah, has been discussed in Chapter 9. When efforts were made in 1895 to enroll all Weenuches, some chose not to be enrolled by the federal government, even though they were unable to receive rations and other supplies as a result.

It has been said that Indians around Blanding, Utah, included not only Weenuches but also some Muache Utes who had fled at the time of enrollment at Ignacio because they feared retaliation for a wrong one of their families had committed against another.[33] Another possibility is that Utes around Utah's Blue Mountains included a core group of Seuvarits who seemed to have disappeared from southeastern Utah. Although it is impossible to find agreement on the tribal affiliations of the "renegades," as they were informally called, some of San Juan County's Utes contend today that they have been in Blue Mountain area forever and that they, not the Towaoc people, are the real Weenuches. To add further to the confusion, intermixed with the Utah Utes were Navajos and Southern Paiutes of the San Juan Band. In the Navajo Mountain region, where Navajos were predominant, Utes and Paiutes came to be called "Navajos."[34] The people living at Allen Canyon are considered to be predominantly Southern Paiute with Ute intermixture. Today's White Mesa Indians assert firmly that they are Ute Indians, although some have Navajo or Paiute ancestry as well.

Material evidence of intertribal relations is seen in trade items. Not only had Utes throughout their entire territory exchanged buckskins for Navajo blankets for centuries, but, in a newer development, Utes and Southern Paiutes were also producing Navajo wedding baskets by the late 1890s.[35] Always manufacturers of excellent, functional basketry for their own use, the two tribes began to craft ceremonial baskets for Navajos as a trade item. Why many Navajos ceased making their own baskets has sometimes been explained by Navajo taboos surrounding the making of ceremonial goods that made it cumbersome for members of the tribe to manufacture such items. Another explanation might be that the Navajos were kept busy with the more profitable production of handwoven blankets and rugs, as well as silver work, for the tourist trade. In any case, it is apparent that Utes and Southern Paiutes were sharing a new type of activity in a craft in which they already had considerable skill. In the 1930s Ute women from Blanding to Ignacio were still fashioning Navajo wedding baskets, and Southern Paiutes were similarly engaged, as both still are to a lesser extent.

Among the Utes in Utah, campsites of the several leaders of the groups in the Four Corners were fairly well established around 1900, although the occupants moved about to herd their flocks of sheep and goats within their own territories. Well-known figures were Johnny Benow, Polk, Posey, and Wash (George Washington) on Utah's Montezuma Creek. Mancos Jim was nearby in Yellow Jacket Canyon and later at Allen Canyon west of Blanding. Modern scholars identify all of these men as Ute Indians, but traditional lore refers to Posey as a Paiute. He married one of Polk's daughters, and it seems likely that he was a Paiute who became a Ute by marriage. Posey has often been described as more of a troublemaker than most others. He was accused of stealing a horse in 1903 and of escaping from Monticello's jail while awaiting trial.[36]

In the Four Corners where these Indians circulated, owners of cattle resented the use of the public domain by Utes and Navajos with their horses and flocks of sheep and goats, especially in Montezuma Canyon. Although the big cattle outfits like the Carlisle and LC Ranches had left the region by 1890, smaller livestock owners remained, and the racially diverse users of the range continued to antagonize one another. In 1907 four cowboys burned a brush fence surrounding Johnny Benow's compound and, in so doing, lit more than a fire. Polk, Posey, Wash, and Mancos Jim, led by Johnny Benow, charged the cowboys.[37] Fortunately, no one was killed in this encounter, but it inspired a hot debate between the ranchers' political allies and the Indians' administrators regarding the right of Native Americans to graze livestock on the public domain. The ranchers' chief argument was that Indians had their reservation land on which to graze their animals. Fort Lewis's Superintendent J. S. Spear, still the Weenuches' overseer, talked to Johnny Benow, who blamed all the trouble on Mormons who were trying to force out the Utes. Benow and the others stubbornly remained in Montezuma Canyon.

Elsewhere, some cattlemen were able to get along with Indians. Henry McCabe, whose family lived around Dolores, recalled in later years that when McCabe cattle strayed onto Ute land, his father gave some cowhides and meat as payment for the grass that had been eaten and thereby avoided the kind of fate that befell trespassing cattle that belonged to others.[38] McCabe remembered Polk and Posey, whom he knew, as being friendly, despite their reputation for being "mean." Also, around trading posts at Mexican Hat, Bluff, and Kayenta, where Polk and Posey often showed up, the two were considered friendly.

Polk had a son named Tsenegat (Everett Hatch), who was generally not considered a troublemaker, but in 1914 he was suspected of having killed a Mexican sheepherder southwest of Sleeping Ute Mountain. Although he later denied guilt, he became the subject of a manhunt by a deputy marshal with a posse who went to Bluff in hopes of arresting Tsenegat and Polk. Some of the posse members were drunk and recklessly shot up a nearby Ute encampment, killing and wounding some innocent occupants and arresting others. The prisoners were confined in the upper story of the local cooperative store, from which they attempted to escape, and one of the escapees, a son-in-law of Polk, was killed. One hundred Indians, led by Polk and Posey, fled to the area of Navajo Mountain for safety.[39]

The episode gained considerable public attention. Ute sympathizers blamed local cattlemen for the tragedy at Bluff. Nevertheless, in early 1915 an assiduous United States marshal set out once more with a posse from the Mancos and Dolores neighborhood to arrest Tsenegat, who by then was camping with Polk on Montezuma Creek near Bluff. The posse shot up the camp and then rode off to find Posey's camp in Allen Canyon, where they also scattered the Indians. Indians and white men were killed in these encounters. The army then sent a detachment to restore peace to San Juan County. Posey's Utes surrendered and were taken by train from Thompson, Utah, to Salt Lake City. Tsenegat was taken to Denver for trial in Federal Court. Acquitted of murder charges, he and the prisoners at Salt Lake City were set free.

During this turmoil more than a hundred Utes left San Juan County and went to the reservation in western Colorado, although most soon returned. Back in Utah the Indians separated into two groups, one led by Polk and Mancos Jim. The other, composed of cocky young men, was led by Posey who became increasingly troublesome in following years until, in 1923, he became embroiled in a conflict that has been called the "Last Indian War," which is described in Chapter 11.[40]

The trouble in southeastern Utah was only one situation in which chaos was enveloping the Ute Indians. Conflicting and frequently changing policies dictated in Washington led to much confusion and despair during this period. To impatient administrators on the East Coast, only obstinacy and laziness explained the Utes' dilatory rate of assimilation into America's agrarian society. Washington bureaucrats ignored the fact that many who were trying to farm lacked sufficient water for success and were unable to produce enough to meet even a subsistence level. Overlooked also was the fact that Utes were already losing their allotments. To force the Utes to improve their ways, it was decided that rations had to be earned with labor.[41]

This policy was certain to increase suffering on the reservation, because many Utes had never overcome their deep-seated aversion to manual labor, which was associated with the white man's culture. When sympathetic outcries went up, such repressive decisions were reversed.

In these years of turmoil, even the great Bear Dance had been given up at a time when it was needed more than ever, but it returned to sustain the Núu-ci, as did the Sun Dance and others.

As government pressure to force the Utes to change increased, many became more determined to retain their identity with their old ways and with some new ones, too, that could be shared with other Native Americans. The Utes were joined in a powerful pan-Indian religious movement that bolstered their identity and self-esteem while providing spiritual sustenance as well. The new way was the peyote ritual, a path that was greeted with dismay by the Bureau of Indian Affairs and by the public in general but was met with respect and hope by Native American people.

11
▼ ▼ ▼

From the Ashes: Today's Ute Indians

Although disastrous changes had come to the Ute Indians and other Native American tribes in the nineteenth century, a new religion centered on peyote ceremonies brought from Mexico and the southwestern United States stirred a sense of unity, consolation, and vision. The Native American Church, a pan-Indian religious movement that grew out of this ritual, was born about 1918, but by the turn of the century Ute Indians had already learned from others about peyote and how to use its buttonlike stems.

Members of the Plains Indians tribes living in Oklahoma and South Dakota had introduced peyote to the Southern Ute Buckskin Charlie, who is believed to have been the first Ute leader of the new cult. He learned about peyote when he visited the Cheyenne and Arapaho reservation in the 1890s, and an Arapaho named Henry Lincoln came to Ignacio to lead meetings in 1900.[1] Most likely, Sioux practices became well-known to Northern Utes who went to South Dakota in 1906–1908, and from them the religion soon spread all the way to Nevada's Paiutes. Among Ute people the cult was well established by the second decade of the twentieth century. Peyote "beans" were then being sold around Dragon, Utah, and rumors were spreading that some peyote users had died there.[2] A Sioux, Sam Lone Bear, also known as Cactus Pete and Pete Phillips, introduced a ritualistic variation called Cross Fire among the Northern Utes, and about half of those Indians were soon holding weekly meetings.[3] Although many of the "best men" were participants, Sam Lone Bear's personal life, which involved relationships with young girls, tarnished both his reputation and that of the new religion. Replacing Sam Lone Bear was another Lone Bear, Raymond, who then became the Uintah road chief.

Many authorities frowned on the entire cult, citing the hallucino-
genic effects of chewing peyote, and by the mid-1920s Fort Duchesne's
superintendent and the United States Postal Service were attempting
to intercept peyote being sent by mail and by express from South Dakota to Utah.[4] Other administrators appeared ignorant of what was
taking place in their midst. For instance, among Ute Mountain Utes
the peyote religion took a firm hold, and annual visits by a Southern
Cheyenne road chief began about 1917, but Bureau of Indian Affairs
officials still reported that the cult had not reached either Towaoc or
Ignacio.[5] Soon afterward, Navajos started to go to Towaoc for meetings,
and the Utes began to supply Navajos with peyote for use on their
reservation. By the late 1930s the peyote cult was so firmly entrenched
on the Ute Mountain Ute Reservation that the subagent there reported
that all but about fifty Utes were practitioners, as were almost all Indians at Blanding.[6]

Government employees and missionaries among Utes and other
Indians sought to stamp out the practice, which they perceived as fraught
with intoxicated orgies and pagan heresy, not to mention physical dan-
gers leading to death, and the use of peyote was banned in some states,
but ceremonies of the Native American Church eventually became legal
and continue today.

Not all Utes accepted the peyote religion, and some adopted it while
also subscribing to other spiritual practices. As Catholic, Protestant,
and Mormon activities increased near or on reservations during the early
1900s, many Ute Indians were attracted to the Christian faith. Finding
no conflict between the different religious expressions, Native Americans adopted some Christian symbols and terminology in their peyote
ceremonies. Other Ute converts, particularly those around the Episcopal missions on the Uintah and Ouray Reservation, staunchly opposed
the Native American Church, however.

In addition to observances of the peyote cult and Christianity, Ute
Indians were regularly holding Sun Dances on their reservations, too.
The Sun Dance religion took a firm hold, sometimes among people who
also belonged to the peyote cult. On the Southern Ute Reservation,
peyote practitioner Buckskin Charlie was the leader.[7] Some Ute Indians, though, believed the Sun Dance was the only true way. As in other
Indian ceremonials, where purification prepares the individual for inner
and outer healing, sweat lodges preceded the dance. Among Ute Indians
the dance was performed without piercing of the skin by thongs, a form
of self-mortification viewed by the dance's critics as outrageous torture.
Ute dancers still suffered three or sometimes four days of thirst, hunger,

and exhaustion with the goal of acquiring spiritual power and the gift of healing.

The number of dancers each year was small, but the crowds of witnesses were large, as groups of Utes traveled from one reservation to another for dances. They brought gifts, even horses, to the hosts, and feasting followed a dance, with watermelon a popular food. Although the government was trying to halt these events, along with others, a large Sun Dance in 1913 drew hundreds to the Uintah and Ouray Reservation where the leaders of all three bands gave talks denouncing the government's policies. A firsthand description of Whiterock's Sun Dance in 1919, written by the son of a homesteader, tells of the arrival of riders on horseback from the Four Corners.[8] In 1930, during their annual visit to Fish Lake, the Ute-Paiute people of southern Utah held a Sun Dance.[9]

Along with other dances, in the early 1900s the Bear Dance was revived after a hiatus on the Southern Ute Reservation. Each center of Ute populations, even Dragon, Utah, had a Bear Dance arbor, separate from the Sun Dance arbor. By the 1930s Jicarilla Apaches were holding Bear Dances at Dulce, New Mexico, too. Many strictly social dances—precursors of today's powwows—brought out participants with their best shawls, their feathered headdresses, and their beaded fans, vests, moccasins, buckskin shirts, doeskin dresses, and other finery.

Whereas these traditions kept the pride of the Núu-ci alive, the Bureau of Indian Affairs continued to advocate education as one of the tools to economic independence and assimilation into America's mainstream. Many Ute Indians resisted schools, which they believed were bad medicine for their people. A federal law in 1921 that required school attendance by all Indians received limited obedience, even when rations were cut if a family failed to comply and when tribal police were ordered to enforce attendance. Language alone was a deterrent. The 1930 census revealed that, with the population of Ute Indians living in Colorado and Utah totaling about 2,000, with fifty percent under the age of twenty, a third were unable to speak English. Southern Utes were above this rate, and Ute Mountain Utes fell below it.

Indian schools had a checkered history. In 1916 twenty-eight boys and twenty-three girls were attending the Southern Ute Boarding School at Ignacio. Four years later it ceased to function as a boarding school and became a day school. In 1930 it again became a boarding school, attended chiefly by Navajo children. The Allen Day School near Bayfield also taught Ute pupils. In 1956 the public school system took over the education of Ignacio's Indian children along with Hispaños and Anglos.[10]

At Towaoc, where a boarding school was built at the time of the subagency's move from Navajo Springs, enrollment soon approached the institution's capacity of 150, but many students were Navajo children. To enforce Ute attendance, officials in automobiles gathered small children from their homes against their will, dressed then in white children's clothing, and brought them to the school where they received English names. A program with continuity was difficult to achieve, for as they grew older some students elected to attend various boarding schools, often Ignacio's, from time to time. Under Presbyterian auspices, a day school also operated at Towaoc, but distances from homes of the seminomadic Ute Mountain Utes made the school impractical. In the 1940s schools on the reservation closed along with the rest of the agency's facilities because of a lack of water. By the 1950s only five Ute Mountain Ute youngsters had a high school education, thirty had elementary schooling, and many were unable to speak English.[11] Little wonder, then, that children from this reservation had difficulty when they began to attend public schools in Cortez in the 1950s and asked, although in vain, to have their own school restored.[12]

In the early 1900s Utes and Paiutes near Blanding, Utah, could choose between a local day school and boarding schools until public schools took over. The boarding schools proved an unhappy choice for some, as exemplified by one girl who attended such schools at Ignacio, Towaoc, and Blanding, as well as the public school at Cortez. Later, she remembered more about homesickness than about her classes.[13]

Children on the Uintah and Ouray Reservation had similar experiences. Those living in outlying sectors chose the boarding school at Whiterocks or no school at all, whereas pupils close to Randlett could attend the state-operated day school at the former boarding school property. In 1952 all schools came under public school administration. Until then, mixed school enrollments were nearly nonexistent. Thereafter, some Ute students attended Roosevelt's or Vernal's high school, but many preferred segregated schools and elected to go to out-of-state Indian schools instead. When Dragon had a little schoolhouse that was for white pupils only, friendly children of both races played together outside of school hours. Left to themselves, youngsters learned about one another's cultures. As Ila Bowman Powell recalled in later years, children from the Ute camp about a mile from Dragon and those from the mining camp shared meals at each other's homes. Ute families cooked meat and bread wrapped on sticks over open fires, she recollected, and the white people donated deer meat and potatoes to the Indians when they gave berries to their friends.[14]

In Indian schools programs included a variety of foreign and frequently unpleasant activities besides learning the "three Rs." To learn horticultural skills and to produce food for the schools' dining rooms, the children worked in gardens and dairy barns. Girls made things such as aprons and dish towels, and boys learned mechanical skills. To counteract the spread of infectious diseases, hygiene was emphasized. With contagious trachoma still rampant, everyone lined up to receive eye drops twice a day. Hair was doused with smelly solutions to control lice. The children slept in crowded dormitory rooms on bunk beds where transmission of germs and pests was unimpeded.

Health care was important. It was handled by the Bureau of Indian Affairs, the Indian Health Services, and, ultimately, the Public Health Service in succession. Many Indians still turned to their medicine men early in the century, but they gradually accepted the care of doctors and nurses. By the 1930s Ignacio and Towaoc had hospitals. Although Ute Mountain Utes suffered from high disease rates, health care at Towaoc was curtailed when the rest of its services were terminated in the 1940s, and for the next two decades personnel from Ignacio made periodic visits to Towaoc.

Prevalent diseases on the reservations were tuberculosis, arthritis, venereal diseases, and trachoma.[15] The influenza epidemic of 1918–1919 struck Ute Indians but in smaller numbers than found elsewhere, perhaps because of the isolation of the homes of many tribal members. Alcoholism was rampant among Ute Indians along with other Native Americans. Socioeconomic factors are often offered as an explanation for this malady, but the legalization of liquor sales to Indians in the 1950s aggravated this problem, which had begun more than a century earlier when the first trappers and traders introduced liquor.

Indian census figures suggest the impact of disease and, later, of improved health care, but other factors also affected tallies—departures of Utes from reservations, refusal to become enrolled, and administrators' inability to count some of the remote families. The censuses do show beyond doubt that there were drastic pre-1900 reductions in Ute population and that stabilization began in the second quarter of the twentieth century.[16] Significant population increases followed later in the century.

Censuses of the Bureau of Indian Affairs reveal numbers of Ute Indians. From a peak population of 8,000 to 10,000 at the time of first contact with white people, the number of Núu-ci dwindled by seventy-five or eighty percent in the following centuries. Sharp reductions took place in the early 1900s. Southern Utes in 1923 numbered

359, a decrease of about fifteen percent among Muaches and Capotes who had been present at the time of allotment in the 1890s, but they increased slightly to 392 in the 1937 census and doubled by the end of the twentieth century. Ute Mountain Utes totaled 433 in 1923, with a loss of roughly eighteen percent since the 1890s. Of these, 347 were living in Colorado, and 86 were in Utah, apparently with only the Montezuma Creek residents being counted. In 1931 the census reported ten families, or forty-two individuals, living at Allen Canyon near Blanding, these being mixed Paiute-Ute Indians, predominantly Paiute. The Utes counted in southeastern Utah grew to about 200 during the twentieth century. Ute Mountain Utes, including those in southeastern Utah, tripled in number by the end of the century. The number of Utes counted on the Uintah and Ouray Reservation doubled in the 1900s. The count in 1921 showed plummeting figures, down to a total of 1,127, which increased to 1,347 in 1940, with the Uintah Utes comprising the largest group followed by Uncompahgre Utes who had been by far the largest band in 1881. The White River Band had dropped to less than twenty percent of the total. By the end of the twentieth century there were more than 3,000 Ute people on the Uintah and Ouray Reservation.

Total numbers of off-reservation Utes and mixed bloods are not available, but some who were living off the Ute reservation in Utah were counted in 1940's census of the Paiute Tribe. At the Kanosh settlement there were twenty-eight Indians, fifteen designated as Utes and three as Paiute-Utes or Ute-Paiutes. At Koosharem there were twenty-seven Indians—all but one, a Paiute, designated as Utes.

Taken as a whole, the numbers of Ute Indians in Colorado and Utah were small when compared with other Native American tribes that had many thousands of people. This circumstance helps to explain why the Ute people have been relatively unknown in American history and perhaps why the federal government's administration often was negligent. An assignment to serve a small tribe probably did not always attract the best professionals among career civil servants, who sometimes performed only perfunctory work at best or had negative attitudes at worst. For instance, the superciliousness of Superintendent E. E. McKean at the Consolidated Ute Agency at Ignacio was obvious when he wrote in 1925 to Superintendent F. A. Gross at the Uintah and Ouray Agency in Fort Duchesne: "Two of your thriving wards, Edgar Unca Sam and Peter Patterson, having enjoyed the hospitality of our fair country for some time past, desire now to return to the bosom of your family, and further extend a wish that you send them $25.00 each in order that their journey homeward may not be deprived of the pleasures of which they are so worthy."[17]

Perhaps McKean also felt superior to Gross because the Colorado office administered two subagencies in southern Colorado as well as the Indians in southeastern Utah. The name of the agency at Ignacio was changed to the Consolidated Ute Agency in 1923. Together, the Southern Ute Reservation and the Ute Mountain Ute Reservation were officially called the Consolidated Ute Reservation until 1968, when the Ute Mountain Ute Agency was established as a separate entity. The Southern Ute Agency then took its present name. The comparative neglect of the more remote Ute Mountain Utes in the meantime was predictable.

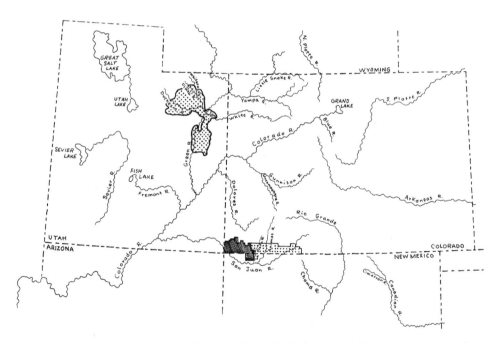

By the mid-1900s reservations in Utah and Colorado had assumed this approximate configuration. In 1911 the western portion of Colorado's reservation, later known as the Ute Mountain Ute Reservation, lost some land to Mesa Verde National Park and in exchange gained the irregularly shaped acreage on its northern boundary. The eastern, allotted portion of the Southern Ute Reservation, which retained that name, lost land through allotment, but some of its acreage has been regained. Utah's reservation, called the Uintah and Ouray Ute Indian Reservation since 1886, also lost land through allotment, but in 1948 the Hill Creek Extension was added at the southern end of the original Ouray Reservation.

While Ute populations were declining and then growing again, Indian lands also were suffering severe losses followed by increases. Of the vast domain once occupied by Ute Indians from central Utah to Colorado's Front Range and nearly from Wyoming south into New Mexico, the Ute Indians of Utah and Colorado held less than a million acres by 1930, much of it semiarid or arid land suitable at best for grazing if anything. Great losses had accompanied allotment, and many Indian allotments were later alienated, for when the Utes signed up for parcels the federal government held the land in trust for twenty-five years. The government sometimes sold land belonging to "incompetents" or to those without heirs, and some Indians who did own their land outright sold it. Assessments by irrigation districts forced impoverished owners of small plots to give them up.

On the Southern Ute Reservation, almost half of the allotted land was lost—chiefly through sale—by the end of the 1920s. The reservation's tribally owned land increased in the 1930s, however, when public lands within the reservation's boundaries that had not been taken up were restored to the tribe. Although these lands were usually those least suited to farming, they proved to contain important oil and gas reserves, as well as some coal, timber, and grazing land. From about 40,000 acres of tribal land in the 1930s, Southern Ute holdings have grown to more than 300,000 acres through purchases during the remainder of the twentieth century. In the 1930s nearly two-thirds of Southern Ute people were living on their own land in houses—often small log cabins—and were farming. They were raising a few milk cows, beef cattle, sheep, and horses but were primarily growing alfalfa, wheat, and oats on fields averaging about forty acres per farm. Sales of crafts, which some other Native American tribes relied on, were discouragingly unprofitable for Southern Ute women, who tended to depend more on leasing their allotments if they needed cash.[18]

Tribal funds enabling modern economic growth came largely from judgments received in the 1950s. In the 1990s an Indian-owned casino joined the tribe's Pino Nuche motel and community center and has augmented important oil and gas royalties. The tribe has an excellent museum and a gift shop where handicrafts are sold. Today, Southern Ute Indians have one of the highest per capita incomes of all Native American tribes.

Weenuches, who held about 550,000 unallotted acres when they separated from the Muache and Capote Bands in the 1890s, still had most of their land intact in the 1900s, but for many years a lack of water and other resources on the land limited its economic potential to sheep and wool. Tribally owned cattle, augmented by trespassing Navajo- and Anglo-owned livestock, resulted in overgrazing, so cattle herds owned communally by the tribe were sold off. In the 1930s there were still many Ute-owned sheep and about four hundred head of cattle whose seminomadic owners lived in tents and sometimes earthen hogans as they moved around, depending on seasonal sources of water and forage.

Material culture, dances, courtship accompanied by flute playing, and other aspects of traditional life continued among the Weenuches more strongly than elsewhere, for isolation and poverty contributed to traditionalism, as did the leadership of conservative tribal chief John Miller. He fought against government interference during his tenure, which lasted into the mid-1930s, and his successor, Jack House, who lived until 1971, also had a conservative influence.

Lacking farms and resisting schools, the Weenuches remained dependent on government rations and thus suffered more than some others when the federal government abruptly cut off distributions of rations to all Native Americans in 1931. Sources of native foods such as game, berries, and roots had been severely reduced by that time. The discovery of oil and gas reserves on the reservation lands in the 1950s began to produce some royalties for the tribe, and moneys from the judgment against the government in the same decade also provided income, however. Some of the Weenuches' judgment funds went directly to Ute Mountain Ute tribal members, and some went into the tribal trust fund. A portion of the money was used to lease additional land—notably a 20,000-acre parcel for grazing south of Blue Mesa Reservoir—beginning in the 1950s.

In the 1970s, when the United States Supreme Court settled a dispute between Navajos and Ute Mountain Utes regarding ownership of 15,000 acres of oil and gas land in northwestern New Mexico by awarding it to the Navajo Nation, Pinecrest Ranch near Blue Mesa Reservoir was awarded to the Weenuches, along with off-season hunting rights on adjoining Bureau of Land Management range land. At the close of the twentieth century, the Ute Mountain Ute Tribe owned about 70,000 acres less than it had in 1896, but the tribe was developing other sources of income such as oil and gas, a gambling casino, commercial manufacture of pottery, construction, and some agriculture that was made possible in the 1990s with irrigation waters from the Dolores Project.

Economic survival had remained an even greater problem for the small groups of Utes and Paiute-Utes still living in Utah's San Juan County. Without reservation land, these people had led a seminomadic lifestyle, grazing flocks on the public domain with various locations customarily used not only by them but also by Navajos and Anglo livestock owners. Some conflicts like those during the late 1800s continued, as camping places, watering places, pastures, and routes overlapped. Local settlers constantly complained of theft, vandalism, horse stealing, and the killing of cattle for food by Indians, who, in turn, accused their white neighbors of unjust persecution.[19] During these confrontations, a few murders occurred.

Antagonism in southeastern Utah reached a climax in an episode called the Posey War, or the Last Indian War, in 1923, which drew attention to San Juan County's Indians and resulted in their being given land. Most accounts say Posey was directly involved in this "war"; others say he was not.[20] Whatever the truth, Posey had gained such a reputation as a troublemaker that it was predictable that he would be accused of complicity. In January 1923 two young Indians killed a sheep and sent the sheepherder running for his life. The culprits were arrested, but the Indians escaped during their trial in March. Posey joined the escapees, who were chased through the rough canyon country southwest of Blanding, and he was shot early in the chase. He hid in a remote place and died there of his wound, although his pursuers did not know his fate. While the hunt for Posey was taking place, a crowd of Indians who had gathered for the trial and others who were rounded up were corralled in a wire enclosure at Blanding. Only after Posey's body was found several weeks later were they released from the makeshift stockade.

Because the Indian "war" and the unsavory events accompanying it in San Juan County occurred at a time when contemporary Americans were living modern lives, it caught widespread publicity. At last, in 1923 the Utes and Paiute-Utes in southeastern Utah got much-needed attention from Washington. They were given allotments, on which they were ordered to remain with their livestock and to plant gardens, and a government farmer was assigned to assist them. A dozen Paiute-Ute people at Allen Canyon received allotments near the Blue Mountains, where they gained some success as farmers and crafted baskets for trade as well as for their own use, but the group remained slow to adopt new ways. The Utes who had centered around Montezuma Creek were given land on White Mesa south of Blanding, with a few additional allotments in Montezuma and Cross Canyons. They have done some basketry and beadwork for cash and operate a gas station with a small store beside the Bluff-Blanding highway that runs through their land.

Collectively, all of these people of San Juan County—Ute, Ute-Pauite, Paiute-Ute, with some Navajo intermixture—are called White Mesa Utes or sometimes Blanding Utes. In 1925 they were enrolled with the Ute Mountain Ute Tribe, and they later would have one representative on that tribe's council when it was created. Paiutes who were not related to Utes and who were not affiliated with the Ute Mountain Ute Tribe suffered more poverty than did the others, who received a very small monthly check.

The 360,000 acres remaining in 1908 of the original four-million-acre Uintah and Ouray Reservation, meanwhile, had dwindled to about 83,000 acres by the 1930s. As compensation for the loss of one million of their former acres, the Northern Utes' trust fund received more than a dollar per acre in 1933, but many individuals had sold their allotments or were leasing them to non-Indians. Added to these losses was curtailment of grazing lands in the public domain after the Taylor Grazing Act of 1934 required leases, and white livestock owners quickly signed up for a third of the grazing land the Utes had been using. In 1948 the federal government ceded more than 400,000 acres of grazing land, called the Hill Creek Extension, to the reservation. This extension was at the southern end of what remained of the old Ouray Reservation.

A major liability was the hundreds of dollars many Utes owed for assessments from irrigation projects, regardless of whether the water was being used. Following the judgment in the 1950s, payments on such debts came out of a Tribal Family Plan, which reduced the cash and capital available to many individuals. By the mid-1900s Utes were farming only 7,000 acres, whereas non-Utes were farming twice as many acres on reservation land. Although white-painted, government-owned structures used by the agency dominated Whiterocks and Fort Duchesne, Ute housing on the reservation was still deplorable in the mid-1900s. Doors, windows, water, and electricity were rare.

A glimpse of life among pastoral Utes in northeastern Utah in the second and third decades of the 1900s is seen in Chipeta's family life, although it must be remembered that her group enjoyed a few benefits accruing to her status and fame, for she was still a highly respected, even legendary figure in both Colorado and Utah. She and her people, led by Chief John McCook, had a fairly good range for summer grazing on the Uncompahgre Grazing Reserve at Bitter Creek, about sixty-five miles from Ouray. In 1948 the area became the Hill Creek Extension. The group had semipermanent camps, in which Chipeta lived part of the time in a canvas tepee and part of the time in a small cabin where she had some dishes, a little table, and boxes for seats.[21] By 1924, totally blind and nearly eighty years old, Chipeta died of chronic gastritis, and her family buried her without fanfare in a shallow grave in a nearby sandy wash near her camp, as was the custom for Ute women.

The stark contrast between Ute life and Anglo life at the time is revealed by ceremonies honoring Chipeta in Colorado. By then, civilization was flourishing back in the Uncompahgre Valley, where towns had sprung up in 1881 before the dust of Chipeta's departure had settled. Learning of the death of "Queen Chipeta," the citizens of Montrose set up a clamor to have her remains returned there for burial with proper ceremony and a tomb. While the tomb was being built near her old home in the winter of 1925, Superintendent Gross at Fort Duchesne made arrangements for the removal of her remains and their transportation by railroad to Montrose. Her body was accompanied by the Episcopal Reverend M. J. Hersey of Randlett's mission, Chief McCook, Ute Yagah, and an agency employee and was welcomed to Montrose by a crowd of 5,000 spectators. (When McCook died in 1937, he was buried in the same memorial park near Montrose.) Part of Ouray and Chipeta's nearby farmhouse remained until 1944, when it burned. In 1945 the property was deeded to the State Historical Society of Colorado, which later built a Ute Museum to exhibit Ute possessions, including some of Ouray's and Chipeta's.

Public ceremonies for Chipeta's reburial were matched when Ouray's remains were moved a few weeks later. The Southern Utes honored the famous Tabeguache chief of all Utes by reburying his remains in the Ute cemetery near Ignacio, across the Los Pinos River from the site where he died in 1880. The location of his original burial was known only to those few, including McCook and Buckskin Charlie, who had accompanied his body there forty-five years earlier, and they were part of the group who in the summer of 1925 went to the place and removed bones and a skull for reburial. A question about the bones lingered because McCook was said to have visited the original burial place in 1916 and found bones scattered on the ground. He believed they were Ouray's, but there was no skull.[22] The fact that Ouray's original burial was at a place previously occupied by another Ute Indian may solve this mystery. Regardless, the ceremonies at Ignacio, attended by a large crowd of Indians and white people, lasted for four days. Later, in Ignacio, a monument was erected across the river at the agency park to honor not only Ouray but also Ignacio, Buckskin Charlie, and Severo.

Although people of both races honored these famous Ute Indians, other tribal members were experiencing qualified acceptance by white newcomers. For instance, the people on the Uintah and Ouray Reservation sometimes enjoyed tolerance from their neighbors but also experienced strained relations. A unique problem involved the creation of the town of Roosevelt in 1905 on patented land that previously had been part of the reservation. Moreover, this new town, only seven miles from Fort Duchesne, diverted water from Dry Gulch that was needed by downstream Utes.

Roosevelt grew quickly, with land purchased from Ute holdings, and it became the undisputed commercial center for the reservation, Myton, and other communities. Duchesne County, created in 1915, consisted entirely of former or remaining reservation land, and jurisdictional issues have plagued the area. Economic development on the reservation was hindered by the fact that businesses in Roosevelt provided necessary goods and services to the tribe and profited from the Utes' money in return, a sore point among the Indians.

Tribal funds have come from a large claims judgment, oil and mineral leases, cattle, a little farming, and, late in the 1990s, a large store and service station that will keep more cash on the reservation. The store was built at a time when the reservation's Utes were boycotting Roosevelt businesses because of a dispute related to law enforcement jurisdiction.

The 1940s brought sweeping changes to all of the Ute reservations, as well as to Native Americans everywhere. The paternalistic policies of the 1800s and the early 1900s, sometimes called "internal colonialism," had kept Native Americans dependent on the federal government. The persistent reform movement had made some but only small changes in national attitudes. For instance, all Native Americans were granted United States citizenship in 1924, but they were not allowed to vote until 1948. The stroke that brought dramatic change was the publication in 1928 of the Meriam Report, or Meriam Survey, entitled *The Problem of Indian Administration*. Conducted by the Institute for Government Research, an arm of the Brookings Institution, at the behest of Department of the Interior Secretary Hubert Work, the report described economic and social conditions of Native Americans. The survey exposed not only the shocking health, educational, and economic state of the nation's Indians but also the federal government's defective policies and administration, particularly as they had resulted in the loss of Indian lands without improvement in the Indians' economic well-being. Solutions to the problems were proposed in the document, although little was achieved until 1933 when John Collier became commissioner of Indian Affairs during the Roosevelt administration. During Collier's tenure pride was fostered by encouraging indigenous culture through Native American crafts programs, ceremonies, and sacred beliefs.

Most important, the Wheeler-Howard Act, also known as the Indian Reorganization Act of 1934, brought a sharp turn onto a new road that affected every phase of Native American life. The act has been called the "Indian New Deal." The Reorganization Act provided for self-government by Indian tribes through business committees, now usually called tribal councils, composed of elected members and a chairperson. The groups were to function under a tribal constitution and by-laws, which required approval by the Bureau of Indian Affairs prior to adoption. Women, who had occasionally participated in traditional Ute council meetings, have been among the members elected to the governing groups. Existing tribal chiefs' titles would be used throughout their lifetimes, and their role would then cease to exist. Tribal budgets were subject to approval by the secretary of the interior. A provision that had a major impact was the authorization to hire legal council to assert tribal interests. Nevertheless, radical change was not achieved until the passage of the Indian Self-Determination and Education Act in 1972, giving tribal governments responsibility for programs previously administered by federal agencies and their employees. Since then, using tribal funds, the tribal governments have contracted for specific services such as law enforcement, courts, social services, education, and range credit management.

The Indian Reorganization Act of 1934, reversing the General Allotment Act of 1887, halted the creation of new allotments and alienation of tribal lands that had not previously been filed on. In ensuing years Congress passed restoration acts returning thousands of acres of land, although the federal government retained responsibility for protecting Indian lands and resources. The return of former Indian lands began through purchases from tribal funds held in trust, and compensation for some lost land also was made.

Increased means for economic development with credit becoming available resulted in the beginning of tribal businesses, particularly the development of natural resources such as oil and gas reserves, and a greater voice in planning public water projects, although the Utes' share of water often turned out to be less than expected. For instance, when Colorado's Vallecito Reservoir on the Los Pinos came into being, it was assumed there would be sufficient irrigation water to meet the Southern Utes' needs, but that has not been true. Another proposed project in southwestern Colorado, called the Animas–La Plata Project, in the 1960s allocated diverted water to both the Southern Ute and Ute Mountain Ute Reservations, but three decades of arguing among Washington politicians, Durango promoters, environmentalists, and the agencies kept the project in limbo.

Changes did not occur simultaneously on the three Ute reservations. With their constitution approved, Southern Ute Indians established their tribal business committee in 1936. When Buckskin Charlie died in 1936, before the committee was established, Antonio Buck Sr. became the last traditional chief of the Southern Ute Tribe. He held that position until his death in 1961, after which the tribe had no chief.

The Ute Mountain Ute constitution was approved in 1940, and the business committee was established, although until 1968 the Bureau of Indian Affairs' Consolidated Ute Agency at Ignacio still served Towaoc, too. Meanwhile, Towaoc also had a traditional chief, Jack House, who continued to have much influence, if not official authority, until his death in 1971.

The Uintah and Ouray Reservation, where a headman had served each of the three bands, had no single tribal chief. In 1936 Lawrence Appah was leading the White River Utes, Jim Atwine the Uintahs, and John Pawwinnee (McCook) the Uncompahgres. The constitution formulated by the three bands and approved in 1937 created the business committee for the entity called the Ute Indian Tribe of the Uintah and Ouray Reservation, Utah, and provided that each band would elect two representatives to the business committee.

In Utah, factionalism created trouble, for it was contended that the Uncompahgre Utes and mixed bloods were dominating tribal government. Disagreement came to a head regarding the status of mixed bloods, those with fifty percent or less Ute blood, and in 1954 mixed bloods were expelled as members of the tribe. During the Eisenhower administration, termination of small Native American tribes was advocated, principally by Utah's Senator Arthur Watkins, and the plan was implemented for some of Utah's tribes. Originally all Ute Indians of the Uintah and Ouray Reservation were on the drawing board for termination, but membership in the tribe was severed only for mixed bloods, of whom the majority were Uintahs. Understandably, wrangling over termination caused much divisiveness on the reservation before and after the final plan was put into effect.

A True Ute movement developed in the Uintah and White River Bands with the intent of disrupting tribal affairs, which, it was felt, were being dominated by Uncompahgre Utes and the BIA. The True Utes' unrest reached a climax in 1960 with a march on tribal headquarters that was broken up with tear gas and arrests.[23] Meanwhile, attempting in vain to protect their interests, mixed bloods had organized as the Affiliated Ute Citizens of Utah.[24] In 1961 the mixed blood Indians of the Uintah and Ouray Reservation were terminated as tribal members and thereafter became ordinary United State citizens, often cheated, unable to compete in the market place, and deprived of government

services that Ute Indian tribal members in Utah and Colorado continued to have. Neither full- nor mixed-blood Utes of Colorado were terminated.

A change of utmost importance to the tribes accompanied the establishment in 1946 of a special Indian Claims Commission to hear
claims for compensation for lands taken illegally or without adequate
payment, for improper expenditures of tribal funds by the government,
for unfulfilled treaty obligations, and for other unjust dealings.[25] This
was not the first time Ute people had sought redress, for in 1910 the
Confederated Bands of Ute Indians of Colorado and Utah had filed for
awards in the United States Court of Claims and won a judgment of
nearly $3.5 million. Significantly, this event came about as a result of
work by the Indians in council—a quarter century before the government recognized the ability of Native Americans to conduct their own
business.

When the Indian Claims Commission was established, there was a
limit of five years for filing claims, and the Ute tribes immediately went
to work with the assistance of attorneys. The Confederated Ute Bands
of Colorado and Utah, whose claims were the first to be settled, received
almost $32 million. After attorneys' fees of seven percent of the total
were deducted, sixty percent of the remainder went to the Ute Indian
Tribe of the Uintah and Ouray Reservation and forty percent went to
Colorado's Ute tribes.

Before moneys were transferred to the tribes, plans for their use had
to be submitted for approval. The tribes chose to allot some to direct per
capita payments and some to tribal programs. The Southern Ute and
Ute Mountain Ute Tribes divided their share, with the Blanding Utes
receiving a small cash award of $500 per capita and credit for housing,
grazing, and farming needs under the Tribal Family Plan. Similar alloca-
tions for other Utes meant that moneys placed in the tribal fund would
be used to pay personal debts first—as, for example, debts to irrigation
districts in Utah—instead of going directly to individuals. A variety of
development and education projects came from tribal funds. Moreover,
the Uintah and Ouray Ute moneys were divided, with twenty-seven
percent of the total going to about three hundred mixed bloods. For the
duration of their lifetimes, the surviving original mixed bloods were to
continue to receive this percentage of distributions, a source of ongoing
resentment among the reservation's Indians.

Termination of any of Utah's Indians who were not attached to
reservations included off-reservation Paiute settlements, some actually
populated by Paiutes and others by Utes and Ute-Paiutes. Indians in

San Juan County who were enrolled in the Ute Mountain Ute Tribe were not terminated, but other off-reservation Indians lost all government services and suffered much hardship as a consequence. For those groups that were predominantly Ute, although loosely called "Paiute," the government had purchased land at Koosharem and Kanosh, Utah, in 1928 and 1929, respectively, and the Kanosh site was enlarged in 1935 and 1937.[26] During termination the Koosharem group moved away, chiefly to the Richfield area, and the Kanosh group remained near Corn Creek. Mormon relief programs took on importance during this period. Termination of these groups ended in 1980 when the federal government's trust relationship was again established through the Restoration Act of 1980. Since then, the Southern Paiute office at Cedar City has had responsibility for small groups of Paiutes and the settlements at Kanosh and Richfield, with the result that Ute Indians there are known loosely as Paiutes to their neighbors.

In the last half of the twentieth century, major issues affecting Utes have included water rights—especially those related to the Dolores, Animas–La Plata, and Central Utah projects; economic development; education; health problems, such as diabetes and substance abuse; poverty; litigation over land and compensation for lost land; contention over tribal law enforcement versus non-Indian local governments; sovereignty; and intratribal factionalism. As increasing numbers of young people leave the reservations to attend universities and law schools, these problems are receiving attention from well-educated Native Americans who take pride in their identity as Indians and are prepared to work on issues affecting their tribes.

Elders have worried, however, that some young members of the tribe have become too thoroughly assimilated into the white man's ways and are preoccupied with acquiring material goods and engaging in the latest forms of recreation with an accompanying loss of Ute ways. The native language suddenly became almost unknown, and tales were being forgotten, whereas alcoholism, vehicular accidents, and crime increased on the reservation. Counteracting such trends are tribal language and cultural programs in the schools, renewed participation in the Sun Dance and other traditional activities, and powwows to which crowds of handsomely costumed Native Americans travel hundreds of miles in their automobiles, pickup trucks, and vans to share camaraderie and to compete for prizes as dancers. At these colorful gatherings feathers and beaded finery dazzle one's eye, jingles and drums fill fairgrounds and parks with their rhythmic sounds, and singers summon Indians of all ages to join in dances.

Less colorful, like an echo from the past, Bear Dances also continue on each Ute reservation, as well as at Blanding—an assurance that the old culture has not been forsaken. The ancient dance is scheduled later in the year, though, after the warm sun has chased away the bitter winds of late winter, and so it may seem primarily a social dance, just as anthropologists claim it is, rather than a religious ritual to rouse Bear from his cave at the time of the equinox to help the Núu-ci survive.

But down Bear Dance Road a crowd has gathered in a late May rain. Falsetto singing and the eerie growl of rasps are sending their calls from the brush shelter. Without fancy costumes, jingles, or feathers but with the mandatory women's shawls, dancers are moving back and forth, back and forth, slowly, monotonously, insistently, under the leaden clouds.

The Núu-ci are dancing. Something stirs. Something is awakening. Call it continuity. Call it the Circle of Life. Call it Bear.

Notes

▼   ▼   ▼

CHAPTER 1

1. Fred A. Conetah, *A History of the Northern Ute People*, ed. Kathryn L. MacKay and Floyd A. O'Neil (Salt Lake City: University of Utah Printing Service for the Uintah-Ouray Ute Tribe, 1982), 2.

2. Indian Claims Commission, "Commission Findings," in *Ute Indians*, vol. 2 (New York: Garland Publishing, 1974), 384; Joel C. Janetski, *The Ute of Utah Lake*, University of Utah Anthropological Papers, no. 116 (Salt Lake City: University of Utah Press, 1991), 1; Omer C. Stewart, "Ute Indians before and after White Contact," *Utah Historical Quarterly*, 34, no. 1 (1966): 51.

3. An article, "Northern Ute Return to Traditional Homelands at Capitol Reef National Park," appeared in *Ute Bulletin* (September 9, 1997), 1.

4. Ted J. Warner, ed., *The Domínguez-Escalante Journal: Their Expedition through Colorado, Utah, Arizona, and New Mexico in 1776*, trans. Fray Angelico Chavez (Salt Lake City: University of Utah Press, 1995), 52–53, 119–120.

5. Richard E. Fike and H. Blaine Phillips II, *A Nineteenth Century Ute Burial from Northeast Utah*, Cultural Resource Series, no. 16 (Salt Lake City: Utah State Office, Bureau of Land Management, 1984), 91.

6. Ibid.

7. Clement Frost, greetings, Ute Indian Museum ceremonies, Montrose, Colorado, September 27, 1997.

8. James A. Goss, "Through the Eyes of the Utes: Colorado's Sacred Mountains," presentation, Adams State College, April 6, 1998; Kenneth Lee Peterson, "Tabeguache and Elk Mountain Utes: A Historical Test of an Ecological Model," *Southwestern Lore*, 43, no. 4 (1977): 5–21.

CHAPTER 2

1. William Gayl Buckles, "The Uncompahgre Complex: Historic Ute Archaeology and Prehistoric Archaeology on the Uncompahgre Plateau in

West Central Colorado" (Ph.D. diss., University of Colorado, 1971), passim.

2. Steven G. Baker, *Numic Archaeology on the Douglas Creek Arch, Rio Blanco County, Colorado: Ute Rancherías and the Broken Blade Wickiup Village* (Montrose, Colo.: Centuries Research, 1996).

3. Jesse Walter Fewkes, *Antiquities of the Mesa Verde National Park*, Bureau of Ethnology Bulletin, no. 41 (Washington, D.C.: Government Printing Office, 1909), 2; Joyce Kayser, "Phantoms in the Pinyon: An Investigation of Ute-Pueblo Contacts," *American Antiquity*, 26, no. 3 (1961): 82–91; David A. Breternitz, personal communication, September 20, 1998.

4. LaVan Martineau, *The Southern Paiutes: Legends, Lore, Language, and Lineage* (Las Vegas: KC Publications, 1992), 24.

5. Stewart, "Ute Indians before and after White Contact," 47.

6. Anne M. Smith, *Ethnography of the Northern Utes*, Papers in Anthropology, no. 17 (Santa Fe: Museum of New Mexico Press, 1974), 15.

7. J. M. Adovasio and David R. Pedler, "A Tisket, a Tasket: Looking at the Numic Speakers through the 'Lens' of a Basket," in David Madsen and David Rhode, eds., *Across the West: Human Population Movement and the Expansion of the Numa* (Salt Lake City: University of Utah Press, 1994), 114–123.

8. Ernest Wallace and E. Adamson Hoebel, *The Comanches: Lords of the South Plains* (Norman: University of Oklahoma Press, 1986 [1952]), 19.

9. Jean Ormsbee Charney, *A Grammar of Comanche* (Lincoln: University of Nebraska Press, 1993), 2.

10. Wick R. Miller, "Numic Languages," in Warren L. D'Azevedo, ed., *Great Basin*, vol. 11, *Handbook of North American Indians* (Washington, D.C.: Smithsonian Institution, 1986), 98.

11. *Ute Dictionary* (Ignacio, Colo.: Ute Press, Southern Ute Tribe, 1979), 147.

12. Martineau, *Southern Paiutes*, 152; Donald Callaway, Joel Janetski, and Omer C. Stewart, "Utes," in D'Azevedo, ed., *Great Basin*, 364–365; Alden Naranjo, Ignacio, Colorado, personal communication, March 12, 1998; Conetah, *History of the Northern Ute People*, 27–28.

13. P. Clark, *The Indian Sign Language* (Lincoln: University of Nebraska Press, 1982 [1885]), 392.

14. Robert H. Nykamp, "Distribution of Known Ute Sites in Colorado," in Paul R. Nickens, ed., *Archaeology of the Eastern Ute: A Symposium*, Colorado Council of Professional Archaeologists, Occasional Papers, no. 1, 1988.

15. Farren Webb and Rick Wheelock, *The Ute Legacy: A Study Guide* (Ignacio, Colo.: Southern Ute Tribe, 1989), 7.

16. Warner, ed., *Domínguez-Escalante Journal*, 86.

17. Callaway, Janetski, and Stewart, "Utes," 340; Julian Haynes Steward, *Ute Indians*, vol. 1, *Aboriginal and Historical Groups of the Ute Indians of Utah* (New York: Garland Publishing, 1974), 93; *Ute Bulletin*, September 9, 1997, 1.

18. Isabel T. Kelly, *Southern Paiute Ethnography*, University of Utah, Anthropological Papers, no. 69, Glen Canyon Series, no. 21 (Salt Lake City: University of Utah Press, 1964), 54–55, 113.

19. Smith, *Ethnography*, 23.
20. Joseph G. Jorgensen, "The Ethnohistory and Acculturation of the Northern Ute" (Ph.D. diss., Indiana University, 1965), 23.
21. Warner, ed., *Domínguez-Escalante Journal*, 70.
22. Janetski, *Ute of Utah Lake*, 5; Callaway, Janetski, and Stewart, "Utes," 340.
23. Smith, *Ethnography*, iii–iv.
24. Martineau, *Southern Paiutes*, 158; Virginia Cole Trenholm and Maurine Carley, *The Shoshonis: Sentinels of the Rockies* (Norman: University of Oklahoma Press, 1964), 4.
25. Steward, *Ute Indians*, 1: 126; Indian Claims Commission, "Commission Findings," in Steward, *Ute Indians*, 2: 365–366.
26. Martineau, *Southern Paiutes*, 156, 164.
27. Smith, *Ethnography*, iv.
28. Conetah, *History of the Northern Ute People*, 94; Jorgensen, "Ethnohistory and Acculturation," 32.
29. Warner, ed., *Domínguez-Escalante Journal*, 31.
30. Norman Lopez, Towaoc, Colorado, personal communication, February 13, 1998.
31. Albert H. Schroeder, "A Brief History of the Southern Utes," *Southwestern Lore*, 30, no. 4 (1965): 54; Callaway, Janetski, and Stewart, "Utes," 339.
32. Callaway, Janetski, and Stewart, "Utes," 339, 365; Willard Z. Park, "Tribal Distribution in the Great Basin," *American Anthropologist*, 40, no. 4 (1938): 632–633.
33. Joseph P. Sánchez, *Explorers, Traders, and Slavers: Forging the Old Spanish Trail, 1678–1850* (Salt Lake City: University of Utah Press, 1997), 30–32.
34. Callaway, Janetski, and Stewart, "Utes," 348.
35. Anne M. Smith, "Cultural Differences and Similarities between Uintah and White River," in Steward, *Ute Indians*, 2: 330.
36. Marvin K. Opler, "The Southern Ute of Colorado," in Ralph Linton, ed., *Acculturation in Seven American Indian Tribes* (New York: D. Appleton-Century, 1940), 140.
37. Smith, *Ethnography*, 107.
38. Ibid.; Callaway, Janetski, and Stewart, "Utes," 346–350.
39. David V. Hill and Allen E. Kane, "Characterizations of Ute Occupations and Ceramics from Southwestern Colorado," in Paul R. Nickens, ed., *Archaeology of the Eastern Ute*, 72, 74.
40. Marilyn A. Martorano, "Culturally Peeled Trees and Ute Indians in Colorado," in Paul R. Nickens, ed., *Archaeology of the Eastern Ute*, 5, 8, 15.
41. J. W. Powell, *The Exploration of the Colorado River and Its Canyons* (New York: Dover Publications, 1961 [1895]), 62–63.
42. Smith, *Ethnography*, 74–76.

CHAPTER 3

1. Opler, "Southern Ute of Colorado," 170–171.
2. Dorothy Boyd Bowen, "A Brief History of Spanish Textile Production in the Southwest," in *Spanish Textile Tradition of New Mexico and Colorado*

(Santa Fe: Museum of New Mexico Press, 1979), 5; Ward Alan Minge, "Effectos del Pais," in Spanish Textile Tradition, 12.

3. Opler, "Southern Ute of Colorado," 170–171.

4. Harry C. James, Pages from Hopi History (Tucson: University of Arizona Press, 1979 [1974]), 10–11, 60; Jack D. Forbes, Apache, Navajo, and Spaniard (Norman: University of Oklahoma Press, 1960), 173.

5. Frank Raymond Secoy, Changing Military Patterns of the Great Plains Indians (Lincoln: University of Nebraska Press, 1992 [1953]), 28.

6. Ruth Marie Colville, La Vereda: A Trail Through Time (Alamosa, Colo.: San Luis Valley Historical Society, 1996), 210–211, 221–235; Schroeder, "Brief History," 56; Forbes, Apache, Navajo, and Spaniard, 256–257, 263.

7. Charney, Grammar of Comanche, 1–2.

8. Alfred Barnaby Thomas, trans. and ed., Forgotten Frontiers: A Study of the Spanish Indian Policy of Don Juan Bautista de Anza, Governor of New Mexico, 1777–1787 (Norman: University of Oklahoma Press, 1932), 57–58.

9. Alfred Barnaby Thomas, trans. and ed., After Coronado: Spanish Exploration Northeast of New Mexico, 1696–1727 (Norman: University of Oklahoma Press, 1935), 27.

10. Schroeder, "Brief History," 57–58; Albert H. Schroeder and Omer C. Stewart, "Indian Servitude in the Southwest," in Wilcombe E. Washburn, ed., History of Indian-White Relations, vol. 4, Handbook of North American Indians (Washington, D.C.: Smithsonian Institution, 1988), 412.

11. Thomas, After Coronado, 99–116.

12. Frances Leon Swadesh, Los Prímeros Pobladores: Hispanic Americans of the Ute Frontier (Notre Dame: University of Notre Dame Press, 1974), 54, 163.

13. Ibid., 32–35; F. Stanley, The Abiquiu Story (privately printed, 1960?), 10.

14. Wallace and Hoebel, Comanches, 9.

15. James Jefferson, Robert W. Delaney, and Gregory C. Thompson, The Southern Utes: A Tribal History, ed. Floyd A. O'Neil (Ignacio, Colo.: Southern Ute Tribe, 1972), 5, 7.

16. Lynn Robison Bailey, Indian Slave Trade in the Southwest: A Study of Slave-Taking and Traffic of Indian Captives (Los Angeles: Western Lore Press, 1966), 19.

17. Schroeder, "Brief History," 60.

18. Sánchez, Explorers, Traders, and Slavers, 13, 21–27, 30–37.

19. Thomas, Forgotten Frontiers, 163.

20. Sánchez, Explorers, Traders, and Slavers, 5, 6, 8, 159.

21. Warner, ed., Domínguez-Escalante Journal, 19–94. Discussion of Southern Paiutes encountered by Domínguez and Escalante, including the "Yutas Cobardes," is found in Pamela A. Bunte and Robert J. Franklin, From the Sands to the Mountain: Change and Persistence in a Southern Paiute Community (Lincoln: University of Nebraska Press, 1987), 41.

22. Thomas, Forgotten Frontiers, 139.

23. Alfred Barnaby Thomas, trans. and ed., Teodoro de Croix and the Northern Frontier of Spain, 1776–1783 (Norman: University of Oklahoma Press, 1941), 112.

24. Thomas, *Forgotten Frontiers,* 269.
25. Ibid., 292, 318, 329–332.
26. Minge, *"Effectos del Pais,"* 15–16, 20.
27. Schroeder, "Brief History," 62.
28. Ibid., 62–63.
29. Milo Milton Quaife, ed., *The Southwestern Expedition of Zebulon M. Pike* (Chicago: R. R. Donnelly and Sons, 1924), 86–87.
30. S. Lyman Tyler, "The Spaniard and the Ute," *Utah Historical Quarterly,* 22 (1954): 354–355; ibid., 153–158.
31. Eleanor Richie, "General Mano Mocha of the Utes and Spanish Policy in Indian Relations," *Colorado Magazine,* 9 (July 1932): 154–156.

CHAPTER 4

1. Swadesh, Los Prímeros Pobladores, 165–168. Original documents pertaining to prosecutions of illegal traders are in the New Mexico Records Center and Archives, Santa Fe.
2. Joseph J. Hill, "Spanish and Mexican Exploration and Trade Northwest from New Mexico into the Great Basin," *Utah Historical Quarterly,* 3, no. 1 (1930): 16.
3. D. W. Jones, *Forty Years among the Indians* (Salt Lake City: Juvenile Instruction Office, 1890), 49–50, quoted in Leroy R. Hafen and Ann W. Hafen, *Old Spanish Trail: Santa Fe to Los Angeles* (Lincoln: University of Nebraska Press, 1982 [1954]), 268.
4. Schroeder, "Brief History," 63.
5. Conway B. Sonne, *World of Wakara* (San Antonio: Naylor, 1962), 21–43; Paul Bailey, *Walkara, "Hawk of the Mountains"* (Los Angeles: Westernlore Press, 1954), 13–45; Bob Wiseman, "Las Vegas Played Role in Giant Horse-Stealing Raid," *Nevadan Today* (August 21, 1988), 10, 12.
6. Isabel T. Kelly, "Southern Paiute Bands," *American Anthropologist,* 36 (1934): 548–560.
7. Elliott Coues, ed., *The Journal of Jacob Fowler* (Lincoln: University of Nebraska Press, 1970), 106.
8. Dale L. Morgan, ed., "The Diary of William H. Ashley," *Bulletin, Missouri Historical Society,* 12, no. 1 (1955): 173, fn. 84.
9. Ibid., 165.
10. Ibid., 180–182.
11. Dale L. Morgan, *Jedediah Smith and the Opening of the West* (Lincoln: University of Nebraska Press, 1964), 144, 148.
12. Ibid., 195–196, 226, 237, 239; Janetski, *Ute of Utah Lake,* 4.
13. William S. Wallace, "Antoine Robidoux," in LeRoy R. Hafen, ed., *The Mountain Men and the Fur Trade of the Far West* (Glendale, Calif.: Arthur H. Clark, 1965–1972), 4: 261–274.
14. Antoine Leroux, "Slopes and Valleys of the Rocky Mountains," *Western Journal and Civilian* (April 1853), 6–8, quoted in Forbes Parkhill, *The Blazed Trail of Antoine Leroux* (Los Angeles: Westernlore Press, 1965), 52–53.
15. Harvey Lewis Carter, *"Dear Old Kit": The Historical Christopher Carson* (Norman: University of Oklahoma Press, 1968), 55–79.

16. Adolphus Wislizenus, *A Journey to the Rocky Mountains in the Year 1839* (Glorieta, N.M.: Rio Grande Press, 1969 [1912]), 129–131.

17. Rufus B. Sage, *Scenes in the Rocky Mountains* (Philadelphia: 1846), 178.

18. Joseph Williams, *Narrative of a Tour from the State of Indiana to the Oregon Territory in the Years 1841–2*, quoted in Herbert S. Auerbach, "Old Trails, Old Forts, Old Trappers and Traders: History and Romance of the Old Spanish Trail," *Utah Historical Quarterly*, 9, no. 1 (1941): 40–43.

19. Clark, *Indian Sign Language*, 386; Parkhill, *Blazed Trail*, 73.

20. Janet Lecompte, *Pueblo, Hardscrabble, Greenhorn: The Upper Arkansas, 1832–1856* (Norman: University of Oklahoma Press, 1978); Virginia McConnell Simmons, *The Upper Arkansas: A Mountain River Valley* (Boulder: Pruett Publishing, 1990), 28–39.

21. Letter to Ute Chiefs, MS 59, New Mexico State Records Center and Archives, Read Collection; MS 14, New Mexico State Records Center and Archives, Read Collection.

22. Carter, *"Dear Old Kit,"* 85–87.

23. David J. Weber, *The Mexican Frontier, 1821–1846: The American Southwest under Mexico* (Albuquerque: University of New Mexico Press, 1982), 98.

24. MS 82, New Mexico State Records Center and Archives, Read Collection.

25. George P. Hammond, *The Adventures of Alexander Barclay, Mountain Man* (Denver: Old West Publishing, 1976), 143, 198.

26. Janet Lecompte, "Charles Town," in Hafen, ed., *The Mountain Men and the Fur Trade*, 1: 393.

27. Sebastian Greenway interview, January 14, 1919, in Cragin Notebook 14, Colorado Springs Pioneers Museum; Janetski, *Ute of Utah Lake*, 26–27.

28. Charles Preuss, *Exploring with Frémont* (Norman: University of Oklahoma Press, 1958), 88, 89, 132–133, 136–137.

29. P. J. De Smet, *Voyages aux Montagnes Rocheuses, 1841*, 31–35, cited in Steward, *Ute Indians*, 1: 114.

30. P. J. De Smet, "Letters and Sketches," in Reuben Gold Thwaites, ed., *Early Western Travels, 1748–1846* (Cleveland: Arthur H. Clark, 1906), 27: 165–168.

31. John C. Frémont, *Report of Exploring Expedition to the Rocky Mountains in the Year 1842 and to Oregon and Northern California in the Years 1843–44*, 28th Cong., 2d Sess., Doc. 174 (Washington, D.C.: 1845), 396; Preuss, *Exploring with Frémont*, 133.

32. Preuss, *Exploring with Frémont*, 34.

33. Cragin Notebook 18.

34. Weber, *Mexican Frontier*, 120.

35. Antonio José Martínez, *Esposición . . . Propriendo La Civilisación De Las Nacionés Barbaros (1843)*, MS 180, New Mexico State Records Center and Archives, Read Collection.

36. Virginia M. Simmons, "Creative Interpretation of Father Antonio José Martínez" (M.A. thesis, Adams State College, 1981), 76–103.

37. Judge Wilbur Stone in Cragin Notebook 20; P. David Smith, *Ouray, Chief of the Utes* (Ouray, Colo.: Wayfinder Press, 1986), 35.

38. J. M. Manzanares, "Colorado Recollections of a Centenarian," *Colorado Magazine*, 10, no. 3 (1933): 115.
39. Ibid.
40. Schroeder, "Brief History," 64; Felipe Ledoux in Cragin Notebook 8.
41. Ward Alan Minge, "Mexican Independence Day and a Ute Tragedy in Santa Fe, 1844," in Albert H. Schroeder, ed., *The Changing Ways of Southwestern Indians* (Glorieta, N.M.: Rio Grande Press, 1973), 107–123; Swadesh, Los Prímeros Pobladores, 62–65.
42. James, *Pages from Hopi History*, 72.
43. Anne M. Smith, *Ute Tales* (Salt Lake City: University of Utah Press, 1992), 170.
44. Preuss, *Exploring with Frémont*, 137.
45. Hammond, *Adventures of Alexander Barclay*, 150, 204; Mrs. Felipe Ledoux in Cragin Notebook 7.
46. A. L. Kroeber, *American Museum Natural History Bulletin*, 18 (1902), quoted in Ralph L. Beals, "Ethnology of Rocky Mountain National Park: The Ute and Arapaho," MS, National Park Service, 1936.
47. Opler, "Southern Ute of Colorado," 162–166.
48. Smith, *Ethnography*, 239.
49. Clark, *Indian Sign Language*, 390.
50. Opler, "Southern Ute of Colorado," 167–168, 205; Marvin K. Opler, "The Ute and Paiute Indians," in Eleanor Burke Leacock and Nancy O. Lurie, eds., *North American Indians in Historical Perspective* (New York: Random House, 1971), 282.

CHAPTER 5

1. George F. Ruxton, *Adventures in Mexico and the Rocky Mountains* (London: John Murray, 1847), 208–209.
2. George D. Brewerton, "A Ride with Kit Carson through the Great American Desert and Rocky Mountains," *Harper's New Monthly Magazine* (August 1853): 306–334.
3. Alpheus H. Favour, *Old Bill Williams, Mountain Man* (Norman: University of Oklahoma Press, 1962 [1936]), 162–165.
4. Ibid., 205–206.
5. Hammond, *Adventures of Alexander Barclay*, 167; Leo E. Oliva, *Fort Union and the Frontier Army in the Southwest*, Southwest Cultural Resources Center, Professional Papers, no. 41 (Santa Fe: National Park Service, Division of History, 1993), 24, 26.
6. Charles J. Kappler, comp., "Treaty with the Utah, 1849," *U.S. Indian Affairs, Laws, and Treaties*, 2: 585–587.
7. Schroeder, "Brief History," 64–65.
8. Colville, La Vereda, 229.
9. Larry Murphy, *Out in God's Country: A History of Colfax County, New Mexico* (Springer, N.M.: Springer Publishing, 1969), 39, 40.
10. F. Stanley (Stanley Francis Crocciola), *The Grant That Maxwell Bought* (Denver: 1952), 89.
11. Schroeder, "Brief History," 65.

12. This battle is also said to have taken place on Twin Creek at Florissant, Colorado. Virginia McConnell Simmons, *Bayou Salado: The Story of South Park* (Boulder: Fred Pruett Books, 1992 [1966]), 27–29; Celinda Reynolds Kaelin and Leo Kimmett, *Pikes Peak Backcountry* (Florissant, Colo.: 1995), 48.

13. Schroeder, "Brief History," 66.

14. Robert J. Torrez, *The Southern Ute Agency at Abiquiu and Tierra Amarilla*, Research Paper no. 36 (Guadalupita, N.M.: Center for Land Grant Studies, 1994), 6.

15. Brewerton, "Ride with Kit," 323–334. Brewerton mistakenly reversed the names of the Green and Grand Rivers.

16. Sánchez, *Explorers, Traders, and Slavers*, 131.

17. William L. Manly, *Death Valley in '49* (Los Angeles: Borden Publishing, 1949), 92–93, 400–401.

18. Conetah, *History of the Northern Ute People,* 38; Floyd A. O'Neil, "A History of the Ute Indians of Utah Until 1890" (Ph.D. diss., University of Utah, 1973), 189.

19. Steward, *Ute Indians*, 1: 74–75; Madoline Cloward Dixon, *These Were the Utes: Their Lifestyles, Wars and Legends* (Provo, Utah: Press Publishing, 1983), 23–25; U.S. Bureau of Indian Affairs, Letters Received, 1824–1881, Utah Superintendency, M234, Roll 897. Several violent incidents are detailed in Howard A. Christy, "Open Hand and Mailed Fist: Mormon-Indian Relations in Utah, 1847–52," *Utah Historical Quarterly*, 46, no. 3 (1973): 216–235.

20. Albert C. T. Antrei and Ruth D. Scow, eds., *The Other Forty-Niners: A Topical History of Sanpete County, Utah, 1849–1983* (Salt Lake City: Western Epics, 1982) viii–ix, 130–131, 498.

21. Trenholm and Carley, *Shoshonis*, 127.

22. Ibid., 130–132.

23. Steward, *Ute Indians*, 1: 62–63.

24. Letters Received, Utah Superintendency, M234, Roll 898.

25. Sonne, *World of Wakara*, 217–221.

26. Fike and Phillips, *Nineteenth Century Ute Burial*, 99–100; Paul R. Nickens, "Archaeological Evidence for Eastern Ute Mortuary Practice," in *Archaeology of the Eastern Ute: A Symposium*, Colorado Council of Professional Archaeologists, Occasional Papers, no. 1 (1988), 22–44.

27. Conetah, *History of the Northern Ute People*, 83.

28. Josiah F. Gibbs, "Gunnison Massacre, 1853: Indian Mareer's Version of the Tragedy," *Utah Historical Quarterly*, 1 (July 1928): 70.

29. Solomon Nunez Carvalho, *Incidents of Travel and Adventure in the Far West* (New York: Derby and Jackson, 1857), 193–194.

30. Trenholm and Carley, *Shoshonis*, 136–140.

31. Steward, *Ute Indians*, 1: 117–118.

32. Antrei and Scow, *Other Forty-Niners*, 138–140.

33. Letters Received, Utah Superintendency. Brigham Young to George Manypenny, M234, Roll 898.

34. Garland Hurt to J. M. Elliott, ibid.

35. George Armstrong, ibid.
36. Schroeder, "Brief History," 65–66.
37. Gwinn Harris Heap, *Central Route to the Pacific, from the Valley of the Mississippi to California: Journal of the Expedition* (Philadelphia: Lippincott, Grambo, 1854), 33–97.
38. Parkhill, *Blazed Trail*, 172–174.
39. Carvalho, *Incidents*, 152–157.
40. Oliva, *Fort Union*, 83, 122.
41. Frank Hall, *History of the State of Colorado* (Chicago: Blakely Printing, 1889), 4: 92.
42. Cragin Notebooks 1, 2, 8, 9, 10; LeRoy R. Hafen, "The Fort Pueblo Massacre and the Punitive Expedition against the Utes," *Colorado Magazine*, 4 (January 1927): 49–58.
43. Virginia McConnell Simmons, *The San Luis Valley: Land of the Six-Armed Cross*, 2d ed. (Niwot: University Press of Colorado, 1999 [1979]), 94.
44. Morris F. Taylor, "Action at Fort Massachusetts: The Indian Campaign of 1855," *Colorado Magazine*, 42, no. 4 (1965): 297–310; Rafael Chacon, "Campaign against Utes and Apaches in Southern Colorado, 1855," *Colorado Magazine*, 11, no. 3 (1934): 108–112.
45. Gerald T. Hart, LeRoy R. Hafen, and Anne M. Smith, *Ute Indians*, vol. 2, American Indian Ethnohistory: California and Basin-Plateau Indians (New York: Garland Publishing, 1974), 278.
46. U.S. Bureau of Indian Affairs, Records of the New Mexico Superintendency. Christopher Carson to Gov. David Meriwether, January 20, 1854, M-T21, Roll 1.
47. Cragin Notebook 10.
48. Morris F. Taylor, "Ka-ni-ache, Part 1," *Colorado Magazine*, 43, no. 4 (1966): 285.
49. Conetah, *History of the Northern Ute People*, 103.
50. Carter, *"Dear Old Kit,"* 147–149.
51. Schroeder, "Brief History," 68.
52. Torrez, *Southern Ute Agency*, 9.
53. LeRoy R. Hafen, ed., "Colonel Loring's Expedition across Colorado in 1858," *Colorado Magazine*, 23, no. 2 (1946): 49–75.

CHAPTER 6

1. Letters Received, Utah Superintendency, M234, Roll 899.
2. Dixon, *These Were the Utes*, 84.
3. Oliva, *Fort Union*, 154–156.
4. Ibid., 162.
5. Cragin Notebook 17.
6. *Rocky Mountain News* (Denver, Colorado), September 26, 1860, 1.
7. Records of the New Mexico Superintendency of Indian Affairs, 1849–1880, M-T21, Roll 4.
8. Bailey, *Indian Slave Trade*, 106–107.
9. Virginia McConnell, "Captain Baker and the San Juan Humbug," *Colorado Magazine*, 48, no. 1 (1971): 59–75.

10. Letters Received, 1824–1881, New Mexico Superintendency, 1849–1880, M234, Roll 550.
11. U.S. Adjutant General's Office, Returns from U.S. Military Posts, 1800–1916, Fort Garland, 1858–1872, M617, Roll 394.
12. Records of the New Mexico Superintendency, M-T21, Roll 4.
13. Steward, *Ute Indians*, 1: 138.
14. Oliva, *Fort Union*, 254.
15. "Existence of Slavery of Ute Indians by Spanish American Settlers of the San Luis Valley," anonymous MS, University of Colorado at Boulder Libraries, Archives. The author is identified as a grandson of Julian Espinoza. The incident probably occurred in the late 1850s or the 1860s.
16. Peterson, "Tabeguache and Elk Mountain Utes," 11–12.
17. James W. Covington, "Federal Relations with the Colorado Utes, 1861–65," *Colorado Magazine*, 28 (October 1951): 262.
18. U.S. Bureau of Indian Affairs, *Annual Report of the Commissioner of Indian Affairs for 1863* (Washington, D.C.: Government Printing Office, 1864), 121–122.
19. Covington, "Federal Relations," 260–261.
20. Finis E. Downing, "With the Ute Peace Delegation of 1863, across the Plains and at Conejos," *Colorado Magazine*, 22, no. 5 (1945): 193–200.
21. Kappler, comp., *U.S. Indian Affairs, Laws, and Treaties*, "Treaty With the Utah-Tabeguache Band, 1863," 2: 856–859.
22. Records of the New Mexico Superintendency, M-T21, Rolls 5, 6.
23. U.S. Congress, House, *Letter of the Secretary of State Transmitting Correspondence of the Territory of New Mexico, Governor A. Rencher to General Lewis Cass.* 36th Cong., 2d Sess., Exec Doc. 24, 1861.
24. U.S. Congress, Joint Special Committee, *Condition of the Indian Tribes; Report of the Joint Special Committee Appointed under Joint Resolution of March 3, 1865* (Washington, D.C.: Government Printing Office, 1867), 114.
25. Robert S. McPherson, *The Northern Navajo Frontier, 1860–1900: Expansion through Adversity* (Albuquerque: University of New Mexico Press, 1988), 8–10. A careful analysis of the Navajo roundup and the role of Kit Carson in it appears in R. C. Gordon-McCutchan, ed., *Kit Carson: Indian Fighter or Indian Killer?* (Niwot: University Press of Colorado, 1996); see therein Lawrence C. Kelly, "The Historiography of the Navajo Roundup," 49–72.
26. Donald J. Berthrong, *The Southern Cheyennes* (Norman: University of Oklahoma Press, 1963), 175–176, 203.
27. Oliva, *Fort Union*, 309; Carter, *"Dear Old Kit,"* 162–165.
28. D. Gene Combs, "Enslavement of Indians in the San Luis Valley" (M.A. thesis, Adams State College, 1970).
29. Hafen and Hafen, *Old Spanish Trail*, 280–281.
30. Hart, Hafen, and Smith, *Ute Indians*, 2: 52.
31. Covington, "Federal Relations," 265.
32. Steward, *Ute Indians*, 1: 119.
33. Taylor, "Ka-ni-ache, Part 1," 291–292.

34. Oliva, *Fort Union*, 333–334.
35. Records of the New Mexico Superintendency, M-T21, Roll 7.
36. *Condition of the Indian Tribes*, 368.
37. Hart, Hafen, and Smith, *Ute Indians*, 2: 285–286.
38. Letters Received, 1824–1881, Colorado Superintendency, 1861–1880, M234, Roll 199.
39. Irving Howbert, *The Indians of the Pike's Peak Region* (New York: Knickerbocker Press, 1914), 72–73.
40. Letters Received, Colorado Superintendency, M234, Roll 199.
41. Ibid.
42. Swadesh, Los Prímeros Pobladores, 82, 99.
43. Indian Claims Commission, "Commission Findings," in Hart, Hafen, and Smith, *Ute Indians*, 2: 375–376.
44. Letters Received, Colorado Superintendency, M234, Roll 199.
45. Schroeder, "Brief History," 7–8; O'Neil, "History of the Ute Indians"; John A. Peterson, *Utah's Black Hawk War* (Salt Lake City: University of Utah Press, 1998), which provides detailed information about Black Hawk's life and contemporary events.
46. Indian Claims Commission, "Commission Findings," 2: 368.
47. U.S. Bureau of Indian Affairs, *Proposed Paiute Indian Tribe of Utah Reservation Plan* (Washington, D.C.: Government Printing Office, 1982), 29.
48. Antrei and Scow, eds., *Other Forty-Niners*, 140, 142.
49. Leavitt Christensen, *Birth of Kanosh* (Kanosh, Utah: 1995), 10, 17, 41.
50. Peterson, *Utah's Black Hawk War*, 245–248.
51. *Ute Bulletin* (Fort Duchesne, Utah), September 9, 1997, 1, 3.
52. LeRoy R. Hafen and Ann W. Hafen, eds., *The Diaries of William Henry Jackson, Frontier Photographer: To California and Return*, vol. 10 in the Far West and the Rockies Historical Series (Glendale, Calif.: A. H. Clark, 1959), 186.
53. O'Neil, "History of the Ute Indians," 72.

CHAPTER 7

1. Kappler, comp., *U.S. Indian Affairs, Laws, and Treaties*, "Treaty With the Utes, 1868," 2: 990–996.
2. *Rocky Mountain News*, June 6, 1868, 4; Letters Received, Colorado Superintendency, M234, Roll 199.
3. *Colorado Chieftain* (Pueblo), October 8, 1868, 1.
4. Letters Received, Colorado Superintendency, M234, Roll 199.
5. John Lawrence, *Frontier Eyewitness: Diary of John Lawrence, 1867–1908* ed. Bernice Martin (Saguache, Colo.: Saguache County Museum, 1990?), 22.
6. U.S. Bureau of Indian Affairs, *Annual Report of the Commissioner of Indian Affairs for 1868* (Washington, D.C.: Government Printing Office, 1869), 642–643.
7. Ibid., 707–708.
8. Ray D. Lyons and Ann M. Johnson, "The Old Agency Fortified Site," *Southwestern Lore*, 59, no. 2 (1993): 3–17; Howbert, *Indians of the Pike's Peak Region*, 24–26.

9. Michael David Kaplan, "Otto Mears: Colorado's Transportation King" (Ph.D. diss., University of Colorado, 1975), 54; Lois Borland, "The Sale of the San Juan," *Colorado Magazine*, 28, no. 2 (1951): 112.

10. George G. Everett and Wendell F. Hutchinson, *Under the Angel of Shavano* (Denver: Golden Bell Press, 1963), 46–48.

11. Sidney Jocknick, *Early Days on the Western Slope of Colorado* (Glorieta, N.M.: Rio Grande Press, 1968 [1913]), 116–117.

12. Ibid., 33–38, 62.

13. Cragin Notebook 14; A. K. Clarke, "The Utes Visit My Ranch on the Plains," *Colorado Magazine*, 5, no. 4 (1928): 144–146.

14. Thomas F. Dawson, "Major Thompson, Chief Ouray, and the Utes," *Colorado Magazine*, 7, no. 3 (May 1930): 114–115. Some of Thompson's papers are located in the Stephen H. Hart Library of the Colorado Historical Society.

15. Letters Received, Colorado Superintendency, M234, Roll 199.

16. Samuel Bowles, *The Switzerland of America: A Summer Vacation in the Parks and Mountains of Colorado* (Boston: Lee and Shepard, 1869), 74.

17. Jorgensen, "Ethnohistory and Acculturation," 84.

18. Jocknick, *Early Days*, 260–264.

19. Lena M. Urquhart, *Colorow, the Angry Chieftain* (Denver: Golden Bell Press, 1968), 31, 32.

20. Hazel Gresham, *North Park* (Walden, Colo.: 1975), 12.

21. James W. Covington, "Ute Scalp Dance in Denver," *Colorado Magazine*, 30, no. 2 (1953): 119–124.

22. Jorgensen, "Ethnohistory and Acculturation," 102.

23. *Rocky Mountain News*, June 23, 1868, 4.

24. Ibid., October 30, 1868, 1.

25. Morris F. Taylor, "Ka-ni-ache, Part 2," *Colorado Magazine*, 44, no. 2 (1967): 147–148.

26. William A. Keleher, *Maxwell Land Grant: A New Mexico Item* (Santa Fe: William Gannon, 1975), 54–57.

27. Federal Indian Agencies, Agency Reports, located in New Mexico State Records Center and Archives. Thomas A. Dolan to E. P. Smith, December 10 and December 22, 1873.

28. Records of the New Mexico Superintendency, M-T21, Roll 9.

29. Lawrence R. Murphy, ed., *Indian Agent in New Mexico: The Journal of Special Agent W. F. M. Arny* (Santa Fe: Stagecoach Press, 1967); Letters Received, New Mexico Superintendency, M234, Roll 557. Following his service as agent at Cimarrón, Arny became New Mexico's territorial secretary and later was agent at Abiquiú (1867–1868). In 1870 he was appointed special agent to conduct a survey of New Mexico Territory's Indians.

30. Norman J. Bender, "The Battle of Tierra Amarilla," *New Mexico Historical Review*, 63, no. 3 (1988): 248–250; Torrez, *Southern Ute Agency*, 18–22.

31. U.S. Bureau of Indian Affairs, Records of Pueblo Agencies, Cimarron and Abiquiu (Jicarilla) Agencies, 1869–1883, RG-75, Roll 28.

32. Ibid.; see also records pertaining to Ute Indians in U.S. Bureau of Indian Affairs, Records Created by the Pueblo and Jicarilla Indian Agencies, 1874–1900, M1304, Roll 1 (1874–1877) and Roll 2 (1877–1878).

33. Robert W. Delaney, *The Ute Mountain Utes* (Albuquerque: University of New Mexico Press, 1989), 37, 39.

34. Ibid., 120–122; U.S. Bureau of Indian Affairs, *Annual Report of the Commissioner of Indian Affairs for 1871* (Washington, D.C.: Government Printing Office, 1872), 405.

35. McPherson, *Northern Navajo Frontier*, 15.

36. *Ibid.*

37. William H. Jackson and William H. Holmes, *Mesa Verde and the Four Corners: Hayden Survey, 1874–1876* (Ouray, Colo.: Bear Creek Publishing, 1981), 377; Robert S. McPherson, "Canyons, Cows, and Conflict: A Native American History of Montezuma Canyon, 1874–1933," *Utah Historical Quarterly*, 60, no. 3 (1992): 239.

38. U.S. Bureau of Indian Affairs, *Annual Report of the Commissioner of Indian Affairs for 1870* (Washington, D.C.: Government Printing Office, 1871), 627–628.

39. Hart, Hafen, and Smith, *Ute Indians*, 2: 55–57, 291, 293–295.

40. Borland, "Sale of the San Juan," 115–118.

41. Ann Woodbury Hafen, "Efforts to Recover the Stolen Son of Chief Ouray," *Colorado Magazine*, 16, no. 2 (1939): 53–62.

42. Hart, Hafen, and Smith, *Ute Indians*, 2: 319–323.

43. Kappler, comp., *U.S. Indian Affairs, Laws, and Treaties*, 1: 151–152.

44. Hall, *History of Colorado*, 2: 191.

45. Chauncey Thomas, "Indians" (unpublished MS, 1930), 10, located at Stephen H. Hart Library, Colorado Historical Society.

46. Hafen and Hafen, eds., *Diaries of William Henry Jackson*, 286–291.

47. Conetah, *History of the Northern Ute People*, 84–85.

48. Christensen, *Birth of Kanosh*, 22, 23, 62, 109, 157–161.

49. O'Neil, "History of the Ute Indians," 104–105.

50. Jorgensen, "Ethnohistory and Acculturation," 90.

51. Steward, *Ute Indians*, 1: 122–123; U.S. Bureau of Indian Affairs, *Annual Report of the Commissioner of Indian Affairs for 1872* (Washington, D.C.: Government Printing Office, 1873), 291–295, 299–300.

52. Steward, *Ute Indians*, 1: 147; Indian Claims Commission, "Commission Findings," 2: 372.

53. U.S. Congress, House. *Ute, Paiute, Go-si Ute, and Shoshone Indians: Letter from the Acting Secretary of the Interior.* 43rd Cong., 1st Sess., Exec. Doc. 157, 1873.

CHAPTER 8

1. Records Created by the Pueblo and Jicarilla Indian Agencies, Letters Received, Cimarron and Abiquiu Agencies, 1867–78, November 14, 1874, M1304, Roll 1; Brian C. Pohanka, ed., *Nelson A. Miles: A Documentary Biography of His Military Career, 1861–1903* (Glendale, Calif.: Arthur H. Clark, 1985), 87, 141. When Brigadier General Nelson Miles came from Fort Leavenworth to Cimarrón in late 1875 to bring order, he wrote to his wife that the problems arose "from whisky, bad rations and want of proper discretion in their management." The secretary of the interior subsequently

increased rations at Cimarrón. Miles also noted that six Ute Indians had been killed "by lawless white men."

2. Robert Svenningsen, comp., *Preliminary Inventory of the Pueblo Records Created by Field Offices of the Bureau of Indian Affairs*, Record Group 75 (Washington, D.C.: National Archives and Records Service, 1980), 13.
3. Letters Received, Cimarron and Abiquiu Agencies, 1867–78, December 1877, M1304, Roll 2.
4. Ibid., January 15, 1878; National Archives and Records Service, Rocky Mountain Region, Consolidated Ute Service, Box 2, Folder 130.
5. Returns from Military Posts, 1800–1916, Fort Lewis, Colorado, October 1878–August 1891, M617, Roll 624.
6. U.S. Bureau of Indian Affairs, *Annual Report of the Commissioner of Indian Affairs for 1879* (Washington, D.C.: Government Printing Office, 1879), 170–181; U.S. Bureau of Indian Affairs, "Report of the Ute Commission, December 27, 1879," 170–181; Kappler, comp., *Indian Affairs, Laws, and Treaties*, 1: 174, 175; Jefferson, Delaney, and Thompson, *Southern Utes*, 32–33.
7. U.S. Bureau of Indian Affairs, *Annual Report of the Commissioner of Indian Affairs for 1879* (Washington, D.C.: Government Printing Office, 1879), 16–17.
8. *Rocky Mountain News*, September 5, 1875, 4; September 17, 1875, 4; September 21, 1875, 2; Howard E. Greager, *We Shall Fall as the Leaves* (N.p.: 1996), 119, 159–160.
9. Buckley Bangert, "Uncompahgre Statesman: The Life of Ouray," *Journal of the Western Slope*, 1 (spring 1986): 52–54.
10. Howbert, *Indians of the Pike's Peak Region*, 73; U.S. Bureau of Indian Affairs, *Report of the Commissioner of Indian Affairs for 1875* (Washington, D.C.: Government Printing Office, 1875), 230–232; Kaelin and Kimmett, *Pikes Peak Backcountry*, 47–48, 112.
11. Lawrence, *Frontier Eyewitness*, 92–94.
12. S. F. Stacher, "Ouray and the Utes," *Colorado Magazine*, 27 (April 1950): 138–139; Cragin Notebook 16; Richard Duran, personal communication, December 29, 1994. Luis Montoya was the great-grandfather of Richard Duran.
13. Alonzo Hartman, "Memories," Appendix in John B. Lloyd, "The Uncompahgre Utes" (M.A. thesis, Western State College, 1932), 11–12.
14. Cragin Notebook 16.
15. Jocknick, *Early Days*, 119.
16. George M. Darley, *Pioneering in the San Juan* (New York: Fleming H. Revell, 1899), 22, 131.
17. Lloyd, "The Uncompahgre Utes," 30.
18. Ernie Rose, *Utahs of the Rocky Mountains* (Montrose, Colo.: Montrose Daily Press, 1968), 102.
19. John Brown Abbott, "Los Pinos Letters," at Stephen H. Hart Library, Colorado Historical Society.
20. William H. Leckie, *The Buffalo Soldiers: A Narrative of the Negro Cavalry in the West* (Norman: University of Oklahoma Press, 1968), 206.

21. U.S. Congress, House, *Memorial of the Legislative Assembly of Colorado, Calling Attention of Congress to the Grievances of the Ute Indians.* 44th Cong., 1st Sess., Misc. Doc. 86, 1, 1875.

22. *Rocky Mountain News,* April 27, 1876, 4; July 21, 1876, 1; John G. Bourke, *On the Border with Crook* (New York: Charles Scribner's Sons, 1891), 334–343.

23. Bourke, *On the Border,* 350–357, 395–396.

24. John Rolfe Burroughs, *Where the Old West Stayed Young* (New York: Bonanza Books, 1962), 41, 216.

25. U.S. Congress, House, Committee on Indian Affairs, *Testimony in Relation to the Ute Indian Outbreak, Taken by the Committee on Indian Affairs of the House of Representatives* (Washington, D.C.: Government Printing Office, 1880), 37; *Rocky Mountain News,* December 12, 13, and 18, 1877, 4; June 18, 1878, 2.

26. Consolidated Ute Indian Service, Box 3, Folder 175; Cragin Notebook 28; Charles H. Leckenby, comp., *The Tread of the Pioneers* (Steamboat Springs, Colo.: Pilot Press, 1944), 27–29.

27. "Middle Park Indians to 1881," *Grand County Historical Association Journal,* 7, no. 1 (1987): 50; Mike Frary, personal communication, September 17, 1996. Abraham Elliott was Frary's great-great-grandfather.

28. Robert C. Black, *Island in the Rockies: The History of Grand County, Colorado, to 1930* (Boulder: Pruett Publishing for the Grand County Pioneer Society, 1969), 118–120.

29. U.S. Bureau of Indian Affairs, *Report of the Commissioner of Indian Affairs for 1878* (Washington, D.C.: Government Printing Office, 1878), 18–19; Nathan C. Meeker, "The Utes of Colorado," *American Antiquarian,* 1, no. 4 (1879): 224–226.

30. V. S. Fitzpatrick, *Red Twilight: A History of the Northern Utes* (Colorado Springs: Earth Design Systems, n.d.), 53–55.

31. Letter from Mrs. Albert Smart, in Al Look, *Ute's Last Stand at White River and Milk Creek, Western Colorado, in 1879* (Denver: Golden Bell Press, 1972), 82–93.

32. Dawson, "Major Thompson, Chief Ouray, and the Utes," 121–122. Dawson interviewed Thompson on May 23, 1921. A few sources implying that the Thompson property was not destroyed may be incorrect.

33. Marvin K. Opler, "The Ute Indian War of 1879," *El Palacio,* 46 (1939): 257–262.

34. Many books and articles have been published about the events at White River; they include Thomas F. Dawson and F. J. V. Skiff, *The Ute War* (Denver: Tribune Publishing, 1879); Robert Emmitt, *The Last War Trail: The Utes and the Settlement of Colorado* (Norman: University of Oklahoma Press, 1954); Marshall D. Moody, "The Meeker Massacre," *Colorado Magazine,* 30, no. 2 (1953): 91–104; Marshall Sprague, *Massacre: The Tragedy at White River* (Lincoln: University of Nebraska Press, 1980 [1957]); and Fred H. Werner, *Meeker—The Story of the Meeker Massacre and the Thornburgh Battle* (Greeley, Colo.: Werner Publications, 1985). Eyewitness accounts include J. S. Payne, "Incidents of the Recent Campaign

against the Utes," *United Service*, 2, no. 1 (1880): 114–129; *Brave Miss Meeker's Captivity! Her Own Account of It. Also, the Narratives of Her Mother and Mrs. Price* (Philadelphia: Old Franklin Publishing, 1879); M. Wilson Rankin, *Reminiscences of Frontier Days* (Denver: Smith-Brooks, 1935).

35. Smith, *Ouray*, 168.
36. Robert G. Athearn, ed., "Major Hough's March into Southern Ute Country, 1879," *Colorado Magazine*, 25, no. 3 (1948): 105–109.
37. Jocknick, *Early Days*, 197–199.
38. George A. Crofutt, *Crofutt's Gripsack Guide of Colorado* (Denver: Cubar, 1966), 2: 119.
39. Virginia McConnell, " 'H. H.,' Colorado, and the Indian Problem," *Journal of the West*, 12, no. 2 (1973): 272, 275.
40. Moody, "Meeker Massacre," 103. Moody's article is especially useful because the author was supervisor of Indian records at the National Archives.
41. Robert G. Lewis, "Lewis Emery Walker" (unpublished MS). This article relates to a Washington photographer who made portraits of Utes in 1880. The author used items from contemporary newspapers in the nation's capital that contained reports about the Utes' activities.
42. U.S. Congress, House, Testimony in Relation to the Ute Indian Outbreak. Taken by the Committee on Indian Affairs of the House of Representatives (Washington, D.C.: Government Printing Office, 1880), 109.
43. Kappler, comp., *Indian Affairs, Laws, and Treaties*, 1: 180–186.
44. Mrs. C. W. Wiegel, "The Death of Ouray, Chief of the Utes," *Colorado Magazine*, 7 (September 1930): 187, 190. In 1925 Ouray's remains were moved to the Southern Ute Reservation cemetery at Ignacio. Some skepticism lingers about the true identity of the remains.
45. Peter Tawes, "Diary of Peter Tawes, May 17–August 13, 1880," transcript, located in University of Colorado at Boulder, Norlin Library, Archives.
46. Christian J. Buys, "Fort Crawford: A Symbol of Transition," *Journal of the Western Slope*, 8 (spring 1993): 12–15; Richard A. Ronzio, "Fort Crawford on the Uncompahgre," *Denver Westerners' Monthly Roundup*, 19, no. 3 (1963): 5–6.
47. U.S. Adjutant's Office, Returns from Military Posts, Fort Crawford, Colorado, October 1880–August 1890, M617, Roll 263; Jerome W. Johnson, "Murder on the Uncompahgre," *Colorado Magazine*, 43, no. 3 (1966): 209–224.
48. Returns from Military Posts, Fort Lewis, M617, Roll 624.
49. *Rocky Mountain News*, November 28, 1881, 8.
50. "Record of the Fort Duchesne Indian Police," in Work Projects Administration MSS, "Moffat County," located at Stephen H. Hart Library, Colorado Historical Society, and reprinted in *Outlaw Trail Journal* (summer 1996): 2–4.
51. *Solid Muldoon* (Ouray, Colorado), September 2, 1881, 3.
52. Clark, *Indian Sign Language*, 388.

CHAPTER 9

1. Kaplan, "Otto Mears," 78–79, quoting *Ouray Times* (Ouray, Colorado), October 8, 1881.

2. Returns from Military Posts, Fort Thornburgh, 1881–1883, M617, Roll 1272; Thomas J. Alexander and Leonard J. Arrington, "The Utah Military Frontier, 1872–1912: Forts Cameron, Thornburgh, and Duchesne," *Utah Historical Quarterly*, 32, no. 4 (1964): 340–341.
3. Indian Claims Commission, "Commission Findings," 408–410.
4. Ibid.
5. *Rocky Mountain News*, May 2, 1882, 1.
6. "Record of the Fort Duchesne Indian Police," 3.
7. Indian Claims Commission, "Commission Findings," 379–380.
8. O'Neil, "History of the Ute Indians," 162–163.
9. Consolidated Ute Indian Service, J. F. Minniss to Patten, August 1883, Box 3, Folder 175.
10. Clark, *Indian Sign Language*, 303, 353.
11. Arthur C. Moulton, "A Trader with the Utes, and the Murder of Chief Shavano," as told to James R. Harvey, *Colorado Magazine*, 20 (May 1943): 101–103.
12. U.S., Indian Census Rolls, 1885–1940, Uncompahgre Band, 1885, M595, Roll 608.
13. Ibid.
14. Moulton, "Trader with the Utes," 104–107.
15. Returns of Military Post, Fort DuChesne, 1886–1903, M617, Roll 333; Alexander and Arrington, "Utah Military Frontier," 343–345; Gary Lee Walker, "Fort Duchesne's Buffalo Soldiers," *Outlaw Trail Journal* (winter 1994): 30–32, 36; Henry Fiack, "Fort Duchesne's Beginnings," *Utah Historical Quarterly*, 2, no. 1 (1929): 31–32.
16. Norma Denver, "Fort Duchesne," *Ute Bulletin*, March 25, 1998, 7.
17. Returns of Military Posts, Fort DuChesne, 1886–1903, M617, Roll 333; A. Dudley Gardner, *The Ute Indians in Northwestern Colorado After the Meeker Massacre*, Western Wyoming College Contributions to History, no. 1 (1979): 1–5; George Truman Kercheval, "The Wrongs of the Ute Indians," *Forum*, (January 1890): 578–585.
18. Dan A. Freeman, *Four Years with the Utes: The Letters of Dan A. Freeman*, ed. W. M. Morrison (Waco, Texas: W. M. Morrison, 1962), 5.
19. Returns of Military Posts, Fort DuChesne, 1886–1903, M617, Roll 333.
20. U.S. Bureau of Indian Affairs, *Annual Report of the Commissioner of Indian Affairs for 1878* (Washington, D.C.: Government Printing Office, 1878), 127; *Annual Report of the Commissioner of Indian Affairs for 1880* (Washington, D.C.: Government Printing Office, 1880), 178.
21. Conetah, *History of the Northern Ute People*, 114, 130–131.
22. Donald A. MacKendrick, "Cesspools, Alkali, and White Lily Soap: The Grand Junction Indian School, 1886–1911," *Journal of the Western Slope*, 8, no. 3 (1993): 1–41, which provides a comprehensive history of the Teller Institute; U.S. Bureau of Indian Affairs, *Annual Report of the Commissioner of Indian Affairs for 1895* (Washington, D.C.: Government Printing Office, 1895), 364–369.
23. Norma Denver, "Randlett Boarding School," *Ute Bulletin* (April 19, 1998), 5.

24. Smith, *Ethnography*, 216, 217; Michael Hittman, *Wovoka and the Ghost Dance*, ed. Don Lynch (Lincoln: University of Nebraska Press, 1997 [1990]); James Mooney, *The Ghost Dance Religion and the Sioux Outbreak of 1890* (Chicago: University of Chicago Press, 1965).
25. Consolidated Ute Indian Service, Gratuity Lists of the Southern Ute Indians, 1881, 1885, 1889, Box 3.
26. Ibid., Liquor Traffic, 1881–1926, Box 2, Folder 126.
27. Ibid., Commander 13th Infantry to Henry Page, June 9, 1881, Box 2, Folder 125; W. B. Haines to Adjutant General at Santa Fe, New Mexico, May 13, 1881, New Mexico State Records Center and Archives.
28. Consolidated Ute Indian Service, Box 3, Folder 175.
29. Returns of Military Posts, Fort Lewis, 1878–1891, M617, Roll 624.
30. Consolidated Ute Indian Service, Box 2.
31. Indian Census Rolls, Southern Utes, 1885, M595, Roll 543.
32. Laura C. Manson White, "Albert H. Pfeiffer," *Colorado Magazine*, 10 (November 1933): 222; Swadesh, Los Prímeros Pobladores, 102–103.
33. Indian Census Rolls, Southern Utes, M595, Roll 543.
34. Consolidated Ute Indian Service, Box 2, Folder 123.
35. Jefferson, Delaney, and Thompson, *Southern Utes*, 41, 43; Delaney, *Ute Mountain Utes*, 68, 73; Gregory Coyne Thompson, *Southern Ute Lands, 1848–1899: The Creation of a Reservation*, Occasional Papers of the Center of Southwest Studies, no. 1 (Durango, Colo.: Fort Lewis College, 1972), 36; Gregory Coyne Thompson, "The Unwanted Indians: The Southern Utes in Southeastern Utah," *Utah Historical Quarterly*, 49, no. 2 (1981): 189–203.
36. Consolidated Ute Indian Service, Box 2, Folder 125.
37. Swadesh, Los Prímeros Pobladores, 98–100.
38. Consolidated Ute Indian Service, Box 2, Folder 130.
39. Veronica E. Velarde Tiller, *The Jicarilla Apache Tribe*, rev. ed. (Lincoln: University of Nebraska Press, 1992 [1983]), 106–108.
40. "Removal of the Southern Utes" (pamphlet, 1892), 89, in The Colorado College, Tutt Library, Special Collections; "Removal of Southern Utes from Colorado to Utah: Protest of Her Legislature, Governor, Delegates, and Citizens" (pamphlet, n.d.), in The Colorado College, Tutt Library, Special Collections.
41. Verner Z. Reed, "The Southern Ute Indians," *Californian*, 4 (September 1893): 494–495.
42. U.S. Bureau of Indian Affairs, *Annual Report of the Commissioner of Indian Affairs for 1895* (Washington, D.C.: Government Printing Office, 1895), 363–364.
43. Jefferson, Delaney, and Thompson, *Southern Utes*, 41–43.
44. Delaney, *Ute Mountain Utes*, 1, 2, 71–73, 109.

CHAPTER 10

1. U.S. Congress, Senate, Letter from the Secretary of the Interior in Response to Senate Resolution of April 6, 1897, 55th Cong., 1st Sess., Doc. 32, 1897.

2. *Denver Times*, July 26, 1898, 2; August 4, 1898, 6; November 11, 1898, 1; November 12, 1898, 3; December 13, 1898, 3; December 16, 1898, 5; October 5, 1899, 3; October 24. 1900, 7.

3. Florence Hawley, "Culture Process and Change in Ute Adaptation," *El Palacio*, 57, no. 3 (1950): 326–331.

4. U.S. Bureau of Indian Affairs, *Annual Report of the Commissioner of Indian Affairs for 1900* (Washington, D.C.: Government Printing Office, 1900), 389–390.

5. Indian Census Rolls, Uintah and Ouray Utes, 1904, M595, Roll 610.

6. Returns of Military Posts, Fort DuChesne, 1886–1903, M617, Roll 333.

7. H. G. Clark, "Diary, 1903," entries of April 2 and September 7–20, 1903. This unpublished diary is located in the Utah State Historical Society Library.

8. *Denver Times*, December 1, 1898, 2.

9. Henry E. Bender Jr., *Uintah Railway: The Gilsonite Route* (Berkeley: Howell-North Books, 1971), 21, 23, 27, 59.

10. Returns of Military Posts, Fort Duchesne, 1904–1912, M617, Roll 334.

11. Kenneth Earl Batch-Elder, "Revelations from the Shadows of Thunder Butte" (M.A. thesis, University of Colorado, 1994), 4.

12. Several accounts of the Ute experience in South Dakota exist in Batch-Elder's work; David D. Laudenschlager, "The Utes in South Dakota, 1906–1908," *South Dakota History*, 9, no. 3 (1979): 233–247; Robert G. Lewis, "C. C. McBride" (unpublished MS about the photographer at Fort Meade); Floyd A. O'Neil, "An Anguished Odyssey: The Flight of the Utes, 1906–1908," *Utah Historical Quarterly*, 36, no. 4 (fall 1968): 315–327; "Utes Invade Dakota," *Wi-iyohi*, 7, no. 3 (1953): 1-2; U.S. Bureau of Indian Affairs, *Annual Report of the Commissioner of Indian Affairs for 1908* (Washington, D.C.: Government Printing Office, 1908), 118–121.

13. Craig W. Fuller, George D. Kendrick, and Robert W. Righter, "Prelude to Settlement: The Efforts of the U.S. Indian Irrigation Service in the Uinta Basin, Utah," in *Beyond the Wasatch: The History of Irrigation in the Uinta Basin and Upper Provo River Area of Utah* (U.S. Bureau of Reclamation, Upper Colorado Regional Office and National Park Service, Rocky Mountain Regional Office, n.d.), 18–30; U.S. Congress, House, *Letter from the Secretary of the Treasury, Transmitting an Estimate of Appropriation for Protection, etc., of Rights of Uncompahgre, Uintah, and White River Utes in Certain Irrigation Systems*, 60th Cong., 2d Sess., Doc. 1279, 1908; U.S. Congress, House, *Joint Report of E. P. Moulton and James M. McLaughlin . . . on the Conditions Found by Them on the Uinta Indian Reservation, Relating to Irrigation and Other Subjects Affecting These Indians*, 62nd Cong., 2d Sess., Doc. 892, 1914; Kathryn L. MacKay, "The Strawberry Valley Irrigation Project and the Opening of the Uintah Indian Reservation," *Utah Historical Quarterly*, 50, no. 1 (1982): 68–89.

14. Chipeta's letter is found in S. Lyman Tyler, "The Ute People: An Example of Anglo-American Contact with the Indian," *Denver Westerners' Roundup*, 11 (August 1955): 5–9.

15. Bender, *Uintah Railway*, 103.

16. Conetah, *History of the Northern Ute People*, 132–133.
17. Jean Allard Jeançon and F. H. Douglas, *The Ute Indians*, leaflet no. 10 (Denver: Denver Art Museum, 1930), 3; Smith, *Ethnography*, 99.
18. Mrs. W. G. King, "Our Ute Indians," *Colorado Magazine*, 37, no. 2 (1960): 128–130.
19. Albert B. Reagan and Wallace Stark, "Chipeta, Queen of the Utes, and Her Equally Illustrious Husband, Noted Chief Ouray," *Utah Historical Quarterly*, 1 (July 1933): 103–110, citing a letter dated August 21, 1923.
20. *Denver Times*, January 13, 1902, 5.
21. Jefferson, Delaney, and Thompson, *Southern Utes*, 47.
22. Swadesh, Los Prímeros Pobladores, 119.
23. *Rocky Mountain News*, May 5, 1899, 1; Thompson, *Southern Ute Lands, 1848–1899*, 55–56.
24. Clipping, Helen Sloan Daniels Collection, Fort Lewis College, John F. Reed Library, Center of Southwest Studies.
25. Swadesh, Los Prímeros Pobladores, 114.
26. L. G. Moses, *Wild West Shows and the Images of American Indians, 1883–1933* (Albuquerque: University of New Mexico Press, 1996), 206–207.
27. Leslie Karp, "Whose Water Is It, Anyway? Bureaucrats, the Animas–La Plata Project, and the Colorado Utes," *Journal of the Western Slope*, 9, no. 3 (1994): 6; Delaney, *Ute Mountain Utes*, 80.
28. Katherine M. B. Osburn, *Southern Ute Women: Autonomy and Assimilation on the Reservation, 1887–1934* (Albuquerque: University of New Mexico Press, 1998), 149.
29. S. F. Stacher, "Indians of the Ute Mountain Reservation, 1906–9," *Colorado Magazine*, 26 (January 1949): 55, 57.
30. Consolidated Ute Indian Service, Box 3, Folder 175.
31. Helen Sloan Daniels, comp., "The Ute Indians of Southwestern Colorado" (unpublished MS, 1941), Durango, Colorado, Public Library.
32. Delaney, *Ute Mountain Utes*, 2, 85.
33. Martineau, *Southern Paiutes*, 164–165.
34. Similar interrelationships between Navajos and Southern Paiutes existed in northern Arizona. McPherson, *Northern Navajo Frontier*, 54.
35. F. H. Douglas, comp., *Types of Southwestern Coiled Basketry*, leaflet no. 88 (Denver: Denver Art Museum, 1971), 151; Omer C. Stewart, "The Navajo Wedding Basket—1938," *Museum Notes* (Museum of Northern Arizona), 10, no. 9 (1938): 25–28; Harry Tschopik, "Taboo as a Possible Factor Involved in the Obsolescence of Navaho Pottery and Basketry," *American Anthropologist*, 40 (1938): 62.
36. Pearl Baker, *The Outlaw of San Juan: Posey and the Mormons, 1880–1923* (Green River, Utah: 1985), 46–47.
37. McPherson, "Canyons, Cows, and Conflict," 246–247.
38. Henry McCabe, *Cowboys, Indians, and Homesteaders* (Salt Lake City: Deseret Press, 1975), 181–182.
39. Baker, *Outlaw of San Juan*, 58–71; Delaney, *Ute Mountain Utes*, 84; Forbes Parkhill, *The Last of the Indian Wars* (New York: Collier, 1961).
40. Baker, *Outlaw of San Juan*, 73.

41. Richard K. Young, *The Ute Indians of Colorado in the Twentieth Century* (Norman: University of Oklahoma Press, 1997), 54–55.

CHAPTER 11

1. Omer C. Stewart, *Peyote Religion: A History* (Norman: University of Oklahoma Press, 1987), 195, 196.
2. King, "Our Ute Indians," 131.
3. Stewart, *Peyote*, 197.
4. Consolidated Ute Indian Service, Box 2, Folder 153.
5. Stewart, *Peyote*, 196, 294.
6. Consolidated Ute Indian Service, Box 2, Folder 153.
7. Joseph G. Jorgensen, *The Sun Dance Religion: Power for the Powerless* (Chicago: University of Chicago Press, 1972), 24–25.
8. *The Ute System of Government* (Salt Lake City: Uintah-Ouray Ute Tribe, 1977), 13–14; Karl E. Young, "Sun Dance at Whiterocks, 1919," *Utah Historical Quarterly*, 40, no. 3 (1972): 234–235.
9. Ronald L. Holt, *Beneath These Red Cliffs: An Ethnohistory of the Utah Paiutes* (Albuquerque: University of New Mexico Press, 1992), 16.
10. J. Donald Hughes, *American Indians in Colorado*, 2d ed. (Boulder: Pruett Publishing, 1987), 88, 100–101.
11. Delaney, *Ute Mountain Utes*, 100.
12. Ibid.
13. Anna Marie Ketchum Nat, Interview, 1968, Doris Duke Oral History Collection no. 485, Western History Center, Merriott Library, University of Utah.
14. Ila Bowman Powell, "Life," *White River Crier* (Rangely, Colorado, Museum), no. 30 (April 1995): 4, 9.
15. Opler, "Southern Ute in Colorado," 186–187.
16. Indian Census Rolls, 1885–1940, M595, Consolidate Ute Agency, 1923–24, Roll 77, and 1926–31, 1932–39, Roll 78; Southern Ute Agency, 1893–95, 1897–1908, Roll 544 (includes Navajo Springs Subagency); Uintah and Ouray Agency, 1885–89, 1891, 1892, 1894, 1895, Roll 608; Uintah and Ouray Agency, 1903–11, Roll 610; Uintah and Ouray Agency, 1921–29, Roll 612; Paiute and Ute Indians, 1940, 1942–44, Roll 615.
17. Consolidated Ute Indian Service, Box 2, Folder 121.
18. Osburn, *Southern Ute Women*, 54.
19. McPherson, "Canyons, Cows, and Conflict," 251–253.
20. Robert S. McPherson, *A History of San Juan County: In the Palm of Time* (Salt Lake City: Utah State Historical Society and the San Juan County Commission, 1995), 158–159, 161–163; Baker, *Outlaw of San Juan*, 76–79; Albert R. Lyman, "A Relic of Gadianton: Old Posey as I Knew Him," *Improvement Era*, 26, no. 9 (1923): 798–800.
21. Reagan and Stark, "Chipeta," 107, 109–110.
22. King, "Our Ute Indians," 131.
23. Conetah, *History of the Northern Ute People*, 150–153.
24. Larry Cesspuch, personal communication, March 14, 1998; Parker M. Nielson, *The Dispossessed: Cultural Genocide of the Mixed-Blood Utes: An*

Advocate's Chronicle (Norman: University of Oklahoma Press, 1998), for detailed discussion.

25. Young, *The Ute Indians of Colorado*.
26. U.S. Bureau of Indian Affairs, *Proposed Paiute Indian Tribe of Utah Reservation Plan*, 30.

.

Bibliography
▼ ▼ ▼

ARCHIVAL SOURCES

Baptisms and Marriages. Archives of the Archdiocese of Santa Fe.

Doris Duke Oral History Collection. In Western History Collection, Merriott Library, University of Utah.

Federal Indian Agencies. Records. In New Mexico State Records Center and Archives.

H. H. Bancoft Collection, Box 2. In University of Colorado at Boulder Libraries, Archives.

Helen Sloan Daniels Collection. In Fort Lewis College, John F. Reed Library, Center of Southwest Studies.

Leo C. Thorne Collection. In Uintah County Western Heritage Museum, Vernal, Utah.

Myra Ellen Jenkins Collection. In New Mexico State Records Center and Archives.

Omer C. Stewart Southern Colorado Records. In University of Colorado at Boulder Libraries, Archives.

Records of the New Mexico Superintendency. In New Mexico State Records Center and Archives.

U.S. Adjutant General's Office. Returns from U.S. Military Posts. Record Group 94. In National Archives and Records Service, Rocky Mountain Region.

U.S. Bureau of Indian Affairs. Consolidated Ute Indian Service Files, 1879–1952. In National Archives and Records Service, Rocky Mountain Region.

———. Letters Received, 1824–1881. Record Group 75. In National Archives and Records Service, Rocky Mountain Region.

———. Records Created by the Pueblo and Jicarilla Indian Agencies. Record Group 75. In National Archives and Records Service, Rocky Mountain Region.

———. Records of Pueblo Agencies, Cimarron and Abiquiu (Jicarilla) Agencies. Record Group 75. In National Archives and Records Service, Rocky Mountain Region.

U.S. Indian Census Rolls, 1885–1940. Record Group 75. In National Archives and Records Service, Rocky Mountain Region.

GOVERNMENT DOCUMENTS AND PUBLICATIONS

Ahlborn, Richard E. *The Penitente Moradas of Abiquiú*. Contributions from the Museum of History and Technology. Bulletin 250. Washington, D.C.: Smithsonian Institution, 1968.

Baker, Steven G. *Ephemeral Archaeology on the Mountain of the Sorrel Deer, Delta, Colorado*. Denver: Colorado State Office, Bureau of Land Management, 1991.

Civil Works Administration Project, Work Projects Administration, manuscripts, 1933–1934. In Colorado Historical Society, Stephen H. Hart Library; Uintah Regional Library History Center; Museum of Northwest Colorado.

D'Azevedo, Warren L., ed. *Great Basin*, vol. 11 in *Handbook of North American Indians*. Washington, D.C.: Smithsonian Institution, 1986.

Densmore, Frances. *Northern Ute Music*. Bureau of American Ethnology Bulletin 75. Washington, D.C.: Government Printing Office, 1922.

Fewkes, Jesse Walter. *Antiquities of the Mesa Verde National Park*. Bureau of American Ethnology Bulletin 41. Washington, D.C.: Government Printing Office, 1909.

Fike, Richard E., and H. Blaine Phillips II. *A Nineteenth Century Ute Burial From Northeast Utah*. Cultural Resources Series, no. 16. Salt Lake City: Utah State Office, Bureau of Land Management, 1984.

Frémont, John C. *Report of Exploring Expedition to the Rocky Mountains in the Year 1842 and to Oregon and Northern California in the Years 1843–44*. 28th Cong., 2d Sess., Doc. 174. Washington, D.C.: 1845.

Gunnerson, James H. *Ethnohistory of the High Plains*. Cultural Resources Series, no. 26. Denver: Colorado State Office, Bureau of Land Management, 1988.

Kappler, Charles J., comp. *Indian Affairs: Laws and Treaties*. 3 vols. Washington, D.C.: Government Printing Office, 1904–1927.

Kendrick, Gregory D., ed. *Beyond the Wasatch: The History of Irrigation in the Uinta Basin and Upper Provo River Area of Utah*. Denver: National Park Service and Bureau of Reclamation, 1986(?).

LaPoint, Halcyon. *A Class I Overview of the Prehistoric Cultural Resources, Little Snake Resource Area, Moffat, Routt, and Rio Blanco Counties, Colorado*. Cultural Resources Series, no. 20. Denver: Colorado State Office, Bureau of Land Management, 1987.

Martínez, Antonio José. *Esposición . . . Proponiendo La Civilisación De Las Naciónes Barbaros (1843)*. In New Mexico State Records Center and Archives, Benjamin Read Collection.

Mehls, Steven F. *The Valley of Opportunity*. Cultural Resources Series, no. 12. Denver: Colorado State Office, Bureau of Land Management, 1982.

Oliva, Leo E. *Fort Union and the Frontier Army in the Southwest*. Southwest Cultural Resources Center, Professional Papers, no. 41. Santa Fe: National Park Service, Division of History, 1993.

Ortiz, Alfonso, ed. *Southwest*, vols. 9 and 10 in *Handbook of North American Indians*. Washington, D.C.: Smithsonian Institution, 1979 and 1983.

Steward, Julian Haynes. *Notes on Hiller's Photographs of the Paiute and Ute Indians Taken on the Powell Expedition of 1873*. Smithsonian Miscellaneous Collections, vol. 98, no. 18. Washington, D.C.: Smithsonian Institution, 1939.

Svenningsen, Robert, comp. "Introduction" in *Preliminary Inventory of the Pueblo Records Field Created by Field Offices of the Bureau of Indian Affairs*. Record Group 75. Washington, D.C.: National Archives and Records Service, 1980.

U.S. Bureau of Indian Affairs. *Annual Report of the Commissioner of Indian Affairs (for the years 1864–1908)*. Washington, D.C.: Government Printing Office, 1864–1908.

———. *Letter from the Secretary of the Interior Transmitting . . . Correspondence Concerning the Ute Indians in Colorado*. Washington, D.C.: Government Printing Office, 1880.

———. *Proposed Paiute Indian Tribe of Utah Reservation Plan*. Washington, D.C.: Government Printing Office, 1982.

U.S. Bureau of Reclamation, Upper Colorado Regional Office, and National Park Service, Rocky Mountain Regional Office. *Beyond the Wasatch: The History of Irrigation in the Uinta Basin and Upper Provo River Area of Utah*. N.d.

U.S. Congress, House. *Conditions on Uinta Indian Reservation, Utah*. 62nd Cong., 2nd Sess., Doc. 892, 1912.

———. *Indian Disturbances in the Territory of New Mexico: Letter of the Secretary of State*. 36th Cong., 2d Sess., Exec. Doc. 24. 1861.

———. *Joint Report of E. P. Holcombe and James M. McLaughlin . . . on the Conditions Found by Them on the Uinta Indian Reservation in Utah, Relating to Irrigation and Other Subjects Affecting These Indians*. 62nd Cong. 2d Sess., Doc. 892. 1912.

———. *Letter from the Secretary of the Treasury, Transmitting a Copy of a Communication from the Secretary of the Interior, Submitting an Estimate of Appropriations for Protection, etc., of Rights of Uncompahgres, Uintah, and White River Utes in Certain Irrigation Systems*. 60th Cong., 2d Sess., Doc. 1279, 1908.

———. *Letter of the Secretary of State Transmitting the Correspondence of the Territory of New Mexico, Governor A. Rencher to General Lewis Cass*. 36th Cong., 2d Sess., Exec. Doc. 24, 1861.

———. *Memorial of the Legislative Assembly of Colorado, Calling Attention of Congress to the Grievances of the Ute Indians*. 44th Cong., 1st Sess., Misc. Doc. 86, 1875.

———. *Testimony Taken in Relation to the Ute Indian Outbreak, Taken by the Committee on Indian Affairs of the House of Representatives*. Washington, D.C.: Government Printing Office, 1880.

———. *Uncompahgre, Uintah, and White River Ute Indians in Utah*. 60th Cong., 2d Sess. Doc. 1279, 1910.

———. *Ute, Pai-ute, Go-si Ute and Shoshone Indians; Letter From the Acting Secretary of the Interior*. 43rd Cong., 1st Sess., Exec. Doc. 157, 1873.

U.S. Congress, Joint Special Committee. *Condition of the Indian Tribes; Report of the Joint Special Committee Appointed under Joint Resolution of March 3, 1865.* Washington, D.C.: Government Printing Office, 1867.

U.S. Congress, Senate. *Gilsonite Lands within the Former Uncompahgre Indian Reservation, Utah.* 63rd Cong., 3rd Sess., Calendar 891, Report 1002, 1915.

————. *Letter from the Secretary of the Interior in Response to Senate Resolution of April 6, 1897.* 55th Cong., 1st Sess., Doc. 32, 1897.

————. *Opening of the Uintah Indian Reservation in Utah: Letter from the Secretary of the Interior.* 58th Cong., 3rd Sess., Doc. 159, 1905.

U.S. Ute Commission. *Message from the President of the United States, Communicating a Report of the Commission . . . Entitled: An Act to Make Certain Negotiations with the Ute Indians in the State of Colorado.* Washington, D.C.: Government Printing Office, 1879.

U.S. White River Commission. *Letter from the Secretary of the Interior, Transmitting a Copy of Evidence Taken before the White River Ute Commission.* Washington, D.C.: Government Printing Office, 1880.

Washburn, Wilcombe E., ed. *History of Indian-White Relations,* vol. 4 in *Handbook of North American Indians.* Washington, D.C.: Smithsonian Institution, 1988.

UNPUBLISHED MANUSCRIPTS, THESES, AND DISSERTATIONS

Abbott, John Brown. "Los Pinos Letters." In Colorado Historical Society, Stephen H. Hart Library.

Arnold, Margaret M. "Ute Trade, 1750–1821: At the Core of Economic, Political, and Cultural Change." M.A. thesis, University of Wyoming, 1995.

Barnes, Sharon. "Petroglyphs of the San Luis Valley." M.A. thesis, Adams State College, 1982.

Batch-Elder, Kenneth Earl. "Revelations from the Shadows of Thunder Butte." M.A. thesis, University of Colorado, 1994.

Beals, Ralph L. "Ethnology of Rocky Mountain National Park: The Ute and Arapaho." National Park Service, 1936.

Buckles, William Gayl. "The Uncompahgre Complex: Historic Ute Archaeology and Prehistoric Archaeology on the Uncompahgre Plateau in West Central Colorado." Ph.D. diss., University of Colorado, 1971.

Clark, H. G. "Diary, 1903." In Utah State Historical Society Library.

Combs, D. Gene. "Enslavement of Indians in the San Luis Valley." M.A. thesis, Adams State College, 1970.

Covington, James Warren. "Relations between the Ute Indians and the United States Government, 1848–1900." Ph.D. diss., University of Oklahoma, 1949.

Cragin, Francis W. "Notebooks: Early Far West Interviews." In Colorado Springs Pioneers Museum, Starsmore Library.

Daniels, Helen Sloan, comp. "The Ute Indians of Southwestern Colorado." Durango, Colorado, Public Library, 1941.

De Vel, Lawrence, and Rhoda De Vel, comps. "Catalogue of Ute and Fremont Indians." In Uintah County Western Heritage Museum, Vernal, Utah.

"Existence of Slavery of Ute Indians of the San Luis Valley." In University of Colorado Libraries at Boulder, Archives.

Gibson, Charles F., Jr. "Alamosa, Conejos, and Costilla Counties." Pamphlet no. 349. In Colorado Historical Society, Stephen H. Hart Library.

Goss, James A. "Through the Eyes of the Utes: Colorado's Sacred Mountains." In Goss files, Lubbock, Texas.

"History of Pike National Forest." In Penrose Public Library, Colorado Springs.

Howbert, Irving. "The Marking of the Ute Pass Trail." In Colorado Springs Pioneers Museum, Starsmore Library.

———. "References in Spanish Archives to Expeditions in the 18th and 19th Centuries to the Territory Now Included in the State of Colorado, Secured by Irving Howbert in the Library of Congress." In The Colorado College, Tutt Library, Special Collections.

Huffman, Mrs. Walter. "Saguache County during Ute Uprising." Colorado State Society, NSDAR, 1989. In Denver Public Library, Western History and Genealogy Department.

Jorgensen, Joseph G. "The Ethnohistory and Acculturation of the Northern Ute." Ph.D diss., Indiana University, 1965.

Kaplan, Michael David. "Otto Mears: Colorado's Transportation King." Ph.D. diss., University of Colorado, 1975.

Lewis, Robert G. "C. C. McBride." In Robert G. Lewis files, Denver.

———. "Lewis Emery Walker." In Robert G. Lewis files, Denver.

Lloyd, John B. "The Uncompahgre Utes." M.A. thesis, Western State College, 1932.

Norman, Georgina. "The White Settlement of the Ute Reservation, 1880–1885." M.A. thesis, University of Colorado, 1957.

O'Neil, Floyd A. "A History of the Ute Indians of Utah until 1890." Ph.D. diss., University of Utah, 1973.

———. "The Utes of Eastern Colorado." In University of Utah, Marriott Library, American West Center.

Reynolds, Mary Stephanie. "Dance Brings about Everything: Dance Power in the Ideologies of Northern Utes of the Uintah and Ouray Reservation and Predominantly Mormon Anglos of Adjacent Uintah Basin Community." Ph.D. diss., University of California, Irvine, 1990.

Richie, Eleanor Louise. "Spanish Relations with the Yutah Indians, 1680–1822." M.A. thesis, University of Denver, 1932.

Simmons, Virginia McConnell. "Creative Interpretation of Father Antonio José Martínez." M.A. thesis, Adams State College, 1981.

Spiva, Agnes Elizabeth. "The Utes in Colorado." M.A. thesis, University of Colorado, 1929.

Tawes, Peter. "Diary of Peter Tawes, May 17–August 13, 1880." 1930. In University of Colorado at Boulder, Norlin Library, Archives.

Thomas, Chauncey. "Indians." In Colorado Historical Society, Stephen H. Hart Library.

Tyler, S. Lyman. "Before Escalante: An Early History of the Yuta Indians and the Area North of New Mexico." Ph.D. diss., University of Utah, 1951.

PUBLISHED BOOKS, PAMPHLETS, AND ARTICLES

Alexander, Thomas G., and Leonard J. Arrington. "The Utah Military Frontier, 1872–1912: Forts Cameron, Thornburgh, and Duchesne." *Utah Historical*

Quarterly, 32, no. 4 (1964): 330–354.

Annand, Richard E. "A Description and Analysis of Surface Collected Pottery from the Collbran Region, Colorado." *Southwestern Lore*, 33, no. 2 (1967): 47–59.

Antrei, Albert C. T., and Ruth D. Scow, eds. *The Other Forty-Niners: A Topical History of Sanpete County, Utah, 1849–1983*. Salt Lake City: Western Epics, 1982.

Athearn, Robert G., ed. "Major Hough's March into Southern Ute Country, 1879." *Colorado Magazine*, 25, no. 3 (1948): 97–109.

Auerbach, Herbert S. "Old Trails, Old Forts, Old Trappers and Traders: History and Romance of the Old Spanish Trail." *Utah Historical Quarterly*, 9, no. 1 (1941): 13–63.

Ayers, Mary C. "History of Fort Lewis, Colorado." *Colorado Magazine*, 8, no. 3 (1931): 81–92.

Bailey, Lynn Robison. *Indian Slave Trade in the Southwest: A Study of Slave-Taking and Traffic of Indian Captives*. Los Angeles: Westernlore Press, 1966.

Bailey, Paul. *The Claws of the Hawk: The Incredible Life of Walker the Ute*. Los Angeles: Westernlore Press, 1966.

———. *Walkara: "Hawk of the Mountains."* Los Angeles: Westernlore Press, 1954.

Bailey, William McCrae. *Fort Uncompahgre*. Silverton, Colo.: Silverton Standard and Miner, 1990.

Baker, Pearl. *The Outlaw of San Juan: Posey and the Mormones, 1880–1923*. Green River, Utah: 1985.

Baker, Steven G. "Archaeological Disenfranchisement of the Colorado Utes." *Southwestern Lore*, 61, no. 3 (1985): 1–9.

———. *Numic Archaeology on the Douglas Creek Arch, Rio Blanco County, Colorado: Ute Rancherías and the Broken Blade Wickiup Village*. Montrose, Colo.: Centuries Research, 1996.

———. *The Uncompahgre Valley Historic Ute Project: First Interim Report and Executive Summary*. Montrose, Colo.: Centuries Research, 1991.

Bangert, Buckley. "Uncompahgre Statesman: The Life of Ouray." *Journal of the Western Slope*, 1 (spring 1986): iii–76.

Bender, Henry E., Jr. *Uintah Railway: The Gilsonite Route*. Berkeley: Howell-North Books, 1971.

Bender, Norman J. "The Battle of Tierra Amarilla." *New Mexico Historical Review*, 63, no. 3 (1988): 241–256.

Berthrong, Donald J. *The Southern Cheyennes*. Norman: University of Oklahoma Press, 1963.

Bettinger, Robert C., and Martin A. Baumhoff. "The Numic Spread: Great Basin Cultures in Competition." *American Antiquity*, 47 (1982): 485–503.

Beyond the Wasatch: The History of Irrigation in the Uinta Basin and Upper Provo River Area of Utah.

Black, Robert C. *Island in the Rockies: The History of Grand County, Colorado, to 1930*. Boulder: Pruett Publishing for the Grand County Pioneer Society, 1969.

Borland, Lois. "Ho for the Reservation: Settlement of the Western Slope." *Colorado Magazine*, 29 (1952): 56–75.

———. "The Sale of the San Juan." *Colorado Magazine*, 28, no. 2 (1951): 107–127.

Bourke, John G. *On the Border with Crook*. New York: Charles Scribner's Sons, 1891.

Bowen, Dorothy Boyd. "A Brief History of Spanish Textile Production in the Southwest." In *Spanish Textile Tradition of New Mexico and Colorado*. Santa Fe: Museum of New Mexico Press, 1979.

Bowles, Samuel. *The Switzerland of America. A Summer Vacation in the Parks and Mountains of Colorado*. Boston: Lee and Shepard, 1869.

Boyd, Henrietta H. "Saguache Antelope Traps." *Southwestern Lore*, 6, no. 2 (1940): 28–34.

Brave Miss Meeker's Captivity! Her Own Account of It. Also, the Narratives of Her Mother and Mrs. Price. Philadelphia: Old Franklin Publishing, 1879.

Breternitz, David A., comp. *Archaeological Excavation in Dinosaur National Monument, Colorado-Utah, 1964–1965*. University of Colorado Studies, Series in Anthropology, no. 17. Boulder: University of Colorado, 1970.

Brewerton, George Douglas. "A Ride with Kit Carson through the Great American Desert and Rocky Mountains." *Harper's New Monthly Magazine* (August 1853): 306–334.

A Brief History of the Ute People. Salt Lake City: Uintah-Ouray Ute Tribe, 1977.

Buckles, William G. "Archaeology in Colorado: Historic Tribes." *Southwestern Lore*, 34, no. 3 (1968): 53–67.

Bunte, Pamela A., and Robert J. Franklin. *From the Sands to the Mountains: Change and Persistence in a Southern Paiute Community*. Lincoln: University of Nebraska Press, 1987.

Burgh, Robert F., and Charles R. Scoggin. *The Archaeology of Castle Park, Dinosaur National Monument*. University of Colorado Studies, Anthropological Series, no. 2. Boulder: University of Colorado, 1948.

Burroughs, John Rolfe. *Where the Old West Stayed Young*. New York: Bonanza Books, 1962.

Burton, Doris Karren. "Chinese Laundryman Comes to Fort Duchesne." *Outlaw Trail Journal*, 7 (summer 1997): 2–11.

———. *A History of Uintah County*. Salt Lake City: Utah State Historical Society, 1996.

Burton, Lloyd. *American Indian Water Rights and the Limits of Law*. Lawrence: University Press of Kansas, 1991.

Buys, Christian J. "Fort Crawford: A Symbol of Transition." *Journal of the Western Slope*, 8 (spring 1993): i–29.

Campbell, Rosemae Wells. *Crystal River Valley, Jewel or Jinx?* Denver: Sage Books, 1966.

Carter, Harvey Lewis. *"Dear Old Kit": The Historical Christopher Carson*. Norman: University of Oklahoma Press, 1968.

Cartwright, Willena D. *The Peyote Cult*. Denver: Denver Art Museum and Denver Public Schools, 1950.

Carvalho, Solomon Nunez. *Incidents of Travel and Adventure in the Far West*. New York: Derby and Jackson, 1857; Philadelphia: Jewish Publication Society of America, 1953.

Chacon, Rafael. "Campaign against Utes and Apaches in Southern Colorado, 1855." *Colorado Magazine*, 11, no. 3 (1934): 108–112.

"Charles Kelly Discovers Chief Walker's Grave." *Utah Historical Quarterly*, 39, no. 2 (1971): 197–198.

Charney, Jean Ormsbee. *A Grammar of Comanche*. Lincoln: University of Nebraska Press, 1993.

Christensen, Leavitt. *Birth of Kanosh*. Kanosh, Utah: 1995.

Christy, Howard A. "Open Hand and Mailed Fist: Mormon-Indian Relations in Utah, 1847–52." *Utah Historical Quarterly*, 46, no. 3 (1973): 216–235.

Clark, W. P. *The Indian Sign Language*. Lincoln: University of Nebraska Press, 1982 [1885].

Clarke, A. K. "The Utes Visit My Ranch on the Plains." *Colorado Magazine*, 5, no. 4 (1928): 144–146.

Coel, Margaret. *Chief Left Hand: Southern Arapaho*. Norman: University of Oklahoma Press, 1981.

Cole, Sally J. *Legacy on Stone: Rock Art of the Colorado Plateau and Four Corners Area*. Boulder: Johnson Books, 1990.

Collins, Thomas W. "Behavioral Change and Ethnic Maintenance among the Northern Ute: Political Considerations." In John W. Bennett, ed., *The New Ethnicity: Perspectives From Ethnology*. St. Paul: West Publishing, 1975.

Colville, Ruth Marie. *La Vereda: A Trail Through Time*. Alamosa, Colo.: San Luis Valley Historical Society, 1996.

Conetah, Fred A. *A History of the Northern Ute People*. Ed. Kathryn L. MacKay and Floyd A. O'Neil. Salt Lake City: University of Utah Printing Service for the Uintah-Ouray Tribe, 1982.

Conetah, Fred A. *A History of the Northern Ute People*. Ed. Kathryn L. MacKay and Floyd A. O'Neil. Salt Lake City: University of Utah Printing Service for the Uintah-Ouray Tribe, 1982.

Coues, Elliott, ed. *The Journal of Jacob Fowler*. Lincoln: University of Nebraska Press, 1970.

———. "Ute Scalp Dance in Denver." *Colorado Magazine*, 30, no. 2 (1953): 119–124.

Crampton, C. Gregory, and Steven K. Madsen. *In Search of the Spanish Trail: Santa Fe to Los Angeles, 1829–1848*. Salt Lake City: Gibbs-Smith, 1994.

Crofutt, George A. *Crofutt's Grip-Sack Guide to Colorado*, vol. 2. Denver: Cubar, 1966 [1895].

Crum, Sally. *People of the Red Earth: American Indians of Colorado*. Santa Fe: Ancient City Press, 1996.

Darley, George M. *Pioneering in the San Juan*. Chicago: Fleming H. Revell, 1899.

Daughters of Utah Pioneers of Uintah County, Utah. *Builders of Uintah*. Springville, Utah: Daughters of Utah Pioneers, 1947.

Dawson, Thomas F. "Major Thompson, Chief Ouray, and the Utes." *Colorado Magazine*, 7, no. 3 (May 1930): 113–122.

Dawson, Thomas F., and F. J. V. Skiff. *The Ute War*. Denver: Tribune Publishing, 1879.

Delaney, Robert W. "The Southern Utes a Century Ago." *Utah Historical Quarterly*, 39, no. 2 (1971): 114–128.

————. *The Ute Mountain Utes.* Albuquerque: University of New Mexico Press, 1989.

Denver, Norma. "Fort Duchesne." *Ute Bulletin,* March 25, 1998, 7.

————. "Randlett Boarding School." *Ute Bulletin,* April 29, 1998, 5.

————. "Whiterocks." *Ute Bulletin,* April 15, 1998, 6.

De Smet, P. J. *Letters and Sketches: With a Narrative of a Year's Residence among the Indian Tribes of the Rocky Mountains.* Philadelphia: M. Eathian, 1843.

Dixon, Madoline Cloward. *These Were the Utes: Their Lifestyles, Wars, and Legends.* Provo: Press Publishing, 1983.

Douglas, F. H. *Many Types of Indian Cradles.* Leaflet no. 115. Denver: Denver Art Museum, 1952.

————, comp. *Types of Southwestern Coiled Basketry.* Leaflet no. 88. Denver: Denver Art Museum, 1971.

————. *War Bonnets.* Leaflet no. 110. Denver: Denver Art Museum, 1951.

Downing, Finis E. "With the Ute Peace Delegation of 1863, across the Plains and at Conejos." *Colorado Magazine,* 22, no. 5 (September 1945): 193–205.

Duke, Philip, and Barbara Blackshear. "Public Archaeology in the San Juan National Forest: The 1990 Grenadier Archaeological Project." *Southwestern Lore,* 63, no. 3 (1992): 15–34.

Dunmire, William W., and Gail D. Tierney. *Wild Plants and Native Peoples of the Four Corners.* Santa Fe: Museum of New Mexico Press, 1997.

Dutton, Bertha Paulin. *The Ranchería, Ute, and Southern Ute Peoples.* Englewood Cliffs, N.J.: Prentice-Hall, 1975.

Emmitt, Robert. *The Last War Trail: The Utes and the Settlement of Colorado.* Norman: University of Oklahoma Press, 1954.

Everett, George C., and Wendell F. Hutchinson. *Under the Angel of Shavano.* Denver: Golden Bell Press, 1963.

Favour, Alpheus H. *Old Bill Williams, Mountain Man.* Norman: University of Oklahoma Press, 1962 [1936].

Fay, George E., comp. *Land Cessions in Utah and Colorado by the Ute Indians, 1861–1899.* Museum of Anthropology, Miscellaneous Series, no. 13. Greeley: University of Northern Colorado, Museum of Anthropology, 1970.

Fiack, Henry. "Fort Duchesne's Beginnings." *Utah Historical Quarterly,* 2, no. 1 (1929): 31–32.

Fitzpatrick, V. S. *Red Twilight: A History of the Northern Utes.* Ed. Laura Watts and Harold Babcock. Colorado Springs: Earth Design Systems, n.d.

Forbes, Jack D. *Apache, Navajo, and Spaniard.* Norman: University of Oklahoma Press, 1960.

Fowler, Don D., and Catherine S. Fowler. "Notes on the History of the Southern Paiutes and Western Shoshones." *Utah Historical Quarterly,* 39, no. 2 (1971): 95–113.

Freeman, Dan A. *Four Years with the Utes: The Letters of Dan A. Freeman.* Ed. W. M. Morrison. Waco, Texas: W. M. Morrison, 1962.

Fuller, Craig. "The Rush for Land: Opening of the Uintah Indian Reservation." *Outlaw Trail Journal,* 2, no. 2 (1992): 2–9.

Gardner, A. Dudley. *The Ute Indians in Northwestern Colorado after the Meeker Massacre*. Western Wyoming College, Contributions to History, no. 1 (1979).

Gibbs, Josiah F. "Black Hawk's Last Raid." *Utah Historical Quarterly*, 4 (October 1931): 99–108.

Gordon-McCutchan, R. C., ed. *Kit Carson: Indian Fighter or Indian Killer?* Niwot: University Press of Colorado, 1996.

Goss, James A. "Ute Linguistics and Anasazi Abandonment of the Four Corners Area." *American Antiquity*, 26, no. 3 (1961): 73–81.

Greager, Howard E. *We Shall Fall as the Leaves*. N.p.: 1996.

Greiser, Sally T., and T. Weber Greiser. "Archaeological Reconnaissance in the Marshall Pass Area." *Southwestern Lore*, 43, no. 4 (1977): 22–31.

Gresham, Hazel. *North Park*. Walden, Colo.: 1975.

Hafen, Ann Woodbury. "Efforts to Recover the Stolen Son of Chief Ouray." *Colorado Magazine*, 16, no. 2 (1939): 53–62.

Hafen, LeRoy R., ed. "Colonel Loring's Expedition across Colorado in 1858." *Colorado Magazine*, 23, no. 2 (1946): 49–75.

———. "The Fort Pueblo Massacre and the Punitive Expedition against the Utes." *Colorado Magazine*, 4 (January 1927): 49–58.

———, ed. *The Mountain Men and the Fur Trade in the Far West*. Glendale, Calif.: Arthur H. Clark, 1965–1972.

———. *Ruxton of the Rockies*. Norman: University of Oklahoma Press, 1950.

Hafen, LeRoy R., and Ann W. Hafen. *Old Spanish Trail: Santa Fe to Los Angeles*. Lincoln: University of Nebraska Press, 1993 [1954].

———, eds. *The Diaries of William Henry Jackson, Frontier Photographer: To California and Return*, vol. 10 in The Far West and the Rockies Historical Series. Glendale, Calif.: A. H. Clark, 1959.

Hagan, William T. *Indian Police and Judges: Experiments in Acculturation and Control*. Lincoln: University of Nebraska Press, 1966.

Hall, Frank. *History of the State of Colorado*. Vols. 1, 2, and 4. Chicago: Blakely Printing, 1889 and 1890.

Hammond, George P. *The Adventures of Alexander Barclay, Mountain Man*. Denver: Old West Publishing, 1976.

Harrington, H. D. *Edible Plants of the Rocky Mountains*. Albuquerque: University of New Mexico Press, 1967.

Hart, Gerald T., LeRoy R. Hafen, and Anne M. Smith. *Ute Indians*, vol. 2 in *American Indian Ethnohistory: California and Basin-Plateau Indians*. New York: Garland Publishing, 1974.

Harvey, James Rose. "*El Cerrito de Los Kiowas*." *Colorado Magazine*, 19 (1942): 213–215.

Hawley, Florence. "Culture Process and Change in Ute Adaptation." *El Palacio*, 57, no. 3 (October 1950): 311–331; 57, no. 11 (November 1950): 345–361.

Heap, Gwinn Harris. *Central Route to the Pacific, from the Valley of the Mississippi to California: Journal of the Expedition*. Philadelphia: Lippincott, Grambo, 1854.

Hill, David V., and Allen E. Kane. "Characterizations of Ute Occupations and Ceramics from Southwestern Colorado." *Archaeology of the Eastern Ute: A*

Symposium. Colorado Council of Professional Archaeologists Occasional Papers, no. 1. Ed. Paul R. Nickens. 1988.

Hill, Joseph J. "Antoine Robidoux, Kingpin in the Colorado River Fur Trade, 1824–44." *Colorado Magazine*, 7, no. 4 (1930): 125–132.

———. "Spanish and Mexican Exploration and Trade Northwest from New Mexico into the Great Basin." *Utah Historical Quarterly*, 3, no. 1 (1930): 16.

Hittman, Michael. *Wovoka and the Ghost Dance*. Ed. Don Lynch. Lincoln: University of Nebraska Press, 1997 [1990].

Holt, Ronald L. *Beneath These Red Cliffs: An Ethnohistory of the Utah Paiutes*. Albuquerque: University of New Mexico Press, 1992.

Howbert, Irving. *The Indians of the Pike's Peak Region*. New York: Knickerbocker Press, 1914.

Hughes, J. Donald. *American Indians in Colorado*, 2d ed. Boulder: Pruett Publishing, 1987 [1977].

Huscher, Harold A. "Influence of the Drainage Pattern of the Uncompahgre Plateau on the Movements of Primitive Peoples." *Southwestern Lore*, 5, no. 2 (1939): 22–41.

Indian Claims Commission. "Commission Findings." In Gerald T. Hart, LeRoy R. Hafen, and Anne M. Smith. *Ute Indians*, vol. 2 in *American Indian Ethnohistory: California and Basin-Plateau Indians*. New York: Garland Publishing, 1974.

Ingersoll, Ernest. *The Crest of the Continent*. Chicago: R. R. Donnelly and Sons, 1885.

Jackson, W. H. "A Visit to the Los Pinos Indian Agency in 1874." *Colorado Magazine*, 15 (November 1938): 201–209.

Jackson, William Henry, and William H. Holmes. *Mesa Verde and the Four Corners: Hayden Survey, 1874–1876*. Ouray, Colo.: Bear Creek Publishing, 1981.

James, Harry C. *Pages from Hopi History*. Tucson: University of Arizona Press, 1979 [1974].

Janetski, Joel C. *The Ute of Utah Lake*. University of Utah Anthropological Papers, no. 116. Salt Lake City: University of Utah Press, 1991.

Jeançon, Jean Allard. *Archaeological Research in the Northeastern San Juan Basin of Colorado*. Ed. Frank H. H. Roberts. Denver: State Historical and Natural History Society of Colorado and the University of Denver, 1922.

———. "Pictographs of Colorado." *Colorado Magazine*, 3 (1926): 33–45.

Jeançon, Jean Allard, and F. H. Douglas. *Southwestern Indian Dwellings*. Leaflet no. 9. Denver: Denver Art Museum, 1930.

———. *The Ute Indians*. Leaflet no. 10. Denver: Denver Art Museum, 1930.

Jefferson, James, Robert W. Delaney, and Gregory C. Thompson. *The Southern Utes: A Tribal History*. Ed. Floyd A. O'Neil. Ignacio, Colo.: Southern Ute Tribe, 1972.

Jennings, Jesse D. *Prehistory of Utah and the Eastern Great Basin*. University of Utah Anthropological Papers, no. 98. Salt Lake City: University of Utah Press, 1978.

Jocknick, Sidney. *Early Days on the Western Slope of Colorado*. Glorieta, N.M.: Rio Grande Press, 1968 [1913].

Johnson, Jerome W. "Murder on the Uncompahgre." *Colorado Magazine*, 43, no. 3 (1966): 209–224.

Jones, Daniel W. *Forty Years among the Indians*. Salt Lake City: Juvenile Instruction Office, 1890.

Jorgensen, Joseph G. "Sovereignty and the Structure of Dependency at Northern Ute." *American Indian Culture and Research Journal*, 10, no. 1 (1986): 75–94.

———. *The Sun Dance Religion: Power for the Powerless*. Chicago: University of Chicago Press, 1972.

Kaelin, Celinda Reynolds, and Leo Kimmett. *Pikes Peak Backcountry*. Florissant, Colo.: 1995.

Karp, Leslie. "Whose Water Is It, Anyway? Bureaucrats, the Animas–La Plata Project, and the Colorado Utes." *Journal of the Western Slope*, 9, no. 3 (1994): 1–22.

Kayser, Joyce. "Phantoms in the Pinyon: An Investigation of Ute-Pueblo Contacts." *American Antiquity*, 26, no. 3 (1961): 82–91.

Keleher, William A. *Maxwell Land Grant: A New Mexico Item*. Santa Fe: William Gannon, 1975.

Keller, Robert H., Jr. *American Protestantism and United States Indian Policy, 1869–82*. Lincoln: University of Nebraska Press, 1983.

Kelly, Isabel T. "Southern Paiute Bands." *American Anthropologist*, 36 (1934): 548–560.

———. *Southern Paiute Ethnography*. University of Utah Anthropological Papers, no. 69; Glen Canyon Series, no. 21. Salt Lake City: University of Utah Press, 1964.

Kelsey, Harry E., Jr. *Frontier Capitalist: The Life of John Evans*. Denver and Boulder: Colorado State Historical Society and Pruett Publishing, 1969.

King, Mrs. W. G. "Our Ute Indians." *Colorado Magazine*, 37, no. 2 (1960): 128–132.

Kushner, Ervan F. *Otto Mears: His Life and Times*. Frederick, Colo.: Jende-Hagan Bookcorp, 1979.

Larsen, Wes. *A Field Folio of Indian and Pioneer Medicinal Plants as Found in the Deserts and Plateaus*. Toquerville, Utah: Third Mesa Publishing, 1992.

Larson, Gustive O. "Walkara's Half Century." *Western Humanities Review*, 6, no. 3 (1952): 235–259.

Laudenschlager, David D. "The Utes in South Dakota, 1906–1908." *South Dakota History*, 9, no. 3 (1979): 233–247.

Lawrence, John. *Frontier Eyewitness: Diary of John Lawrence, 1867–1908*, Ed. Bernice Martin. Saguache, Colo.: Saguache County Museum, 1990(?).

Leckenby, Charles H., comp. *The Tread of the Pioneers*. Steamboat Springs, Colo.: Pilot Press, 1944.

Leckie, William H. *The Buffalo Soldiers: A Narrative of the Negro Cavalry in the West*. Norman: University of Oklahoma Press, 1968.

Lecompte, Janet. *Pueblo, Hardscrabble, Greenhorn: The Upper Arkansas, 1832–1856*. Norman: University of Oklahoma Press, 1978.

Londoner, Wolfe. "Colorow, Renegade Chief Dines Out." *Colorado Magazine*, 8, no. 3 (1931): 93–94.

Look, Al. *Utes' Last Stand at White River and Milk Creek, Western Colorado, in 1879*. Denver: Golden Bell Press, 1972.

Lotrich, Victor F. "Indian Terms for the Cradle and the Cradleboard." *Colorado Magazine*, 18 (May 1941): 81–109.

Lyman, Albert R. "A Relic of Gadianton: Old Posey as I Knew Him." *Improvement Era*, 26, no. 9 (1923): 791–801.

Lyman, June, and Norma Denver, comps. *Ute People: An Historical Study*. Ed. Floyd A. O'Neil and John D. Sylvester. Salt Lake City: University of Utah Press, 1970.

Lyons, Ray D. "Floral Resources in the Vicinity of Old Agency Fortified Site." *Southwestern Lore*, 59, no. 2 (1993): 19–22.

Lyons, Ray D., and Ann M. Johnson. "The Old Agency Fortified Site." *Southwestern Lore*, 59, no. 2 (1993): 3–17.

MacKay, Kathryn L. "The Strawberry Valley Irrigation Project and the Opening of the Uintah Indian Reservation." *Utah Historical Quarterly*, 50, no. 1 (1982): 68–89.

MacKendrick, Donald A. "Cesspools, Alkali and White Lily Soap: The Grand Junction Indian School, 1886–1911." *Journal of the Western Slope*, 8, no. 3 (1993): 1–4.

Madsen, David, and David Rhodes, eds. *Across the West: Human Population Movement and the Expansion of the Numa*. Salt Lake City: University of Utah Press, 1994.

Manly, William L. *Death Valley in '49*. Los Angeles: Borden Publishing, 1949.

Manzanares, J. M. "Colorado Recollections of a Centenarian." Interview by LeRoy R. Hafen. *Colorado Magazine*, 10, no. 3 (1933): 114–115.

Marsh, Charles S. *People of the Shining Mountains*. Boulder: Pruett Publishing, 1982.

Martineau, LaVan. *The Southern Paiutes: Legends, Lore, Language, and Lineage*. Las Vegas: KC Publications, 1992(?).

Martorano, Marilyn A. "Culturally Peeled Trees and Ute Indians in Colorado." In *Archaeology of the Eastern Ute: A Symposium*. Colorado Council of Professional Archaeologists, Occasional Papers, no. 1. Ed. Paul R. Nickens. 1988.

McCabe, Henry. *Cowboys, Indians, and Homesteaders*. Salt Lake City: Deseret Press, 1975.

McConnell, Virginia. "Captain Baker and the San Juan Humbug." *Colorado Magazine*, 48, no. 1 (1971): 59–75.

———. " 'H. H.,' Colorado, and the Indian Problem." *Journal of the West*, 12, no. 2 (1973): 272–280.

McPherson, Robert S. "Canyons, Cows, and Conflict: A Native American History of Montezuma Canyon, 1874–1933." *Utah Historical Quarterly*, 60, no. 3 (1992): 238–258.

———. *A History of San Juan County: In the Palm of Time*. Salt Lake City: Utah State Historical Society and the San Juan County Commission, 1995.

———. *The Northern Navajo Frontier, 1860–1900: Expansion through Adversity*. Albuquerque: University of New Mexico Press, 1988.

———. "The Ute Invasion of San Juan County, 1894: A Study in Differing Perceptions." *Blue Mountain Shadows*, 17 (summer 1996): 46–50.

Meeker, Nathan C. "The Utes of Colorado." *American Antiquarian*, 1, no. 4 (1879): 224–226.

"Middle Park Indians to 1881." *Grand County Historical Association Journal*, 7, no. 1 (1987): 2–89.

Miller, Wick R. "Indian Languages of the Great Basin." *Southwestern Lore*, 31, no. 4 (1966): 81–83.

———. "Numic Languages." In Warren L. D'Azevedo, ed., *Great Basin*, vol. 11, *Handbook of North American Indians* (Washington, D.C.: Smithsonian Institution, 1986).

Minge, Ward Alan. "*Efectos del Pais*." In *Spanish Textile Tradition of New Mexico and Colorado*. Santa Fe: Museum of New Mexico Press, 1979.

———. "Mexican Independence Day and a Ute Tragedy in Santa Fe, 1844." In *The Changing Ways of Southwestern Indians*. Ed. Albert H. Schroeder. Glorieta, N.M.: Rio Grande Press, 1973.

Moody, Marshall D. "The Meeker Massacre." *Colorado Magazine*, 30, no. 2 (1953): 91–104.

Mooney, James. *The Ghost Dance Religion and the Sioux Outbreak of 1890*. Intro. by Anthony F. C. Wallace. Chicago: University of Chicago Press, 1965 [1896].

Moore, Michael. *Medicinal Plants of the Mountain West*. Albuquerque: University of New Mexico Press, 1979.

Morgan, Dale L. *Jedediah Smith and the Opening of the West*. Lincoln: University of Nebraska Press, 1964.

———, ed. "The West of William Ashley." *Bulletin, Missouri Historical Society*, 12, no. 1 (1955): 158–186.

Moses, L. G. *Wild West Shows and the Images of American Indians, 1883–1933*. Albuquerque: University of New Mexico Press, 1996.

Motter, John M. *Pagosa Country*. Marceline, Mo.: Walsworth, n.d.

Moulton, Arthur C. "A Trader with the Utes, and the Murder of Chief Shavano," as told to James R. Harvey. *Colorado Magazine*, 20 (May 1943): 99–108.

Murphy, Larry. *Out in God's Country: A History of Colfax County, New Mexico*. Springer, N.M.: Springer Publishing, 1969.

Murphy, Lawrence R., ed. *Indian Agent in New Mexico: The Journal of Special Agent W. F. M. Arny*. Santa Fe: Stagecoach Press, 1967.

Nickens, Paul R. "Archaeological Evidence for Eastern Ute Mortuary Practice." In *Archaeology of the Eastern Ute: A Symposium*. Colorado Council of Professional Archaeologists, Occasional Papers, no. 1. Ed. Paul R. Nickens. 1988.

Nielson, Parker M. *The Dispossessed: Cultural Genocide of the Mixed-Blood Utes: An Advocate's Chronicle*. Norman: University of Oklahoma Press, 1998.

Nykamp, Robert H. "Distribution of Known Ute Sites in Colorado." In *Archaeology of the Eastern Ute: A Symposium*. Colorado Council of Professional Archaeologists, Occasional Papers, no. 1. Ed. Paul R. Nickens. 1988.

Oberndorf, Michael R. "Two Hunting Blinds in Boulder County, Colorado." *Southwestern Lore*, 63, no. 2 (1997): 27–39.

O'Neil, Floyd A. "An Anguished Odyssey: The Flight of the Utes, 1906–1908." *Utah Historical Quarterly*, 36, no. 4 (1968): 315–327.

———. "The Reluctant Suzerainty: The Uintah and Ouray Reservation." *Utah Historical Quarterly*, 34, no. 2 (1971): 129–144.

Opler, Marvin K. "The Character and History of the Southern Ute Peyote Rite." *American Anthropologist*, 42 (1940): 463–478.

———. "A Colorado Ute Indian Dance." *Southwestern Lore*, 7, no. 2 (1941): 21–30.

———. "The Origins of Comanche and Ute." *American Anthropologist*, 45, no. 1 (1943): 155–158.

———. "The Southern Ute Dog Dance and Its Reported Transmission to Taos." *New Mexico Anthropologist*, 3, no. 5 (1939): 66–72.

———. "The Southern Ute of Colorado." In *Acculturation in Seven American Indian Tribes*. Ed. Ralph Linton. New York: D. Appleton-Century, 1940.

———. "The Ute and Paiute Indians." In *North American Indians in Historical Perspective*. Eds. Eleanor Burke Leacock and Nancy O. Lurie. New York: Random House, 1971.

———. "The Ute Indian War of 1879." *El Palacio*, 46 (1939): 255–262.

Osburn, Katherine M. B. *Southern Ute Women: Autonomy and Assimilation on the Reservation, 1887–1934*. Albuquerque: University of New Mexico Press, 1998.

Palmer, Edward. *Notes on the Utah Utes by Edward Palmer, 1866–1877*. University of Utah Anthropological Papers, nos. 17–19. Salt Lake City: University of Utah Press, 1954.

Park, Willard Z. "Tribal Distribution in the Great Basin." *American Anthropologist*, 40, no. 4 (1938): 622–638.

Parkhill, Forbes. *The Blazed Trail of Antoine Leroux*. Los Angeles: Westernlore Press, 1965.

———. *The Last of the Indian Wars*. New York: Collier, 1961.

Payne, J. S. "Incidents of the Recent Campaign against the Utes." *United Service*, 2, no. 1 (1880): 114–129.

Peterson, John A. *Utah's Black Hawk War*. Salt Lake City: University of Utah Press, 1998.

Peterson, Kenneth Lee. "Tabeguache and Elk Mountain Utes: A Historical Test of an Ecological Model." *Southwestern Lore*, 43, no. 4 (1977): 5–21.

Pettit, Jan. *Utes: The Mountain People*, rev. ed. Boulder: Johnson Books, 1990.

Pohanka, Brian C., ed. *Nelson A. Miles: A Documentary Biography of His Military Career, 1861–1903*. Glendale, Calif.: Arthur H. Clark, 1985.

Powell, Ila Bowman. "Life." *White River Crier*, no. 30 (April 1995): 1–10.

Powell, J. W. *The Exploration of the Colorado River and Its Canyons*. New York: Dover Publications, 1961 [1895].

Preuss, Charles. *Exploring with Frémont*. Norman: University of Oklahoma Press, 1958.

Quaife, Milo Milton, ed. *The Southwestern Expedition of Zebulon M. Pike*. Chicago: R. R. Donnelly and Sons, 1924.

Rankin, M. Wilson. *Reminiscences of Frontier Days*. Denver: Smith-Brooks, 1935.

Reagan, Albert B. "Collections of Ancient Artifacts from the Ashley–Dry Fork District of the Uintah Basin with Some Notes on the Dwellings and Mortuary Customs of the Ouray Indians of the Ouray (Utah) Region." *El Palacio*, 31, no. 26 (1931): 407–412.

Reagan, Albert B., and Wallace Stark. "Chipeta, Queen of the Utes, and Her Equally Illustrious Husband, Noted Chief Ouray." *Utah Historical Quarterly*, 1 (July 1933): 103–110.

"Record of the Fort Duchesne Indian Police" (reprint). *Outlaw Trail Journal* (summer 1996): 2–4.

Reed, Alan D. *West-Central Colorado Prehistoric Context*. Denver: State Historical Society of Colorado, 1984.

Reed, Verner Z. "The Southern Ute Indians." *Californian*, 4 (September 1893): 488–505.

"Removal of the Southern Utes." Pamphlet, 1892. In the Colorado College Tutt Library, Special Collections.

"Removal of Southern Utes from Colorado to Utah: Protest of Utah by Her Legislature, Governor, Delegates, and Citizens." Pamphlet, n.d. In the Colorado College Tutt Library, Special Collections.

Richie, Eleanor. "General Mano Mocha of the Utes and Spanish Policy in Indian Relations." *Colorado Magazine*, 9 (July 1932): 150–157.

Rockwell, Wilson. *Sunset Slope: True Epics of Western Colorado*. Denver: Big Mountain Press, 1956.

———. *Uncompahgre Country*. Denver: Sage Books, 1965.

———. *The Utes: A Forgotten People*. Denver: Sage Books, 1956.

Ronzio, Richard A. "Fort Crawford on the Uncompahgre." *Denver Westerners' Monthly Roundup*, 19, no. 3 (1963): 3–9.

Rose, Ernie. *Utahs of the Rocky Mountains*. Montrose, Colo.: Montrose Daily Press, 1968.

Ruxton, George F. *Adventures in Mexico and the Rocky Mountains*. London: John Murray, 1847.

Sage, Rufus. *Scenes in the Rocky Mountains*. Philadelphia: 1846.

Sánchez, Joseph P. *Explorers, Traders, and Slavers: Forging the Old Spanish Trail, 1678–1850*. Salt Lake City: University of Utah Press, 1997.

Schroeder, Albert H. "A Brief History of the Southern Utes." *Southwestern Lore*, 30, no. 4 (1965): 53–78.

Scott, Douglas D. "Robidoux's Fort on the Uncompahgre and the Matlock Homestead." *Southwestern Lore*, 48, no. 4 (1932): 25–31.

Secoy, Frank Raymond. *Changing Military Patterns of the Great Plains Indians*. Lincoln: University of Nebraska Press, 1992 [1953].

Selman, Mormon V. *Dictionary of the Ute Language*. Provo: M. H. Graham Printing, 1900.

Shoemaker, Len. *Roaring Fork Valley*. Denver: Sage Books, 1958.

Simmons, Virginia McConnell. *Bayou Salado: The Story of South Park*. Boulder: Fred Pruett Books, 1992 [1966].

———. *The San Luis Valley: Land of the Six-Armed Cross*, 2d ed. Niwot: University Press of Colorado, 1999 [1979].

———. *The Upper Arkansas: A Mountain River Valley*. Boulder: Pruett Publishing, 1990.

Smith, Anne M. *Ethnography of the Northern Utes*. Papers in Anthropology, no. 17. Santa Fe: Museum of New Mexico Press, 1974.

———. *Ute Tales*. Salt Lake City: University of Utah Press, 1992.

Smith, P. David. *Ouray, Chief of the Utes*. Ouray, Colo.: Wayfinder Press, 1986.

Snow, William J. "Utah Indians and Spanish Slave Trade." *Utah Historical Quarterly*, 2, no. 3 (1929): 67–73.

Sonne, Conway B. *World of Wakara*. San Antonio: Naylor, 1962.

Sprague, Marshall. *Massacre: The Tragedy at White River*. Lincoln: University of Nebraska Press, 1980 [1957].

Stacher, S. F. "Indians of the Ute Mountain Reservation, 1906–9." *Colorado Magazine*, 26 (January 1949): 52–61.

———. "Ouray and the Utes." *Colorado Magazine*, 27 (April 1950): 134–140.

Stanley, F. (Stanley Francis Crocchiola). *The Abiquiu Story*. N.p.: 1960(?).

———. *Fort Bascom, Comanche-Kiowa Barrier*. Pampa, Texas: Pampa Print Shop, 1961.

———. *The Grant That Maxwell Bought*. Denver: 1952.

———. *The Jicarilla Apaches of New Mexico, 1540–1967*. Pampa, Texas: Pampa Print Shop, 1967.

———. *One Half Mile From Heaven, or the Cimarron Story*. Denver: World Press, 1949.

Steward, Julian Haynes. "Linguistic Distributions and Political Groups of the Great Basin Shoshoneans." *American Anthropologist*, 39, no. 4 (1937): 625–634.

———. *Ute Indians*, vol. 1 in *Aboriginal and Historical Groups of the Ute Indians of Utah*. New York: Garland Publishing, 1974.

Stewart, George Emery, Jr. *Tales From Indian Country*. Orem, Utah: Sun Rise Publishing, 1997.

Stewart, Omer C. "Escalante and the Ute." *Southwestern Lore*, 18, no. 3 (1952): 47–51.

———. *Ethnohistorical Bibliography of the Ute Indians of Colorado*. University of Colorado Studies, Series in Anthropology, no. 18. Boulder: University of Colorado Press, 1971.

———. "The Navajo Wedding Basket—1938." *Museum Notes* (Museum of Northern Arizona), 10, no. 9 (1938): 25–28.

———. *Peyote Religion: A History*. Norman: University of Oklahoma Press, 1987.

———. "Ute Indians: Before and after White Contact." *Utah Historical Quarterly*, 34, no. 1 (1966): 38–61.

———. *Ute Peyotism*. University of Colorado Studies, Series on Anthropology, no. 1. Boulder: University of Colorado Press, 1948.

Stobie, Charles S. "With the Indians in Colorado." *Colorado Magazine*, 7 (March 1930): 75–76.

Stollsteimer, Robert Samuel, and Dorothy Causey. *Christian and Amanda: The Life and Times of a Pioneer Family*. Montrose, Colo.: FERS Books, 1996.

Sumner, Edwin Vose. "Besieged by the Utes: The Massacre of 1879." Illustrated by Frederick Remington. *Century Illustrated Magazine*, 42, no. 6 (1891): 837–847.

Swadesh, Frances Leon. *Los Prímeros Pobladores: Hispanic Americans of the Ute Frontier*. Notre Dame: University of Notre Dame Press, 1974.

Tanner, Fran McConkie. *The Far Country: A Regional History of Moab and La Sal, Utah*. Salt Lake City: Olympus Publishing, 1976.

Taylor, Morris F. "Action at Fort Massachusetts: The Indian Campaign of 1855." *Colorado Magazine*, 42, no. 4 (1965): 292–310.

———. "Ka-ni-ache, Part 1." *Colorado Magazine*, 43, no. 4 (1966): 275–302.

———. "Ka-ni-ache, Part 2." *Colorado Magazine*, 44, no. 2 (1967): 139–161.

Thomas, Alfred Barnaby. "Spanish Expedition into Colorado." *Colorado Magazine*, 1, no. 7 (1924): 289–300.

———, trans. and ed. *After Coronado: Spanish Exploration Northeast of New Mexico, 1696–1727*. Norman: University of Oklahoma Press, 1935.

———. *Forgotten Frontiers: A Study of the Spanish Indian Policy of Don Juan Bautista de Anza, Governor of New Mexico, 1777–1787*. Norman: University of Oklahoma Press, 1932.

———. *Teodoro de Croix and the Northern Frontier of Spain, 1776–1783*. Norman: University of Oklahoma Press, 1941.

Thompson, Gregory Coyne. *Southern Ute Lands, 1848–1899: The Creation of a Reservation*. Occasional Papers of the Center of Southwest Studies, no. 1. Durango, Colo.: Fort Lewis College, 1972.

———. "The Unwanted Indians: The Southern Utes in Southeastern Utah." *Utah Historical Quarterly*, 49, no. 2 (1981): 189–203.

Thompson, Gregory C., and Floyd A. O'Neil. "Fort Lewis Military Records." *Colorado Magazine*, 44, no. 2 (1969): 166–168.

Thwaites, Reuben Gold, ed. *Early Western Travels, 1748–1846*. Vols. 27–30. Cleveland: Arthur H. Clark, 1904–1907.

Tiller, Veronica E. Velarde. *The Jicarilla Apache Tribe*, rev. ed. Lincoln: University of Nebraska Press, 1992 [1983].

Torrez, Robert J. *The Southern Ute Agency at Abiquiu and Tierra Amarilla*. Research Paper no. 36. Guadalupita, N.M.: Center for Land Grant Studies, 1994.

Trenholm, Virginia Cole, and Maurine Carley. *The Shoshonis: Sentinels of the Rockies*. Norman: University of Oklahoma Press, 1964.

Trimble, Stephen. *The People: Indians of the American Southwest*. Santa Fe: School of American Research, 1993.

Tschopik, Harry. "Taboo as a Possible Factor Involved in the Obsolescence of Navaho Pottery and Basketry." *American Anthropologist*, 40 (1938): 257–262.

Tyler, S. Lyman. "The Spaniard and the Ute." *Utah Historical Quarterly*, 22 (October 1954): 343–361.

———. *The Ute People: A Bibliographical Checklist*. Institute of American Indian Studies. Provo: Brigham Young University, 1964.

———. "The Ute People: An Example of Anglo-American Contact with the Indian." *Denver Westerners' Roundup*, 11 (August 1955): 5–9.

———. "The Yuta Indians Before 1680." *Western Humanities Review*, 5 (spring 1951): 153–163.

Urquhart, Lena M. *Colorow, The Angry Chieftain*. Denver: Golden Bell Press, 1968.

The Ute Bulletin, March 26, 1996; July 8, 1998 (Special information handouts).

Ute-Comanche Peace Treaty Ceremony and Powwow. Program. Ignacio, Colo.: 1977.

Ute Dictionary. Ignacio, Colo.: Ute Press, Southern Ute Tribe, 1979.

The Ute Massacre: Brave Miss Meeker's Captivity! Her Own Account of It. Philadelphia: Old Franklin Publishing, 1879.

Ute Photo Album: The Elders, "Nahnpuchew." Fort Duchesne, Utah: Ute Indian Tribe, 1985.

Ute Reference Grammar. Ignacio, Colo.: Ute Press, Southern Ute Tribe, 1980.

The Ute System of Government. Salt Lake City: Uintah-Ouray Ute Tribe, 1977.

Ute Traditional Narratives. Ed. T. Givón. Ignacio, Colo.: Ute Press, 1985.

Ute Ways. Salt Lake City: Uintah-Ouray Ute Tribe, 1977.

"Utes Invade Dakota." *Wi-iyohi,* 7, no. 3 (1953): 1–6.

Vandenbusche, Duane. *Early Days in the Gunnison Country.* Gunnison, Colo.: B and B Printers, 1974.

Walker, Gary Lee. "Fort Duchesne's Buffalo Soldiers." *Outlaw Trail Journal* (winter 1994): 29–38.

————. "The Outlaw Strip." *Outlaw Trail Journal,* 3, no. 1 (1993): 3–11.

Wallace, Ernest, and E. Adamson Hoebel. *The Comanches: Lords of the South Plains.* Norman: University of Oklahoma Press, 1986 [1952].

Warner, Ted. J., Jr., ed. *The Domínguez-Escalante Journal: Their Expedition through Colorado, Utah, Arizona, and New Mexico in 1776.* Trans. Fray Angelico Chavez. Salt Lake City: University of Utah Press, 1995.

Webb, Farren, and Rick Wheelock. *The Ute Legacy: A Study Guide.* Ignacio, Colo.: Southern Ute Tribe, 1989.

Weber, David J. *The Mexican Frontier, 1821–1846: The American Southwest under Mexico.* Albuquerque: University of New Mexico Press, 1982.

————. *The Taos Trappers: The Fur Trade in the Far Southwest.* Norman: University of Oklahoma Press, 1968.

Weenoocheeyoo Peesadueynee Yak:anup: Stories of Our Ancestors. Illustrations by Clifford Duncan. Salt Lake City: Uintah-Ouray Ute Tribe, 1974.

Werner, Fred H. *Meeker—The Story of the Meeker Massacre and Thornburgh Battle.* Greeley, Colo.: Werner Publications, 1985.

White, Laura C. Manson. "Albert H. Pfeiffer." *Colorado Magazine,* 10 (November 1933): 217–222.

Whittier, Florence E. "The Grave of Chief Ouray." *Colorado Magazine,* 1, no. 7 (1924): 312–319.

Wiegel, Mrs. C. W. "The Death of Ouray, Chief of the Utes." *Colorado Magazine,* 7 (September 1930): 187–191.

Wiseman, Bob. "Las Vegas Played Role in Giant Horse-Stealing Raid." *Nevadan Today* (August 21, 1988), 10, 12.

Wislizenus, Adolphus. *A Journey to the Rocky Mountains in the Year 1839.* Glorieta, N.M.: Rio Grande Press, 1969 [1912].

Witherspoon, Y. T., ed. *Conversations with Connor Chapoose, a Leader of the Ute Tribe of the Uintah and Ouray Reservation.* Recorded in 1960. University of Oregon Anthropological Papers, no. 47. Eugene: University of Oregon Press, 1993.

Wood, Nancy. *War Cry on a Prayer Feather: Prose and Poetry of the Ute Indians.* Garden City, N.Y.: Doubleday, 1979.

————. *When Buffalo Free the Mountains.* Garden City, N.Y.: Doubleday, 1980.

Wormington, H. M., and Robert H. Lister. *Archaeological Investigations on the Uncompahgre Plateau in West Central Colorado*. Denver: Denver Museum of Natural History, 1956.

Young, Karl E. "Sun Dance at Whiterocks, 1919." *Utah Historical Quarterly*, 40, no. 3 (1972): 233–241.

Young, Richard K. *The Ute Indians of Colorado in the Twentieth Century*. Norman: University of Oklahoma Press, 1997.

NEWSPAPERS

Colorado Chieftain (Pueblo)
Denver Post
Denver Times
Rocky Mountain News (Denver)
Solid Muldoon (Ouray, Colorado)
Southern Ute Drum (Ignacio, Colorado)
Ute Bulletin (Fort Duchesne, Utah)
Weenuche Smoke Signals (Towaoc, Colorado)

Index

▼ ▼ ▼